A . Ji

Novi

11- 3- 09.

International Organizations in Global Environmental Governance

This book provides a comparative study of the role of international organizations in environmental governance.

Whilst a growing body of literature considers global governance in a number of policy areas, this volume delivers one of the first comprehensive accounts of international organizations in relation to environmental policy. Providing the reader with key insights within this area of global governance, the book focuses on policies developing in relation to climate change, biodiversity and international environmental funding. Presenting a compelling and up-to-date account of developments within this burgeoning policy area, the volume:

- includes a range of case studies including the World Bank, UNEP and the OECD
- presents quantitative and qualitative research that advances understanding of international organizations in the field of international relations
- delivers contributions from a range of internationally renowned academics and specialists within the field

International Organizations in Global Environmental Governance will be of interest to students and scholars of international relations theory, international economics, environmental policy, organizational theory and environmental studies.

Frank Biermann is Professor of Political Science and of Environmental Policy Sciences at the Vrije Universiteit in Amsterdam, The Netherlands.

Bernd Siebenhüner is Professor of Ecological Economics at Oldenburg University, Germany.

Anna Schreyögg is Researcher at the Climate Change Division, Federal Environment Agency, Germany.

Environmental politics / Routledge research in environmental politics
Edited by Matthew Paterson, University of Ottawa and Graham Smith, University of Southampton

Over recent years environmental politics has moved from a peripheral interest to a central concern within the discipline of politics. This series aims to reinforce this trend through the publication of books that investigate the nature of contemporary environmental politics and show the centrality of environmental politics to the study of politics per se. The series understands politics in a broad sense and books will focus on mainstream issues such as the policy process and new social movements as well as emerging areas such as cultural politics and political economy. Books in the series will analyse contemporary political practices with regards to the environment and/or explore possible future directions for the 'greening' of contemporary politics. The series will be of interest not only to academics and students working in the environmental field, but will also demand to be read within the broader discipline.
The series consists of two strands:

Environmental Politics addresses the needs of students and teachers, and the titles will be published in paperback and hardback. Titles include:

Global Warming and Global Politics
Matthew Paterson

Politics and the Environment
James Connelly and Graham Smith

International Relations Theory and Ecological Thought
Towards synthesis
Eric Laferrière and Peter Stoett

Planning Sustainability
Edited by Michael Kenny and James Meadowcroft

Deliberative Democracy and the Environment
Graham Smith

EU Enlargement and the Environment
Institutional change and environmental policy in Central and Eastern
Europe
Edited by JoAnn Carmin and Stacy D. VanDeveer

The Crisis of Global Environmental Governance
Towards a new political economy of sustainability
Edited by Jacob Park, Ken Conca and Matthias Finger

Routledge Research in Environmental Politics presents innovative new
research intended for high-level specialist readership. These titles are
published in hardback only and include:

1 The Emergence of Ecological Modernisation
Integrating the environment and the economy?
Stephen C. Young

2 Ideas and Actions in the Green Movement
Brian Doherty

3 Russia and the West
Environmental cooperation and conflict
Geir Hønneland

4 Global Warming and East Asia
The domestic and international politics of climate change
Edited by Paul G. Harris

5 Europe, Globalization and Sustainable Development
Edited by John Barry, Brian Baxter and Richard Dunphy

6 The Politics of GM Food
A comparative study of the UK, USA and EU
Dave Toke

7 Environmental Policy in Europe
The Europeanization of national environmental policy
Edited by Andrew Jordan and Duncan Liefferink

8 A Theory of Ecological Justice
Brian Baxter

9 Security and Climate Change
International relations and the limits of realism
Mark J. Lacy

International Organizations in Global Environmental Governance

Edited by Frank Biermann,
Bernd Siebenhüner and Anna Schreyögg

Routledge
Taylor & Francis Group

LONDON AND NEW YORK

First published 2009
by Routledge
2 Park Square, Milton Park, Abingdon, Oxon OX14 4RN

Simultaneously published in the USA and Canada
by Routledge
270 Madison Avenue, New York, NY 10016

Routledge is an imprint of the Taylor & Francis Group, an informa business

Typeset in Times New Roman by
Swales & Willis Ltd, Exeter, Devon
Printed in the UK by the
MPG Books Group

British Library Cataloguing in Publication Data
A catalogue record for this book is available from the British Library

Library of Congress Cataloging in Publication Data
International organizations in global environmental governance /
edited by Frank Biermann, Bernd Siebenhüner and Anna Schreyögg.
    p. cm. – (Routledge research in environmental politics ; 17)
  Includes bibliographical references and index.
    1. International agencies – Environmental aspects. 2. Environmental policy – International cooperation. 3. Environmental protection – International cooperation. I. Biermann, Frank, 1967– II. Siebenhüner, Bernd. III. Schreyögg, Anna.
  JZ1324.I58 2008
  333.7 – dc22
  2008032291

ISBN 10: 0–415–46925–2 (hbk)
ISBN 10: 0–203–88315–2 (ebk)

ISBN 13: 978–0–415–46925–8 (hbk)
ISBN 13: 978–0–203–88315–0 (ebk)

Contents

Figures

Tables

Notes on contributors

Camilla Adelle, Policy Analyst, Institute for European Environmental Policy, London, United Kingdom.

Liliana B. Andonova, Assistant Professor of Government and Environmental Studies at Colby College, United States of America.

Steinar Andresen, Senior Research Fellow at Fridtjof Nansen Institute; former Professor of Political Science at University of Oslo, Norway.

Steffen Bauer, Research Associate at the German Institute for Development Studies.

Frank Biermann, Professor of Political Science and Professor of Environmental Policy Sciences, and head of the Department of Environmental Policy Analysis, at the Vrije Universiteit Amsterdam, The Netherlands. Director of the Global Governance Project, a joint research programme of ten European institutions. Principal investigator (with B. Siebenhüner), research project 'Managers of Global Change: Effectiveness and Influence of International Environmental Organizations'.

Per-Olof Busch, Research Associate and Coordinator of the working group on Global Environmental Governance at the Freie Universität Berlin, Germany.

Axel Dreher, Professor of Economics at the Georg-August University, Göttingen, Germany.

Maria Ivanova, Assistant Professor of Government and Environmental Policy at the College of William and Mary, United States of America. Director of the Global Environmental Governance Project at Yale University.

Andrew Jordan, Senior Researcher at the Centre for Social and Economic Research on the Global Environment (CSERGE), University of East Anglia, United Kingdom.

Markku Lehtonen, Research Fellow with the Sussex Energy Group, Science and Technology Policy Research (SPRU), University of Sussex, United Kingdom.

Susan Park, Lecturer in International Relations, Department of Government and International Relations, University of Sydney, Australia.

Philipp Pattberg, Research Fellow at the Institute for Environmental Studies at the Vrije Universiteit, Amsterdam, The Netherlands, and Research Coordinator of the Global Governance Project, a joint research programme of ten European institutions in the field of global environmental governance.

Magdalena Ramada y Galán Sarasola, Research Fellow at the University of Konstanz, Germany.

Kristin Rosendal, Senior Research Fellow and coordinator of the working area on biodiversity governance, the Fridtjof Nansen Institute, Norway.

Anna Schreyögg, Researcher, Climate Change Division, Federal Environment Agency, Germany.

Bernd Siebenhüner, Professor of Ecological Economics at Oldenburg University, Germany, principal investigator (with F. Biermann), research project 'Managers of Global Change: Effectiveness and Influence of International Environmental Organizations'.

Vanessa Timmer, Post-Doctoral Research Fellow at the University of British Columbia, Canada.

Christopher Wright, Research Fellow at the Grantham Institute on Climate Change and the Environment, London School of Economics, and Visiting Researcher at the Center for the Environment and Development, University of Oslo.

Preface

The pressing problems of global environmental change have challenged the international research community to generate new theoretical understandings, methodological refinements and empirical knowledge of its institutional dimensions. Most of this work, however, has concentrated on the principles, norms, rules and decision-making procedures that underlie the emerging system of global environmental governance. More systematic work will be necessary to better understand the actors at the international level that identify, analyse, manage and evaluate the problems of global environmental change. This particularly applies in the case of the plethora of intergovernmental organizations and programmes that are entrusted with assisting in the mitigation of, and adaptation to, global environmental change. These organizations are hence in the central focus of this book.

All contributions to this volume were first presented at the 2005 Berlin Conference on the Human Dimensions of Global Environmental Change, which was held in December 2005 under the overall theme of 'International Organizations and Global Environmental Governance'. What became clear during this conference was the broad and rising scholarly interest in the work, influence and deficiencies of international organizations in particular in the field of global environmental governance. In total, more than 150 papers were presented at this conference. The studies in this book were selected as the best conference papers by the two conference chairs – who served as editors of the present volume – and their international advisory group. All papers were subsequently revised, submitted to peer review, and subsequently further amended and updated.

The conference was supported financially or in kind by the Volkswagen Stiftung, the Freie Universität Berlin and the Vrije Universiteit Amsterdam, which is gratefully acknowledged. The organizers particularly thank the Potsdam Institute for Climate Impact Research for hosting this event.

Frank Biermann (Amsterdam)
Bernd Siebenhüner (Oldenburg)
Anna Schreyögg (Dessau and Berlin)

1 Global environmental governance and international organizations

Setting the stage

Frank Biermann, Bernd Siebenhüner and Anna Schreyögg

International organizations in a changing world

The history of international organizations dates back hundreds of years, with a major growth in their number, size and mandate since 1945. While there were merely 37 international organizations in 1909, today more than 250 major agencies are in place, along with hundreds of smaller bureaucracies such as treaty secretariats or United Nations programmes. International organizations, like most other actors in world politics, have been challenged in the last decades through major transformations in the international system, ranging from economic globalization to the end of the bipolar order, global environmental degradation, the information revolution, or the rise of transnational terrorism.

Two transformations, we argue, are particularly relevant for the way in which international organizations function: (1) the general shift from intergovernmental politics to global governance, and (2) the increasing functional differentiation of international decision-making, including the emergence of environmental policy as a distinct field of international politics. It is these transformations and their impacts on international organizations that are at the centre of this book.

From intergovernmental politics to global governance

As for the first transformation, 'global governance' is now a key term of the discourse on world politics. Global governance became a rallying call for policy advocates who hail it as panacea for the evils of globalization; a global menace for opponents who fear it as the universal hegemony of the many by the powerful few; and an analytical concept that has given rise to much discussion among scholars of international relations. As is typical for new terms that rise in popularity within a short time in different communities and literatures, no clear definition exists yet. While some see global governance as an emerging new *phenomenon* of world politics that can be described and analysed, others conceptualize global governance as a political *programme* or *project* that is needed to cope with problems of modernity (the affirmative-normative perspective) or that is to be criticized for its flaws and attempts at global domination of weak states by the powerful few (the critical-normative perspective) (for reviews of the literature see Biermann 2006; Dingwerth and Pattberg 2006; Biermann and Pattberg 2008).

We do not propose an exclusive conceptualization of global governance here. All current definitions have pros and cons depending on the context in which they are used. Given the increasing complexity and interdependence of world society in the face of economic and ecological globalization, more effective global regimes and organizations are needed. There is little contestation that this political reform programme can be called 'global governance'. In addition, today's international relations differ from the 1950s and 1960s in many respects, and it seems appropriate to denote these new observable forms of international regulation as 'global governance'. In particular, we see 'global governance' as being defined by three new phenomena that make the world of today different from what it used to be in the 1950s (see in more detail Biermann and Pattberg 2008). First, 'global governance' describes world politics that are no longer confined to nation states but characterized by increased participation of actors other than central governments, including networks of experts, environmentalist organizations and multinational corporations as well as new agencies set up by governments. Here, intergovernmental organizations are among the most important. Second, global governance is characterized through the rise of new forms of institutions in addition to the traditional system of legally binding documents negotiated by states. Politics is now often organized in networks and in new forms of public–private cooperation negotiated between states *and* non-state entities. Intergovernmental organizations, again, play a major role in these new mechanisms. Third, global governance is marked by an increasing segmentation of different layers and clusters of rule-making and rule-implementing, fragmented both vertically between supranational, international, national and subnational layers of authority and horizontally between different parallel rule-making systems maintained by different groups of actors. Again, the role of intergovernmental organizations is key in this respect.

This system of global governance poses particular challenges for international organizations. On the one hand, the rising influence of international organizations in itself is part of, and one of the driving forces behind, the emerging 'multiactor' global governance and new systems of fragmented, 'multilayered' global governance with diffuse authority. Yet international organizations are also affected by the changing context of world politics, in which lines of authority blur, levels of governance change and multiply, and in which the traditional principals of international organizations – the national governments – are accompanied by a variety of other actors that are at times equally influential, even though building on different, and usually informal, sources of power and influence. The chief bureaucrats of international organizations operate today in an environment of network-based interactions that is increasingly shaped not only by governments, but also by new and diffuse new actors as diverse as Amnesty International, the Gates or Turner foundations, scientific networks or CNN.

Functional differentiation of governance

The second major transformation in world politics with particular relevance for international organizations is the functional differentiation of the system. The increased complexity of the modern world has led to a host of new policy issues to emerge on the agenda of international organizations that continuously have to adapt to new developments and policy demands. Central to this book is one newly emerged core policy issue that was not yet salient when most UN agencies were set-up: the local and increasingly global degradation of the environment. Because the charter of the United Nations was negotiated in 1945 and has hardly been amended since then, the word 'environment' does not even appear in this constitutive document. Given the complexities of environmental degradation, international organizations became over time differently involved in this emerging policy field. While some, notably the World Bank, are often viewed as part of the problem, others have built up a reputation as proponents of international environmental cooperation.

These responses by international organizations and by the overall system of international organizations to the challenges brought about by the emergence of global governance and of environmental policy as a new policy field form a major focus of the book. The range of cases studied goes beyond intergovernmental organizations in the traditional understanding, but also includes intergovernmental agencies that are not organizations in the traditional sense of international law, such as the UN Environment Programme and the secretariats to major international agreements, as well as non-state hybrid organizations, which have often developed characteristics that make them very similar, in many respects, to traditional international organizations.

In view of the body of literature these studies could build on, it is striking that the theoretical and empirical understanding of international organizations is still limited, especially if compared to the significantly larger research area of the study of international regimes (for a review of international relations literature on international organizations see Bauer *et al.* 2009). Until a few years ago, the study of international organizations was a rather peripheral subject of research in the study of international relations. Following the general conviction, especially in the paradigms of realism and rational institutionalism, that states are the key actors in international relations, international organizations were often seen as by-products of international cooperation with little autonomy and limited external influence. Surely, they were never entirely neglected. A first peak of interest in international organizations after 1945 focused on a functionalist approach that analysed the emergence of inter- and supranational bodies mainly in Western Europe (e.g. Haas 1958). A second wave of interest emerged in the 1970s, when international relations scholars became more sensitive to the role of international organizations. For example, Cox and Jacobson (1973) and colleagues studied how and to what extent international organizations can take autonomous decisions vis-à-vis national delegates, and Weiss (1975) studied attitudes of staff members of and delegates to international organizations. A related discourse on international organizations emerged in organizational theory, the proponents of which include: Jervis (1976), who used the concept of organizational learning to analyse how perceptions and misperceptions within international organizations shape international politics; Ness and Brechin (1988), who used an organizational perspective on international bureaucracies; or similarly Dijkzeul (1997), who highlighted the fact that international organizations and business organizations have different opportunities of internal evaluation and assessment in human resource management and in their autonomy; and Jordan (2001), who analysed the emergence and management of international cooperation through international organizations.

More recent approaches employ institutional and organizational theories to understand the emergence, growth and behaviour of international organizations (Jönsson 1986; Haas 1990; Haas and Haas 1995; Reinalda and Verbeek 1998, 2004; Barnett and Finnemore 2004; Biermann and Siebenhüner 2009). In this literature, scholars approached international organizations as collective actors in their own right (see Underdal 2001: 27; Barnett and Finnemore 2004: 16–20). Within the discourse on global governance beginning in the 1990s, the predominant focus on states in international relations theory was opened up to also include non-state actors in the analysis. This research addressed, in particular, transnational nongovernmental organizations in areas such as environmental policy or human rights (for example Ghils 1992; Clark 1995; Dingwerth 2007; Pattberg 2005, 2006, 2007). Yet considering the entire discipline, international organizations have remained a rather neglected field in the study of international relations compared with other, more established areas of inquiry. This volume is thus designed to provide fresh analysis to the study of international organizations, in particular in the area of environmental policy.

The volume is based on the premise that the transformation from intergovernmental politics to global governance and the emergence of environmental policy as a distinct arena of conflict and cooperation has brought about three major types of responses from the community of international organizations. These three responses guide the book's overall structure.

First, many international organizations have had to adjust and adapt to changes in their external context: Part I examines the rise of environmental policy as a major issue of international cooperation and conflict. Second, several new international organizations have been set up in the last decades with the sole purpose of advancing environmental protection, including the UN Environment Programme and the secretariats of multilateral environmental agreements (Part II). Finally, new types of international organizations emerged that are no longer fully within the realm of public actors, such as institutionalized networks of public and private actors, and even entirely private international organizations, such as Greenpeace or the Friends of the Earth (Part III).

Adaptation to global transformations

The first chapters in this volume study how international organizations have adapted their core functions, procedures and policies in order to support the new and emerging issues of environmental policy at all levels. Even during the creation of the League of Nations in 1919, early environmental groups had argued – unsuccessfully – for the inclusion of environmental problems in the League's mandate (Wöbse 2003). In the United Nations Organization, environmental debates first emerged during the 1949 United Nations Scientific Conference on the Conservation and Utilization of Resources (Kilian 1987). However, it was not until the 1960s that the United Nations and other international organizations actively took up the issue and adapted their activities. Facing rising demand for transboundary, coordinated environmental protection measures, a number of international organizations widened their original mandate throughout the late 1960s and early 1970s. The International Maritime Organization (IMD), for example, extended its functions in 1967 to cover not only the safety of shipping, but also environmental pollution. A number of environmental treaties on ship-based pollution have since then been negotiated under the auspices of the IMO (Campe 2009). The World Meteorological Organization, originally concerned only with weather and climate research, integrated environmental problems in its work in the 1960s and widened its focus to address global environmental transformations such as the destruction of the ozone layer. In 1970, the Organization for Economic Cooperation and Development enlarged its mandate and included environmental policy objectives in its work programme, even though questions of economic development remained the core of its activity (Long 2000; Busch 2009b; Lehtonen, this volume). Even the North Atlantic Treaty Organization now covers environmental degradation within its activities, under the umbrella of its Committee on the Challenges of Modern Society, which covers international cooperation on air and marine pollution among many other issues.

While many organizations adopted new functions of actively pursuing environmental policy, others had to react to the perceived environmental harmfulness of their core function. Private environmentalist groups and some national governments pressurized these organizations to develop environmental policies and to withdraw from controversial and environmentally damaging projects. Major international organizations such as the World

Bank and other development banks were forced to establish environmental departments and environmental policies (Marschinski and Behrle 2009).

The book offers five in-depth case studies on international organizations and their environmental policies and programmes. At a more general level, Axel Dreher and Magdalena Ramada y Galán Sarasola (Chapter 2) conclude from a quantitative study that almost all organizations analysed – the International Monetary Fund, the World Bank, regional multilateral development banks, the World Trade Organization, and the Global Environment Facility – have had a sizeable impact on the natural environment as well as on environmental governance. They analyse, for example, the effects of international organizations on the environment through their impact on carbon dioxide emissions. Projects financed by development banks and agencies in most cases increase emissions, while the European Bank for Reconstruction and Development and the UN Environment Programme had no significant effect on carbon dioxide emissions. The authors also found a positive correlation between WTO membership and emission reductions through the indirect effect of trade liberalization on domestic emissions.

Christopher Wright (Chapter 3) studies in more detail the role of multilateral financial institutions in shaping the content and institutional design of global environmental governance. Wright analyses the International Finance Corporation's (IFC) role in the emergence of the Equator Principles, a voluntary code of conduct aimed at multinational banks that stipulates how environmental and social concerns should be considered in preparing and implementing project finance loans. According to Wright, the IFC's direct influence on the Equator Principles manifested itself in three ways. First, it convened and encouraged an initial pool of multinational banks to discuss environmental and social management issues, which eventually led to the launch of the Equator Principles in June 2003. Second, the framework's specific provisions are directly derived from the IFC's own environmental and social policies and procedures. Third, by virtue of the Equator Principles, the IFC has effectively become an environmental and social standard-setter in the global project finance market, as signatory banks are expected to harmonize their practices in accordance with any future revisions or updates of the IFC's policies and procedures. The emergence of the Equator Principles also provides an example of the growing discursive power of multilateral financial institutions. While having their credibility continuously challenged by environmental advocacy groups, the IFC's policies and procedures nevertheless enjoy considerable legitimacy, and came to define how private multinational banks harmonized their environmental and social practices. Wright argues that this form of knowledge-based power will become increasingly significant, as multilateral financial institutions continue to embrace a development agenda that emphasizes knowledge generation, management and diffusion.

Markku Lehtonen (Chapter 4) offers an in-depth study of the Organization for Economic Cooperation and Development (OECD). Lehtonen distinguishes diffusion, harmonization and coercion as three key mechanisms that enhance the spread of environmental policy innovations at the international level. The OECD has practically no coercive power, and little capacity to promote legal harmonization, but a strong potential for promoting policy diffusion through 'idea games'. Yet, the concept of 'peer pressure' is precisely based on the desire to combine policy diffusion and learning with 'soft coercion' and accountability through moral persuasion, transparency and public pressure. This chapter examines the potential of the 'peer review logic' in combining the three mechanisms, looking more closely at the OECD Environmental Performance Reviews. The Environmental Performance Reviews influence policies in the reviewed countries through different pathways. The relative importance of these pathways depends not only on the review design, but also on the country-specific context, notably the different expectations, worldviews and positions of actors. The OECD peer reviews have succeeded in avoiding some of the negative impacts associated with the more coercive mechanisms, but, according to Lehtonen, compromise the relevance and credibility of the reviews in the absence of innovation and a more rigorous, comparative approach.

Susan Park (Chapter 5) analyses two banks within the World Bank Group. Based on a constructivist approach, Park studies their roles in diffusing norms throughout the international system, and in spreading ideas through their actions. She identifies processes of socialization whereby both state and non-state actors, such as transnational advocacy networks, interact and diffuse norms within international organizations, changing their identities. Both banks' interactions with transnational environmental advocacy networks are taken as examples to demonstrate how socialization processes, both direct and indirect, are performed and how unevenly they shape the identities of international organizations. As shown in this chapter, 'becoming green' requires a constant process.

Similar trends are observable at the regional level, for example in Europe. The Council of Europe began to address environmental problems in 1968. The European Community included environmental protection in its mission and enlarged its environmental competences in the 1987 Single European Act. In 1969, the United Nations founded the Economic Commission for Europe that helped to coordinate meetings of environmental experts from East and West. The commission was deemed credible by both sides and could thus advance international agreements on transboundary environmental problems, notably the first international binding agreements on transboundary air pollution across Europe and North America.

The European Union is the focus of the study of Camilla Adelle and Andrew Jordan (Chapter 6). They scrutinize the European Union's sustainable development policies. Since 2001, sustainable development has been a fundamental goal of the Union. In its Sustainable Development Strategy, the European Union committed itself to the simultaneous pursuit of social, environmental and economic objectives. At the same time it claimed to consider the effect of its policies – e.g. the Common Agricultural Policy – on the ability of other countries to develop sustainably, especially those in the developing world. This link between the so-called 'external' and 'internal' dimensions of sustainability represents an ambitious policy objective, and Adelle and Jordan examine how the European Union has interpreted and operationalized its commitment to sustainable development especially regarding the 'external dimension'. They trace the historical evolution of the European Union's thinking in this area and identify a number of underlying drivers behind the emergence of the 'external' dimension. The Union's relationship with developing countries is discussed by examining key policy statements and strategies, as well as the main implementing mechanisms. This analysis reveals that the European Union's interpretation of sustainable development has, until recently, mostly focused on its environmental and internal dimensions. Thus far, progress towards addressing the external dimension has been slow, partial, and disparate from the Union's development agenda.

Creation of new specialized agencies and programmes

A second consequence of the emergence of environmental policy as an area of international conflict and cooperation is the emergence of new organizations created exclusively for the support of environmental policy-making. This process started at the 1972 UN Conference on the Human Environment in Stockholm, which led to a new emphasis on environmental protection in the system of international organizations and to the creation of the United Nations Environment Programme (UNEP) to coordinate environment-related activities of states and international organizations and catalyse processes towards regional and global environmental protection (see Andresen and Rosendal, Chapter 7; Ivanova, Chapter 8; Bauer 2009b).

In addition, the steep increase in the number of international environmental agreements beginning in the 1970s led to a rise also in the number of international secretariats, committees and panels in support of these agreements. Notably, in the early 1990s, three international conventions on climate change, biodiversity and desertification were agreed. Each of them now has a sizable new international bureaucracy to serve the implementation of the conventions (see Busch 2009a on the climate secretariat; Siebenhüner 2009 on the biodiversity secretariat; Bauer 2009a on the desertification secretariat). While these secretariats are not international organizations in the legal sense, they are often rather large agencies, with at times over a hundred employees, and they exert a noticeable influence on environmental negotiations (Biermann and Siebenhüner 2009; Bauer, Busch and Siebenhüner, Chapter 9). Finally, discussions on UNEP and the various treaty secretariats also need to be seen in light of ongoing discussions about the need of a larger, more powerful agency for global environmental policy. While proponents of such a 'world environment organization' invoke the need for strong international organizations to counter environmental degradation on a global scale (see Biermann 2000; Esty and Ivanova 2001; Biermann and Bauer 2005), others express scepticism about the feasibility of such proposals (e.g. Najam 2005). The three studies in Part II of this volume, while not addressing the debate on a world environment organization directly, can also be seen in this context.

Maria Ivanova (Chapter 8) assesses the role of UNEP as an anchor organization for the global environment. Many have called for a strengthening of global environmental governance by transforming the United Nations Environment Programme into a more powerful global environmental organization. Institutional reform, however, necessitates an understanding of where UNEP has succeeded, where and why it has failed, and what the leverage points are to increase effectiveness, efficiency and equity. Ivanova examines how UNEP has performed as the anchor organization for the global environment and identifies a set of core factors that affect UNEP's effectiveness and need to be considered both in the theoretical and practical context of organizational reform.

Steinar Andresen and Kristin Rosendal (Chapter 7) also analyse UNEP, drawing on a larger research programme on the effectiveness of the United Nations in global environmental governance. They do not evaluate the entire work of UNEP, but focus on its performance in relation to multilateral environmental agreements. Their findings are nuanced. In terms of agenda setting and regime creation, the score of UNEP is very high, in terms of governing and coordination of relevant multilateral environmental agreements the picture is mixed, but more on the negative side. In terms of the emerging role of UNEP in implementation, the picture is bound to be more inconclusive, but there are some promising signs. Andresen and Rosendal explain this pattern by focusing on both the interest and power of major member states, and the ability of UNEP as an organization in its own right to perform these functions. In conclusion, they discuss potential improvements on part of UNEP and position them in the broader discussion of global environmental governance.

Embedded in a larger interdisciplinary qualitative research framework on organizational effectiveness (Biermann *et al.* 2009), Steffen Bauer, Per-Olof Busch and Bernd Siebenhüner (Chapter 9) analyse the specific role of treaty secretariats – conceptualized as a distinct type of intergovernmental organization – in international environmental politics. Theoretically and methodologically, the chapter employs organizational theories and sociological institutionalism for qualitative case study research. Empirically, the chapter assesses variances in the influence of three environmental treaty secretariats, namely the secretariats to the UN Framework Convention on Climate Change, the UN Convention to Combat Desertification, and the Convention on Biological Diversity. While the organizational design of all three secretariats is similar, their institutional histories and political influence differ markedly. This research addresses in particular the variation in the normative influence of the secretariats' activities, that is, its rule-setting functions. From a larger set of variables, the chapter emphasizes the salience of autonomy and authority as well as leadership in exploring the capacities of intergovernmental treaty secretariats to influence rule setting and compliance in their respective treaty regimes.

New public–private hybrid organizations

A third consequence of the increasing trend towards multi-actor global governance and the emergence of environmental policy is seen in the increasing interactions and interplay of international organizations with civil society organizations through public–private partnerships. This evolution has gained increased momentum through the 2002 World Summit on Sustainable Development in Johannesburg (Glasbergen *et al.* 2007). The numbers and sizes of transnational civil society organizations have significantly increased since the 1990s, with more and more participating in international environmental policy-making. While at the 1992 Rio conference 1,400 registered nongovernmental organizations participated, ten years later at the Johannesburg conference this number was ten times higher with over 15,000 registered nongovernmental organizations – among them also many business organizations (Falkner 2007). The proliferation of private actor participation gave rise to new modes of governance such as public–private partnerships. International organizations often play a leading role in these partnerships and developed novel means of implementing international environmental policy goals.

Part III thus covers the new and growing area of public–private cooperation. It covers both conventional environmentalist nongovernmental organizations and novel hybrid forms that include business-related nongovernmental organizations.

First, Liliana Andonova (Chapter 10) examines the emergence and role of international organizations within public–private partnerships in global environmental governance. She finds that international organizations have been among the most active entrepreneurs of partnerships. Through their initiative, the partnership movement was able to respond to public pressure and strategic organizational incentives. Departing from the commonly held view of partnerships as an alternative governance mechanism, she conceptualizes them as complements and additions to the formal operations of intergovernmental organizations and regimes. Her analysis of five large international partnership initiatives shows that the initiative often comes from within international organizations. As a consequence, partnerships are often guided by specific organizational objectives and tend to be supply-driven by the resources and organizational interests of the dominant international organizations. Her empirical cases include the United Nations Fund for International Partnerships (UNFIP), the Prototype Carbon Fund of the World Bank, the Small Grants Programmes of the Global Environment

Facility, the Equator Initiative of UNDP, and the WSSD partnerships, endorsed at the Johannesburg Summit in 2002.

Philipp Pattberg (Chapter 11) argues that organization, as a key concept for understanding the current global order, does not only exist on the inter-state level, but increasingly manifests itself on the transnational level. Trans-national organization has many sources and appears in many forms. As a relatively recent phenomenon, transnational rule-making processes could be considered the most apparent expression of the shift from state-driven polit-ics and intergovernmental cooperation to non-state-driven governance in world affairs. In recent years, a number of rule-making processes have emerged around issues of global sustainability politics. However, most research on non-state actors and their roles in environmental politics has focused on rather traditional forms of policy-making firmly directed towards states and embedded in the international paradigm. Pattberg's chapter assesses the roles and functions that transnational forms of organization perform in world politics. As most research in this field has hitherto focused either on business self-regulation or public–private cooperation, this contri-bution takes a closer look at forms of transnational organization that include both the profit as well as the non-profit side of transnational society (business co-regulation). Empirically, the chapter analyses the Coalition for Environ-mentally Responsible Economies as an example of a business-related transnational organization with regard to its role and function in global environmental governance.

The final chapter by Vanessa Timmer (Chapter 12) leaves the area of public actors entirely behind. Instead, she is looking at transnational nongovern-mental organizations that have become increasingly prominent and influen-tial players in global environmental governance in recent years. She questions their accountability and effectiveness in creating value, building legitimacy and support and enhancing operational capacity, and then investigates the influence of agility on the performance and organizational effectiveness of transnational nongovernmental organizations. She sees agility as the ability of a nongovernmental organization to learn, adapt and adjust in strategic ways while maintaining organizational relevance, quality and reputation. Timmer studies agility and its counterpart, resilience, in two case studies, namely Friends of the Earth International and Greenpeace International. With more than three decades of involvement in global environmental governance, both organizations are interesting cases for tracing the long-term influence of agility and resilience on effectiveness.

Methodology

This book builds on methodological diversity, which reflects the complex nature of its subject, one that can be fully understood only through combin-ing different methods. In particular, the book brings together contributions that use single-case study designs, multiple-case studies, and quantitative comparative studies. Through these lenses, different facets of organizations, their roles and functions are brought to the surface with the particular strengths and weaknesses embodied in these methods.

Quantitative methods using statistical data have rarely been used in the study of international organizations in environmental politics. The chapter by Dreher and Sarasola is thus a pioneering contribution. They use data on environmental indicators at national and global levels to measure the influence of international organizations. With regard to the independent variable (activities of international organizations), they then measure the average yearly number of programmes or projects started by an organization. This approach allows some rough assessment of the performance of international organizations in capacity building and implementation, yet cannot capture the size and quality of the projects and softer forms of activity such as influence on international negotiations. Regression analysis is also not sufficient to elucidate causal relationships between the activities of international organizations and observed changes in environmental quality. Thus, while the types and quality of organizational influence can and should be further studied in quantitative analysis, a more complete understanding will require also continued qualitative work.

Such qualitative research methods are used by the other studies included here. The single-case study design allows deeper analyses into the processes and structures of an international organization and its external relations and effects. Nevertheless, methodological demands on single-case studies are substantial, in particular when it comes to the study of large organizations such as the World Bank, the OECD or UNEP. In this book, Wright, Lehtonen, Adelle and Jordan, as well as Andresen and Rosendal, Ivanova and Pattberg all employ single-case study designs.

Since most of these case studies draw on interview data, the size of the organization poses a challenge to the researcher, who has to address numerous individuals within and outside the organization. Conducting larger numbers of interviews increases the effort in data analysis and aggregation. In particular, triangulation of the data (Yin 1994) through other sources such as written documents or external views requires substantial resources from the researcher. In addition, the focus on a single organization hardly allows for comparative conclusions. Findings can only be generalized for all or other specific organizations if framework conditions are largely similar. This renders case selection rather difficult. Scholars therefore show a tendency towards the bigger and better known international organizations since findings seem here more useful or interesting than findings on smaller bodies in international politics. Because there is thus more knowledge on larger international organizations, case studies on smaller and less well-known organizations may broaden insights on the roles and activities of international organizations.

Another strategy is multiple-case study designs, employed by a number of contributors. Comparative case study designs require rather strong analytical frameworks that are applied consistently over the cases. This places high demands on data collection and quality. Multiple-case study designs often address a small number of cases that restricts research efforts to a manageable size. Park and Timmer apply their general framework to two cases; Bauer, Busch and Siebenhüner study three treaty secretariats with a consistently applied analytical framework; and Andonova compares five public–private partnership initiatives. They all share the major strength of multiple-case study designs, namely the formulation of more general hypotheses to be applied to other similar organizations. Park's results can be applied to other development banks under the umbrella of the World Bank, while Timmer's findings can provide fruitful starting points for the study of other transnational nongovernmental environmental organizations. While Andonova's study deals with significant heterogeneity among five cases, one common feature shared by all allows her to compare and to draw general conclusions.

Taken together, while all the chapters study international organizations in the field of environmental policy from different angles, theoretical perspectives and methodological approaches, all testify to the increasing role of international organizations for global environmental protection as well as to the increasing relevance of global environmental protection for international organizations. In times of global environmental change, almost all international organizations are challenged to take part in joint efforts to find effective, efficient and equitable solutions. These chapters are thus part of a fast growing literature on international organizations and global environmental change, and are also part of larger research programmes that promise to provide more detailed analyses in the future. At times when the global environmental crisis has become a regular topic of the headlines of mainstream newspapers, international organizations must react and act. It is today one of the core challenges of the UN system and all its specialized agencies and programmes to develop and implement within their responsibilities effective, timely, and equitable solutions to the global environmental crisis. The contributions to this book show many examples of problems and shortcomings. Yet the analysis gives also much hope that international bureaucracies will live up to the challenge that lies ahead.

References

Barnett, M.N. and Finnemore, M. (2004) *Rules for the World: International Organizations in Global Politics*, Ithaca, NY: Cornell University Press.

Bauer, S. (2009a) 'The Desertification Secretariat: A Castle Made of Sand', in Biermann, F. and Siebenhüner, B. (eds) (2009) *Managers of Global Change: The Influence of International Environmental Bureaucracies*, Cambridge, MA: MIT Press (in press).

Bauer, S. (2009b) 'The Secretariat of the United Nations Environment Programme:

Tangled up in Blue', in Biermann, F. and Siebenhüner, B. (eds) (2009) *Managers of Global Change: The Influence of International Environmental Bureaucracies*, Cambridge, MA: MIT Press (in press).

Bauer, S., Biermann, F., Dingwerth, K. and Siebenhüner, B. (2009) 'Understanding International Bureaucracies: Taking Stock', in Biermann, F. and Siebenhüner, B. (eds) (2009) *Managers of Global Change: The Influence of International Environmental Bureaucracies*, Cambridge, MA: MIT Press (in press).

Biermann, F. (2000) 'The Case for a World Environment Organization', *Environment*, 20: 22–31.

Biermann, F. (2006) 'Global Governance and the Environment', in Betsill, M., Hochstetler, K. and Stevis, D. (eds) *International Environmental Politics*, New York: Palgrave Macmillan.

Biermann, F. and Bauer, S. (eds) (2005) *A World Environment Organization. Solution or Threat for Effective International Environmental Governance?*, Aldershot, UK: Ashgate.

Biermann, F. and Pattberg, P. (2008) 'Global Environmental Governance: Taking Stock, Moving Forward', *Annual Review of Environment and Resources 33* (in press).

Biermann, F. and Siebenhüner, B. (eds) (2009) *Managers of Global Change: The Influence of International Environmental Bureaucracies*, Cambridge, MA: MIT Press (in press).

Biermann, F., Siebenhüner, B., Bauer, S., Busch, P.-O., Campe, S., Dingwerth, K., Grothmann, T., Marschinski, R. and Tarradell, M. (2009) 'Studying the Influence of International Bureaucracies: A Conceptual Framework', in Biermann, F. and Siebenhüner, B. (eds) *Managers of Global Change: The Influence of International Environmental Bureaucracies*, Cambridge, MA: MIT Press (in press).

Busch, P.-O. (2009a) 'The Climate Secretariat: Making a Living in a Straitjacket', in Biermann, F. and Siebenhüner, B. (eds) (2009) *Managers of Global Change: The Influence of International Environmental Bureaucracies*, Cambridge, MA: MIT Press (in press).

Busch, P.-O. (2009b) 'The OECD Environment Directorate: The Art of Persuasion and its Limitations', in Biermann, F. and Siebenhüner, B. (eds) (2009) *Managers of Global Change: The Influence of International Environmental Bureaucracies*, Cambridge, MA: MIT Press (in press).

Campe, S. (2009) 'The Secretariat of the International Maritime Organization: A Tanker for the Tankers', in Biermann, F. and Siebenhüner, B. (eds) (2009) *Managers of Global Change: The Influence of International Environmental Bureaucracies*, Cambridge, MA: MIT Press (in press).

Clark, A.M. (1995) 'Non-governmental Organizations and their Influence on International Society', *Journal of International Affairs*, 48: 507–25.

Cox, R.W. and Jacobson, H.K. (eds) (1973) *The Anatomy of Influence: Decision-Making in International Organization*, New Haven: Yale University Press.

Dijkzeul, D. (1997) *The Management of Multilateral Organizations*, The Hague: Kluwer.

Dingwerth, K. (2007) *The New Transnationalism. Transnational Governance and Democratic Accountability*, Basingstoke: Palgrave Macmillan.

Dingwerth, K. and Pattberg, P. (2006) 'Global Governance as a Perspective on World Politics', *Global Governance*, 12: 185–203.

Esty, D.C. and Ivanova, M.H. (2001) 'Making Environmental Efforts Work: The Case for a Global Environmental Organization', *Working Paper 2/01*, New Haven, CT: Yale Center for Environmental Law and Policy.

Falkner, R. (2007) *Business Power and Conflict in International Environmental Politics*, Basingstoke: Palgrave Macmillan.

Ghils, P. (1992) 'International Civil Society: International Non-governmental Organizations in the International System', *International Social Science Journal*, 133: 417–31.

Glasbergen, P., Biermann, F. and Mol, A.P.J. (2007) *Partnerships for Sustainable Development. Reflections on Theory and Practice*, Cheltenham: Edward Elgar.

Haas, E.B. (1958) *The Uniting of Europe. Political, Social and Economical Forces 1950–1957*, London: Stevens.

Haas, E.B. (1990) *When Knowledge is Power: Three Models of Change in International Organizations*, Berkeley: University of California Press.

Haas, P.M. and Haas, E.B. (1995) 'Learning to Learn: Improving International Governance', *Global Governance*, 1: 255–85.

Jervis, R. (1976) *Perception and Misperception in International Politics*, Princeton, NJ: Princeton University Press.

Jönsson, C. (1986) 'Interorganization Theory and International Organization', *International Studies Quarterly*, 30(1): 39–57.

Jordan, R.S. (2001) *International Organizations: A Comparative Approach to the Management of Cooperation*, Westport, CT: Praeger.

Kilian, M. (1987) *Umweltschutz durch internationale Organisationen: die Antwort des Völkerrechts auf die Krise der Umwelt?*, Berlin: Duncker & Humboldt.

Long, B.L. (2000) *International Environmental Issues and the OECD 1950–2000*, Paris: OECD.

Marschinski, R. and Behrle, S. (2009) 'The World Bank: Making the Business Case for the Environment', in Biermann, F. and Siebenhüner, B. (eds) (2009) *Managers of Global Change: The Influence of International Environmental Bureaucracies*, Cambridge, MA: MIT Press (in press).

Najam, A. (2005) 'Neither Necessary, nor Sufficient: Why Organizational Tinkering will not Improve Environmental Governance', in Biermann, F. and Bauer, S. (eds) *A World Environment Organization. Solution or Threat for Effective International Environmental Governance?*, Aldershot: Ashgate: 231–50.

Ness, G.D. and Brechin, S. (1988) 'Bridging the Gap: International Organizations as Organizations', *International Organization*, 42(2): 245–73.

Pattberg, P. (2005) 'The Institutionalization of Private Governance: How Business and Non-profits Agree on Transnational Rules', *Governance: An International Journal of Policy, Administration and Institutions*, 18(4): 589–610.

Pattberg P. (2006) 'The Influence of Global Business Regulation: Beyond Good Corporate Conduct', *Business and Society Review*, 111: 241–68.

Pattberg, P. (2007) *Private Institutions and Global Governance. The New Politics of Environmental Sustainability*, Cheltenham, UK and Northampton, MA: Edward Elgar.

Reinalda, B. and Verbeek, B. (eds) (1998) *Autonomous Policy Making by International Organizations*, London: Routledge.

Reinalda, B. and Verbeek, B. (eds) (2004) *Decision Making Within International Organizations*, London: Routledge.

Siebenhüner, B. (2009) 'The Biodiversity Secretariat: Lean Shark in Troubled Waters', in Biermann, F. and Siebenhüner, B. (eds) (2009) *Managers of Global Change: The*

Influence of International Environmental Bureaucracies, Cambridge, MA: The MIT Press (in press).

Underdal, A. (2001), 'One Question, Two Answers', in Miles, E.L., Underdal, A., Andresen, A., Wettestad, J., Skjærseth, J.B. and Carlin, E.M. (eds) *Environmental Regime Effectiveness. Confronting Theory with Evidence*, Cambridge, MA: MIT Press.

Weiss, T.G. (1975) *International Bureaucracy*, Lexington, MA: Lexington Books.

Wöbse, A.-K. (2003) 'Der Schutz der Natur im Völkerbund – Anfänge einer Weltumweltpolitik', *Archiv für Sozialgeschichte*, 43: 177–90.

Yin, R.K. (1994) *Case Study Research: Design and Methods*, Thousand Oaks, CA: Sage.

Part I

Intergovernmental organizations

2 The impact of international organizations on the environment

An empirical analysis

Axel Dreher and Magdalena Ramada y Galán Sarasola

Introduction

In the last two decades, or at least since the release of the Brundtland Report (World Commission of Environment and Development 1987), international organizations (IOs) have started considering the importance of environmental concerns in their policies. Multilateral Development Banks (MDBs) have tried to embody environmental policies in their lending programs, both through conditionality and through the institutionalization of environmental impact assessment procedures within the project release process. In the early 1990s the International Monetary Fund (IMF) also decided to include environmental considerations in its lending programs, since major environmental problems could affect macroeconomic variables, thereby threatening stability. International organizations have also developed purely environmental facilities – such as the Global Environment Facility (GEF) – making environmental governance and policy an issue of its own in international lending, and not only a side issue to be taken into account among other things.

However, although IOs have been developing environmental issues in their policy making, critics still consider their programs and policies to have mainly adverse effects on the environment. The World Trade Organization (WTO) has been heavily criticized by environmental NGOs for neglecting the environmental impact of its policies. IOs are criticized for being badly coordinated and even for not considering environmental problems as their priority in their relations with borrowing countries. Particularly via their impact on trade liberalization and their promotion of growth-oriented policies, IOs are accused of harming the natural environment. Clearly, the question whether international organizations harm or benefit the environment is empirical in nature. This chapter tries to answer this question; it includes IOs whose main task is promoting economic development, growth and trade, and tests whether their presence and projects in different countries have on average significant effects on environmental governance and outcomes. Specifically, the analysis covers the IMF, World Bank, WTO, Inter-American

Development Bank (IADB), Asian Development Bank (ADB), African Development Bank (AfDB) and European Bank for Reconstruction and Development (EBRD). Furthermore, our analysis includes facilities that are specifically designed for environmental purposes – the United Nations Development and Environmental Programs' GEF.[1]

To quantify the presence and influence of an IO in a specific country, we focus on the number of programs that the IO has implemented there. Regarding the WTO, we use the membership status of the country and also the duration of membership, which produce similar results. To assess the impact on environmental outcomes we employ four dependent variables measuring the degree of water and air pollution and round wood production. Environmental governance is captured by a composite index intended to measure environmental sustainability.

Where data availability allows, we employ panel data to test our hypotheses. Regarding environmental governance, however, we are restricted to relying on cross-section regressions. Our results show that the international organizations affect the environment directly via their impact on CO_2 emissions. Projects financed by the World Bank, ADB and UNDP, and membership in the WTO, increase emissions, while IADB projects reduce emissions. EBRD and UNEP do not significantly affect CO_2 emissions, while the AfDB increases emissions after 1985 only. Taking the indirect impact through trade liberalization into account, however, the WTO reduces emissions, while the IADB increases emissions. Environmental governance is not affected by the international organizations investigated here.

The chapter is organized as follows. The next section presents our hypotheses for the individual organizations covered under this study. The third section describes data and methodology used in the empirical investigation, while the results are shown in the fourth section. Finally, the fifth section contains a short summary.

Hypotheses

International Monetary Fund

In early 1991, the IMF's Executive Board decided the Fund should take environmental issues into account when they are crucial for a country's macroeconomic stability (Gandhi 1998). In fact, IMF Policy Framework Papers and Poverty Reduction Strategy Papers (PRSPs) frequently include a discussion of environmental policies (Gandhi 1998 and Friends of the Earth 1999 provide specific examples). In countries with active discussions about green taxes or energy reforms, the IMF also takes these issues into account in its regular review of its members' economies (Gandhi 1998).

According to the IMF (2004), the links between its macroeconomic mandate and the natural environment are substantial. IMF programs address policies in borrower countries; policies – in turn – can affect the environment.

Clearly, environmental aspects are rarely covered directly under the Fund's conditionality (Dreher 2002 gives a detailed overview of conditions included in IMF and World Bank programs). However, policies included on efficiency grounds are often also beneficial for the environment. Conditions and advice aim at promoting a more rational use of resources and discourage waste, and may thereby benefit environmental quality.

The IMF (2004) gives three examples (see Gandhi 1998 for more examples). First, subsidies and tax relief on agricultural inputs are frequently subject to conditionality – they are inefficient; and often they harm the environment. Second, taxes yielding substantial revenue can sometimes also be used to discourage environmentally harmful activities. And third, publicly owned natural resources can be a significant source of revenues. Even without explicit environmental conditionality, then, IMF programs could benefit the environment by addressing these areas.

IMF policies, however, have always been subject to criticism, and such criticism also refers to the Fund's role vis-à-vis the natural environment. For example, NGOs blame its programs for leading to reductions in environmental spending, increasing natural resource exploitation, and weakening environmental laws (e.g. Gandhi 1998; Friends of the Earth 1999). Spending cuts can adversely affect level and quality of services such as waste management, sanitation, and environmental regulation standards (Gueorguieva and Bolt 2003). Capacity to monitor and regulate polluters is reduced. Decentralization and privatization redistribute power in favour of the private sector, undermining the state's ability to protect the environment and regulate industries (Killick 1993). The urban poor may be forced, for example, to cut forests for fuelwood or exploit marginal lands for food. Reductions in interest rate subsidies can cut farmers' access to the credit markets and make them switch to intensive farming techniques, thereby contributing to deforestation and soil erosion.

IMF programs aim at increasing exports and generating foreign reserves. As a consequence, countries may over-exploit their natural resources, generating excessive pollution and environmental destruction (Friends of the Earth 1999). Pandey and Wheeler (2001) show that currency devaluations – these have been a frequent IMF condition until the 1980s – significantly increase deforestation over a sample of 112 developing countries and 38 years. Trade liberalization – which is a frequent condition in IMF programs – may imply negative consequences for the natural environment when 'dirty' industries migrate to liberalized developing countries, where environmental standards and thus the costs of pollution are lower ('pollution haven hypothesis').[2]

Clearly, trade liberalization also implies effects that are beneficial for environmental protection. As one specific example, liberalization can increase the profitability of raising herbs, leading to preservation of forests as trees are necessary to protect the herbs (Jayarajah and Branson 1995). Overall, however, world market demand for commodities destructive for the environment is much higher than that for more benign products (Battikha 2002).

Another channel by which the IMF may influence the natural environment is its impact on external debt. It has been argued that developing countries are forced into pursuing environmentally damaging activities in order to be able to service their debt, particularly regarding tropical deforestation (see, e.g., Capistrano 1990). The direction of the Fund's impact is, however, not obvious. While its loans alleviate short-term pressure, the medium and long-term consequence of an IMF loan may well be an increase in indebtedness, and in debt service payments.

Summarizing the discussion, the direction of the overall impact of the IMF on the environment is not obvious *a priori*. We derive two alternative hypotheses from this:

> Hypothesis 1a: IMF involvement improves environmental governance and outcomes.

> Hypothesis 1b: IMF involvement worsens environmental governance and outcomes.

World Bank

The World Bank implements projects and provides loans for structural adjustment. Both project loans and program loans are subject to conditionality, which is to some extent similar to the conditions set by the IMF (see Dreher 2002). However, whereas the majority of the Fund's conditions focus on macroeconomic targets, World Bank conditionality is more structural in nature. Bank programs include conditions directly referring to the natural environment – in the 1990s, 23 per cent of its Structural Adjustment Loans (SALs) contained such conditions (World Bank 2001). Policies like the creation and strengthening of environmental institutions, the implementation of policies for environmental protection, or environmental taxation are explicitly covered.[3] Our second hypothesis is therefore:

> Hypothesis 2: World Bank involvement improves environmental governance.

Apart from conditions referring directly to the environment, World Bank programs cover a range of other areas that have indirect positive environmental consequences. For example, measures increasing the prices of agricultural products might increase incentives and abilities to conserve soil. Higher energy prices are likely to promote conservation of fossil fuels (Hansen and Hansen 1999). The introduction of electricity tariffs can increase energy efficiency (Gueorguieva and Bolt 2003). The Bank's programs sometimes imply declining use of fertilizers and pesticides, which is likely to improve water quality (Hughes and Lovei 1999).[4] All those conditions imply:

Hypothesis 3a: World Bank involvement improves environmental outcomes.

However, World Bank projects have frequently been criticized. Much of its lending supports projects and programs in environmentally sensitive areas, such as energy, agriculture and transport.

Conditions included under the Bank's programs and projects may also imply negative environmental consequences. For example, measures increasing the prices of agricultural products could lead to intensified cultivation and erosion (Hansen and Hansen 1999). The same might happen as a consequence of increased input prices. The impact of structural adjustment on energy use can also be negative, as the introduction of electricity tariffs may imply increasing use of traditional fuels, in turn increasing air pollution (Munasinghe and Cruz 1994, Gueorguieva and Bolt 2003 provide case study evidence).

World Bank conditionality frequently aims at reducing the size of the public sector. The private sector, however, is less likely to internalize environmental costs (Battikha 2002). Export promotion, trade liberalization and privatization may also damage the environment, as was mentioned before. As Pandey and Wheeler (2001) argue, the World Bank's structural adjustment measures may increase deforestation in the program country.[5] Thus:

Hypothesis 3b: World Bank involvement worsens environmental outcomes.

Regional Multilateral Development Banks

We focus on the Inter-American Development Bank, the Asian Development Bank, the African Development Bank and the European Bank for Reconstruction and Development. Although these regional Multilateral Development Banks (MDBs) all rely on comparable structures and operating systems and conduct similar policies as the World Bank, there are important differences. Above all, MDBs do not exert comparable pressure on their borrowers to implement structural and macroeconomic conditionality (Mikesell and Williams 1992). They mostly engage in project lending or concentrate on certain economic areas like, e.g. agriculture or energy.

In all four regional MDBs analysed in this chapter, environmental issues became prominent in the late 1980s, even though these issues did not directly influence their policies until many years later.[6] They all included the preparation of Environmental Impact Assessments (EIA) in their project analysis procedure and institutionalized environmental issues through internal units designed for that purpose. Moreover, they allow or even encourage participation by national experts and institutions to different degrees in their analysis of the environmental impact of lending projects. In this way the MDBs intend to enhance and promote environmental governance and try to integrate national organizations and institutions into the environmental assessment process.

Accordingly, the Environmental Protection Division of the IADB, founded in 1989, analyses the potential environmental consequences of a project together with the project team, in order to identify necessary studies to be carried out by the borrower countries in order to formulate the EIA. Based on both the EIA and the project team's analysis, the Environmental Management Committee (EMC) elaborates the loan report that is to be approved by the director's board (IADB 2003). A similar procedure is followed at the ADB, where the Environmental Division (formerly the Office of the Environment) has analysed the environmental consequences of projects since 1988 (ADB 1986, 1995a, 2003). Because of its initial difficulties in raising funds and the late incorporation of non-African donors to the AfDB, the environmental issue was implemented there only in 1991, when EIA started to be part of the standard procedure in structural loans (Mikesell and Williams 1992). Finally, although the EBRD has been heavily criticized for its environmental policies because of lending projects in respect of old Soviet-built nuclear plants and because environmental projects amount to only about 10 per cent of its lending portfolio, it has environmental procedures similar to the other MDBs and played an important role as advisor of the Preparation Committee for the Environment for Europe Process (Gutner 2002).

In this way, every regional MDB included in our analysis has an institutionalized procedure concerning the environmental impact analysis of its lending projects and is therefore supposed to positively impact on environmental outcomes and governance. Particularly, the incorporation and strengthening of national institutions in the EIA process, extensive research about the natural environment, training public sector officials in environmental policy,[7] and their function as knowledge centres for future environmental issues (AfDB 2001) imply:

> Hypothesis 4: Regional MDB involvement improves environmental governance.

Following the same line of reasoning as for the World Bank above, we derive two further hypotheses referring to environmental outcomes. Regional MDBs may in fact influence environmental quality directly and indirectly by implementing programs with medium or high environmental sensitivity. Examples are projects in the agro-industry, fish farming, small-scale irrigation, water supply and power generation, and particularly large-scale irrigation, hydropower and water management, resettlement, new ports, airports and harbours, forestry or livestock projects (Mikesell and Williams 1992).

Again, the potential impact and its positive or negative implications are not obvious *a priori*. Agricultural credit loans, for example, can on one side mitigate rural-urban migration processes, alleviating waste and water management problems in overcrowded cities or reducing urban pollution, but – on the other hand – can also produce intensified cultivation and soil erosion. As irrigation projects can improve agricultural output and create incentives to remain in rural regions, they may also damage soil through salinization, displace families from the water reservoir areas or pollute downstream waterways (ADB 1995b). Hydropower dams can improve energy efficiency. However, they negatively affect wildlife, wildlands, fishery or other downstream water projects, as turbidity will deteriorate aquatic life recreation or soil erosion and chemical pollution of upland streams could finally be stored in the water delivery system and then be carried downstream affecting other water uses (Goldsmith and Hildyard 1984; Dixon *et al.* 1998). Even forestry projects directly intending the conservation of a certain ecosystem or the protection of water resources may have adverse impacts, as the modification of migration trends through population resettlement, the destruction of indigenous cultures living in primary forests or the modification of the ecosystem affecting species in their composition or number (ADB 1999).[8]

Hence, we can formulate the alternative hypotheses:

Hypothesis 5a: Regional MDB involvement improves environmental outcomes.

Hypothesis 5b: Regional MDB involvement worsens environmental outcomes.

Global Environment Facility

The Global Environment Facility (GEF) was proposed in 1990 by the World Bank, as a consequence of the discussion distinguishing between domestic and global environmental impact and the increasing concern about global environmental issues. Since implementing projects to increase global environmental quality is not always profitable for developing – and other – countries, the idea of providing funds at low interest rates for these kinds of loans arose. The GEF was created in World Bank resolution 91–5, under the management of the World Bank itself and to be executed through three implementing agencies, the World Bank, the United Nations Development Program (UNDP) and the United Nations Environmental Program (UNEP).

The direct involvement of the World Bank in the GEF has been heavily criticized. According to some NGOs, the World Bank hardly managed to care about environmental issues in its 'own' programs and should therefore not lead an environmental 'agency' as the GEF was understood to be. The NGOs stressed the need for independent implementing agencies (Mikesell and Williams 1992), particularly as they feared any World Bank involvement would allow the Bank to expand its conditionality to 'green areas' (Streck 2001).[9]

Other critics of the GEF requested a larger number of implementing agencies to improve the efficacy and the quality of the projects through the competition for GEF funds, since they predicted a leading role of the World Bank in the GEF distribution (Streck 2001) and a suboptimal aid allocation.[10]

Given that GEF is directly designed to promote environmental governance[11] we hypothesize:

Hypothesis 6: GEF improves environmental governance.

Hypothesis 7: GEF improves environmental outcomes.

World Trade Organization

The impact of the WTO on the natural environment has also been subject to heated debate (for an in-depth discussion, see MacMillan 2001). A vast array of environmental NGOs blame the WTO for neglecting the environmental consequences of its policies (examples are Friends of the Earth, Greenpeace, One World and World Wildlife Fund). However, the WTO has also been defended. According to Oxley (2001), the WTO gives great latitude to its members to restrict trade to protect the environment (see also Sampson 2003). In the Marrakech Agreement (establishing the WTO) there is explicit reference to sustainable development as one of the WTO's general objectives. Its article XX.g permits restrictions if they complement national programs for conservation of resources.[12] WTO members are allowed to adopt national environmental protection policies, provided they do not discriminate between imported and domestic products (WTO 2004).

Clearly, the main channel by which the WTO might affect the natural environment is its impact on trade liberalization. However, the direction of the impact of the WTO on liberalization is not obvious *a priori*. For example, Guisinger (2001) does not find empirical evidence suggesting that WTO membership is a significant determinant of the rate of trade liberalization. On the contrary, the WTO affects the level of trade protection (Guisinger 2005).

Whether liberalization is actually beneficial or detrimental to the environment is also subject to considerable controversy (Alpay 2002). According to the WTO (2004), trade liberalization improves the allocation and efficient use of natural resources. The Secretariat of the WTO identifies a range of channels through which the removal of trade restrictions improves environmental quality.[13] Among them is a more efficient factor use through enhanced competition, poverty reduction through trade expansion and encouragement of a sustainable rate of natural resource exploitation, and an increase in the availability of environment-related goods and services through market liberalization. Firms from developed countries may find it cheaper to use the same technology for production in developing countries they use at home, thus contributing to cleaner production in the developing country. In their review article, Beghin and Potier (1997) conclude that trade liberalization does not induce wholesale specialization in dirty manufacturing industries in the developing world. Wheeler and Martin (1992) show that liberalization contributed to the international diffusion of clean technology in wood pulp production.

By expanding the scale of production, liberalization can, however, also decrease environmental quality. According to Reed (1996) and Daly (1996), trade liberalization discourages the internalization of environmental costs in developing countries as a consequence of increased competition from developed countries. Environmental standards may be considered as being non-tariff barriers so they would be discouraged. As Killick (1993) points out, liberalization is likely to induce a shift in production towards tradable goods, increasing pressure to exploit natural resources.

Evidence in favour of a negative link from liberalization to environmental quality is provided by Mani and Wheeler (1999). Their cross-section analysis shows that pollution intensive production has fallen considerably in the OECD while it has risen in the developing world.[14] Giordano (1994) suggests that free trade can compound over-exploitation of natural resources in countries without clearly defined property rights.

In summary, the previous discussion implies two alternative hypotheses:

Hypothesis 8a: WTO involvement improves environmental governance and outcomes.

Hypothesis 8b: WTO involvement worsens environmental governance and outcomes.

Data and method

Our regressions employ cross-sectional and pooled time-series cross-sectional data. The panel data are averages over five years. They cover the time period 1970–2000 and extend to a maximum of 112 countries. Since some of the data are not available for all countries or periods, the panel data are unbalanced and the number of observations depends on the choice of explanatory variables. The cross-section-analysis uses the most recent data available for the dependent variables and averages over the last 30 years for the explanatory variables. The analysis refers to about 90 countries.

The panel regressions are estimated using Feasible Generalized Least Squares (FGLS). This allows estimation in the presence of cross-sectional heteroscedasticity across panels and AR(1) autocorrelation. We impose the additional assumption that the first order autoregressive process is homogenous across countries, i.e. we only estimate one common AR(1) term.[15]

Our cross-section regressions are estimated by OLS and robust regressions. The robust regression technique weighs observations in an iterative process.

Starting with OLS, estimates are obtained through weighted least squares where observations with relatively large residuals get smaller weight. This results in estimates not being overly influenced by any specific observation.

We employ five dependent variables to test our hypotheses. The first is biochemical oxygen demand (BOD), which is a proxy for water pollution. According to the European Environment Agency, a high demand can indicate falling levels of dissolved oxygen, implying dangerous consequences for river diversity.[16] BOD is available for a maximum of 114 countries over the period 1980–2001 (World Bank 2005). We employ the logarithm of emissions in kilogram per day and per capita. In the literature on air pollution, the most frequently used measures are carbon dioxide (CO_2) and sulphur dioxide (SO_2) emissions (Gassebner *et al.* 2006). We include the logarithm of CO_2 and SO_2 (in metric tons per capita) in our empirical analysis. Data for CO_2 are available for up to 188 countries covering the years 1970–2000 (World Bank 2005). However, as Gassebner *et al.* (2006) point out, these data are based on calculations instead of being measured directly.

The source for SO_2 data is Stern (2005). It is available over the period 1970–2000 for a maximum of about 200 countries. In constructing the dataset, Stern combined various sources and interpolated or extrapolated missing data:

> For the remaining countries and for missing years for countries with some published data, [he] interpolate[s] or extrapolate[s] estimates using either an econometric emissions frontier model, an environmental Kuznets curve model, or a simple extrapolation, depending on the availability of data.
>
> (Stern 2005: 163)

While these data give a decent overview of the evolution of sulphur emissions in the past decade for a substantial part of the world, employing the environmental Kuznets curve in their construction makes them to some extent problematic (Gassebner *et al.* 2006).

As our fourth measure of environmental quality we employ round wood production (measured as the log of thousand cubic meters produced per capita). Data is available from the Food and Agriculture Agency of the United Nations (FAO) over the period 1970–2003, for about 170 countries (FAO 2004).

The fifth measure is no outcome variable but a composite index intended to measure environmental sustainability. The Environmental Sustainability Index (ESI) is calculated by the Environmental Performance Measurement Project in collaboration with the Center for International Earth Science Information Network (CIESIN) and the World Economic Forum (Esty *et al.* 2005). The ESI is a composite index tracking a diverse set of socioeconomic, environmental and institutional indicators that characterize and influence environmental sustainability at the national level.[17] As these data are not available prior to 2001, we cannot employ panel data methods to analyse them. We employ the most recent (2005) data for our cross-section analysis.

Our selection of control variables follows the previous literature as closely as possible. In choosing the covariates for the CO_2, SO_2 and BOD equations, we rely on the robustness analysis of Gassebner *et al.* (2006).[18] We employ those variables that have been shown to be robust and are available for a sufficient number of countries and years. We use the level and square of (the logarithm of) GDP per capita to take account of the environmental Kuznets curve. Openness to trade is also included.[19] The effect of trade may occur via the scale effect, the composition effect, and the technique effect.[20] *A priori*, trade may thus increase or reduce pollution.[21]

A dummy for left-wing governments is included to account for their prefer-ence for environmental protection. A dummy for dictatorships is employed, as dictators may take greater care of the environment to verify their leading position than democratically elected leaders would (Gassebner *et al.* 2006). We include population density and the share of urban population in total population to account for demographic factors. Higher population density and greater urbanization are likely to increase pollution. The value added in the manufacturing industry (in percent of GDP) takes account of a country's industrialization. It is hypothesized to increase pollution. Finally, fertilizer consumption (in 100 grams per hectare of arable land) is employed. Accord-ing to Gassebner *et al.* (2006), fertilizer consumption can be interpreted as reflecting a country's general attitude towards environmental protection. In low income countries, fertilizer is relatively easy and cheap to produce but its production is pollution intensive. The presence of these 'dirty' industries is likely to be associated with greater water and air pollution.[22]

The panel regressions also include regional dummy variables for Africa, Eastern and Central Europe, Asia, and Latin America (which turn out to be jointly significant in almost all regressions).[23] However, the coefficients of the dummies are not reported in the tables. Appendix A lists all variables with their exact sources and definitions, while Appendix B provides descriptive statistics.

In choosing the covariates for the analysis of round wood production we follow Pandey and Wheeler (2001). We therefore include (the log of) the export and import prices for round wood, the quantity of world exports of round wood and the oil price in our list of explanatory variables. As none of these additional variables turns out to be significant at conventional levels, we stick to the model introduced for CO_2, SO_2 and BOD. We employ the same covariates when analysing the environmental sustainability index.

Given the potential indirect effect of the international organizations on environmental quality via trade liberalization discussed above, we also include an index of liberalization. The index has been developed by Gwartney and Lawson (2004) as part of their economic freedom index. It reflects the free-dom to trade internationally, where higher scores reflect greater freedom. The index ranges from 1 to 10 and comprises taxes on international trade, regulatory trade barriers, the actual size of the trade sector as compared to its expected size, the difference between the official exchange rate and the black market rate, and international capital market controls. It is available over the period 1970–2002 for a maximum of 123 countries.

Turning to the impact of international organizations, we employ a range of dummy variables. Most of these variables have been coded according to the organizations' annual reports. Data on regional development banks has been provided by Hicks *et al.* (2005). The influence of the IMF and the development banks is captured by the average yearly number of programs (or projects) starting in the preceding five-year period.[24] This is meant to capture the overall influence of the financial institutions, i.e. the impact of available or disbursed money, the policy conditions they attach to their loans and their policy advice.[25] An alternative possibility to capturing the environmental impact of the Development Banks would be to classify their projects according to category, and focus on those with direct environmental relevance. For example, Nielson and Tierney (2003) coded (World Bank) projects as either predominantly environmental or not. However, projects attempting to improve the environment on paper may not be implemented as agreed, and thus may not be a good proxy for the international organizations' impact on the natural environment. IOs may also take environmental issues into account in their non-environmental projects. Projects may thus affect the environment independent of whether they are classified as being primarily environmental or not (Gutner 2005b). Using overall project dummies is preferable.[26] We construct variables for the UN development program and environment program along the same lines.

With respect to the WTO, two variables have been employed. The first is the average number of years the country has been a WTO member in the preceding five-year period.[27] The second is the total number of years the country has been a WTO member since 1970. As the results are very similar, we only report those for the former.

As one problem with measuring the influence of international organizations on environmental quality, countries with poorer environmental records may self select into (the programs of) these institutions. However – except for the Global Environmental Facility – the international organizations included in our analysis do not primarily address environmental issues. As we control for other factors of development, such self-selection is unlikely to be an issue here. We thus disregard the potential endogeneity in our analysis.

When estimating the regressions, we not only want to capture the direct impact of the international organizations on environmental quality, but also their indirect effect via trade liberalization. We therefore estimate 2SLS in addition to FGLS and, respectively, OLS. In our 2SLS regressions, we follow Guisinger (2005: 128: Table 1) in selecting potential determinants of trade liberalization. Again we do not include variables that are not available for a sufficient number of countries and years. We include a countries' (log) GDP per capita (World Bank 2005), its democracy score (Marshall and Jaggers

2000), a dummy that takes the value one for countries with a presidential system (Beck *et al.* 2001), and dummies that are one if a country's exports are mainly manufactured goods, mainly fuel, and, respectively, if the country is undeveloped (all Easterly and Sewadeh 2002). Regarding the impact of international organizations, we employ the same variables as in the environmental quality regressions.

Results

This section reports the results of the empirical analysis. We start with the determinants of trade liberalization. Table 2.1, at the end of the chapter, reports the results. Our panel analysis refers to 90 countries. We include the number of projects agreed on for each international organization one at a time. The final column includes all organizations. As can be seen, more trade liberalization is induced by high GDP per capita, with a coefficient significant at the 1 per cent level in all specifications. In most regressions, trade liberalization is also positively linked to democracy. Manufactured exports, fuel exports and the dummies for development and presidential systems have no robustly significant impact. A Wald test shows that all variables are jointly significant at the 1 per cent level in all regressions.[28] Turning to the impact of the international organizations, the results show that the ADB significantly promotes trade liberalization according to both specifications. The same is true for the UNDP and WTO membership. EBRD and UNEP have a significantly positive impact when included individually, but not in the full model specification of column 10.[29] In the final equation, the number of AfDB and IADB projects induces less trade liberalization. According to the estimates of column 10, one additional ADB project over the whole five-year period increases the index of trade liberalization by 0.07 points: an additional UNDP GEF loan by 0.54 points. WTO membership increases the index by 0.03 points, while an additional AfDB (IADB) project reduces the index by 0.09 (0.07) points. The impact of the international organizations on trade liberalization is jointly significant at the 1 per cent level.

We now turn to the impact of the international organizations on the environment. Table 2.2 reports (panel) results for CO_2, SO_2, BOD and round wood production, with and without employing instruments for trade liberalization. As can be seen, the results show some support for the environmental Kuznets curve hypothesis. In most regressions per capita GDP increases environmental damage, while its square has a significantly negative coefficient in some. The obvious exception is round wood production, where production is not significantly affected by GDP and its square. The results also show that CO_2 emissions are higher with greater economic openness, with a coefficient significant at the 1 per cent level. In line with our expectations, bigger manufacturing sectors and more intensive use of fertilizer generally harm the environment. Regarding population density, the results are mixed, while greater urbanization significantly increases CO_2 and SO_2 emissions, but significantly reduces round wood production and water pollution. Left-wing governments significantly reduce CO_2 emissions in the 2SLS regression and have no significant impact in relation to the other specifications. Dictatorships exert a significantly negative impact on the amount of CO_2 emissions and water pollution, but increase round wood production (according to the IV estimates). The index of trade liberalization is significant at least at the 5 per cent level in two equations only. According to the 2SLS results of column 2, an increase in the index by 0.1 points reduces CO_2 emissions by about 8 per cent. Column 8 shows that the same increase raises round wood production by 5 per cent. In calculating the total impact of the international organizations we have to keep their indirect effects via this channel into account.

The results show a substantial impact of the international organizations considered here. In all regressions this impact is jointly significant at the 5 per cent level. Generally, the impact of the international organizations is strongest when it comes to CO_2 emissions and round wood production. However, the results are rarely consistent across the GLS and 2SLS specifications. The exceptions refer to the impact of the EBRD and WTO on SO_2 emissions. As can be seen, at least at the 5 per cent level of significance, EBRD projects and WTO membership reduce emissions. An additional EBRD project reduces emissions by between 4 and 10 per cent, while the impact of WTO membership ranges from 1 to 2 per cent. The following discussion refers to the 2SLS regressions, where the endogeneity of trade liberalization is taken into account.

Regarding CO_2 emissions, column 2 shows a substantial impact of the international organizations on the environment. CO_2 emissions rise significantly with a greater number of World Bank and ADB projects, and fall with the number of IADB projects. According to the results, the direct quantitative impact of an additional project is smallest for the IADB, where an additional project reduces emissions by 5 per cent. IMF programs reduce air pollution at the 1 per cent level of significance, with an additional IMF program implying a reduction in emissions by 17 per cent over a five-year period. Also at the 1 per cent level, WTO membership increases emissions, and the same is true for UNDP projects.

When we take the indirect effect of the organizations via their impact on trade liberalization into account, however, the direct impact of IADB projects on CO_2 emissions is reversed. One additional five-year project by the IADB increases emissions by 1 per cent in total, since it produces a reduction of the liberalization index of 0.086 points, leading to an indirect effect on emissions of 6 per cent. Taking the indirect effect via trade liberalization into account for all significant coefficients, the impact of ADB and UNDP is reduced to about one third of their direct impact. The total effect of WTO membership on emissions is also reversed. Overall, an additional ADB project increases CO_2 emissions by 3 per cent over the five-year-period. A project financed by the UNDP increases emissions by 21 per cent, while WTO membership reduces emissions by 1 per cent in total.

Regarding SO_2 emissions and water pollution, the results show that the international organizations rarely have a significant impact. There are three exceptions: BOD demand is significantly reduced by IADB projects, with a coefficient significant at the 1 per cent level. This influence is quantitatively relevant – one additional IADB project each year reduces BOD demand (in metric tons per capita) by more than 4 per cent. SO_2 emissions decrease significantly with EBRD projects and WTO membership, at least at the 5 per cent level of significance.

Turning to round wood production, finally, the results are again ambiguous. Production rises significantly with IMF and IADB projects, while it is reduced by World Bank and UNDP projects. The direct quantitative impact of an additional project lies between 3 per cent (for the World Bank) and more than 50 per cent (UNDP). Again, given the significant impact of trade liberalization on round wood production, however, we have to take the indirect effect of the international organizations via liberalization into account. The indirect impact is quantitatively relevant. It even reverses the negative impact of the IADB on environmental quality, so that an additional five-year-project reduces emissions by 0.6 per cent in total. The impact of the UNDP is substantially reduced, amounting to about 25 per cent in total.

To summarize, the international organizations investigated here affect the natural environment predominantly via their impact on CO_2 emissions. The World Bank, ADB, UNDP, and WTO membership increase emissions, while the IMF and IADB reduce emissions. The EBRD, AfDB and UNEP do not significantly effect CO_2 emissions.

Arguably, as many international organizations took environmental issues into account starting in the mid-1980s only, the negative results presented here may be driven by the choice of sample period. Table 2.3 therefore replicates the analysis for the 2SLS regressions over the period 1985–2000. The substantially reduced number of observations results in generally higher standard errors, implying a greater number of insignificant coefficients. As can be seen, the major results regarding the impact of the international organizations on the environment, however, remain. In the more recent period though, the AfDB seems to have increased CO_2 emissions and water pollution, while the results for round wood production are generally less significant.

Table 2.4, finally, shows the results of our cross-section estimates. As can be seen, these results also show some support for the Kuznets curve hypothesis, implying an increase in air pollution with increasing per capita GDP, whereas its square has a significantly negative coefficient in the case of CO_2. BOD is the exception here: production is significantly reduced by higher GDP and increases with its square. Greater economic openness, larger manufacturing sectors and more intensive use of fertilizer affect the natural environment adversely, whilst population density and fertilizer use have a significantly negative impact on environmental sustainability which is in line with Gassebner *et al.* (2006). In their interpretation, the use of fertilizer is a proxy for the attitude towards environmental protection in a specific country. Greater urbanization significantly increases SO_2 emissions, and also BOD demand. The dummies for left-wing governments and dictatorships have a significantly negative effect on environmental governance and sustainability, contradicting our *a priori* expectations.

The tests for joint significance of the impact of international organizations in the cross-sectional analysis are in most regressions significant at the 1 per cent level. In the long run, however, the individual impact of the international organizations seems to be much more limited as compared to the medium-term effects reported above. The results show that CO_2 emissions rise significantly with projects by the Word Bank, and are significantly reduced with programs by the IMF, AfDB and IADB. The EBRD significantly increases round wood production. Finally, BOD demand falls significantly with IADB programs. Most of these results are in line with those of the panel approach reported above.[30]

With regard to the environmental sustainability index, we fail to find a consistent picture among the different specifications and organizations. None of the coefficients is significant at the 1 per cent significance level and none of the organizations and programs included was significant in more than one regression.

Summary

This study empirically investigated the impact of key international organizations on environmental governance and outcomes. Overall, we find that international organizations significantly affect the natural environment. Although the impact of IOs on the environment is found to be jointly significant in all regressions, many results are not entirely consistent among the different specifications analysed for each international organization and environmental measure.

Turning to UNEP, there are no significant coefficients for the number of GEF projects implemented through the UNEP in the panel studies. In the cross-section analysis, our results even show that UNEP projects significantly increase water pollution. As this result does not hold in the robust regression, however, it seems to be driven by outlying observations.

The natural environment improves only slowly. The ineffectiveness of UNEP in achieving significant improvements may thus reflect its short period of operation. Moreover, as Andresen and Rosendal (2005) point out, the UNEP's small budget limits its impact. Maybe the UNEP is simply too small to make a difference.

To summarize, we find that the international organizations affect the natural environment directly via their impact on CO_2 emissions. Projects financed by World Bank, ADB and UNDP, and membership in the WTO, increase emissions, while IADB projects reduce emissions. EBRD and UNEP do not significantly affect CO_2 emissions, while the AfDB increases emissions after 1985 only. Taking the indirect impact through trade liberalization into account, however, the WTO reduces emissions, while the IADB increases emissions. Regarding environmental governance – as proxied by the environmental sustainability index – our results show no significant impact of the international organizations investigated here.

Notes

1 The study does not include international non-governmental organizations. For an interesting analysis of these organizations see Timmer in this volume. We do not include the OECD's Environmental Performance Reviews in this study. For an analysis of the OECD's influence on environmental governance see Lehtonen in this volume.

2 According to the pollution haven hypothesis globalization causes dirty industrial sectors to be located in countries with low environmental standards. See Beghin (2000) for a summary of this literature. See also Cole (2004) and Gassebner *et al.* (2008).

3 Nielson and Tierney (2003) provide a description and explanation of recent environmental policies at the Bank. See also Gutner (2005a, 2005b).

4 For case studies regarding the evidence of structural adjustment on water quality see Munasinghe and Cruz (1994) and Goldin and Roland-Host (1994).

5 Apart from its influence on the program country's wood production, the Bank may influence wood production in other countries, when exports and imports of the program country change (Pandey and Wheeler 2001).

6 According to Runnals (1986), for example, the IADB did not have an adequate system of environmental impact analysis in 1985 although the Environmental Management Committee (EMC) had been founded two years before. Analogously, project environmental reports have been made by the ADB since 1981, but without an adequate framework and in-depth analysis (Mikesell and Williams 1992).

7 As, for example, in the Development Management Training of the AfDB or through the Joint African Institute (AfDB 2001).

8 For a detailed description on the effects of multipurpose dams, irrigation, forestry and livestock projects, agricultural credit loans and loans for infrastructure and extractive industry see Mikesell and Williams (1992). They also present several case studies on different MDB projects in these areas. See also Hansen and Hansen (1999).

9 In this context the benefits and drawbacks of an independent World Environmental Organization (WEO) have also been discussed. The main arguments in favour of a WEO can be found in Biermann (2001). For further discussion see von Moltke (2001) and Lodefalk and Whalley (2002).

10 The optimality of GEF allocation and the role of agency problems in this context is analysed by Congleton (2002) and Lewis (2003). Congleton (2002, 2006) shows that the GEF does not maximize international environmental quality. According to his estimates, countries directly represented on GEF's decision making bodies obtain more money than environmental factors can account for. As Andresen and Rosendal (2005) point out, the UNEP is far from being effective in reaching its goals in coordinating multilateral environmental agencies. Ivanova (2005) discusses institutional factors to be considered in the context of organizational reform necessary to enhance UNEP's role as anchor institution for global environmental issues.

11 The facilities have to belong to one of four focal areas, (1) climate change, (2) biological diversity, (3) international waters and (4) ozone layer depletion.

12 WTO policies are therefore much in line with the preferences of most environmental NGOs. Cone (2002) provides an interesting illustration.

13 WT/CTE/W/67, 7 November 1997, 'Environmental Benefits of Removing Trade
Restrictions and Distortions', Note by the Secretariat.

14 However, Mani and Wheeler (1999) also show that the tendency to form pollution
havens is quite limited. See also Cole (2004).

15 Note that the FGLS correction for a single AR(1) term is unlikely to cause the
standard errors to be flawed as would be the case employing the Parks correction
with individual AR(1) terms for each country (Beck and Katz 1995: 637).

16 <http://themes.eea.eu.int/Specific_media/water/indicators/bod/index_html>

17 While the ESI is used as an index of environmental sustainability in a substantial
number of recent articles (see <http://sedac.ciesin.columbia.edu/citations/cita-
tions_esi.html>), it has also been criticized. See Jha and Bhanu Murthy (2003) for
critical comments regarding choice of method and inclusion of variables,

18 See Table 2 of Gassebner *et al.* (2006) for an overview of the empirical literature.
For an excellent robustness test employing Bayesian Averaging of Classical Estimates see Lamla (2006).

19 Note that GDP may also be affected by the involvement of international organizations (e.g. Dreher 2006). If, for example, IMF programs increase economic growth
in the program countries, the scale effect of higher GDP may worsen environmental quality. We disregard this channel here.

20 The scale effect refers to the negative environmental quality arising from an
increase in production. The composition effect results from trade-induced changes
in the composition of output that affects the environment. The technique effect
arises from a shift towards cleaner technology resulting from shifting preferences
in line with higher incomes.

21 Clearly, the level of trade can also be endogenous to environmental quality. However, the instrumental variables approach of Frankel and Rose (2002) shows very
similar effects among their OLS and IV estimates. We therefore disregard this
potential endogeneity here.

22 All variables are taken from the World Bank's (2005) World Development Indicators. The exceptions are the dummies for left-wing governments and the dictator-
ship dummy. The former is from Beck *et al.* (2001), the latter has been constructed
employing the Polity IV index of democracy (Marshall and Jaggers 2000). It
takes the value one for scores smaller than three on the Polity index, and zero
otherwise.

23 The dummies showed to be insignificant in the cross-section regressions, so we
exclude them there.

24 Arguably, program dummies are imperfect proxies to capture the impact of international organizations on policy and outcome measures, ignoring both the
amount of resources made available and the degree to which associated conditions
have been implemented. Still, this proxy is standard in the recent empirical literature. Atoyan and Conway (2006) and Dreher (2005, 2006) are recent examples.

25 See Boockmann and Dreher (2003) for an attempt to separate out these effects of
the international organizations on economic freedom. Dreher (2005, 2006) analyses the impact of those channels of IMF involvement on fiscal and monetary
policy and, respectively, economic growth.

26 Clearly, dummies for program agreements cannot take the degree to which the
program is implemented into account. Ideally, we would also want to control
for the degree of compliance with program conditionality. Unfortunately, no
appropriate data exist.

27 The WTO replaced the GATT in 1995. We treat GATT and WTO membership as
continuous.

28 We do not report the R-squared statistic as with GLS the total sum of squares

cannot be broken down in the same way as with OLS, making the R-square statistic less useful as a diagnostic tool for GLS regressions. Specifically, an R-square statistic computed from GLS sums of squares need not be bounded between zero and one and does not represent the percentage of total variation in the dependent variable that is accounted for by the model. Additionally, eliminating or adding variables in a model does not always increase or decrease the computed R-square value.

29 Clearly, the projects of some organizations are to some extent correlated. Correlation, however, never exceeds 0.50 and is well below 0.15 in most cases.

30 Only the effects that are significant in all three regressions or at least in two of them – but including the robust regression – were taken into account here.

Table 2.1 Trade liberalization, 1980–2000, 90 countries (panel data)

	(1)	(2)	(3)	(4)	(5)	(6)	(7)	(8)	(9)	(10)
(log) GDP p.c.	0.771 (11.72***)	0.770 (11.53***)	0.821 (12.9***)	0.819 (12.64***)	0.814 (12.68***)	0.805 (13.58***)	0.871 (12.66***)	0.799 (12.79***)	0.786 (11.55***)	0.964 (6.66***)
Exports primarily manufactured, dummy	0.592 (2.23**)	0.562 (2.09**)	0.180 (1.39)	0.186 (1.45)	0.191 (1.47)	0.153 (1.29)	0.175 (1.23)	0.173 (1.36)	0.223 (1.83*)	0.138 (0.21)
Exports primarily fuel, dummy	-0.422 (1.86*)	-0.430 (1.9*)	-0.499 (2.16**)	-0.520 (2.3**)	-0.532 (2.31**)	-0.538 (2.52**)	-0.561 (2.34**)	-0.468 (2.09**)	-0.332 (1.39)	-0.368 (0.55)
Developing country, dummy	0.312 (0.87)	0.332 (0.92)	0.526 (1.61)	0.665 (2.12**)	0.678 (2.11**)	0.689 (2.36**)	0.701 (2.04**)	0.658 (2.18**)	0.822 (2.43**)	0.710 (0.58)
Democracy, Index	0.038 (2.99***)	0.039 (3.04***)	0.036 (2.69***)	0.033 (2.52**)	0.034 (2.6***)	0.033 (2.63***)	0.021 (1.5)	0.033 (2.58***)	0.027 (1.94*)	0.025 (1.43)
System Presidential, dummy	0.049 (0.77)	0.042 (0.67)	0.045 (0.86)	0.045 (0.87)	0.043 (0.82)	0.041 (0.82)	0.087 (1.51)	0.060 (1.18)	0.065 (1.08)	0.214 (2.95***)
IMF programs (t-1)	-0.012 (0.08)									0.018 (0.15)
World Bank programs (t-1)		0.011 (0.5)								0.024 (0.94)
ADB (t-1)			0.086 (2.89***)							0.066 (2.09**)
AfDB (t-1)				0.024 (0.65)						-0.086 (3.07***)
IADB (t-1)					-0.021 (0.69)					-0.071 (2.73***)
EBRD (t-1)						0.061 (2.6***)				0.027 (1.24)

UNDP (t-1)						0.818 (4.94***)			0.543 (3.16***)
UNEP (t-1)							0.802 (2.34**)		0.261 (0.78)
WTO membership (t-1)								0.021 (5.85***)	0.027 (3.53***)
Number of observations	461	461	599	599	599	599	599	599	461
Wald Test (Prob>chi2)	0.00	0.00	0.00	0.00	0.00	0.00	0.00	0.00	0.00

Notes: Estimated using Feasible Generalized Least Squares (FGLS). Corrected for cross-sectional heteroskedasticity across panels and first order autocorrelation.

All regressions include regional dummy variables for Africa, Eastern and Central Europe, Asia, and Latin America. Levels of significance: 1 per cent (***), 5 per cent (**), 10 per cent (*)

t-statistics in parentheses.

Table 2.2 Environmental quality, 1970–2000, 112 countries (panel data)

	CO_2		SO_2		BOD		Round Wood	
	(1)	(2)[a]	(3)	(4)[a]	(5)	(6)[a]	(7)	(8)[a]
(log) GDP p.c.	1.680 (6.24***)	0.810 (2.34**)	0.851 (2.05**)	1.233 (2.76***)	1.515 (5.62***)	1.313 (4.23***)	-0.437 (1.47)	-0.346 (0.83)
(log) squared GDP p.c.	-0.054 (2.91***)	0.023 (0.89)	-0.008 (0.25)	-0.049 (1.45)	-0.074 (4.23***)	-0.060 (2.65***)	0.020 (0.9)	0.006 (0.18)
Openness	0.002 (3.32***)	0.020 (6.65***)	0.001 (1.14)	0.002 (0.4)	0.002 (2.11**)	0.004 (1.34)	0.001 (1.7*)	-0.009 (2.69***)
Manufacture, value added	0.009 (2.74***)	0.008 (2.47**)	0.004 (1.38)	0.011 (2.71***)	0.035 (8.97***)	0.054 (12.23***)	-0.002 (0.61)	0.000 (0.00)
Fertilizer (per hectare)	0.000 (1.71*)	0.000 (2.2**)	0.000 (3.01***)	0.000 (3.15***)	0.000 (2.18**)	0.000 (1.23)	0.000 (0.17)	0.000 (0.00)
Population density	0.000 (2.57***)	-0.002 (5.15***)	-0.007 (14.01***)	-0.001 (1.62)	0.000 (1.03)	0.000 (0.06)	-0.003 (0.17)	-0.001 (1.03)
Urbanization	0.014 (7.59***)	0.022 (10.14***)	0.005 (1.55)	0.012 (4.6***)	-0.006 (2.65***)	-0.005 (2.05**)	-0.017 (8.07***)	-0.022 (9.24***)
Government left-wing, dummy	0.006 (0.18)	-0.199 (3.92***)	0.028 (0.8)	0.012 (0.19)	0.062 (1.55)	0.081 (1.33)	-0.057 (7.55***)	0.002 (0.04)
Dictatorship, dummy	0.021 (0.63)	-0.353 (4.87***)	0.049 (1.63)	0.034 (0.32)	-0.096 (2.24**)	-0.188 (2.18**)	0.012 (0.39)	0.270 (3.35***)
Trade liberalization, index	0.009 (0.87)	-0.838 (6.06***)	-0.008 (0.87)	-0.047 (0.22)	-0.001 (0.08)	-0.035 (0.26)	0.010 (1.16)	0.515 (3.7***)
IMF programs (t-1)	-0.054 (1.48)	-0.170 (3.84***)	-0.112 (1.31)	-0.059 (1.1)	-0.009 (0.13)	-0.021 (0.21)	0.013 (0.4)	0.098 (1.81*)

World Bank programs (t-1)	0.006	0.053	0.005	-0.005	-0.005	-0.013	0.001	-0.030
	(0.89)	(4.95***)	(0.79)	(0.33)	(0.63)	(1.11)	(0.16)	(2.95***)
ADB (t-1)	-0.006	0.090	0.004	0.030	-0.020	-0.021	0.008	-0.025
	(0.93)	(5.06***)	(0.34)	(1.12)	(1.83*)	(1.1)	(0.91)	(1.26)
AfDB (t-1)	-0.019	-0.019	0.003	-0.009	-0.021	0.033	0.005	0.002
	(1.57)	(1.52)	(0.44)	(0.95)	(0.7)	(1.25)	(0.85)	(0.15)
IADB (t-1)	-0.004	-0.047	-0.008	-0.002	-0.013	-0.042	0.006	0.031
	(0.85)	(5.61***)	(1.21)	(0.19)	(1.58)	(3.49***)	(1.05)	(2.66***)
EBRD (t-1)	-0.033	0.004	-0.096	-0.036	-0.010	0.006	0.039	0.025
	(3.85***)	(0.3)	(6.36***)	(2.06**)	(1.25)	(0.13)	(5.85***)	(1.36)
UNDP (t-1)	-0.100	0.663	0.045	-0.017	-0.228	-0.034	-0.056	-0.532
	(2.09**)	(4.88***)	(0.7)	(0.08)	(2.46**)	(0.11)	(1.1)	(3.71***)
UNEP (t-1)	0.095	0.042	-0.081	0.187	0.057	-0.609	-0.101	-0.212
	(0.87)	(0.34)	(0.7)	(1.29)	(0.24)	(0.3)	(0.92)	(1.07)
WTO membership (t-1)	0.003	0.008	-0.020	-0.012	0.000	0.006	0.005	0.003
	(1.52)	(2.89***)	(3.28***)	(3.51***)	(0.1)	(1.6)	(2.28***)	(1.17)
Number of observations	417	393	412	393	269	260	398	381
Wald Test (Prob>chi2)	0.00	0.00	0.00	0.00	0.00	0.00	0.00	0.00

Notes: Estimated using Feasible Generalized Least Squares (FGLS). Corrected for cross-sectional heteroskedasticity across panels and first order autocorrelation.

a Estimated with 2SLS; trade liberalization predicted with equation of Table 1, column 10.

All regressions include regional dummy variables for Africa, Eastern and Central Europe, Asia, and Latin America.

t-statistics in parentheses. Levels of significance: 1 per cent (***), 5 per cent (**), 10 per cent (*).

Table 2.3 Environmental quality, 1985–2000, 75 countries (panel data)

	CO_2 (1)	SO_2 (2)	BOD (3)	Round Wood (4)
(log) GDP p.c.	0.310	0.187	0.129	−2.024
	(0.68)	(0.38)	(0.41)	(2.92***)
(log) squared GDP p.c.	0.056	0.029	0.034	0.131
	(1.63)	(0.8)	(1.46)	(2.41**)
Openness	0.023	0.009	0.006	0.000
	(5.89***)	(2.31**)	(2.47**)	(0.04)
Manufacture, value added	0.005	0.024	0.057	−0.019
	(1.3)	(3.7***)	(11.39***)	(2.49**)
Fertilizer (per hectare)	0.000	0.000	0.000	0.000
	(1.58)	(4.59***)	(1.38)	(1.48)
Population density	−0.003	−0.003	0.000	−0.003
	(4.38***)	(4.6***)	(0.62)	(2.56***)
Urbanization	0.030	0.025	−0.007	−0.020
	(9.92***)	(7.61***)	(2.65***)	(4.92***)
Government left-wing, dummy	−0.199	0.069	0.155	−0.131
	(3.34***)	(0.98)	(2.62***)	(1.44)
Dictatorship, dummy	−0.333	−0.086	−0.128	0.131
	(3.56***)	(0.78)	(1.5)	(0.81)
Trade liberalization, index	−0.993	−0.435	−0.135	0.247
	(5.62***)	(2.57***)	(0.87)	(0.92)
IMF programs (t-1)	−0.242	−0.003	−0.112	0.233
	(4.6***)	(0.02)	(0.16)	(1.73*)
World Bank programs (t-1)	0.060	−0.012	0.014	−0.021
	(4.9***)	(0.6)	(1.24)	(1.16)
ADB (t-1)	0.095	0.005	0.012	−0.004
	(3.47***)	(0.13)	(0.47)	(0.1)
AfDB (t-1)	0.034	0.032	0.060	−0.007
	(2.95***)	(1.22)	(2.33**)	(0.32)
IADB (t-1)	−0.027	−0.002	−0.009	0.005
	(3.29***)	(0.16)	(0.95)	(0.27)
EBRD (t-1)	−0.006	0.021	0.002	0.018
	(0.76)	(0.92)	(0.21)	(0.72)
UNDP (t-1)	0.670	0.222	−0.043	−0.344
	(4.29***)	(1.12)	(0.39)	(1.38)
UNEP (t-1)	−0.100	−0.088	0.195	−0.038
	(1.28)	(0.26)	(0.94)	(0.21)
WTO membership (t-1)	0.010	0.003	−0.009	0.012
	(3.29***)	(0.98)	(3.37***)	(2.38**)
Number of observations	206	206	133	202
Wald Test (Prob>chi2)	0.00	0.00	0.00	0.00

Notes: Estimated with 2SLS; trade liberalization predicted with equation of Table 1, column 10. All regressions include regional dummy variables for Africa, Eastern and Central Europe, Asia, and Latin America. t-statistics in parentheses. Levels of significance: 1 per cent (***), 5 per cent (**), 10 per cent (*).

Table 2.4 Environmental quality, 1970–2000 (cross section)

	CO_2			SO_2			BOD			Round Wood			Sustainability		
	(1)	(2)	(3)	(4)	(5)	(6)	(7)	(8)	(9)	(10)	(11)	(12)	(13)	(14)	(15)
(log) GDP p.c.	2.306 (3.26***)	2.205 (2.61**)	2.518 (2.81***)	1.250 (1.29)	0.647 (0.59)	0.980 (0.69)	-1.428 (0.65)	-2.332 (2.28**)	-1.358 (0.84)	-1.907 (1.12)	-1.000 (0.65)	-1.726 (0.88)	-0.027 (0.05)	0.366 (0.78)	3.776 (0.41)
(log) squared GDP p.c.	-0.097 (2.21**)	-0.094 (1.68*)	-0.108 (1.82*)	-0.066 (1.04)	-0.014 (0.19)	-0.038 (0.4)	0.120 (0.85)	0.159 (2.42**)	0.117 (1.11)	0.129 (1.07)	0.063 (0.6)	0.118 (0.89)	0.044 (0.17)	0.111 (3.3***)	-0.257 (0.42)
Openness	0.006 (1.8*)	0.005 (1.44)	0.009 (1.87*)	0.000 (0.05)	-0.001 (0.29)	0.008 (1.02)	0.009 (3.11***)	0.009 (2.74***)	0.010 (2.58**)	0.002 (0.28)	0.006 (1.1)	-0.006 (0.74)	0.035 (0.25)	0.175 (1.25)	0.015 (0.31)
Manufacture, value added	0.021 (1.06)	0.017 (1.03)	0.024 (1.35)	0.023 (0.87)	0.038 (1.76*)	0.032 (1.15)	0.043 (3.15***)	0.040 (4.92***)	0.046 (2.87**)	0.007 (0.21)	0.033 (1.32)	-0.022 (0.66)	-0.001 (0.74)	0.000 (0.36)	-0.050 (0.28)
Fertilizer (per hectare)	0.000 (0.98)	0.000 (0.94)	0.000 (0.45)	0.000 (0.55)	0.000 (1.58)	0.000 (0.66)	0.000 (0.91)	0.000 (2.57**)	0.000 (0.87)	0.000 (1.61)	0.000 (1.39)	0.000 (1.28)	-0.027 (1.77*)	-0.068 (7.52***)	-0.001 (0.65)
Population density	0.000 (1.08)	0.000 (0.58)	0.000 (0.32)	0.000 (0.17)	0.000 (0.52)	-0.001 (0.78)	-0.002 (1.53)	0.000 (0.17)	-0.002 (1.24)	-0.004 (2.13**)	-0.004 (3.05***)	-0.002 (0.87)	-0.005 (0.07)	-0.057 (0.8)	-0.022 (1.77*)
Urbanization	0.013 (1.46)	0.013 (1.51)	0.011 (1.3)	0.028 (2.01**)	0.018 (1.67*)	0.026 (1.92*)	0.022 (1.79*)	0.021 (3.45***)	0.021 (2.14*)	-0.022 (1.48)	-0.012 (0.95)	-0.022 (1.37)	-0.862 (0.5)	-0.905 (0.5)	0.007 (0.08)
Government left-wing, dummy	0.072 (0.38)	0.044 (0.21)	0.037 (0.16)	0.076 (0.26)	-0.076 (0.28)	0.023 (0.06)	0.341 (1.23)	0.480 (2.95**)	0.292 (1.03)	-0.089 (0.31)	-0.500 (1.67*)	0.132 (0.33)	-5.516 (2.36**)	-7.576 (3.21***)	-0.386 (0.16)
Dictatorship, dummy	0.057 (0.22)	0.132 (0.49)	0.122 (0.46)	0.528 (1.48)	0.294 (0.83)	0.471 (1.12)	-0.364 (1.53)	-0.265 (1.75)	-0.357 (1.51)	-0.552 (1.06)	-0.100 (0.24)	-0.447 (0.87)	-0.353 (0.28)	-2.193 (1.92*)	-5.015 (1.75*)
Trade liberalization, index	-0.102 (0.81)	-0.033 (0.26)	-0.194 (0.93)	0.120 (0.67)	0.135 (0.78)	-0.279 (0.84)	-0.274 (2.53**)	-0.169 (1.31)	-0.301 (2.07*)	0.355 (1.54)	0.072 (0.39)	0.831 (2.23**)	1.000 (0.13)	-4.423 (0.63)	1.303 (0.59)
IMF programs (t-1)	-0.652 (2.02**)	-0.712 (1.69*)	-0.786 (1.92*)	-0.558 (0.85)	0.178 (0.32)	-0.557 (0.86)	-0.114 (0.32)	0.011 (0.05)	-0.090 (0.24)	0.888 (1.79*)	0.637 (1.03)	0.702 (0.93)	8.680 (1.62)	1.627 (0.44)	8.230 (1.93*)
World Bank programs (t-1)	0.133 (3.22***)	0.123 (2.15**)	0.128 (2.3**)	-0.001 (0.02)	0.001 (0.01)	0.008 (0.09)	-0.061 (1.02)	-0.107 (2.16*)	-0.057 (0.95)	-0.049 (0.82)	-0.037 (0.46)	-0.043 (0.44)	0.638 (1.64)	0.861 (1.8*)	0.696 (1.22)
ADB (t-1)	0.058 (1.28)	0.046 (0.63)	0.052 (0.75)	0.018 (0.021)	-0.082 (0.87)	0.030 (0.27)	0.291 (3.05***)	0.004 (0.03)	0.290 (3.29***)	0.082 (1.17)	0.022 (0.22)	0.079 (0.66)	-0.335 (0.5)	0.113 (0.19)	-0.423 (0.61)

(Continued Overleaf)

Table 2.4 Continued

	CO₂			SO₂			BOD			Round Wood			Sustainability		
	(1)	(2)	(3)	(4)	(5)	(6)	(7)	(8)	(9)	(10)	(11)	(12)	(13)	(14)	(15)
AfDB (t-1)	-0.176 (1.53)	-0.189 (1.7*)	-0.198 (1.79*)	0.017 (0.09)	-0.208 (1.43)	-0.026 (0.15)	0.063 (0.27)	0.148 (0.66)	0.067 (0.34)	0.157 (1.17)	0.125 (0.79)	0.237 (1.22)	0.775 (1.33)	0.993 (1.09)	0.804 (0.72)
IADB (t-1)	-0.101 (2.89***)	-0.094 (2.09***)	-0.105 (2.44***)	-0.092 (1.5)	-0.133 (2.25**)	-0.110 (1.61)	-0.078 (1.92*)	-0.068 (2.5**)	-0.078 (1.7)	0.162 (2.65***)	0.073 (1.15)	0.204 (2.67***)	0.348 (0.74)	0.721 (1.89*)	0.437 (0.97)
EBRD (t-1)	0.070 (0.7)	0.076 (0.63)	0.068 (0.59)	0.046 (0.34)	-0.026 (0.16)	0.047 (0.25)	0.127 (1.67)	0.071 (0.98)	0.137 (1.6)	0.583 (2.43**)	0.406 (2.34**)	0.591 (2.88***)	0.575 (0.62)	1.510 (1.45)	0.471 (0.39)
UNDP (t-1)	-0.425 (0.81)	-0.315 (0.46)	-0.550 (0.85)	-0.219 (0.3)	0.166 (0.18)	-0.411 (0.4)	1.823 (2.05*)	0.718 (0.58)	1.858 (2.47**)	1.126 (1.47)	0.992 (1.01)	1.554 (1.37)	2.997 (0.5)	1.916 (0.34)	3.676 (0.56)
UNEP (t-1)	1.442 (0.77)	0.662 (0.12)	1.389 (0.27)	-2.851 (1.06)	-5.091 (0.73)	-1.314 (0.16)	11.305 (2.79**)	3.372 (1.24)	11.242 (2.82**)	-2.431 (0.95)	-2.621 (0.35)	-2.924 (0.33)	-39.763 (2.17**)	-15.818 (0.36)	-47.994 (0.94)
WTO membership (t-1)	-0.157 (0.67)	-0.111 (0.47)	-0.031 (0.13)	0.020 (0.06)	0.216 (0.71)	0.017 (0.05)	-0.672 (2.29**)	-0.217 (1.44)	-0.696 (2.56**)	0.761 (1.95*)	0.159 (0.47)	0.773 (1.83*)	-1.221 (0.58)	-1.112 (0.57)	-0.580 (0.24)
Method	OLS	Robust	IV	OLS	Robust	IV	OLS	Robust	IV	OLS	Robust	IV	OLS	Robust	IV
Adjusted R2	0.84		0.84	0.44		0.38	0.79		0.78	0.28		0.26	0.22		0.19
Observations	89	89	80	88	88	80	33	30	32	83	83	75	82	82	76
F-test (Prob>F)	0.00	0.00	0.00	0.00	0.00	0.00	0.00	0.00	0.00	0.00	0.01	0.01	0.00	0.00	0.03
Normality test (Prob>chi2)	0.89	0.90	0.85	0.00	0.00	0.00	0.00	0.00	0.00	0.00	0.00	0.56	0.01	0.00	0.00
Heteroscedasticity test (Prob>chi2)	0.44			0.14			0.44			0.00			0.75		
RESET (Prob>F)	0.11			0.64			0.23			0.01			0.00		

Notes: IV Estimates: trade liberalization predicted with equation of Table 1, column 10. (robust) t-statistics in parentheses. Levels of significance: 1 per cent (***), 5 per cent (**), 10 per cent (*).

Appendix A: Sources and definitions

Variable	Description	Source
Trade liberalization	Composite index measuring the freedom to trade internationally. Ranges from 1 to 10, with 10 showing more freedom.	Gwartney and Lawson (2004)
Exports primarily manufactured, dummy	Dummy that is one for countries exporting primarily manufactured goods and zero otherwise.	Easterly and Sewadeh (2002)
Exports primarily fuel, dummy	Dummy that is one for countries exporting primarily fuel and zero otherwise.	Easterly and Sewadeh (2002)
Developing country, dummy	Dummy that is one for developing countries and zero otherwise.	Easterly and Sewadeh (2002)
Democracy, Index	Measures the general openness of political institutions on a score of 0–10, with higher values representing more democracy.	Marshall and Jaggers (2000)
System Presidential, dummy	Dummy that is 1 for countries with presidential system and zero otherwise.	Beck *et al.* (2001)
IMF	Number of loan approvals in a certain year.	IMF Annual Reports (various years)
World Bank	Number of loan approvals in a certain year.	www.worldbank.org
ADB	Number of loan approvals in a certain year.	Hicks *et al.* (2005)
AfDB	Number of loan approvals in a certain year.	Hicks *et al.* (2005)
IADB	Number of loan approvals in a certain year.	Hicks *et al.* (2005)
EBRD	Number of loan approvals in a certain year.	Hicks *et al.* (2005)
UNDP	Number of loan approvals in a certain year.	www.gefonline.org/home.cfm
UNEP	Number of loan approvals in a certain year.	www.gefonline.org/home.cfm
WTO	Dummy for membership in GATT/WTO.	www.wto.org
CO_2	Carbon dioxide in logarithm of metric tons per capita.	World Bank (2005)
SO_2	Sulphur dioxide in logarithm of metric tons per capita.	Stern (2005)
BOD	Biochemical oxygen demand in logarithm of emissions in kilogram per day and capita.	World Bank (2005)

Variable	Description	Source
Round wood	Round wood production in logarithm of thousand cubic meters per capita.	FAO (2004)
Environmental sustainability, index	Composite index tracking a diverse set of socioeconomic, environmental, and institutional indicators that characterize and influence environmental sustainability at the national level	Esty *et al.* (2005)
(log) GDP p.c.	GDP per capita in constant 2000 US$.	World Bank (2005)
Openness	Sum of exports and imports in percent of GDP.	World Bank (2005)
Manufacture, value added	Manufacturing value added in percent of GDP.	World Bank (2005)
Fertilizer (per hectare)	Fertilizer consumption in 100 grams per hectare of arable land.	World Bank (2005)
Population density	Population density in people per sq km.	World Bank (2005)
Urbanization	Urban population in percent of total population.	World Bank (2005)

Appendix B: Descriptive statistics

Variable	Mean	Minimum	Maximum	Standard Deviation
Trade liberalization	5.72	1.70	9.60	1.53
Exports primarily manufactured, dummy	0.10	0.00	1.00	0.31
Exports primarily fuel, dummy	0.12	0.00	1.00	0.32
Developing country, dummy	0.94	0.00	1.00	0.24
Democracy, Index	3.98	0.00	10.00	3.75
System Presidential, dummy	0.55	0.00	1.00	0.81
IMF	0.14	0.00	1.00	0.21
World Bank	2.01	0.00	15.20	2.30
ADB	0.57	0.00	15.80	1.86
AfDB	0.61	0.00	7.60	1.28
IADB	1.06	0.00	15.80	2.53
EBRD	0.23	0.00	15.00	1.17
UNDP	0.08	0.00	1.20	0.18
UNEP	0.02	0.00	0.08	0.08
WTO	0.58	0.00	1.00	0.48
CO_2	−0.05	−4.47	3.96	1.22
SO_2	−5.34	−9.34	−1.71	1.32
BOD	−5.84	−10.19	−3.71	1.01

Round wood	−7.64	−13.82	−4.87	1.35
Environmental sustainability, index	49.94	36.30	71.80	7.07
(log) GDP p.c.	50.43	19.80	113.48	17.42
Openness	74.89	9.55	231.97	39.05
Manufacture, value added	15.15	0.63	39.20	7.60
Fertilizer (per hectare)	1000.94	0.90	30583.00	1965.14
Population density	99.82	1.44	1146.21	159.76
Urbanization	44.77	3.67	95.72	21.53

References

African Development Bank (2001) *Environmental and Social Assessment Procedures for African Development Bank's Public Sector Operations*, Abidjan, Côte d'Ivoire: African Development Bank.

Alpay, S. (2002) 'How Can Trade Liberalization Be Conducive to a Better Environment? A Survey of the Literature', mimeo, Beykent University.

Andresen, S. and Rosendal, K. (2005) 'The UN Environment Programme: Achievements and Challenges', International Organisations and Global Environmental Governance Conference Papers, Berlin.

Asian Development Bank (1986) 'Environmental Planning and Development', Conference Papers and Proceedings, Manila, Philippines: Asian Development Bank.

Asian Development Bank (1995a) 'Economic Assessment of Environmental Impacts (Supplementary Budget)', *JSF Reports*, Manila, Philippines: Asian Development Bank.

Asian Development Bank (1995b) 'Water Resources Development and Management', *Technical Assistance Reports*, Manila, Philippines: Asian Development Bank.

Asian Development Bank (1999) 'Water Resources Management in Southeast Asia – Phase 2', *Technical Assistance Reports*, Manila, Philippines: Asian Development Bank.

Asian Development Bank (2003) *ADB Environmental Assessment Guidelines*, Manila, Philippines: Asian Development Bank.

Atoyan, R. and Conway, P. (2006) 'Evaluating the Impact of IMF Programs: A Comparison of Matching and Instrumental-Variable Estimators', *Review of International Organizations*, 1(2): 99–124.

Battikha, A. (2002) 'Structural Adjustment and the Environment: Impacts of the World Bank and IMF Conditional Loans on Developing Countries', mimeo, Virginia Polytechnic Institute and State University.

Beck, N. and Katz, J. (1995) 'What to Do (and not to Do) with Time-Series Cross-Section Data', *American Political Science Review*, 89(3): 634–47.

Beck, T., Clarke, G., Groff, A., Keefer, P. and Walsh, P. (2001) 'New Tools in Comparative Political Economy: The Database of Political Institutions', *World Bank Economic Review*, 15(1): 165–76.

Beghin, J. (2000) 'Environment and Trade in Developing Economies: A Primer for the World Bank's Global Economic Prospects 2001', *Department of Economics Research Papers 1872*, Iowa State University.

Beghin, J. and Potier, M. (1997) 'Effects of Trade Liberalization on the Environment in the Manufacturing Sector', *The World Economy*, 20(4): 435–56.

Biermann, F. (2001) 'The Emerging Debate on the Need for a World Environmental Organization: A Commentary', *Global Environmental Politics*, 1(1): 45–55.

Boockmann, B. and Dreher, A. (2003), 'The Contribution of the IMF and the World Bank to Economic Freedom', *European Journal of Political Economy*, 19(3): 633–49.

Capistrano, A. (1990) 'Macroeconomic Influences on Tropical Forest Depletion: A Cross Country Analysis', Ph.D. dissertation, University of Florida, Gainesville.

Cole, M.A. (2004) 'Trade, the Pollution Haven Hypothesis and the Environmental Kuznets Curve: Examining the Linkages', *Ecological Economics*, 48: 71–81.

Cone, S.M. (2002) 'The Environment and the World Trade Organization', *Research Paper Series 02–10*, New York Law School.

Congleton, R.D. (2002) 'Agency Problems and the Allocation of International Environmental Grants: The Return to Rio', *Journal of Public Finance and Public Choice/Economia delle Scelte Pubbliche*, 20(2–3): 125–46.

Congleton, R.D. (2006) 'Public Goods and Agency Problems in Treaty Organizations, Analysis and Evidence', mimeo.

Daly, H. (1996) *Beyond Growth*, Boston, MA: Beacon Press.

Dixon, J.A., Talbit, L.M. and Le Moigne, G.J.M. (1998) 'Dams and the Environment', *Technical Paper No. 110*, Washington, DC: World Bank.

Dreher, A. (2002) 'The Development and Implementation of IMF and World Bank Conditionality', *HWWA Discussion Paper 165*, Hamburg: Hamburgisches Welt-Wirtschafts-Archiv.

Dreher, A. (2005) 'Does the IMF Influence Fiscal and Monetary Policy?' *The Journal of Policy Reform*, 8(3): 225–38.

Dreher, A. (2006) 'IMF and Economic Growth: The Effects of Programs, Loans, and Compliance with Conditionality', *World Development*, 34(5): 769–88.

Easterly, W. and Sewadeh, M. (2002) *Global Development Network Growth Database*, Washington, DC: World Bank.

Esty, D.C., Levy, M., Srebotnjak, T. and de Sherbinin, A. (2005) *2005 Environmental Sustainability Index: Benchmarking National Environmental Stewardship*, New Haven, CT: Yale Center for Environmental Law and Policy.

Food and Agriculture Organization of the United Nations (FAO) (2004) *FAOSTAT on-line statistical service*, online. Available HTTP: <http://apps.fao.org>.

Frankel, J. and Rose, A. (2002) 'Is Trade Good or Bad for the Environment? Sorting Out the Causality', *NBER Working Paper 9021*, Cambridge MA: National Bureau of Economic Research.

Friends of the Earth (1999) 'The IMF: Selling the Environment Short', Report, online. Available HTTP: <http://www.foe.org/international>.

Gandhi, V.P. (1998) *The IMF and the Environment*, Washington, DC: External Relations Department, IMF.

Gassebner, M., Lamla, M. and Sturm, J. (2006) 'Economic, Demographic and Political Determinants of Pollution Reassessed: A Sensitivity Analysis', *KOF Working Paper 129*, Zurich: Swiss Federal Institute of Technology (ETH Zurich).

Gassebner, M., Gaston, N. and Lamla, M. (2008) 'Relief for the Environment? The Importance of an Increasingly Unimportant Industrial Sector', *Economic Inquiry*, 46: 160–78.

Giordano, M. (1994) 'Tropical Forest Policy and Trade: A Case Study of Malaysia', in Sullivan, J. (ed.) *Environmental Policies: Implications for Agricultural Trade*, USDA-ERS FAER, 252.

Goldin, I. and Roland-Host, D. (1994) 'Economic Policies for Sustainable Resource Use in Morocco', mimeo.

Goldsmith, E. and Hildyard, N. (1984) *The Social and Environmental Effects of Large Dams*, San Francisco, CA: Sierra Club Books.

Gueorguieva, A. and Bolt, K. (2003) 'A Critical Review of the Literature on Structural Adjustment and the Environment', *Environmental Economics Series No. 90*, Washington, DC: The World Bank.

Guisinger, A. (2001) 'The Determinants of Trade Tariff Liberalization', mimeo, Yale University.

Guisinger, A. (2005) 'Understanding Cross-Country Patterns in Trade Liberalization', Ph.D. Thesis, Yale University.

Gutner, T. (2002) *Banking on the Environment: Multilateral Development Banks and their Environmental Performance in Central and Eastern Europe*, Cambridge, MA and London: MIT Press.

Gutner, T. (2005a) 'World Bank Environmental Reform: Revisiting Lessons from Agency Theory', *International Organization*, 59: 773–83.

Gutner, T. (2005b) 'Explaining the Gaps between Mandate and Performance: Agency Theory and World Bank Environmental Reform', *Global Environmental Politics*, 5(2): 10–35.

Gwartney, J. and Lawson, R. (2004) *Economic Freedom of the World: 2004 Annual Report*, Calgary *et al.*, Canada: The Fraser Institute.

Hansen, J.K. and Hansen, S. (1999) 'Integrating Environmental Concerns into Economy-Wide Policies in Developing Countries: The Role of Multilateral Development Banks', *Environment and Development Economics*, 4(1): 45–68.

Hicks, R., Nielson, D., Parks, B., Roberts, T. and Tierney, M. (2005) *Project Level Aid (PLAID) Database*.

Hughes, G. and Lovei, L. (1999) 'Economic Reform and Environmental Performance in Transition Countries', *World Bank Technical Paper 446, Eastern Europe and Central Asia Pollution Management Series*, Washington, DC: World Bank.

Inter-American Development Bank (2003) *Environment Strategy Document*, Washington, DC: Inter-American Development Bank.

International Monetary Fund (2004) *The IMF and the Environment, A Factsheet*, Washington, DC: IMF

Ivanova, M. (2005) 'Moving Forward by Looking Back: Assessing UNEP as Anchor Institution for the Global Environment', International Organisations and Global Environmental Governance Conference Papers, Berlin.

Jha, R. and Bhanu Murti, K.V. (2003) 'A Critique of the Environmental Sustainability Index', Australian National University, mimeo.

Jayarajah, C. and Branson, W. (1995) *Structural Adjustment and Sectoral Adjustment – World Bank Experience, 1980–1992*, Washington DC: World Bank.

Killick, T. (1993) *The Adaptive Economy – Adjustment Policies in Small, Low-Income Countries*, Washington, DC: World Bank.

Lamla, M. (2006) 'Long-run Determinants of Pollution: A Robustness Analysis', ETH Zurich, mimeo.

Lewis, T. (2003) 'Environmental Aid: Driven by Recipient Need or Donor Interests?', *Social Science Quarterly*, (84)1: 144–61.

Lodefalk, M. and Whalley, J. (2002) 'Reviewing Proposals for a World Environmental Organisation', *World Economy*, 25(5): 601–17.

MacMillan, F. (2001) *WTO and the Environment*, London: Sweet & Maxwell.

Mani, M. and Wheeler, D. (1999) 'In Search of Pollution Havens? Dirty Industry in the World Economy, 1960–1995', in Fredriksson, P. (ed.) *Trade, Global Policy, and the Environment*, Washington, DC: World Bank.

Marshall, M.G. and Jaggers, K. (2000) *Polity IV project: political regime characteristics and transitions, 1800–2000*, online. Available HTTP: <http://www.cidcm.umd.edu/inscr/polity/>.

Mikesell, R.F. and Williams, L. (1992) *International Banks and the Environment: From Growth to Sustainability: An Unfinished Agenda*, San Francisco, CA: Sierra Club Books.

Moltke, K. von (2001) 'The Organization of the Impossible', *Global Environmental Politics*, 1(1): 23–8.

Munasinghe, M. and Cruz, W. (1994) *Economywide Policies and the Environment: Emerging Lessons from Experience*, Washington, DC: World Bank.

Nielson, D.L. and Tierney, M.J. (2003) 'Delegation to International Organizations: Agency Theory and World Bank Environmental Reform', *International Organizations*, 57(2): 241–76.

Oxley, A. (2001) 'WTO and the Environment', *Contributions from The Australian APEC Study Centre 2001–11*, Melbourne: The Australian APEC Study Centre.

Pandey, K. and Wheeler, D. (2001) 'Structural Adjustment and Forest Resources: The Impact of World Bank Operations', *Policy Research Working Paper 2584*, Washington, DC: World Bank.

Reed, D. (1996) *Structural Adjustment, the Environment, and Sustainable Development*, London: Earthscan Publications.

Runnals, D. (1986) 'Factors Influencing Environmental Policies in International Development Agencies', in Asian Development Bank (ed.) *Environmental Planning and Management (Proceedings of the 1986 Regional Symposium on Environmental and Natural Resources Planning)*, Manila: ADB.

Sampson, G.P. (2003) 'WTO, Trade, and the Environment', Symposium WTO Research Center Globalization and Consumer Benefits, Aoyama Gakuin University.

Stern, D.I. (2005) 'Reversal in the Trend of Global Anthropogenic Sulfur Emissions', *Rensselaer Working Papers in Economics 0504*, Troy, NY: Rensselaer Polytechnic Institute, Department of Economics.

Streck, C. (2001) 'The Global Environment Facility – A Role Model for International Governance?', *Global Environmental Politics*, 1(2): 71–94.

Wheeler, D. and Martin, P. (1992) 'Prices, Policies, and the International Diffusion of Clean Technology: The Case of Wood Pulp Production', in Low, P. (ed.) *World Bank Discussion Paper*, Washington, DC: World Bank.

World Bank (2001) *Adjustment Lending Retrospective*, Washington, DC: World Bank.

World Bank (2005) *World Development Indicators*, CD-Rom, Washington, DC: World Bank.

World Commission of Environment and Development (1987) *Our Common Future*, Oxford: Oxford University Press.

World Trade Organization (2004) *Trade and Environment at the WTO: Background Document*, Geneva: WTO.

3 Setting standards for responsible banking

Examining the role of the International Finance Corporation in the emergence of the Equator Principles

Christopher Wright

Introduction

Voluntary business regulation is becoming an increasingly prominent feature of global environmental governance (Falkner 2003; Levy and Newell 2005; Pattberg 2006). Underpinning this trend is a deepening institutional relationship between international organizations, transnational corporations and civil society groups, which has placed the private sector at the centre of global responses to environmental problems (Ruggie 2004). In this policy space, international organizations are playing a leading role in directly facilitating the creation and administration of voluntary codes of conduct that aim to integrate environmental and social norms into business practices, particularly in developing countries (Utting 2005). Through such institutional arrangements, they seek to contribute to defining and diffusing international best practices for private companies.

Most international organizations facilitate the emergence of voluntary initiatives in their capacity as international bureaucracies governing particular issue areas. As a result, voluntary initiatives, such as the UN Global Compact, the *OECD Guidelines on Multinational Enterprises*, and the statements of United Nations Environment Program's Finance Initiative (UNEP FI), most often take the form of 'principled codes' that primarily contain aspirational principles affirming the moral responsibilities of private companies, yet often lack specific guidelines on how individual commitments will be put into practice (Bondy *et al.* 2004). Changes to corporate behaviour are expected to result from a process of social learning, in which private companies are provided with a forum for sharing and gaining knowledge and information about incorporating various aspirational environmental and social goals into their business operations (Ruggie 2002).

In stark contrast to the UN and the OECD, several multilateral development banks are mandated to provide financing directly to private sector companies or projects in developing countries. As participants in financial markets, these international organizations enjoy strong operational relationships with commercial banks and private companies, which allow them to directly shape corporate practices in their countries of operations. Therefore, while other international organizations' interaction with the private sector is limited to facilitating interactions between businesses and harmonizing practices around specific ethical principles, multilateral development banks can leverage their commercial relationships and internal business expertise to influence corporate practices in much more fundamental ways.

This chapter will discuss the role of the International Finance Corporation (IFC), the private sector lending arm of the World Bank Group, in facilitating the emergence of the Equator Principles, a voluntary code of conduct that stipulates how financial institutions should incorporate environmental and social concerns into project lending (Equator Principles 2003, 2006). Launched in June 2003, the framework is based on the internal operational policies and procedures of the IFC, and has to date been adopted by sixty private financial institutions, whose combined market share exceeds 85 per cent of the global project finance market. The analysis will consider how and on what basis the IFC influenced the drafting of the framework, and in particular, why commercial banks chose its operational standards and procedures as a blueprint for devising common environmental and social standards for the commercial project finance industry.

Evaluating the influence of voluntary business regulation is difficult. In the case of the Equator Principles, the task of conducting an accurate assessment of influence on the development impact of projects is severely undermined by the lack of independent data on project-level compliance. But despite the absence of this, it is possible to gauge the influence of the Equator Principles by using a number of other metrics. First, the commitment to adopting the Equator Principles among market participants is significant and growing. One estimate suggests that total debt amount for Equator Principles debt financing in developing countries was $28 billion, or 93 per cent of the market (IJ Research & Analysis 2006). Secondly, alongside the hiring of environmental and social risk specialists in commercial banks, a new industry of consulting, training and legal advisory services has emerged to meet demands for support in applying and interpreting the framework. This suggests that the framework has led to a growth in both the supply of and demand for environmental and social risk management training and expertise. Third, legal analysts have predicted that the Equator Principles may significantly inform the future development of lender liability in developing countries by exhibiting 'law-like' characteristics and setting a global benchmark for acceptable or responsible financing practices (Boisson de Chazournes 2000; FBD 2005). Fourth, some adopting banks are using the Equator Principles to inform the integration of environmental and social considerations into asset classes other than project financing, suggesting that the influence of the framework may go beyond the narrow confines of project finance. And fifth, there is evidence that some transnational corporations in environmentally-sensitive industries are recognizing that compliance with the Equator Principles may in the future be a condition for accessing long-term capital (see FBD 2005: 118–21; Lazarus 2004).

The chapter will be divided into four sections. The first section will briefly introduce the IFC and the unique organizational features of multilateral development banks that provide direct financing to private sector companies and projects in developing countries. The second section will discuss the recent growth of the project finance market in developing countries, and the emergence of environmental and social norms in multilateral project financing. The third section will consider the rise of environmental advocacy campaigns against commercial project finance banks and briefly describe the Equator Principles. And finally, the fourth section will consider why the IFC's environmental and social standards became recognized as the global standard in the project finance market.

The IFC and the promotion of globalization

In 1951, a US development policy advisory panel first endorsed the idea of establishing a public financial institution affiliated with the World Bank mandated to encourage private sector growth and investment in developing countries. In 1956, separate Articles of Agreement were drafted for an International Finance Corporation (IFC), mandating it to promote private sector development by 'encouraging the growth of productive private enterprise in member countries, particularly in the less developed areas'. While a formal member of the World Bank Group, alongside the International Bank for Reconstruction and Development (IBRD), the International Development Agency (IDA) and the Multilateral Investment Guarantee Agency (MIGA), the IFC operates as a separate legal entity, with its own operational mandate, professional staff and financial resources. As with the World Bank, voting power on its Board of Directors is weighted according to the amount of paid-in-capital from each country, with the United States enjoying a voting share of 23.66 per cent in 2005 (IFC 2005). As of 2008, it has a staff of 3,325, just over half of which are located in its Washington DC headquarters, the remainder divided among its 70 international field offices. And its relative autonomy is secured by the financing of the organization, which relies extensively on public borrowing and private placements in international capital markets for financing its lending operations, and total capital and retained earning for equity investments.

As a corporation, the IFC has experienced tremendous growth in recent years, in parallel with many commercial banks in OECD countries prior to the recent financial crisis. Since its inception in 1956, the IFC has committed US$49 billion in loan and equity investments to 3,319 private companies, with a six-fold increase in annual commitments since the late 1970s (IFC 2005). During the 1990s, the IFC accounted for nearly one-quarter of the total multilateral- and bilateral financing to private sector entities in developing countries (IFC 2002a). In 2005 alone, it financed 236 projects across 67 developing countries, amounting to $5.4 billion in financing of IFC's own account (IFC 2005). Financing to developing countries is provided in various forms; long-term project loans typically ranging from 7 to 20 years in maturity, equity stakes in financial institutions and other private companies, partial credit guarantees to help clients access additional long-term capital and diversify their funding sources, and technical assistance in the form of staff training, organizational capacity building and restructuring (IFC 2005). In addition to its direct financing, the IFC mobilizes private investment through its loan syndications program, in which commercial banks are invited to provide debt financing alongside IFC loans, thereby benefiting from the IFC's preferred creditor status as a multilateral lender.

Underlying its private sector financing is a strong commitment to promoting a neo-liberal economic order through its investments and advisory services. The combination of its governance structure and operational mandate produced an international organization that was 'owned by governments but acted as a corporation', taking on the full commercial risks of its investments, accepting no government guarantees, and earning profits from its financing operations (IFC 1996). By focusing on transaction-based financing to private sector projects, its operations were meant to supplement those of the World Bank, which lends exclusively to member state governments. In this context, its financing activities are intimately tied to establishing and maintaining a neo-liberal economic order conducive to accelerating transnational private capital flows and private sector growth. Symptomatically, on its 40th anniversary in 1996, the IFC proclaimed with content that its investments had collectively promoted 'an economic model based on privatization, liberalization of trade and investment regimes, establishment of domestic capital markets, and encouragement of a dynamic, competitive local private sector with a growing export base' (IFC 1996: 10).

Understanding multilateral financing to the private sector

Spanning more than a half-century, the IFC has a long history that predates all other multilateral development banks, or divisions within them, providing financing directly to the private sector. This underscores the fact that multilateral financing to the private sector at a significant scale is a relatively recent phenomenon. Indeed, the IFC's annual commitments did not exceed $1 billion until the mid-1980s, when there was a notable shift in multilateral financing towards private sector investments and economic reform programs designed to encourage private sector growth. In 1989, the Inter-American Development Bank (IDC Group) established the Inter-American Investment Corporation (IIC) to primarily finance small business growth through financial intermediaries, and in 1994, it created the Private Sector Development Department (PRI) to financially support the privatization of large-scale infrastructure in Latin America. In 1991, the European Bank for Reconstruction and

Development (EBRD) was established to promote market reforms and private sector growth in the former planned economies of Eastern Europe and the republics of the former Soviet Union. During this time, the Asian Development Bank (ADB) and the African Development Bank (AfDB) also obtained authorisation to lend for non-guaranteed private investments.

Whether lending to the public or the private sector, multilateral development banks are amongst the most formally institutionalized features of the international economic regime. As international bureaucracies, they comprise of large bodies of professional staff that work within an array of operational procedures and bureaucratic routines, managing the transfer of vast financial resources to developing countries. In this context, decision-making follows a distinctly technocratic logic, as it is rooted in professional expertise and management practices that aim to produce measurable results, quickly and efficiently (Gulrajani 2006). The focus on quantitative analysis means they engage in the collection, production, manipulation and dissemination of vast amounts of information, which provides the basis for developing and demonstrating specialized competency in particular professional fields. In turn, by being large depositories of technical knowledge that informs policy-making and investment decisions, they significantly influence the development and diffusion of international best practices in both the public and private sectors.

While all multilateral development banks generally share these organizational characteristics, those that predominately finance private sector entities have a distinctly commercial orientation to their operational mandate and organizational structure. Their financing operations are overwhelmingly transaction-based and revolve around the identification, assessment and approval of profitable investment projects. While they do offer advisory services to government entities in support of regulatory reforms that further private sector development, they generally do not provide policy loans or sector loans that address the broader institutional context of development. By implication, lending and equity financing is provided under a narrower mandate, carried out in sector-based banking divisions run by finance professionals that are trained in investment and risk management practices.

Furthermore, while they do operate within a broader mission to promote sustainable development, commercial viability is the overarching criterion for selecting projects and negotiating financing terms, as projects do not benefit from host government guarantees. When financing development projects, they often take on the same commercial risks as private lenders do, and seek to operate within the constraints and opportunities of the marketplace in order to demonstrate the commercial viability of developing country investment. Under these circumstances, managing and mitigating investment risk by carefully structuring the transaction and involving a multitude of different financial institutions becomes central to realizing individual projects. By implication, they are therefore more 'bank-like' than public sector lenders, with an organizational culture, operational structure and professional staff more narrowly attuned to identifying and assessing commercial investment opportunities (Gutner 2002).

Project finance and sustainable development

Since the early 1990s, market reforms in developing countries have resulted in the widespread privatization of traditional public sector industries, harmonization of tax regimes, and lower restrictions on foreign capital all contributed to the growth in long-term private capital flows to infrastructure projects, including power plants, roads, ports and telecommunication (World Bank 2004). By implication, transnational corporations and commercial banks increasingly presided over the construction and implementation of projects that not only contributed to the economic transformation of entire sub-national regions and industry sectors, but also had a profound impact on the environment and local communities. Between 1990 and 1997, commercial bank financing for infrastructure in developing countries increased nine-fold, and the annual volume of project finance deals exploded from less than $5 billion to over $50 billion (Esty 2004; World Bank 2004). The growth was led by commercial banks from OECD countries – principally Japan, the United States, France, Germany, the Netherlands, and the United Kingdom – which accounted for roughly three-quarters of all commercial infrastructure finance in developing countries. In addition, local capital markets in the fastest growing economies, led by regional and public development agencies, became a significant source of long-term financing for capital-intensive projects.

The growth in financing to the private sector in developing countries also manifested itself in the composition of aid and financing from official sources. Between 1991 and 1997, long-term official capital flows to developing countries declined nearly 40 per cent and the World Bank withdrew almost entirely from large-scale public infrastructure lending. Meanwhile, during the same period, multilateral and bilateral financing to private entities in developing countries nearly tripled, growing from US$ 9 billion to US$25 billion (IFC 2002a). This underscores how multilateral lenders and official export credit agencies were critical to mobilizing commercial bank lending to the private sector in so-called high-risk sectors and regions by way of loan syndications (World Bank 2004). As an example, the recently completed Baku-Tblisi-Ceyhan oil pipeline project, which included an oil-field and a pipeline stretching 1760 kilometres from Azerbaijan to Turkey, had a total project cost of $3.6 billion and was financed by syndications which included the IFC and the EBRD, seven export credit agencies, and fifteen commercial banks. In this case and other large projects, commercial banks took comfort in the participation of a multilateral lender, as they enjoyed a 'preferred creditor status' and were in position to secure a political commitment from host governments not to introduce policies or regulations that would adversely affect the borrowers' future capacity to service loan payments.

The IFC's environmental and social policy reforms

Not surprisingly, the systematic consideration of environmental and social issues in private sector financing arrived much later than in public sector lending. As an indication, whereas the World Bank hired its first environmental specialist as early as 1971, the IFC did not do so until 1989. In general terms, the notion that the consideration of environmental and social issues is political territory and falls outside of the commercial mandate of private sector financing was for long the prevailing view, and remains contested. Among multilateral development banks that predominately finance the private sector, the EBRD is the only one officially mandated to promote sustainable development. Yet, all multilateral development banks have made a commitment to protect the environment and reduce poverty in some form, primarily by institutionalizing environmental and social review procedures in their project cycles, aimed at detecting and mitigating any adverse environmental and social impacts that may arise as a result of their investment projects (for overviews, see Kennedy 1999; IFC 2002a; Gutner 2002; Park 2006; and Park in this volume).

Relative to its half-century long history, the IFC only recently established an internal environmental and social policy framework. Until the late 1980s, the selection of projects was overwhelmingly based on a combination of technical criteria and internal rates of return. It was not until the early 1990s that the IFC began using environmental review procedures similar to those of the World Bank on an ad hoc basis, and started adding a number of environmental specialists to oversee the due diligence process. Its own explanation for introducing environmental review of projects pointed to five developments; the growth in scientific knowledge about environmental issues, regulatory developments in the United States and the European Union, an internal learning process, a strategic desire to manage economic transitions in a sustainable manner; and the influence of the NGO community (IFC 2002a).

While all of these factors contributed to raising awareness and mobilizing political will, the timing of the environmental and social reforms was undoubtedly in large part due to external calls for greater accountability and transparency. In 1995, it came under immense pressure from civil society groups alleging that the IFC was violating the World Bank's environmental and social policies in a Chilean hydropower project (Park 2006). The controversy resulted in a scathing independent report criticizing the IFC's conduct, triggering an internal re-examination of its policies and procedures (Hair *et al.* 1997; IFC 2002a). It emerged on the heels of two independent reports on the World Bank's compliance with its own operational policies – the *Morse Report* and the *Wapenhaus Report* – which highlighted the importance of strengthening internal quality controls at the World Bank to ensure that projects contribute to the broader objectives of the organization (see Boisson de Chazournes 2000).

In 1998, the IFC formally adopted most of the World Bank's *Environmental and Social Safeguard Policies*, an umbrella term used for the set of thematic policies that provide internal staff with guidance on how to manage a variety of adverse environmental and social impacts associated with projects (Boisson de Chazournes 2000). Its main element was the *Operational Policy on Environmental Assessment* (OP 4.01), which listed environmental screening, public consultation, information disclosure and implementation require-ments, and identified the *World Bank's Pollution Prevention and Abatement Handbook* and *Occupational Health and Safety Guidelines* as benchmarks for IFC's private sector projects. Furthermore, it introduced the *Procedures for Environmental and Social Review*, which outlined the internal procedures by which environmental specialists would assess environmental assessments provided by borrowers.

The main component of these reforms was an environmental screening process whereby each project proposal would be assigned a category – A, B, C or FI – according to its level of expected environmental impact, and the financing modality ('FI' was assigned to projects involving a financial inter-mediary). In turn, the category assigned to each project would determine the scale and scope of environmental assessment and public consultation. Finally, the set of nine operational policies laid out the minimum environ-mental and social standards that all projects would be subjected to. As examples, it included the *Operational Policy on Natural Habitats* (OP 4.04) barred the IFC from financing projects that involved the significant conver-sion or degradation of critical natural habitats, as defined by the World Con-servation Union (IUCN), and the *Operational Policy on Dam Safety* (OP 4.37) required the technical aspects of hydropower construction to be overseen by an independent panel of experts, amongst other things.

The rise of NGO campaigns against commercial banks

Given that many of the projects with the most widespread adverse environ-mental and social impacts also happen to generate the most revenue, it is not surprising that the management of environmental and social issues remains a very controversial issue. Yet, until recently, most of the public scrutiny of the environmental and social impacts of project finance deals was directed towards multilateral development banks, and to a lesser extent to bilateral export credit agencies (Wade 1997; Gutner 2002; Schaper 2007). Since they held strong positions in the market and had certain obligations as publicly mandated institutions to ensure that investments did not negatively impact local communities and the environment, they became natural targets for critics. But the expansion of the project finance market in the early 1990s, and the growing public visibility of commercial banks as arrangers and financiers of large projects, revealed the extent to which the decisions regarding the management of environmental and social impacts of large projects were often taken by commercial banks and private borrowers.

Starting in the late 1990s, a series of well-publicized civil society campaigns against a number of large commercial banks accused them of financing projects that were violating the rights of local communities and harming the environment. In numerous cases, commercial banks were alleged to have financed a project even though a multilateral development bank had refused to do because they were in violation of their environmental and social policies (Missbach 2004). Milieudefensie, the Dutch chapter of Friends of the Earth, together with other NGOs, targeted ABN Amro for its lengthy involvement as a co-financier of mines in Papua New Guinea operated by Freeport-McMoRan, and for financing, alongside other Dutch commercial lenders, the conversion of Indonesian forests to oil palm plantations (FOE 2001).

In 2000, the Rainforest Action Network (RAN) launched a public advocacy campaign against industry leader Citigroup for its involvement in numerous projects, including the Chad–Cameroon pipeline, and the Oleoducto de Crudos Pesados (OCP) pipeline and Camisea gas fields in Peru, which over a three-year period included consumer boycotts and targeted media campaigns. Similarly, German NGOs and parliamentarians criticized West Deutsche Landesbank, the quasi-public German bank, for arranging the highly controversial Peruvian pipeline, whereas Barclays's reputation was adversely affected by its financial involvement with the large-scale forestry projects of Asia Pulp and Paper, the conglomerate that financially collapsed in 2001. In these and other cases, NGOs alleged that the commercial banks bore some responsibility for the adverse impacts of their project financing, and demanded that they directly confront irresponsible or negligent borrowers.

In 2002, a senior executive at ABN Amro met with IFC's executive vice-president and discussed the growing criticism levied against commercial banks for financing projects in developing countries with significant adverse environmental and social impacts. In many cases, civil society groups had attempted to mobilize bank customers to support their advocacy campaigns, adversely affecting retail banking operations. In October 2002, following additional discussions, the IFC and ABN Amro decided to convene a meeting of leading project finance banks in London to discuss the management of environmental and social issues in projects. Co-chaired by the IFC and ABN Amro, the meeting gathered project finance and risk management executives of numerous commercial banks to share their experiences with 'problem projects'. In turn, the four banks that gave presentations – ABN Amro, Barclays, Citigroup and West LB – formed a working group to explore the formulation of a common set of environmental and social review procedures for commercial project finance banks (Lazarus 2004).

During the ensuing four months, the working group collaborated with a technical advisor from the IFC to consider a set of environmental and social standards for project finance investments that would be suitable for commercial banks. Through meetings with the working group and in bilateral talks with individual banks, IFC presented and discussed how it applied the *Safeguard Policies* to high-risk projects. Initially, the working group briefly considered devising an entirely new set of standards, but over time, the impracticality of starting from scratch, and the objective to maximize the appeal and utility of the framework, led them to base a draft framework on the IFC's *Safeguard Policies*.

In February 2003, a second meeting was hosted by Citigroup to discuss a set of draft standards named the 'Greenwich Principles', in reference to the meeting location's proximity to Greenwich, near Central London (Lazarus 2004). The representatives of commercial banks were presented with the draft standards, and most of them gave their tentative support, subject to discussions with internal corporate relations and legal departments, senior management, and clients. Subsequently, the draft standards were circulated to a select group of NGOs for consultation. While generally positive about the standards themselves, the NGOs highlighted several shortcomings regarding implementation and governance, including the lack of a reporting requirement or compliance mechanism to ensure transparency and accountability, and the absence of a secretariat to facilitate communication between the banks and stakeholders. These concerns had been previously articulated in the *Collevecchio Declaration on Financial Institutions and Sustainability*, a policy statement issued jointly by over 100 civil society groups at the World Economic Forum in Davos, January 2003 (see Missbach 2004).

In April 2003, the four commercial banks of the working group formally announced they would adopt the framework, and hosted a consultation meeting with a selection of NGOs in London. A month later, a fourth meeting was held in Düsseldorf at the headquarters of WestLB. In the meeting, the IFC gave a series of presentations on the process of environmental screening and the application of its *Safeguard Policies* to individual projects. It also affirmed its interest in providing environmental management training to adopting banks, in order to increase their capacity to implement their new commitments (Lazarus 2004). By then, the standards had been renamed the Equator Principles so as to reflect the joint intention among adopting banks to produce a global framework applicable to all industry sectors. Less than one month later, senior executives of ten commercial banks gathered at the IFC's headquarters in Washington DC alongside its chief executive to officially launch the Equator Principles.

Since June 2003, more than 60 financial institutions have adopted the Equator Principles, representing over 85 per cent of the global project finance market in financing volume. In October 2005, leading Equator banks began revising the framework, in anticipation of the IFC's released of new *Policy and Performance Standards on Social and Environmental Sustainability*, replacing the *Safeguard Policies* upon which the original Equator Principles were based. In July 2006, the new Equator Principles were released and readopted by the commercial banks that had pledged their commitment to the original framework, who began to refer to themselves as the Equator Principles Financial Institutions (EPFIs). In May 2008, the EPFIs announced a new governance structure in which the operating structure, voting procedures and annual meeting arrangements have been formalized, and groups of EPFIs have been given formal responsibilities in areas such as communications, outreach and stakeholder engagement.

The Equator Principles

In reality, the formal existence of the Equator Principles is limited to a publicly available document that spells out the normative and business rationale for undertaking environmental and social risk management, and specific operational standards that adopting banks commit to using in their project finance activities. Notwithstanding the formal governance structure introduced in May 2008, it is a strictly non-binding framework in which '[financial] institutions are adopting and implementing [the] Principles voluntarily and independently, without reliance on or recourse to IFC or the World Bank' (Equator Principles 2003: 4, 2006: 5). Furthermore, it has no independent monitoring mechanism mandated to verify that projects have been prepared according to the relevant provisions. As is stated, compliance with host country laws and regulations and relevant World Bank and IFC guidelines will be addressed to the satisfaction of the financier.

Yet, by adopting the Equator Principles, financial institutions make a public commitment to take on a variety of tasks and responsibilities related to preparing and managing project investments. Previously, these would not have been performed at all, or in most cases, less systematically. For projects in developing countries predicted to have significant adverse environmental and social impacts (or those assigned environmental screening category A or B), the financial institution must require the borrower to complete and disclose an environmental assessment that addresses relevant impacts and risks, including proposals for mitigation and management. Commonly, this includes establishing baseline conditions, identifying relevant host country laws and regulations and applicable international agreements and treaties, and evaluating project design in a number of areas, including resource efficiency, environmental health and safety, biodiversity protection, and involuntary settlement. And significantly, the assessment needs to consider the industry-specific standards of the World Bank and IFC *Pollution Prevention Handbook* (World Bank Group 1999), and for projects located in low- and low-middle-income countries, the applicable IFC Performance Standards.

Subsequently, the assessment, or a non-technical summary of it, is released for public consultation, and borrowers or a commissioned third party are required to prepare an environmental management plan (EMP) which addresses mitigation, monitoring, management of risk and schedules. Significantly, the action plan has to be covenanted in loan agreements, embedding it in the contractual arrangements between the commercial banks and the borrower. Furthermore, borrowers have to consult with project-affected groups, including indigenous people and local NGO, early in the assessment process and on an ongoing basis, and establish a grievance mechanism for stake-holders. In turn, if a borrower fails to comply with the EMP, financial institutions have committed 'to bring it back into compliance *to the extent feasible*, and if the borrower fails to re-establish compliance within an agreed grace period, [signatory banks] reserve the right to exercise remedies, *as they consider appropriate*' (emphasis added, Equator Principles 2006: 4).

While the qualifying language gives financial institutions significant flexibility and discretion in crafting responses to compliance breaches, financial institutions do accept some responsibility for ensuring that the environmental and social loan conditions are adhered to. Nevertheless, the risk of a damaged reputation for failing to implement the Equator Principles is not likely to be an adequate substitute for an effective, independent monitoring mechanism that enjoys the legitimacy and trust of stakeholders.

The IFC and the Equator Principles: exploring the links

While the need to mitigate the reputational risks associated with project financing in developing countries represents that primary reason why the original ten commercial banks initially created and adopted the Equator Principles, the choice of the IFC's policy framework as a blueprint for creating their own was not inevitable. This section will make an argument as to why the IFC's environmental and social policies and procedures became recognized as 'best practice standards' in the global project finance market, manifested in the widespread adoption of the Equator Principles among leading project finance banks. It identifies two developments that were crucial to this outcome, the IFC's involvement as a meeting facilitator and a technical advisor during the drafting stages of the Equator Principles, and the eventual decision among commercial banks to base a set of common environmental and social standards for commercial project lenders on the IFC's internal operational policies. Both developments speak to rising influence of the IFC in the global economy during a time of globalization.

The commercial orientation of the IFC's financing operations

As the largest provider of multilateral finance to the private sector in developing countries, the IFC is a significant market actor in its own right. The IFC's involvement as a technical advisor in the drafting stages of the Equator Principles reflects the extent to which leading commercial banks identified with its operational experiences as a project lender in developing countries, and considered it as a valuable source of expertise for managing environmental and social risks in developing country projects. These perceptions were grounded in several characteristics of the IFC as an international organization.

First, the IFC's organizational structure and professional practices centre on identifying, evaluating, negotiating and closing financially viable investment projects which broadly resemble those of commercial banks. Given this transactional orientation, the IFC's operational staff primarily consists of business professionals with advanced degrees in corporate finance or business management. Its financing operations are organized in nine industry departments, each charged with identifying and completing investment projects in particular industries, such as agribusiness, infrastructure and global financial markets. Tasks associated with identifying and mitigating the environmental and social impacts of project proposals are primarily handled by environmental specialists working in a separate support department.

Secondly, apart from an organizational structure that focuses on project transactions, the IFC's investment decisions are primarily made on the basis of commercial viability. While its mission to foster sustainable development is much broader than that of commercial banks, it remains firmly wedded to its original purpose of mobilizing financial resources in support of productive private sector projects in developing countries. Indeed, profitability is considered a prerequisite for a project to make a positive contribution to development (Jaabre 2002). This emphasis effectively means that IFC financing and commercial bank lending is broadly driven by the same organizing principle, which in turn guaranteed that the IFC's technical advice to commercial banks would not directly conflict with their profit motive.

Third, given its focus on identifying financially viable transactions, the IFC engages with the environmental and social dimension of private sector development on a project-by-project basis, and increasingly, with business profitability in mind. While a significant purpose of its environmental and social policy framework is for minimum standards to increase the development impact and accountability of its financing operations, the IFC is increasingly arguing for the existence of a 'business case' for managing environmental and social issues in project investments (IFC 2002b; Wright 2006). By having adopted this distinctly corporate perspective on environmental and social issues, the IFC is not only aligning its environmental and social mission with the concept of corporate social responsibility, but also reinforcing the notion that private sector growth and investment is a prerequisite for reversing environmental degradation and reducing poverty.

Finally, the commercial orientation of the IFC's financing activities means its operational knowledge and experiences are directly relevant to commercial banks. During the last decade in particular, the IFC has amassed considerable expertise in environmental and social risk management by increasing the number of in-house environmental specialists from under 10 to over 100 (IFC 2002a; Park 2006). In doing so, it frequently promoted its specialized expertise in environmental and social risk management, and positioned itself as 'a partner of choice' for private borrowers in developing countries (IFC 2003: 2; Wright 2006). And in the context of its financial sector investments, it has provided environmental risk management training to financial institutions, produced guidance material diffusing its own operational experiences and made the case for considering environmental and social issues in investments. More recently, the IFC has exploited its enhanced leverage and expertise to form a partnership with the UN Global Compact and the UNEP Finance Initiative (UNEP FI) to further the integration of environmental and social issues in financial markets.

Financial partnerships in a global marketplace

By virtue of its financing operations, the IFC has long had operational relationships with private financial institutions, as a provider of debt or equity financing, or as a co-financier in large development projects. Since the mid-1990s, the financial sector has been a strategic priority sector for the IFC, and has received between two-thirds and one-half of its annual financing. These investments often take the form of intermediary financing schemes, in which the IFC provides debt or equity financing to a financial institution or investment fund operating in a developing country, which in turn provides financing to multiple private companies. Such intermediary financing schemes sometimes include staff training and corporate restructuring programs aimed at improving corporate governance and commercializing risk management practices in private financial institutions.

Apart from providing financing or technical assistance to private financial institutions operating in domestic markets, it also enjoys close, operational relationships with many of the world's largest commercial banks with significant global investment portfolios. These interactions are in large part a product of the IFC's long-standing loan syndications program – also referred to as its B-Loan program – through which it co-finances development projects with commercial banks. The program necessitates frequent interactions between project finance executives in commercial banks and operational staff at the IFC, which provided the backdrop for the initial discussions that eventually led to the drafting of the Equator Principles.

In fact, among the ten commercial banks that adopted the framework at its inception in June 2003, six had participated in IFC syndications signed that year, including all four of the banks that constituted the working group in charge of the drafting process. As frequent participants of the program, commercial banks had regularly been in communication with the IFC's internal B Loan Management division that disseminates progress reports on syndicated loans and keeps participating banks informed of potential syndications opportunities. It also organizes an annual participants meeting for private financial institutions, investment funds and development agencies to showcase its loan syndication program and provide a forum for discussing opportunities and obstacles to investing in developing countries. Not coincidentally, the Equator Principles were launched at the IFL's Annual Participants Meeting in June 2003.

Global standards for a global industry

While the IFC's operational mandate, financial strength, and risk management expertise may explain why the IFC became involved as a technical advisor in the drafting stages, this does not by itself reveal why commercial banks chose the IFC's environmental and social policy framework as the blueprint for the Equator Principles. To understand their appeal among leading commercial banks, it is necessary to consider the characteristics of the IFC's *Safeguard Policies* from the commercial vantage point of financial institutions in position to decide whether or not to apply them to their project finance lending.

First, choosing to base the common industry standards on the IFC's environmental and social policy framework guaranteed that they would draw a certain amount of immediate and unconditional recognition and legitimacy. As the IFC's Board of Directors, representing over 170 governments, formally approves changes or additions to the IFC's operational policies and procedures, the *Safeguard Policies* enjoyed a multilateral endorsement, albeit perhaps not equally supported by all governments. And as they give affirmation to well-recognized norms and rules in the international system, such as human rights, protection of sensitive ecosystems and public access to decision-making, they also enjoy relatively strong support among environmental NGOs campaigning for better protection for the environment and local communities (EDF 2005).

While environmental NGOs frequently criticized the scope of *Safeguard Policies*, and particularly the way the World Bank and the IFC applied them to projects, they nevertheless had come to define responsible lending and symbolized the influence of environmental NGOs on development financing. Thus, when leading commercial banks were first confronted by public advocacy campaigns over their involvement in projects that adversely affected the environment and local communities, they were often criticized for failing to abide by the environmental and social policies of the World Bank and the IFC (see Missbach 2004). Given that preventing damages to their corporate reputation was a primary concern for commercial banks, the legitimacy that the *Safeguard Policies* enjoyed among their chief critics was a significant factor in deciding to use them as a blueprint for developing an industry standard for commercial project lending (Amalric 2005; Wright and Rwabizambuga 2006).

Secondly, the fact that many commercial banks were quite familiar with the IFC's environmental and social policy framework provided a strong rationale for aligning industry standards with it. Although the IFC has less financial strength than many commercial banks, it enjoys unique privileges as a multilateral institution that allow it to significantly influence how environmental and social issues are managed in large-scale infrastructure projects in developing countries. (see Schaper 2007). By determining the financing conditions attached to its own loans, and in the context of syndications, to commercial bank loans as well, the IFC can influence the standardization of contracting practices and commercial legal obligations in developing countries, particularly those that lack access to private financing. By implication, frequent borrowers in environmentally sensitive industries, such as oil, gas, mining and infrastructure, and commercial banks participating in loan syndications, have become familiar with the IFC's environmental and social policies and the World Bank's environmental standards and guidelines.

And finally, given the global reach of the project finance market, there was a purely functional argument for commercial banks to choose a policy framework that could be applied to project investments in all industry sectors globally. In fact, gaining the support of a significant share of market participants was as important for the working group as the selection of standards. In contrast to those of regional development banks, the IFC's operational policies and procedures were not designed to respond to the institutional conditions of particular geographic regions, but meant to be applicable and equally effective in all of its countries of operation. In turn, this universal logic was well suited for a globally integrated industry, in which the project finance portfolios of commercial banks differed widely in their geographic and sectoral concentrations. In this context, drawing on the IFC's framework was meant to ensure the widest possible participation in the Equator Principles, as it would not in principle discriminate against financial institutions from any region.

Conclusion

By being based on the IFC's environmental and social policy framework, the widespread support for the Equator Principles has effectively made the IFC a *de facto* standard-setter in the global project finance market. Overall, the Equator Principles reflects the growing discursive and structural influence of the IFC in the global economy, and has undoubtedly raised its public profile as an international organization. In a lead editorial, the *Washington Post* went so far as proclaiming that the Equator Principles 'demonstrate that the [World Bank Group] can remain relevant in a world awash in private capital' (Washington Post 2006).

However, notwithstanding such media reports, the influence of the IFC should not be overestimated. Once commercial project financing was negatively affected by a growing reputational risk, commercial banks drove the cooperative and deliberative process that eventually led to the launch of the Equator Principles. Without commercial banks voluntarily committing to a common industry standard and offering their widespread endorsement of the framework, it would not have materialized. Yet, despite being industry-driven, the Equator Principles do have a significant public dimension, as the standards themselves were originally developed within multilateral institutions and were designed under a public mandate to ensure that project loans would not harm the environment and local communities.

In attaining its influential position in the global project finance market, the IFC draws on three main sources of power. First, the IFC influences corporate practices, by collecting, organizing and manipulating knowledge and information about the relationship between private sector investment, environmental degradation and poverty, and advocating certain kinds of corporate interventions (see IFC 2002b). Second, this influence is reinforced by its operational mandate and financing operations, which allow it to exert structural power in the global economy by arranging project financing and placing environmental and social conditions on the disbursement of project loans, thereby diffusing its own operational policies and procedures in the marketplace. Third, by virtue of its public mandate, technical expertise and market influence, the IFC enjoys significant convening power in the global project finance market, manifested in attendance figures for its Annual Participants Meeting for syndicating banks, gathering leading financial institutions operating in developing countries.

In the context of the Equator Principles, the IFC's convening power proved instrumental for bringing together otherwise fiercely competitive financial institutions to share their experiences with project finance investments in developing countries. Yet, far from playing an entirely neutral role, IFC was in a privileged position relative to other international organizations, able to directly influence finance executives in an operational setting. The subsequent participation of the IFC in the drafting stages influenced the eventual decision among leading commercial banks to make the *Safeguard Policies* the blueprint for a common industry framework, as it convinced them that the IFC's framework was the most effective in mitigating the environmental and social risks associated with project financing globally, across all industry sectors.

As the Equator Principles have been widely embraced by financial institutions, project sponsors and third parties such as international law firms and environmental consultancies, the framework has shaped the environmental and social risk management in the project finance market and enjoys legitimacy as a voluntary initiative. The recent formalization of its governance structure reflects its transition from a loose network of commercial banks to an industry association cooperating on achieving common objectives, and marks a new phase in the framework's history.

However, environmental NGOs have argued that the lack of the accountability and transparency makes it nearly impossible for external observers to pass judgement on the effectiveness of the framework (see Banktrack 2006). In an attempt to respond to such criticisms, an additional principle was inserted in the 2006 revision of the framework that requires financial institutions to report, at least annually, on 'Equator Principles implementation processes and experience', which should at a minimum include the number of transactions screened, and their environmental screening category (Equator Principles 2006: 5). However, this requirement falls short of disclosure practices at multilateral lenders, which notify the public of projects that are under consideration for financing. The weakness of the reporting requirement in the

Equator Principles reflects the fact that commercial banks remain reluctant to publicly disclose which projects they are financing, much less how they apply the Equator Principles to particular projects. In support of their stance, there is evidence that the disclosure of project-level information would be considered illegal or highly unprofessional in most jurisdictions (FBD 2005). Yet, notwithstanding this obstacle, to instil public confidence in the voluntary framework, it is necessary for commercial banks to disclose how the standards and procedures are applied to the most controversial projects.

References

Amalric, F. (2005) 'The Equator Principles – A Step Towards Sustainability?', in Center for Corporate Responsibility and Sustainability (ed.) *Working Paper Series 01/05*, Zurich: University of Zurich.

Banktrack (2006) *Shaping the Future of Sustainable Finance – Moving From Paper Promises to Performance*, Amsterdam: Banktrack.

Boisson de Chazournes, L. (2000) 'Policy Guidance and Compliance: The World Bank Operational Standards', in Shelton, D. (ed.) *Commitment and Compliance: The Role of Non-binding Norms in the International Legal System*, Oxford: Oxford University Press.

Bondy, K., Matten, D. and Moon, J. (2004) 'The Adoption of Voluntary Codes of Conduct in MNCs – A Three Countries Comparative Study', *Business and Society Review*, 109(4): 449–77.

Environmental Defense Fund (EDF) (ed.) (2005) *Retreat from the Safeguard Policies – Recent Trends Undermining Social and Environmental Accountability at the World Bank*, New York: EDF.

Equator Principles (2003) *The Equator Principles – An Industry Approach for Financial Institutions in Determining, Assessing and Managing Environmental and Social Risk in Project Financing*, online. Available HTTP: <http://www.equator-principles.com> (June).

Equator Principles (2006) *The Equator Principles – A Financial Industry Benchmark for Determining, Assessing and Managing Social and Environmental Risk in Project Financing*, online. Available HTTP: <http://www.equator-principles.com> (July 2006).

Esty, B.C (2004) 'Why Study Large Projects? An Introduction to Research on Project Finance', *European Financial Management*, 10(2): 213–24.

Falkner, R. (2003) 'Private Environmental Governance and International Relations: Exploring the Links', *Global Environmental Politics*, 3(2), May: 72–87.

FOE (2001) 'Paper Tigers, Hidden Dragons', by Ed Matthew (Friends of the Earth, England, Wales and Northern Ireland) and Jan Willem van Gelder (Profundo), May.

Freshfields Bruckhaus Deringer (FBD) (2005) *Banking on Responsibility, Part One of Freshfields Bruckhaus Deringer Equator Principles Survey 2005*, The Banks: FBD.

Gulrajani, N. (2006) 'The Art of Fine Balances: The Challenge of Institutionalizing the Comprehensive Development Framework Inside the World Bank', in Stone, D. and Wright, C. (eds) *The World Bank and Governance: A Decade of Reform and Reaction*, CSGR Series in Globalisation and Regionalisation, London: Routledge.

Gutner, T.L. (2002) *Banking on the Environment – Multilateral Development Banks and*

Their Environmental Performance in Central and Eastern Europe, Cambridge, MA: MIT Press.

Hair, J., Dysart, B., Danielson, L.J. and Rubaleava, A.O. (1997) 'Pangue Hydroelectric Project (Chile): An Independent Review of the International Finance Corporation's Compliance with Applicable World Bank Group Environment and Social Requirements', IFC Internal Document, April 4 1997, Santiago, Chile: World Bank.

International Finance Corporation (IFC) (1996) *Annual Report 1996*, Washington DC: IFC.

IFC (2002a) *The Environmental and Social Challenges of Private Sector Projects*, Washington DC: IFC.

IFC (2002b) *Developing Value – The Business Case for Sustainability in Emerging Markets*, Washington DC: IFC, SustainAbility and the Ethos Institute.

IFC (2003) *Sustainability Review 2003*, Washington, DC: IFC.

IFC (2005) *Annual Report 2005*, Washington, DC: IFC.

IJ Research & Analysis (2006) 'IJ First Half Review: Equator Principles Financing', *Infrastructure Journal*, 17 August.

Jaabre, A. (2002) 'Update on IFC Financing', in Lazarus, S. (ed.) *IFC and its Role in Globalization – Highlights from IFC's Participants Meeting, Washington DC, June 6–7, 2001*, Washington, DC: IFC.

Kennedy, W. (1999) 'Environmental Impact Assessment and Multilateral Financial Institutions', in Petts, J. (ed.) *Handbook of Environmental Impact Assessment*, Oxford: Blackwell Science.

Lazarus, S. (2004) 'The Equator Principles: A Milestone or Just Good PR?', *Global Agenda*, March 17.

Levy, D. and Newell, P. (eds) (2005) *The Business of Global Environmental Governance*, Cambridge, MA: MIT Press.

Missbach, A. (2004) 'The Equator Principles: Drawing The Line for Socially Responsible Banks? An Interim Review from an NGO Perspective', *Development*, 47(3), September: 78–84.

Park, S. (2006) 'Becoming Green: The World Bank Group, Norm Diffusion and Transnational Environmental Advocacy Networks', in Stone, D. and Wright, C. (eds) *The World Bank and Governance: A Decade of Reform and Reaction*, CSGR Series in Globalisation and Regionalisation, London: Routledge.

Pattberg, P. (2006) 'The Influence of Global Business Regulation: Beyond Good Corporate Conduct', *Business and Society Review*, 113(3): 241–68.

Ruggie, J. (2002) 'The Theory and Practice of Learning Networks: Corporate Social Responsibility and the Global Compact', *Journal of Corporate Citizenship*, 5, Spring: 27–36.

Ruggie, J. (2004) 'Reconstituting the Global Public Domain – Issues, Actors, and Practices', *European Journal of International Relations*, 10(4): 499–531.

Schaper, M. (2007) 'Leveraging Green Power: Environmental Rules for Project Finance', *Business and Politics*, 9(3), Article 3: 1–27.

Utting, P. (2005) 'Rethinking Business Regulation: From Self-Regulation to Social Control', *Technology, Business and Society Programme Paper No.15*, Geneva: United Nations Research Institute for Social Development (UNRISD).

Wade, R. (1997) 'Greening the Bank: The Struggle over the Environment, 1970–1995', in Kapur, D., Lewis, J. and Webb, R. (eds) *The World Bank: Its First Half Century*, Washington, DC: The Brookings Institution, Vol. 2

Washington Post (2006) 'Managing Globalization', Lead Editorial, 19 February, Section B06.

Watchman, P.Q. and Baines, T. (2007) 'The Equator Principles', client memo publicly released by law firm LeBoeuf, Lamb, Greene and MacRae, 19 January.

World Bank (2004) *Global Development Finance 2004*, Washington, DC: The World Bank.

World Bank Group (1999) *Pollution Prevention and Abatement Handbook 1998, Towards Cleaner Production*, Washington, DC: The World Bank Group.

Wright, C. (2006) 'From "Safeguards" to "Sustainability": The Evolution of Environmental Discourse Inside the International Finance Corporation', in Stone, D. and Wright, C. (eds) *The World Bank and Governance: A Decade of Reform and Reaction*, CSGR Series in Globalisation and Regionalisation, London: Routledge.

Wright, C. and Rwabizambuga, A. (2006) 'Institutional Pressures, Corporate Reputation and Voluntary Codes of Conduct: An Examination of the Equator Principles', *Business and Society Review*, 111(1): 89–117.

4 OECD peer reviews and policy convergence

Diffusing policies or discourses?

Markku Lehtonen

Introduction

The OECD is an international organization in crisis. Its member countries widely agree on the continuing relevance of its original objectives: to promote policies designed to achieve the highest sustainable economic growth; to contribute to sound economic expansion in member as well as non-member countries; and to contribute to the expansion of world trade (e.g. OECD 2003a). However, as a result of changes in the international policy arena, the OECD seems to have somewhat lost its original identity over the past decade or so, and its legitimacy is increasingly being questioned, both within and beyond the member governments. The organization is often seen as a 'club of rich countries' promoting a neo-liberal reform agenda (e.g. Libération 2001; Dostal 2004), its organizational structure and consensual decision-making hampers its capacity to react quickly to new, emerging issues, and its overly prudent communications approach has resulted in low visibility (OECD 2003a: 20).

This loss of legitimacy is reflected in the continuous budget cuts and reductions in the staff numbers, despite the increasing workload stemming from the joining of six new member countries since 1994 (OECD 2003c; Dostal 2004: 465). The OECD must therefore 'fight harder for less' (Julin 2003; OECD 2003a; OECD 2003c: 20) in the context of globalization and increasing number of players in the arena of international policy analysis and advice. Moreover, the urgent short-term issues tending to crowd out the longer term concerns in which the OECD has its comparative advantage. A typical example is the effort that many European governments put into keeping up with the demands from the EU policymaking machinery, contrasted with the voluntary, more long-term OECD work. The changing role of the state in the new context of multi-actor governance; the shift in geopolitical priorities away from the OECD countries since the end of the Cold War; and the general pressure on governments to cut spending have further aggravated the OECD's problems.

In the area of environmental policies, the OECD seems to have lost the role it had in the 1970s and 1980s in leading the way towards more market-oriented and internationally harmonized policy approaches. Today, most of its member countries have well-established environmental institutions and the focus of environmental policy discourse has shifted away from the wider use of economic instruments towards broader approaches, in which the OECD has less specific expertise.

In its recent reform work, the OECD sought to identify its strengths – its 'comparative advantage' and core areas of work. Dismissing most of the charges against the OECD as unfounded, the reform work concluded that the organization possesses a combination of unique qualities, such as: intergovernmental character; broad range of member countries (as compared with, for example, the EU or the G8); focused capacity for policy analysis among a like-minded group (as opposed to the UN agencies); non-negotiating context in which most OECD bodies meet; unique cross-national data sets and deep analytical capacity of many OECD divisions; and highly developed capacity to carry out benchmarking and peer reviews (OECD 2003a).

It is this last aspect – the OECD benchmarking exercises – that the present chapter will focus on. The chapter analyses the potential of the OECD Environmental Performance Reviews to foster policy change through harmonization, imposition and diffusion. Given that environmental policy integration is among the central objectives of the EPRs – promotion of 'policy coherence' across sectors being, in turn, one of the key objectives of the OECD as a whole (OECD 2003c), this analysis also provides clues on the impacts of the peer reviews in promoting policy integration.

The chapter begins by presenting the OECD 'peer review logic', and introduces the concepts of harmonization, imposition and diffusion as a basis for analysing the role of benchmarking in policymaking. It then presents the idea of international organizations as 'norm creators' whose influence largely relies on agenda-setting throughout the 'norm life-cycle', largely brought about by the repetition of their respective 'organizational discourse'. The second part of the chapter first presents the EPR programme, then identifies the main pathways of influence from the reviews, and draws upon the concepts introduced in the first part of the chapter to consider the reasons for the relatively modest impact of the EPRs. The concluding section draws conclusions on the effectiveness of the EPRs and their role in OECD work in general.

The analysis is based on the author's experience as a national delegate to the OECD Working Party on Environmental Performance (WPEP) between May 1996 and June 2005, as a co-ordinator of the Finnish EPR in 1996–1997, as a country expert on three EPRs, and as a representative of the Ministry of the Environment in the preparation of the Economic Survey of Finland in 1998. Empirical data is drawn from the examination of diverse OECD policy documents and from 40 interviews with officials from the OECD Environment Directorate and Economics Department, national delegates and other stakeholders involved in the environmental policy reviews (for further details see Lehtonen 2005a).

Analytical framework

This section provides the analytical framework used in the second part of the article to analyse the OECD Environmental Performance Review Programme. It focuses on the 'ideational' aspects of policy, introducing the concepts used in the analytical part of the chapter: norm creation, norm life-cycle, harmonization, imposition and diffusion, and organisational discourse.

'Peer review logic' and benchmarking

Ranking and rating, evaluation of policies, and performance measurement have over the past decade become increasingly popular as 'new methods of governance' and as a 'regulatory innovation', in the context of changing role of the nation-state, and the emergence of multiactor, multilevel governance (see e.g. Lehmkuhl 2005; Lodge 2005). While peer review has in these traditional fields of application come under threat by the increasing use of performance measurement (e.g. Hansson 2000), in international organizations it seems to be gaining ground, albeit in a different form and on a different level.

The OECD has defined international peer review as 'the systematic examination and assessment of the performance of a State by other States, with the ultimate goal of helping the reviewed State improve its policy making, adopt best practices, and comply with established standards and principles' (OECD 2003b: 9). The examination should be *non-adversarial* and rely on mutual *trust* among the States involved, as well as on their shared *confidence* in the process. With these elements in place, peer review is assumed to create a system of mutual *accountability* (ibid.).

As an assessment process, peer review falls between performance measurement and evaluation. Unlike the former, it does not result in a binding or legal judgement by a superior body, never implies a punitive decision or sanctions, is characterized by dialogue and interactive investigation, and usually does not involve formal reporting by the examined state (ibid.: 5.). Compared with evaluations, in turn, peer reviews pay less attention to the causal mechanisms behind the policy outcomes – the main emphasis is on results rather than explanation.

Peer reviews are expected to exert their influence through *'peer pressure'*. Public scrutiny facilitated by media involvement, dialogue with peer countries, comparisons, and in some cases even ranking of countries, put pressure on the domestic public opinion, national administrations and policymakers (OECD 2003b: 10). A country hardly wants to be seen in a negative light among its peers, and therefore peer pressure might be a powerful tool in promoting compliance, notably in the 'laggard' states (see Beyeler 2002; Marcussen 2001: 8; Strang and Chang 1993). It therefore constitutes an instrument establishing normative criteria of appropriate behaviour

(Lehmkuhl 2005: 2). Peer reviews must balance between on the one hand a high level of ownership felt by the reviewed country, dependent on close involvement of the reviewed country in the process, and on the other, diminished credibility resulting from attempts by the reviewed State to unduly influence the final outcome.

Ideally, peer review can simultaneously serve two distinct objectives of evaluation: learning and accountability (Lehtonen 2005b). The latter perspective is characteristic to performance measurement within the so-called New Public Management, and judges the value of a programme or a policy on the basis of its outcomes, without analysing the causal links between policies and outcomes (e.g. Greene 1999: 162; Thoenig 2000; Feller 2002: 438). The former, by contrast, sees evaluation as a deliberative social learning process, in the context of uncertainty, complexity and plurality of values (e.g. van der Knaap 1995; Baron 1999; Siebenhüner 2001).

Harmonization, imposition and diffusion through benchmarking

The first perspective on the OECD's role in international politics stems from the typology of Busch and Jörgens (2005a, 2005b), consisting of three broad classes of mechanisms – harmonization, imposition and diffusion – through which international processes, actors and institutions contribute to domestic policy change and cross-national policy convergence. Boundaries between the three mechanisms are not always clear, but they often work synergistically, in parallel, in subsequent turns, or constraining each other (Busch and Jörgens 2005a, 2005b).

'Harmonization' integrates mechanisms such as negotiation, legalization, compliance and enforcement. It involves international negotiations among sovereign states leading to policy formulation and subsequent domestic implementation and compliance. While participation in such multilateral decision-making is voluntary, once an agreement has been reached, the states have little room for negotiation, but must comply with the agreement. Compliance is often monitored and enforced by independent institutions (Busch and Jörgens 2005a).

Imposition takes place when external actors intentionally coerce nations, for instance through economic and political conditionality, to adopt policy innovations, which they would not have adopted otherwise. Unlike in the case of harmonization, the motivations of the targeted and 'imposing' countries differ from each other. The weaker actor may reject or accept the demands simply to obtain the political or economic benefits which imposing actors offer in exchange. The stronger countries, in turn, seek to disseminate their fundamental values and principles (Busch and Jörgens 2005a).

Finally, *diffusion* is defined as a 'process by which policy innovations are communicated in the international system and adopted voluntarily by an increasing number of countries over time' (Busch and Jörgens 2005a: 865). At the micro-level, diffusion takes the form of social learning, copying or emulation. Diffusion is basically a horizontal process whereby individually adopted policies and programmes add up to a decentralized regulatory structure (Levi-Faur 2005). National policymakers may wish to emulate other countries' policies for a number of reasons, associated with their self-interest or identity. The former implies looking beyond national borders for effective solutions to domestic problems, and being persuaded – but not forced – by other actors to adopt policies from abroad. The latter refers to the desire to conform with broadly adopted political norms, to gain legitimacy and enhance self-esteem among both the national and international policy community (Finnemore and Sikkink 1998; Marcussen 2001; Busch and Jörgens 2005a).

International organizations as creators of norms and identities

The identity-related, or 'ideational' factors referred to above are a major means whereby international organizations without decision-making power can exert influence. Through 'idea games', such organizations diffuse ideas, shape a certain 'repertoire' of reform, and provide domestic actors with arguments that allow them to legitimize their actions (e.g. Haas 1992; Finnemore and Sikkink 1998; March and Olsen 1998; Marcussen 2001; Dostal 2004). As deliberate *creators of international norms and identities* international organizations 'define problems, construct conceptions of causal knowledge, and create frames for action that integrate across nation states' (March and Olsen 1998: 963). They also socialize individuals, create meaning, and promote specific concepts (ibid.: 964). This perspective not only helps to understand how policy diffusion takes place, but also explains some of the reasons behind harmonization and imposition – reasons that relate to factors such as esteem, legitimacy, and the identities of the states as members of an international society.

Socialization can be defined as a process of learning, whereby interaction with other people leads to the internalization of norms, ideals, and behavioural patterns (Ikenberry and Kupchan 1990: 289; Finnemore and Sikkink 1998: 902; Marcussen 2001: 6). Mechanisms of socialization include both positive and negative feedback – 'stick and carrot' – particularly characteristic of the OECD peer review exercises. *Imitation* (or emulation) is triggered by dissatisfaction or the discovery of new possibilities and does not necessarily involve direct contact between social actors. While an international organization without regulatory power can hardly directly *coerce* its member countries and impose binding sanctions, it can indirectly push them to comply with certain norms and principles (ibid. 2001). Benchmarking, for instance, may amount to *de facto* imposition when embedded in international or national regulation, or when it has a central role in market processes (Lehmkuhl 2005: 26–7).

Norm life-cycle

The processes of socialization, imitation and coercion have different roles depending on the phase of the policy process or 'norm life-cycle' at which they operate. At the earliest stage of the cycle, international organizations can function as *'norm entrepreneurs'*: along with NGOs, as parts of larger transnational advocacy networks – 'epistemic communities' – they can advocate the adoption of certain international norms (see also Haas 1992: 17; Finnemore and Sikkink 1998: 895). For example Dostal (2004: 451) has emphasized the role of the OECD as a 'first mover' in influencing the definition of policy problems.

The second stage, *'norm cascade'*, is a result of an active process of international socialization intended to convert norm breakers to norm followers. International organizations can help in establishing and assuring adherence to international norms, and *legitimizing* or *delegitimizing* state actions. A government can also use external evaluations to acquire legitimacy for its policy (Finnemore and Sikkink 1998).

At the highest level of norm life-cycle, the norm becomes *internalized*, i.e. it acquires a taken-for-granted quality and is no longer subject to broad public debate. Sources and mechanisms of internalization include iterated behaviour and habit, as well as professional training that systematically carries forward different normative biases (Finnemore and Sikkink 1998: 904–5).

Agenda-setting through 'organizational discourse'

The concept 'organizational discourse' allows one to move beyond the procedural aspects and look at the character of and the forces behind the creation of such norms. Organizational discourse can be defined as 'the language and symbolic media used by organizations and the people who manage and work in them' (Grant *et al.* 2001: 8). The concept has to do with the organization's internal value system – it is neither scientific discourse, nor directly comparable with epistemic communities. Rather than being highly discursive, it is based on the power of discursive closure: organizations create their own knowledge based on strategically selected issues and aim to disseminate the resulting expertise in their policymaking environment. Long-term policy change, from this perspective, is characterized by the mutual adaptation of organizational discourse, the agents using the power of discursive repetition to produce lasting changes (Dostal 2004: 445). Such agents can be organizations, as well as individuals or units within an organization.

An international organization such as the OECD therefore influences agenda-setting at different levels of policymaking 'by providing a controlled environment for the creation, development and dissemination of political discourse' (Dostal 2004: 440). Such influence tends to lead to the adoption of a shared terminology, similar methods of inquiry, and unified style of presentation across benchmarking exercises. While the concept of organizational discourse is helpful in understanding an international organization's influence on policy, it still needs to be placed within the context of power relations: how is such a discourse being constituted and whose ideas does it represent? Usually, the 'specific knowledge' with regard to particular political problems and the 'general knowledge' with regard to the overarching framework coexist in an organization, and the latter, as a rule, gains the upper hand (Dostal 2004: 447). As we shall see later on, the influence of the OECD peer reviews is largely conditioned by such tensions between the dominant and marginalized discourses within the organization.

Analysing the OECD and its environmental policy reviews

In the following, the concepts presented above will be used to analyse the role that the OECD Environmental Performance Reviews play in influencing policymaking in its member countries. In particular, this section aims at examining the role of the EPRs in relation to the mechanisms of harmonization, imposition and diffusion; asking what type of norm creation takes place and in which phase of the 'norm life-cycle'; how the OECD organizational discourse manifests itself in the EPRs; and to what extent such discursive elements condition the influence of the reviews.

Four roles of the OECD

Before going into a more detailed analysis of the EPRs, a look at the OECD's role through Marcussen's (2001) typology helps to identify the source of the organizational discourse: whether it emanates from the member countries or is independently advocated by the OECD secretariat.

The basis for the OECD's authority rests on its fundamental 'mission', consisting of two roles. First, as an *'ideational artist'* the organization is an enormous 'think tank' that formulates, tests and diffuses new policy ideas. Thanks to its financial and political independence, the OECD should be able to distance itself from national controversies and possess considerable room for manoeuvre when inventing new ideas in old policy areas. In the area of environmental policies, the OECD's best-known contribution has been the invention and 'marketing' of the concept of polluter pays principle (Marcussen 2001). Second, the OECD plays the role of an *'ideational arbitrator'*, allowing national civil servants to meet each other in supportive surroundings, thereby helping them to acquire skills and competence, and sometimes even develop their personality and feelings of belonging, through *learning processes* such as socialization, imitation and coercion. This is a major feature of OECD work in general, and was evoked by many of the interviewees consulted in this study (see also Marcussen 2001).

These two core functions have over the years been complemented by two other, less 'idealistic' roles, namely those of an 'ideational agent' and an 'ideational agency'. As an *ideational agent*, the OECD picks up ideas prevalent among the most powerful member states, then links these ideas to department-specific areas of activity, and finally transfers the final product to other, less centrally placed member states. In environmental policy, the traditional 'frontrunners' and 'opinion leaders' such as Sweden, Norway and the Netherlands, seem no longer to have the role they used to have, and new concepts such as 'decoupling' or 'dematerialization' tend to emanate from 'think tanks' and other international organizations rather than from specific member countries. Finally, as an *ideational agency*, the OECD constantly surfs around among the national political debates in order to make a good 'business deal'. When it discovers that certain ideas have gained ground among the member states, it operationalizes them into a set of causal ideas that can be marketed to the member states. The OECD provides its clients the kind of products that happen to be in general demand. The attempt to define and operationalize the 'environmental-social interface' is but one example of the OECD acting in this role.

The four roles reflect different perspectives on the independence and autonomy of the OECD, illustrated through Figure 4.1. As an ideational artist, the OECD is a source of new ideas, as an ideational arbitrator it continues to play an important role as innovator and disseminator of policy ideas, while as an ideational agent or agency the OECD is rather on the receiving end in the processes of norm creation.

The independence of the OECD therefore declines as its role shifts from the fully independent 'ideational artist' towards the 'ideational agency' that follows rather than sets the agendas of the member countries. The mechanisms of 'norm creation' – socialization, imitation, coercion – as well

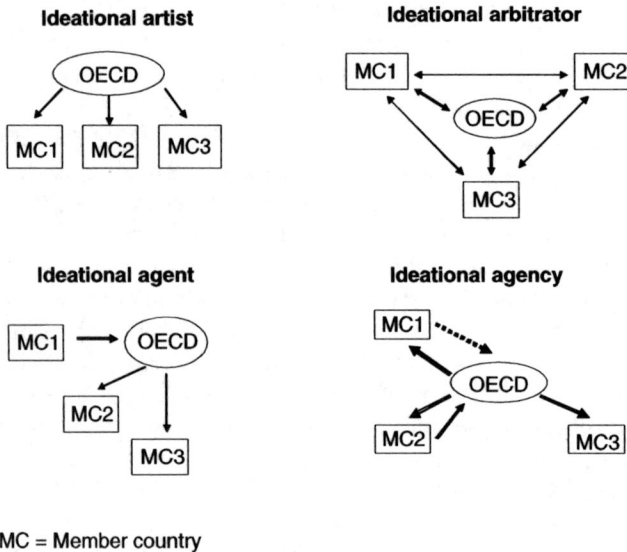

MC = Member country

Figure 4.1 The four roles of the OECD.

as the reasons why such mechanisms are operational (legitimacy, conformity, esteem) remain the same, but their locus moves downstream along the norm life-cycle. While an ideational artist ideally operates as a norm entrepreneur, an ideational agent or agency no longer has the capacity to innovate, but takes up innovations developed elsewhere and contributes to 'norm cascade' and 'norm internalization'. In these two latter roles, the OECD has fully entered the 'power game', in which its independence, legitimacy and credibility in promoting norm adoption may be called into question. Figure 4.2 summarizes the conceptual framework developed so far.

The OECD Environmental Performance Review Programme

The OECD has carried out systematic reviews of its member countries' environmental policies since 1992. The principal objective of the Environmental Performance Reviews (EPR) is 'to help Member countries improve their individual and collective performances in environmental management with the goal of achieving sustainable development' (OECD 1998: 6). More specifically, the EPRs are to help countries assess progress, promote policy dialogue, and stimulate greater accountability of governments towards their peers and constituencies (ibid.).[1] Together with other country reviews, the EPRs are a part of the OECD's efforts to analyse sustainable development in its member countries. The reviews assess performance against three key criteria: (1) countries' own policy objectives and international commitments; (2) commonly agreed OECD policy principles; and (3) the cost-effectiveness of policies.

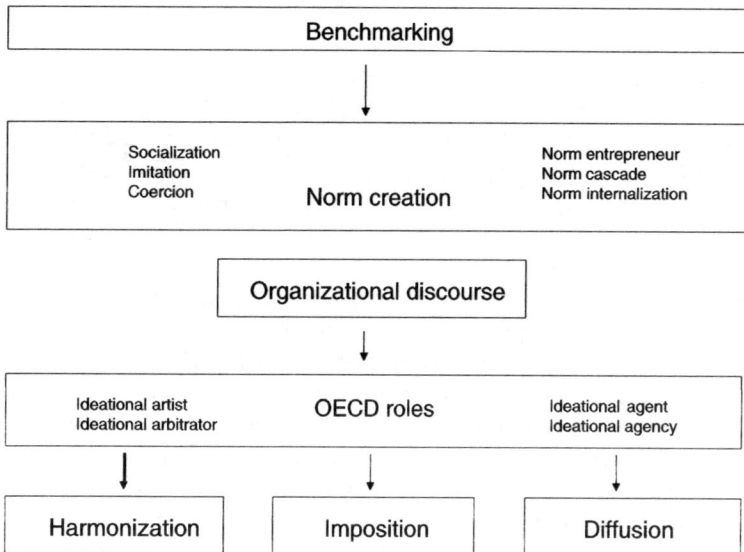

Figure 4.2 Conceptual framework for analysing the impact of OECD reviews.

An Environmental Performance Review begins with a visit by a high-level official from the OECD Environmental Performance and Information (EPI) division to the reviewed country, to agree upon the detailed scope of the review and explain the steps of the process. The country government (usually environment ministry) then prepares background material according to the guidelines and more specific questions sent by the OECD secretariat. The background material mainly comes from the country's environmental authorities, but also includes information from other relevant government bodies, and often also from environmental NGOs.

After having studied the background material, the review team – usually made up of five to eight OECD secretariat members and consultants, and three to four experts of environmental policy from other OECD countries – travels to the country for a six-to-ten-day 'review mission'. The team first meets relevant authorities in thematic meetings on water and air management, nature conservation, integration of environmental issues into other policy sectors, environmental-social interface, international environmental cooperation, and a special issue chosen in collaboration with the country's government (environmental concerns in policy areas such as energy, chemicals, transport, health, agriculture or tourism). These meetings reflect the structure of the review report, which usually consists of seven or eight chapters. The team also meets with NGOs, business representatives, and environmental researchers, in two-to-three-hour sessions in which authorities are not present.

The team then drafts a preliminary review report, which is sent to the reviewed country and to the delegates of the OECD Working Party on Environmental Performance about a month before the final peer review meeting in Paris. Each chapter contains five to eight non-binding policy recommendations. Following an inter-ministerial consultation round, the government sends to the OECD secretariat its comments on and proposals for changes to the report. Those change proposals that the secretariat considers controversial are highlighted in the draft document and discussed among the group. Only a few revisions are usually proposed and accepted, most of the time in the meeting being spent on general dialogue between the working party members and the reviewed country delegation. The Working Party on Environmental Performance then adopts the conclusions and recommendations by consensus.

About three months after the peer review meeting, the report is released in the reviewed country's capital, usually in a press conference and/or a seminar, with presentations and comments given by a high-level OECD official, the minister of the environment (sometimes other ministers participate as well), and representatives from other sectors of government, industry, NGOs, and researchers. The reviewed country government – not the OECD – decides how to organize the release event, disseminate the report, and follow up the implementation of the recommendations. However, the OECD urges countries to draw up a report on the implementation of the recommendations two to three years after the review has been published.

Four pathways of EPR influence

The analysis of the EPRs allows the construction of four 'ideal types' of pathways of EPRs influence on policymaking (Figure 4.3). These pathways operate, on the one hand, through *political pressure* inside the government (A) or among a broader range of stakeholders and the public (B), and, on the other hand, through *learning* concerning the reviewed policies (C) or consisting of more general long-term socialization, 'enlightenment' (e.g. Weiss 1980, 1987, 1999), and modification of mental models or frameworks of thought (D). Which one, if any, of these pathways dominates, depends to a large extent on the 'repertoires' of different actors and potential users of the reviews. Repertoires are 'stabilized ways of thinking and acting (on the individual level) or stabilized codes, operations and technology (on other levels)' (van der Meer 1999: 390). Because of differences in their histories, experiences, and positions in the relations of power, actors have different repertoires, which they use in the process of sense-making and construction of behaviour. These repertoires in turn influence to what degree actors consider reviews as salient, credible and legitimate – seen as key determinants for the usefulness of evaluations and assessments (e.g. Eckley 2001).

Pathway A – *'advocacy through intragovernmental debate'* – corresponds to the expectations of many civil servants in the reviewed countries, and represents 'soft coercion' in its purest sense. Gathering together, around environmental issues, a large number of civil servants from different sectors of administration, the review process and the recommendations from a respected intergovernmental economic organization give visibility and legitimacy to environmental policies, providing environmental authorities with 'ammunition' for inter-ministerial battles. The virtues of the review reports

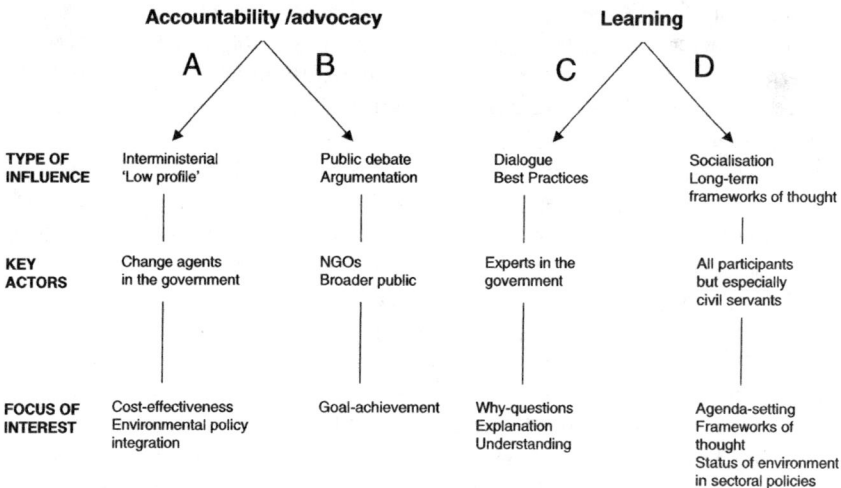

Figure 4.3 Four pathways of influence from the EPRs.

and the recommendations in this perspective are their diplomatic, non-confrontational and fact-based approach, as well as their capacity to appeal to actors that would not listen to pure 'environmentalist' arguments. Policy implementation, cost-effectiveness of policies, and environmental policy integration are among the likely themes of interest.

Pathway B – *'advocacy/accountability through public debate'* – represents a 'tougher' version of advocacy/accountability, since the main influence stems from public debate and argumentation among a broad range of stakeholders – the media and the NGOs playing a key role. The likely users of the reviews focus on goal-achievement and enhanced accountability of the government towards its citizens, rather than on procedural issues and administrative effectiveness.

To be effective, pathways A and B require that the OECD be perceived as an organization with political weight and capacity to persuade through public or intra-governmental pressure. Pathway C – *'learning from best practice'* – by contrast, does not assume that the OECD can exert significant political pressure, but sees it mainly as a forum for dialogue that facilitates mutual learning on technical issues of policy implementation. As opposed to the accountability/advocacy pathways, where pressure is placed on the whole government (pathway B) or on its non-environmental sectors (pathway A) to strengthen environmental policies, here the reviews are supposed to engender dialogue on the reasons for policy success and failure, and in this way promote innovation and learning from best practices. The OECD's credibility would rely on its high level of expertise on relatively technical issues.

The EPR programme has been designed to exploit all three pathways mentioned above. However, it is not uncommon that none of the three operates in an optimal manner. Pathway A ('advocacy through intragovernmental debate') may fail simply because of the lack of motivated change agents in key positions in the government (see also Lodge 2005: 661); pathway B ('advocacy/accountability through public debate') suffers from the lack of comparability and from the highly diplomatic tone of the reports, hardly appealing to the more conflict-oriented 'repertoires' dominant among the media and the environmental NGOs. Often, the EPR process is not sufficiently dialogical to engender genuine learning through pathway C ('learning from best practice'). Many participants see the review processes as excessively formal and ritualistic, characterized by defensive discussions in the peer review meetings. Moreover, the lack of an explanatory element in the reviews does not facilitate learning either (for similar conclusions see Lodge 2005). Yet, the interviews showed that the EPRs are only rarely considered as completely useless, since they help to legitimize environmental policies and authorities on the one hand (pathways A and B), and to instil an OECD-type results-based, market-oriented policy style within environmental administrations on the other (especially through pathway D, to some extent also C).

The EPRs influence depends not only on 'repertoires' and review design, but largely also on the country-specific institutional context, as is the case with evaluations and assessments in general (e.g. Sabatier and Jenkins-Smith 1999; Weiss 1999; Barnes *et al.* 2003; Nilsson 2005: 22). In general, the EPRs appear to be most influential in small countries that are sensitive to outside opinions, have recently joined the OECD, and have relatively poorly developed environmental policy institutions and a weak tradition of environmental policy evaluation. The country-specific context also affects the relative importance of the different pathways of influence. Relevant factors include:

- The degree of networking within the administration. For example, in Japan, the Netherlands, and Portugal, the authorities argued that the EPRs did little to extend or strengthen the already existing networks, whereas the first EPR of Mexico was highly valued as an occasion for building inter-organizational contacts.
- The country's 'discussion culture' and policy style. An outspoken, even confrontational style may be more effective in countries with an 'Anglo-Saxon' discussion culture (see e.g. Gambetta 1998), whereas the Latin countries appreciate a more diplomatic tone. On the other hand, many interviewees stressed the value of the OECD as a forum for frank discussions on 'hot' topics in a relaxed atmosphere – a luxury that negotiators do not have in most arenas of international policy.
- The timing of the release of the report. In Norway and Mexico, for instance, the newly appointed environment ministers were eager to use the reports as a benchmark against which new policies could be assessed, and a source of legitimacy for the new government's policy objectives.

If pathways A, B and C often fail to operate optimally, how about pathway D – *'long-term conceptual learning'*? The reviews gradually shape the frameworks of thought and the relative importance of different policy issues on the policy agenda, notably by strengthening the status of environmental issues in sectoral policies and by promoting results-oriented, efficiency-oriented thinking in environmental policy. Seen from the perspective of 'organizational discourse', the influence therefore goes in both ways: on the one hand, the minority environmentalist discourse – advocated by the epistemic community congregated around the ministries of the environment – gains legitimacy in the national policy debates, while on the other, the dominant organizational discourse of the OECD 'infiltrates' itself into the national environmental administrations. While the motivation of 'change agents' to carry forward the OECD message certainly facilitates this type of impact, its absence is not fatal, unlike in the three other pathways. The mere participation of a large number of stakeholders in the review process – participation that is rather intensive for those most immediately involved – in itself shapes the ways of thought.

Harmonization, imposition and diffusion through the EPRs

In theory, the primary role of the OECD peer reviews is to promote policy *diffusion* through dialogue, socialization and legitimization. The reviews can hardly impose policies on member countries, and do not involve negotiations leading to international *harmonization*. Indirectly, the EPRs support harmonization by monitoring the compliance of states with international treaties, conventions and regulations. The fear of being excluded from the 'good company' constitutes a potentially powerful mechanism of *quasi-imposition* – pathway B clearly involves the idea of indirect imposition through public pressure. However, as non-binding, diplomatic and politically rather low-profile exercises, the EPRs seldom have sufficient leverage to press the countries to change their policies. Moreover, the country's authorities can always refer to 'national specificities' as an excuse to reject the findings, or simply ignore the review. The lack of genuine dialogue throughout the process further reduces the contribution of EPRs to policy diffusion.

Yet, the EPRs clearly play a legitimizing function, as long as the country-specific context is favourable enough to stimulate the emergence of advocacy coalitions willing to push for the adoption of policies recommended by the OECD. On the one hand, the reviews legitimize environmental policies and authorities, and on the other, they disseminate and reproduce the OECD 'organizational discourse' within the reviewed countries. In pathway C, diffusion concerns the specific policies, instruments and 'best practices', whereas pathway D involves diffusion of broader approaches and mindsets. While transfer of 'best practices' is a way of using the EPRs that many prefer in principle, there is scarce evidence of such direct policy transfer. By contrast, the OECD's 'organizational discourse', dominated by liberal economics and characterized by the exclusion of interest groups, is crucial from the perspective of long-term conceptual learning. A typical feature of the dominant OECD discourse is its selective reliance on the authority of academic mainstream economics (see e.g. Dostal 2004: 450–1). The neoclassical belief in market equilibrium outcomes provides a unifying framework for all OECD activities, and a homogeneous discourse in different fields of policymaking, including the environment (e.g. principles of relying on market-based instruments, internalization of external costs, cost-benefit analysis). The EPRs do attempt to expand this perspective, for instance through attempting to see internalization of external costs more broadly than as mere monetary internalization based on calculations of Pareto efficiency. Yet, they frequently adjust their message to suit the dominant discourse, in an attempt to survive in an environment strongly dominated by mainstream economic thinking.

In sum, the EPR experience hardly lends support to Lehmkuhl's (2005) optimism concerning the potential of benchmarking as a powerful mechanism in promoting the convergence of governance practices, thereby leading to harmonization, imposition and diffusion. Rather, the findings justify the scepticism of Lodge (2005) regarding the impacts of the regulatory policy reviews. The OECD Programme for International Student Assessment (PISA)[2] is often brought forward as a 'success story' of OECD benchmarking exercises. The success of PISA has been attributed to the great public interest and political pressure that a clear ranking of countries in function of their educational performance can generate (e.g. Lehmkuhl 2005). A number of factors may explain why the EPRs have failed to have the strong policy influence characteristic of the PISA studies.

The first explanation is obvious but crucial: PISA assessments are not peer reviews in the sense of the term described above, but are conducted by independent bodies in each OECD country, according to an evaluation framework defined by the OECD. This lends PISA greater independence and 'objectivity'. Second, EPRs do not clearly fit into any of Marcussen's (2001) four roles of the OECD. They rarely produce the new and innovative ideas that an 'ideational artist' would be expected to provide, while the review process is not sufficiently dialogical and the conclusions sufficiently 'biting' to make EPRs an instrument useful for an 'ideational arbitrator'. Furthermore, the most powerful countries do not seem to have a disproportionate impact on the reviews – which would imply the OECD playing a role of an 'ideational agent' – and the new issues and approaches usually enter OECD countries' national policy agendas long before they are integrated into the EPR framework, thus calling into question whether the OECD is an 'ideational agency' in conducting the reviews. Third, because of their highly consensual approach, the EPRs hardly represent 'transnational challenger rules' (Lehmkuhl 2005: 12) that would put significant pressure on policymakers. The EPRs neither rank nor rate countries, which makes cross-country comparisons much more difficult than in the PISA studies. Instead of making 'challenger rules' to emerge as models and norms for 'good practice', the EPRs mainly reiterate the OECD discourse. Through constant repetition, perceived by many 'insiders' in the EPR programme as frustrating, the EPRs reproduce the OECD discourse, and promoting its adoption in the member countries. Fourth, the PISA studies link educational achievement with the future economic growth potential, suggesting that a reviewed country's *economic* future strongly depends on the performance of its educational system today. A similar argument is much harder to sustain in the case of environmental policies.

OECD credibility and reputation as an asset or an obstacle to reform?

The EPRs represent environmental policy integration as a two-way learning process whereby the non-environmental authorities learn about environmental policy and the environmental officials about sectoral issues (Nilsson 2005: 21). On the one hand, they are a tool for the environmental authorities in the member countries to strengthen their legitimacy in the face of their more powerful economic counterparts, and, more generally, for the 'environmentalist epistemic community' to gain foothold in an organization dominated by mainstream economic thinking. On the other hand, the EPRs help to instil the dominant OECD discourse into the 'environmentalist' community. To serve their double function of environmental policy advocacy and the promotion of the OECD doctrine, the EPRs need to motivate the potential 'change agents' within the reviewed countries by linking with the dominant 'repertoires' or discourses in the country, yet without losing their integrity and credibility among the 'environmentalist' community. To some extent, the reviews have failed in this task, partly because of the inability of the programme to innovate and renew itself, but also because the EPRs at present do not optimally serve any stakeholder group.

A great deal of the policy impact of the OECD in general, and the EPRs in particular, stems from symbolic power, based on the OECD's prestige, credibility and perceived independence as an 'apolitical', 'neutral', techno-cratic institution (e.g. Dostal 2004; Sharman 2005). A key dilemma for the OECD is how to balance between the conflicting roles of an advocate and a politically neutral, independent evaluator. The authority and credibility of the organization have traditionally rested on the latter, whereas the failure to acknowledge the former would be politically naïve, and would greatly compromise the potential of the reviews to influence policies. The EPRs face formidable challenges in trying to straddle between the contrasting demands from the rather heterogeneous range of OECD member countries, but also from the different repertoires within the environmental administrations, other sectors of government, NGOs, the media, and the other parts of the OECD – the Economics Department and the associated 'economist com-munity' in particular.

Any attempt to change the EPR framework must take into account the degree to which the credibility, salience and legitimacy of the reviews depend on the 'repertoires' of the various stakeholders. For example, sharper and more specific recommendations, as well as a wider use of quantitative indicators and comparison between countries would likely enhance the salience and credibility of the reviews, in particular in the eyes of the NGOs and the media. However, this might weaken the reviews' legitimacy in the eyes of their main clients – the environmental administration of the reviewed country – and engender resistance on the part of sectoral ministries that could feel unjustly 'attacked'. Greater attention to the causal relations between policies and outcomes, in turn, would improve salience and credibility especially to environmental administrations, and strengthen the arguments behind the recommendations. Yet, given the limited resources available for the review programme, this would make it more difficult to improve at the same time cross-country comparability through the use of quantitative indicators. Moreover, the civil servants whose work would thus come under closer scrutiny might perceive such an approach as threatening – and hence less legitimate.

A similar observation is valid for participation and deliberative democracy.

While the EPRs by no means are an example of a truly deliberative process – participation during the review is broad, but relatively 'shallow' – greater stakeholder involvement might not be a key to success. The reviews are strongly government-oriented exercises, whose strength is not their potential to engage a broad range of stakeholders in a dialogue, but rather their capacity to mobilize governmental actors and promote environmental policy integration within the government. More participation might 'politicize' the reviews, compromising their value as a forum for 'cool debates on hot issues' and the credibility of the reviews to some key stakeholders (Lehtonen 2006).

If the EPRs are to play a significant role in promoting policy convergence through harmonization, imposition and diffusion, the OECD must tackle such dilemmas. It must motivate the key change agents, making sure national authorities have a clear picture of what the organization can and cannot achieve. To do so, it must design the EPRs in a manner that allows sufficient flexibility to accommodate national circumstances and yet provide for a rigorous and transparent framework of analysis. Carrying out a 'third cycle' of reviews very similar to the two first ones would be unlikely to receive sufficient support from the member countries. Unless the EPR programme succeeds in renewing itself, it risks being drawn into a self-reinforcing spiral, in which the lack of innovation in the EPRs reduces the utility of the reviews to the governments, which would be less motivated to support the continuation of the programme. The lack of political support would lead to further cuts in budget and/or personnel, thereby reducing the capacity of the secretariat to innovate, and increasing the gap between countries' expectations and what the EPRs can deliver in practice. Moreover, the reduced utility of the reviews would again diminish governments' interest in the whole exercise. The traditional strength of the OECD – its identity as an impartial expert organization – may turn out to be one of its greatest weaknesses as well, any reform of the EPR programme being constrained by the expectations the OECD has built up over the more than forty years of its existence.

Conclusions

If the influence of the OECD in international politics – especially in its old member countries – has declined over the past couple of decades, does this imply that the organizational discourse underpinning the OECD message is irrelevant for global sustainability? A number of reasons suggest otherwise. First, the OECD's influence in terms of 'norm creation' has probably declined much less than its more direct policy impact. The 'OECD message' may sound repetitive, old-fashioned and uninteresting, yet by its very nature, this repetition helps to maintain cohesion among the economic policy elites within the OECD countries. Second, the rather frequent attempts by the reviewed country governments to influence the contents of especially the Economic Surveys, but in some cases also those of the EPRs, proves that the reviews are not perceived as trivial. And third, even if the influence of the

OECD is declining in its old member countries, such is not the case in many of its newest members and in the potential future member countries. The Slovak Republic and Mexico are among the clearest examples of countries whose governments have deliberately used OECD message to support their policy reforms. Such a shift in the 'market' for the OECD message of course raises questions about the identity of the organization: if the main demand for OECD products is in the new member countries, how to retain the interest of the old members, and what happens once the new countries – the current 'laggards' – have been brought to the line, and there are no more frontiers for the OECD to expand?

This chapter has no pretension to judge whether the survival of the EPRs, let alone that of the OECD as a whole, might be desirable from a broader sustainability perspective. To adopt a slightly optimistic position, one can argue that the recent changes in the global policy arena are not a reason to abolish the OECD, but that they have instead made it more important than ever: the accelerating pace of policymaking and the pressures from international organizations – not least the EU – effectively prevent the overburdened policymakers and civil servants from looking back, taking distance, and considering the priorities of their work. There is a definite demand for an organization that can provide such a forum for reflection. Whether the OECD is up to the challenge depends on its capacity to convince its member countries that they have something to gain in the 'idea games'.

Notes

1 The goals of the EPR programme are to (1) *help individual governments assess progress by establishing* baseline conditions, trends, policy commitments, institutional arrangements and mechanisms for evaluating policy results in their social and economic contexts; (2) promote environmental improvements and continuous *policy dialogue* among member countries, through a peer review process and by the transfer of information on policies, approaches, and experiences of reviewed countries; and (3) stimulate greater *accountability* from member country governments towards representatives of all sectors of society both at national and international levels (OECD 1998: 6).
2 PISA is a three-yearly survey of the knowledge and skills of 15-year-olds in the principal industrialized countries aimed at producing valid comparisons across countries and cultures.

References

Barnes, M., Matka, E. and Sullivan, H. (2003) 'Evidence, Understanding and Complexity', *Evaluation*, 9(3): 265–84.
Baron, G. (1999) 'Evaluation, participation, apprentissage: Une conception de l'action publique avec rationalité limitée. Analyse et étude de cas d'une évaluation d'un programme européen', doctoral dissertation, Université de Rennes I.
Beyeler, M. (2002) 'OECD Surveillance and Welfare States in Western Europe – Concepts and Methods of a Comparative Research Project', paper presented at COST A15 Second Conference 'Welfare Reforms for the 21st Century', April 5–6, Oslo.

Busch, P.-O. and Jörgens, H. (2005a) 'The International Sources of Policy Convergence: Explaining the Spread of Environmental Policy Innovations', *Journal of European Public Policy*, 12(5): 860–84.

Busch, P.-O. and Jörgens, H. (2005b) 'Globale Ausbreitungsmuster umweltpolitischer Innovationen', *FFU-Report 02–2005*, Berlin: Forschungsstelle für Umweltpolitik (Environmental Policy Research Centre).

Dostal, J.M. (2004) 'Campaigning on Expertise: How the OECD Framed EU Welfare and Labour Market Policies – And why Success Could Trigger Failure', *Journal of European Public Policy*, 11(3): 440–60.

Eckley, N. (2001) 'Designing Effective Assessments: The Role of Participation, Science and Governance, and Focus', Report of a workshop co-organized by the European Environment Agency and the Global Environmental Assessment Project, Copenhagen, 1–3 March 2001, European Environment Agency Environmental issue report 26.

Feller, I. (2002) 'Performance Measurement Redux', *American Journal of Evaluation*, 23(4): 435–52.

Finnemore, M. and Sikkink, K. (1998) 'International Norm Dynamics and Political Change', *International Organization*, 52(4): 887–917.

Gambetta, D. (1998) ' "Claro!" An Essay on Discursive Machismo', in Elster, J. (ed.) *Deliberative Democracy*, Cambridge: Cambridge University Press.

Grant, D., Keenoy, T. and Oswick, C. (2001) 'Organizational Discourse: Key Contributions and Challenges', *International Studies of Management and Organization*, 31(3): 5–24.

Greene, J. (1999) 'The Inequality of Performance Measurements', *Evaluation*, 5(2): 160–72.

Haas, P.M. (1992) 'Introduction: Epistemic Communities and International Policy Co-ordination', *International Organization*, 46(1): 1–35.

Hansson, F. (2000) 'Research Evaluation: Controlling or Developing the Production of Knowledge. The Peer Review System in the Changing Knowledge Production System', paper presented at Evaluation 2000, Conference of the American Evaluation Association, 1–5 November, Waikiki, Hawaii.

Ikenberry, J.G. and Kupchan, C. (1990) 'Socialization and Hegemonic Power', *International Organization*, 44(3): 283–315.

Julin, J. (2003) 'The OECD: Securing the Future', *OECD Observer*, 240/241, December.

Lehmkuhl, D. (2005) 'Governance by Rating and Ranking', paper presented at the annual meeting of the International Studies Association, Hawaii, 1–6 March.

Lehtonen, M. (2005a) 'Environmental Policy Evaluation in the Service of Sustainable Development: Influence of the OECD Environmental Performance Reviews from the Perspective of Institutional Economics', unpublished doctoral dissertation, Université de Versailles Saint-Quentin-en-Yvelines, U.F.R. des Sciences Sociales et des Humanités, France.

Lehtonen, M. (2005b) 'OECD Environmental Performance Review Programme: Accountability (f)or Learning?', *Evaluation*, 11(2): 169–88.

Lehtonen, M. (2006) 'Deliberative Democracy, Participation, and OECD Peer Reviews of Environmental Policies', *American Journal of Evaluation*, 27(2): 185–200.

Levi-Faur, D. (2005) 'The Global Diffusion of Regulatory Capitalism', *The Annals of the American Academy of Political and Social Science*, 598 (March): 12–32.

Libération (2001) 'L'OCDE est un piston de la mondialisation', le 7 août 2001.

Lodge, M. (2005) 'The Importance of Being Modern: International Benchmarking and National Regulatory Innovation', *Journal of European Public Policy*, 12(4): 649–67.

March, J.G. and Olsen, J.P. (1998) 'The Institutional Dynamics of International Political Orders', *International Organization*, 52(4): 943–69.

Marcussen, M. (2001) 'The OECD: Transnational Regulation Through the Idea-Game', paper prepared for the SCANCOR Workshop 'Transnational Regulation and the Transformation of States', Stanford University, 22–23 June.

Nilsson, M.A. (2005) 'Connecting Reason to Power: Assessments, Learning, and Environmental Policy Integration in Swedish Energy Policy', doctoral dissertation for Technical University of Delft, The Netherlands/Stockholm Environment Institute, Stockholm.

OECD (1997) 'Workshop on the Second Cycle of Reviews/Lessons from the first cycle of reviews', room document No. 12. (document prepared by the Finnish Delegation), OECD Environment Directorate/Environmental Policy Committee, Group on Environmental Performance, Paris, 17 November 1997.

OECD (1998) 'OECD Environmental Performance Reviews: Second Cycle Work Plan', *EPOC Document ENV/EPOC (98)21*, Paris: OECD.

OECD (2003a) 'Future Direction of the OECD: Report on OECD's Role in Global Architecture', report prepared by Julin, J. (ambassador), *HOD(2003)2*, Paris: OECD.

OECD (2003b) *Peer Review: An OECD Tool for Co-operation and Change*, Paris: OECD.

OECD (2003c) 'Maximising the Impact of the OECD: Reorganizing the Committee Structure and Related Matters', report by Nicholson, P., *SG(2003)1*, Paris: OECD.

Sabatier, P.A. and Jenkins-Smith, H.C. (1999) 'The Advocacy Coalition Framework: An Assessment', in Sabatier, P.A. (ed.) *Theories of the Policy Process*, Boulder, CO: Westview Press.

Sharman, J.C. (2005) 'OECD Reputation as OECD Effectiveness', paper presented at the International Studies Association Meeting, Honolulu, Hawaii, 1–5 March.

Siebenhüner, B. (2001) 'How do Scientific Assessments Learn? A Comparative Study of LRTAP and IPCC', paper presented at 'Frontiers 1' European Society for Ecological Economics Conference, Cambridge, 4–7 July.

Strang, D. and Chang, P.M.Y. (1993) 'The International Labour Organization and the Welfare State: Institutional Effects on National Welfare Spending, 1960–1980', *International Organization*, 47(2): 235–62.

Thoenig, J.-C. (2000) 'Evaluation as Usable Knowledge for Public Management Reforms', *Evaluation*, 6(2): 217–29.

Van der Knaap, P. (1995) 'Policy Evaluation and Learning: Feedback, Enlightenment or Argumentation?', *Evaluation*, 1(2): 189–216.

Van der Meer, F.-B. (1999) 'Evaluation and the Social Construction of Impacts', *Evaluation*, 5(4): 387–406.

Weiss, C.H. (1980) 'Knowledge Creep and Decision Accretion', *Knowledge: Creation, Diffusion, Utilisation*, 1(3): 381–404.

Weiss, C.H. (1987) 'The Circuitry of Enlightenment: Diffusion of Social Science Research to Policymakers', *Knowledge: Creation, Diffusion, Utilisation*, 8(2): 274–81.

Weiss, C.H. (1999) 'The Interface Between Evaluation and Public Policy', *Evaluation*, 5(4): 468–86.

5 Socialization, the World Bank Group and global environmental governance

Susan Park [1]

Introduction

The proliferating 'global governance' literature indicates that international order exists in the form of governance rather than government (Rosenau and Czempiel 1992). It has been defined as 'the sum of the many ways individuals and institutions, public and private, manage their common affairs' (Commission on Global Governance 1995). Global *environmental* governance exemplifies this: regimes, often centred on multilateral environmental agreements (MEAs), address environmental degradation and management of the commons at local, national, regional and international levels. Regimes are 'sets of implicit or explicit principles, norms, rules and decision-making procedures around which actors' expectations converge in a given area of international relations' (Krasner 1983: 2). Global environmental governance has therefore been defined as 'the sum of overlapping networks of inter-state regimes on environmental issues' (Paterson *et al.* 2003: 4). This definition downplays the role of non-state actors and internal power dynamics – a criticism leveled against general global governance scholarship (Barnett and Duvall 2005). Some critical scholars argue that nongovernmental organizations (NGOs) remain outside global environmental governance, which they argue is based on hegemonic state and corporate interests (Ford 2003) while others argue that NGOs have been coopted by these hegemonic structures (Goldman 2005). Contra critical approaches, this chapter seeks to demonstrate how international organizations are being reshaped through socialization processes from transnational environmental advocacy networks. As demonstrated below, these processes have succeeded in drawing non-environmental international organizations into global environmental governance, by extending environmental issues into the private sector.

This chapter therefore examines how international organizations within the World Bank Group increasingly constitute part of global environmental governance. The World Bank Group includes the International Bank for Reconstruction and Development (IBRD) and the International Development Association (IDA) (together known as the 'World Bank'); the International Finance Corporation (IFC); the Multilateral Investment Guarantee

Agency (MIGA) and the International Centre for the Settlement of Investment Disputes (ICSID). It argues that environmental networks attempt to socialize IFC and MIGA to 'govern' environmentally. IFC invests in private sector projects in developing countries while MIGA provides political risk insurance to foreign investors in developing countries. The chapter demonstrates how environmental networks attempted to influence IFC and MIGA via direct and indirect socialization. This is evidenced through their core project and policy components. The cases are important because they are under-examined organizations that both facilitate, and have leverage over, private sector development. Environmental networks focus on the World Bank Group because they recognize that international organizations spread ideas through their practices (Finnemore 1996).

The chapter demonstrates that IFC, more so than MIGA, has internalized environmental ideas, which arguably is a result of their different identities. Methods used to establish how IFC but not MIGA has been socialized include gathering primary documents, secondary materials and conducting interviews with both the organizations and environmental networks. This captures organization–network interactions through examining their discussions, meetings, and correspondence. Collecting information on the social interaction between the organizations and the networks furthers understanding of the organizations' responses to network socialization. A change in their routinized discursive practices indicates that they begin to view themselves as sustainable development practitioners. When the organizations understand and interpret their own actions in line with the norms espoused by environmental networks, then a change in their identities is occurring. The changing socio-linguistic routines and the attendant change in actions (and vice versa) determine that an identity shift has taken place. First, however, an analysis of socialization is warranted.

Socialization and international organizations

This analysis proposes that environmental networks shape international organizations via processes of socialization. In turn, international organizations contest and (re)create norms in the international system. They can therefore contribute to global environmental governance by internalizing, interpreting, and diffusing environmental practices to state and non-state actors in their issue area (such as development project financing and political risk insurance). Indeed, international organizations routinely reinforce international norms through socializing states (Johnston 2001; Barnett and Finnemore 2004). Yet how organizations themselves internalize ideas continues to be 'an important theoretical challenge' (Wiener 2003: 254). While states determine an international organization's mandate as laid out in its constitution or charter, of interest here is how an organization interprets it. First an examination is undertaken of how norms of international organization behaviour are created, before arguing that international norms are contested and recreated through constant interaction between organizations, states and non-state actors.

International organizations operate in a social structure of international norms which inform how they behave. Norms are 'shared expectations about appropriate behavior held by a community of actors' (Finnemore 1996: 22–3). In this regard, actors' identities are informed by norms, which in turn define actors' interests. Arguably, international norms are created and contested through constant interaction between states, international organizations and non-state actors, such as environmental networks. Shared understandings of how international organizations should behave are initially created between states on establishing the organization. This is reinforced and recreated through ongoing state-organization interactions and the organization's practices (and as argued below, through interactions with non-state actors). As such, organizational identities are not fixed and may shift to diffuse new norms. Examples of international organization identity shifts include the United Nations High Commissioner for Refugees (UNHCR) and changing refugee norms, the United Nations and peacekeeping, and the International Monetary Fund and the construction of norms of domestic economic intervention (Barnett and Finnemore 2004). The aim here is to examine how international organizations shift to diffuse new norms. We argue that international organizations internalize new norms that arise from engaging with state and non-state actors.

Rationalists have argued that international organizations are autonomous in their decision making but that their actions stem from member state demands. The principal-agent (P-A) model examines dynamics between international organizations and states by examining the agent (organization) and its multiple principals (member states) which are themselves collective principals (different agencies and lobby groups within the state) (Nielson and Tierney 2003: 248). In this way, the P-A model examines the competing pressures on international organizations as agents, yet the model has not been used to examine organizations' interests. Thus far it has only examined the causal pathway from states to international organizations (Barnett and Finnemore 2004: 11). Furthermore, the P-A model overlooks the transnational activities of non-state actors. For example, transnational advocacy networks are fluid, loosely based connections of transboundary non-state actors that come together on issue-based campaigns (Keck and Sikkink 1998: 9).

The P-A model views international organization actions through states but this marginalizes analysis of how non-state actors attempt to influence organizations, not only indirectly through influencing state perceptions of appropriate organizational behaviour but also through direct international organization-non-state actor interactions. Unpacking how networks contest and (re)create norms of appropriate international organization behaviour is an important part of determining the role of international organizations in world politics. In the cases outlined below environmental networks politicized the social and environmental impact of World Bank Group practices (Price

1998: 621). They contested investment and political risk decisions that ignored environmental and social factors. Environmental networks challenged, contested and attempted to recreate norms appropriate for international organizations with development mandates, such as the World Bank Group, through processes of socialization examined below.

Socialization is defined as a process whereby agents internalize ideas into their identities that are constitutive of the social structure in which they exist (Park 2005a). The socialization of international organizations does not occur as an independent action of environmental networks (and/or states). Rather, environmental networks respond to organization actions. If these actions affect communities and ecosystems, environmental networks attempt to reconstitute the international organization's identity such that the organization recognizes its environmental impact and alters its practices accordingly. Therefore, an analysis of how international organizations are shaped by norms is based on the norm entrepreneurship of non-state actors (Finnemore and Sikkink 2001: 400–1). How an organization's practices (actions and ideas) change as a result of engaging with environmental networks, also represent a change in shared understandings of the organization's identity. An organization's identity includes its mandate and bureaucratic culture based on its dominant profession, and is both subjective and intersubjective (Park 2005a: 119).

Socialization, however, is not simply a one-way process: while environmental networks do influence international organizations, the influence may also run in the opposite direction. Rather it is a fluid process, reconstituting norms through contestation. Actors' identities, interests and actions shape norms. For constructivists '[F]undamental change of the international system occurs when actors, through their practices, change the rules and norms constitutive of international interaction' (Koslowski and Kratochwil 1994: 216). Socialization thus creates new organizational identities *and* new social structures.

Direct and indirect paths of socialization can be identified to demonstrate how non-state actors (re)constitute the norms international organizations follow. Direct socialization is where non-state actors such as environmental networks interact with and attempt to influence organizations. This may be through *persuasion* via dialogue such as formal and informal meetings, letters, emails, and phone calls, or *social influence* via protests and petitions at the organization's project sites, offices or headquarters. Persuasion involves 'changing minds, opinions, and attitudes about causality and affect (identity) in the absence of overtly material or mental coercion' (Johnston 2001: 496). Environmental networks are able to persuade international organizations to the relevance of particular norms through ongoing campaigns. Social influence on the other hand, involves distributing social rewards and punishments. Punishments include 'shaming, shunning, excluding, and demeaning, or dissonance derived from actions inconsistent with role and identity' which environmental networks aspire organizations to acquire, while rewards would contribute to 'status, a sense of belonging, and a sense of well-being derived from conformity with role expectations' (Johnston 2001: 499).

Indirect socialization is understood as a process in which member states are first pressured by lobbying (instigating *instrumental pressure*) and then engaged in dialogue (persuasion), in order to then influence the organization.[2] Thus, non-state actors such as environmental networks attempt to reshape organizations such as IFC or MIGA through an indirect process of influencing powerful states. As members, states can assist environmental networks to shape the interests of the international organization to reflect environmental norms. Both processes are necessary in organizational socialization because it demonstrates a convergence of ideas around increasingly accepted alternative norms for the organization. Thus socialization involves challenging the organization's behaviour and engaging with it to establish shared understandings between it, states and environmental networks. This involves a reconstitution of the organization's identity through the internalization of new norms into its practices, such that the international organization shares a new understanding of its role with states and non-state actors.

An additional process is added to the micro-processes of persuasion and social influence: instrumental pressure from states triggered by lobbying. While lobbying states to institute regulations to stop a particular organization's behaviour is not considered part of socialization, the act of changing an organization's actions reshapes its interests and ultimately its identity. Regarding the World Bank Group organizations below, defining certain practices as unacceptable for development-oriented financial and political risk institutions, combined with social influence and persuasion, arguably leads to a re-evaluation by IFC (less so MIGA) about how to meet its mandate (through internalizing and reinterpreting new environmental norms). By promoting new shared meanings through direct and indirect socialization (involving persuasion, social influence and coercive lobbying) environmental networks can reconstitute the identity of international organizations and can extend the global environmental governance structure. Yet organizations do not just conform to these social structures but help mediate and shape them through their responses. This is examined below.

Socializing international organizations: IFC and MIGA

Having outlined the processes of socialization, this section analyses how environmental groups attempted to socialize the World Bank Group organizations in order to reconstitute their identities as green financiers and insurers, inadvertently making them part of global environmental governance. First, the design and operations of IFC and MIGA are outlined before tracing how environmental groups interacted repeatedly with states and the affiliates over their 'problem' projects and social and environmental safeguard policies, with varying outcomes. Environmental groups attempted to directly and indirectly socialize the affiliates which provided opportunities for norm contestation and creation between environmental groups, states and international organizations.

Design and operation of IFC and MIGA

IFC invests and facilitates financing in private sector development projects in developing countries where capital is not available from private investors on reasonable terms. IFC was established in 1956 with its own mandate, operations, Articles of Agreement and funding although it shares its Board of Governors, Directors and its President (currently Robert Zoellick) with the World Bank. IFC currently has 179 members. Each member's voting power is determined by the amount of share capital 'paid in' with the US providing the dominant share of IFC funds at 23.65 per cent (thus replicating the World Bank's organizational structure in membership and voting rights). IFC raises funds through international capital markets and, like the Bank, has a triple-A credit rating.

IFC operations increased significantly in the 1990s and early 2000s. In 2005, IFC's portfolio comprised of loans, equity investments and risk management products totalling $19.3 billion. Since its inception IFC has committed $49 billion of its own funds and arranged syndications of $24 billion. In doing so it has provided guarantees for 3,319 companies and 140 states making it 'the largest multilateral source of loan and equity financing for private sector projects in the developing world' (IFC 2002a: Attachment II; IFC 2005: 1). IFC finances private sector projects in developing countries (usually investing 5 to 20 per cent) and assists private sector companies to attract investors from international financial markets ('B' loans or syndications). It also provides technical assistance to private sector companies and developing states. As such, both private sector corporations (project sponsors) and developing country governments are its clients (IFC 2002b).

MIGA was established by the World Bank's Board of Governors in 1988. MIGA aims to 'promote foreign direct investment into emerging economies to improve people's lives and reduce poverty' (MIGA 2003). It does so through providing non-commercial political risk insurance to investors in developing countries and technical assistance for developing states to attract private investment (World Bank 2001). Like IFC, the agency has its own chairman, board of governors, directors, convention and budget. MIGA's chairman is currently the president of the World Bank, who in turn nominates the agency's executive vice-president. MIGA's 173 members seek either political risk insurance or technical assistance to increase foreign investment. MIGA's underwriting capacity is underpinned by its capital stock, to which all members subscribe. As with IFC, voting within MIGA is weighted according each member's share capital (MIGA 2005b).

Since 1988, the Agency had issued over 800 guarantees amounting to $14.7 billion in insurance coverage for projects in 91 developing countries (MIGA 2005a). By the mid-1990s, MIGA had already grown to be one of the largest investment risk insurers in the world, facilitating $19 billion in FDI between 1988 and 1997 (MIGA 2001). As an affiliate of the World Bank Group, MIGA is central to the insurance industry because it has the ability to reduce exposure for investors and to deter moral hazard on behalf of the investor or the host country (West 1999: 28–30). The Agency's political risk guarantees have drawn environmental network attention and are examined below.

Problem projects

Having outlined the design and operations of IFC and MIGA, this section analyses how environmental networks unevenly influenced these organizations through direct and indirect socialization starting with project campaigns. In the 1990s environmental networks, comprised of local environmental groups, NGOs, media and citizens and northern environmental NGOs, began promoting new environmental norms for IFC and MIGA by opposing 'problem projects' (Wirth 1998).

As stated above, direct socialization influences organizations at the project level through protest (social influence) and through policy-level dialogue (persuasion). Indirect socialization takes place contemporaneously, where environmental networks attempt to influence state perceptions of international organization behaviour (via coercive lobbying and persuasion). Yet, it was never certain that challenging IFC- or MIGA-backed projects would lead to project victories because of IFC's minimal equity percentage in private sector projects and MIGA's underwriting of companies undertaking projects. However, as will be established below, environmental networks reiterated IFC's and MIGA's harmful environmental practices and sought to clarify the link between IFC, MIGA and the World Bank through similar campaigns. The first environmental campaign on IFC, Chile's Pangue Dam, demonstrates how direct and indirect socialization through the US began to reconstitute the organization through its projects (other campaigns emerged after Pangue, see Park 2005b) and later through its policies. This compares to campaigns on MIGA which also attempted direct and indirect socialization but with less success.

IFC

Chile's hydroelectric Pangue Dam is IFC's most controversial project to date (IFC 2005: 1). It sparked changes to IFC's projects, policies and institutions and will be briefly sketched here (for a full account of Pangue see Park 2005b). Although IFC had no environmental and social safeguards at the time, the project was both approved and classified as a World Bank Category A project for its high risk environmental and social impact (compared with Category B projects which have serious but mitigatory impacts and Category C projects which are deemed negligible, IFC 1992). In 1990 the network began opposing the project through petitions (direct socialization).[3] In 1991 environmental networks questioned the US Executive Director's view on IFC's involvement in Pangue (indirect socialization).[4] In January 1992 US Treasury then met IFC to discuss the impacts of the dam. The company, Pangue SA, sent a copy of the Environmental Assessment to the US executive director, and in May the US executive director was one of a number of directors involved in meetings with environmental networks.[5] The US executive director then abstained from voting on the project with the US alternative executive director arguing that the dam demonstrated 'a general failure of recent World Bank hydroelectric projects to assess adequately, and in a timely manner, the likely impacts of proposed projects to fisheries and aquatic biodiversity'.[6] Significantly, the alternate US executive director requested information from Pangue SA including specific reports for the networks.[7] The US Treasury was influenced to advocate to the US executive director in IFC on behalf of environmental networks. While indirect socialization in this project campaign was successful in influencing the US executive director's position on Pangue, it was not able to mitigate the project's environmental effects. However, processes of socialization would continue to shape IFC.

In 1997, IFC threatened to declare Pangue SA's parent company, Endesa, in default for its failure to meet the environmental and social loan conditions. James Wolfensohn urged Chilean government mediation.[8] In doing so, Wolfensohn referred to two independent critical reviews instigated by 'green lobbies' of IFC's 'handling of the environmental appraisal and supervision of the Pangue project and the compliance of . . . Endesa with their obligations under IFC agreement'.[9] The first report documented an independent investigation contracted by IFC in 1995 by the American anthropologist Dr Theodore Downing. Its findings were negative: unchecked in-migration to a previously isolated area, land speculation, deforestation, as well as severe limitation of Pehuenche land rights and the general failure of the Pehuen Foundation to protect the indigenous community (Downing 1996: 5).

In 1995 environmental networks filed a complaint with the World Bank Inspection Panel but were rejected on the basis that the Panel does not have the power to inspect IFC projects, although IFC must meet World Bank policies (GABB 1995: 4–5). The claim argued that IFC had violated eight IFC/Bank environmental and social safeguards (GABB 1995: 6–7). President Wolfensohn then commissioned an autonomous internal review of Pangue in 1996, which was undertaken by Dr Jay Hair. The Hair Report stated that: 'IFC did not follow fundamental World Bank Group requirements in any consistent or comprehensible manner throughout the development and implementation of the Pangue Project' and that 'There was no evidence in the record that comprehensive and systematic monitoring of requirements to determine compliance with relevant World Bank Group requirements were either a) identified within IFC or to the project sponsor or b) subsequently monitored' (Hair 1997: 35, 38). The Hair Report documented fundamental flaws in IFC's implementation of environmental ideas.

IFC attempted to alleviate the negative social implications of the dam. The foundation was innovative although it 'failed miserably' (Robinson 1998). The lack of structural incentives to adhere to the original plans indicated that IFC had not internalized environmental norms. IFC now accepts that the dam's environmental problems were not systematically addressed. Indeed, the project became a 'wake-up call' to IFC over its use of World Bank safeguard policies, revealing inherent weaknesses in adopting but not internalizing environmental ideas. The network subsequently aimed to shape IFC through strengthening its environmental policies. The next section compares MIGA's interactions with environmental networks over 'problem projects'.

MIGA

Beginning again with problem projects, environmental networks attempted direct and indirect socialization of MIGA. They challenged MIGA's underwriting of investments in projects with significant environmental and social impacts. Environmental network campaigns include: in 1995, the Freeport McMoran mine in West Papua, the Omai mine in Guyana, and the Kumtor mine in the Kyrgyz Republic (with the World Bank); in 1997, the Lihir mine in Papua New Guinea; in 1999, the Antamina mine in Peru and the Brazil–Bolivia gas pipeline; in 2000, the Julietta mine in Russia; in 2002, the Buljanhulu mine in Tanzania; in 2005, a paper mill in Uruguay (with IFC) and the Dikulushi mine in the Democratic Republic of Congo. To date the campaigns have had limited effect on project sponsor activities (and therefore have had limited success in preventing environmental degradation). However, the ongoing campaigns are important for highlighting the role of environmental networks in interrupting business as usual and for challenging MIGA to incorporate environmental and social safeguards.

For example, in West Papua the project sponsor Freeport McMoran was pressured to establish environmental and social mitagatory measures but the effect was negligible (Leith 2003). Unlike the Pangue campaign against IFC, MIGA was not the target of the Freeport campaign. However, the networks still engaged with the agency enacting processes of direct socialization via social influence and persuasion. Direct socialization placed the onus on MIGA to examine the network's environmental and human rights concerns. Yet, Freeport cancelled the Agency's underwriting of the mine before its investigation – attracting negative publicity in the process. Most likely, the company was worried about meeting MIGA's environmental provisions as well as those of its main insurer the Overseas Private Investment Corporation (OPIC – which had threatened to cancel Freeport's coverage on environmental grounds).[10]

If Freeport had not cancelled its coverage, both MIGA and OPIC would have increased their environmental and social safeguard monitoring as a result of socialization from environmental networks. Indeed, in 1998 OPIC tightened its safeguards (OPIC 1999) while MIGA began devising its own as campaigns against the Agency mounted. Direct socialization was therefore influential, as was indirect socialization: the networks engaged in socializing the US government-owned OPIC (although it is privately operated). Conceivably, MIGA was influenced by OPIC's decision to strengthen its environmental standards to the point where it decided to establish its own. MIGA thus adopted safeguard policies soon after the eruption of campaigns.

Environmental networks have challenged MIGA on these problem projects in order to halt environmental degradation and to diffuse environmental norms throughout the political risk industry via socialization. By including MIGA in international project campaigns, environmental networks inched towards bringing a pivotal political risk insurer under the global environmental governance umbrella. The problem project campaigns instigated by environmental networks are vital for our understanding of MIGA practices because it was during the wave of campaigns against the organization that the agency established its environmental and social safeguard policies, and is discussed next.

Safeguard policies

Environmental networks also aimed to spread environmental norms within IFC and MIGA through their safeguard policies, again through direct and indirect socialization. Environmental networks attempted to shape the organizations through directly influencing and persuading staff on environmental policy and indirectly by influencing the US to mandate the organizations to strengthen their safeguards. IFC incorporated environmental and social safeguard policies in the wake of increased scrutiny into 'problem projects', demonstrating how environmental networks diffused norms throughout IFC, while MIGA resisted.

IFC

IFC created an Environment Division including the appointment of its first environmental advisor in 1989 as well as introducing environmental categories (A to C) for its projects according to their environmental impact. Yet in 1990, only 7 of 160 projects reviewed were deemed to have potentially significant environmental impacts. The volume of projects to review was beyond the capacity of its one permanent staff member (IFC 2002b: 30). In 1993, during the Pangue project campaign, IFC began to revise its use of World Bank policies. Prior to this there was the assumption that IFC would adhere to Bank standards. Indirect socialization also shaped the US who supported a sustainable IFC. Environmental networks assisted the US Congress to pass a law requiring IFC (and MIGA) to improve information disclosure (the Pelosi Amendment).[11]

IFC adapted and incorporated the safeguards in 1993 rather than maintain the ill-defined use of Bank policies that had been in place since 1988 with minor amendments in 1990 and 1992. The Pangue Inspection Panel claim convinced IFC to overhaul its approach to environmental and social issues. It was not until direct and indirect socialization by environmental networks culminated in the Inspection Panel claim in 1995 that IFC began to realize the significance of environmental and social aspects of development. Indeed, according to one IFC staff member, the Pangue campaign really affected IFC's outlook.[12] Environmental networks recognized that IFC became much more responsive after the Pangue claim.[13] Indeed, the 1997 Hair Report's recommendations lead to a wide-scale review and comprehensive establishment of IFC's own safeguard policies in 1998 (IFC 2002b: 31). Environmental networks therefore helped reconstitute IFC by pressing for the organization to have its own environmental and social policies. While there remain concerns about the implementation of the safeguard policies and existing 'problem projects', IFC has become a leader in integrating environmental and social considerations into its operations and lending requirements.[14] From 1998, IFC became committed to incorporating social and environmental concerns into its operations.[15]

IFC has since established the independent Operations Evaluation Group (OEG) as well as other internal monitoring mechanisms.[16] Between 2001 and 2004 the OEG concluded that two-thirds of projects were deemed satisfactory or excellent for their environmental, social, and health and safety requirements (Park 2007b). A 2004 report notes that unsatisfactory projects continue to be improved and, as of 2005, the group intends to link environmental evaluations back into the project cycle (IFC 2004: 40–1). Other review mechanisms have been instituted to assist IFC staff, including the establishment of a quality portfolio management system in 2000 for environment and social specialists, and the introduction of an environment and social risk rating system in 2001 to identify projects with a high risk of non-compliance (CAO 2002a: 19).

In 2001, IFC senior management asked the Compliance Advisor/ Ombudsman (CAO) to undertake a review of its 1998 safeguard policies. The CAO Office was established by James Wolfensohn in 1999 with assistance from environmental networks, at the same time that IFC appointed its first NGO liaison officer (Park 2005b). The review noted that there was no drastic shift in practice before and after the 1998 adoption of the safeguard policies, but a 'steady progression and evolution of practice' and that safeguard policies are having an overall positive effect, contributing to positive environmental and social impacts (CAO 2002a: 23–42). It also states that the safeguards often go beyond the 'do no harm' approach (CAO 2003a: 6). In February 2006, IFC approved new environmental and social performance standards to replace its safeguard and information disclosure policies as a result of the 2003 CAO report.

IFC has undertaken substantial changes since 1989. It incorporated environmental ideas into its mission statement; it dramatically increased environmental and social staff; it introduced safeguard policies into the project finance industry via the Equator Principles (see Wright, this volume). These changes demonstrate a normative shift in IFC's identity: from having no social and environmental conscience, to a position of 'do no harm' to the present 'do good' (IFC 2002b: 2). Further changes verify IFC's commitment to sustainable development norms: IFC now reports on its own greenhouse gas emissions and its environmental footprint (IFC 2002c: 57). It instituted a Sustainability Initiative in 2001 to embody a triple bottom line approach based on a commitment to 'people, the planet and profits' (IFC 2002b). Its success will be determined by IFC's marketing of sustainable development to project sponsors. This is already being addressed by the adoption of the Equator Principles by investment banks in 2003. These Principles were initiated by IFC in conjunction with private banks and demonstrate how IFC has begun to diffuse sustainable development throughout the project finance industry.

Importantly, environmental networks recognize a change in IFC. The networks state that the organization seems genuine in its concern for its environment impact.[17] IFC is viewed as less bureaucratic and more responsive in incorporating environmental norms into IFC operations, although environmental networks opposed the new performance standards in favour of retaining the safeguard policies.[18] Yet its new performance standards instituted in 2006 demonstrate how IFC's identity has both reproduced and transformed environmental norms. The changes outlined throughout demonstrate how IFC has fundamentally reoriented itself to become part of global environmental governance. How this differs from MIGA's incorporation of environmental norms is discussed below.

MIGA

The networks aimed to shape MIGA in the same way that they had IFC: through processes of direct and indirect socialization. Yet MIGA's response, as evidenced below, was far less engaging than IFC's. The networks claimed that the political risk identity of the organization is diametrically opposed to the organization's development mandate as a member of the World Bank Group. In doing so, the network argued that MIGA's limited and belated attempts to improve accountability and transparency remains superficial (Friends of the Earth *et al.* 2001).[19]

MIGA introduced environmental and social policies in 1999. Before then, it was assumed that the agency would follow IFC policies as IFC had followed the World Bank's. MIGA had been using Bank/IFC safeguards since 1991 (OEU 2003: 7). By 1996, environmental networks were highlighting 'a series of double standards between the World Bank's public and private sector lending operations' (Bosshard 1996a: n.p.). Environmental networks claimed that MIGA's environmental assessment procedures were less comprehensive, took place too late, and were given too little time. At that time the agency was subcontracting its environmental analysis to IFC even though

IFC's small department (of seven staff and three consultants) was reviewing 200 to 250 new projects a year while supervising approximately 1,000 ongoing projects. Environmental networks stated that before 1993, only 10 of MIGA's 185 projects were classified as category A even though MIGA guarantees environmentally risky projects in extractive and infrastructure industries (Bosshard 1996b).

In 1997 MIGA established an environmental unit, now comprising two environmental and one social specialist. In May 1999, MIGA's Board adopted interim environmental and social policies adapted from IFC's safeguards (Van Veldhuizen 2000: 54). In doing so, MIGA opened a 50-day window for comments on the draft policies from stakeholders including investors, insurers, project sponsors, and civil society. In 2002 MIGA permanently endorsed the safeguards (MIGA 2003). MIGA's lead environmental specialist argued that 'the environmental assessment policy formalizes an approach to environmental review that has been taken by MIGA for many years' and that '[I]t is MIGA's policy that all the investments it facilitates through its guarantee program are carried out in an environmentally and socially responsible manner' (Van Veldhuizen 2000: 54). MIGA's implementation of safeguard policies can be seen as a response to environmental network influence although it does not signify that an identity shift has occurred. There is little indication of their actual impact on the organization. This contrasts with the extensive internal and external discussions and reviews that have taken place within IFC since 1998.

MIGA itself noted the 'less than satisfactory' process of adopting IFC environmental safeguard policies to MIGA-insured investments. MIGA stated that progress was limited while awaiting IFC's safeguard policy review (2001–2003). MIGA waited for IFC's conversion because its private sector needs are similar to IFC, and the agency has limited capacity to undertake these conversions itself. IFC approved its new performance standards in February 2006. From then on, MIGA had 12 months to adapt IFC's standards to its specific needs as mandated by its Board of Directors.

Yet environmental networks argue that MIGA had done little to monitor the impacts of the investment projects it underwrites. In 2001, a development impact review was undertaken evaluating 52 projects from 27 states and representing 75 per cent of all active projects backed by MIGA between 1990 and 1996 (West and Tarazona 2001: 25). The review included the environmental impacts of MIGA backed projects but only 10 projects (17 per cent) were visited by environmental specialists. Environmental specialists involved in the evaluation process identified 10 of the 52 projects as requiring environmental monitoring (West and Tarazona 2001: 29). No projects failed on environmental grounds. Of the 52 projects analysed, 22 were not measured, none failed, and none were deemed 'untraceable' (or unable to measure). Significantly, little explanation is provided regarding the projects not measured for their environmental impact. The fact that 60 per cent of the projects evaluated are in the manufacturing, mining, infrastructure and tourism sectors (West and Tarazona 2001: 26–7), which generally have large environmental and social impacts, demonstrates the need for further analysis on assessing sustainable development.

At the very heart of the network critique of MIGA is the agency's under-writing of projects in traditionally environmentally degrading industries such as oil, gas and mining. How this is reconciled to environmentally sustainable development is not mentioned within MIGA reports. Notably, the OEU states in response to the recent extractive industries review that 73 per cent of MIGA's oil, gas and mining projects met the safeguard policy requirements, but that more attention is required on identifying issue specific safeguards and their implementation, in addition to information disclosure, due dili-gence, monitoring compliance and reviewing social safeguard outcomes (Liebenthal *et al.* 2003: 147; OEU 2003: 9–13).

Specifically, the networks argue that the agency is not accountable for the social and environmental impacts of the projects it insures (Friends of the Earth *et al.* 2001). The networks state that MIGA's monitoring capacity remains weak because it has few staff and no ongoing monitoring system. Environmental networks therefore argue that MIGA is 'not equipped pro-perly to continue monitoring . . . [so that] the project[s] it insures adhere to MIGA's standards and policies, especially in environmental and social areas' (Down to Earth 2001: n.p.). This is demonstrated, they claim, by the fact that MIGA's clients are not screened on the basis of their previous social, environmental, labour and human rights record. The agency refutes this claim, pointing out that it

> has turned down and cancelled projects that have not complied with our environmental and social requirements. Companies know that they have to be environmentally and socially responsible if they come to any of the institutions of the World Bank Group for support.[20]

MIGA's trenchant response in September 2001 demonstrated increasingly strained interactions with environmental networks:

> MIGA's activities do not promote or subsidize poor corporate behavior at the expense of people and the environment. The broad statements made in the report that MIGA's activities are anti-environmental . . . are untrue. And there is no evidence to support the claims that MIGA's clients have poor environmental and human rights records.[21]

In turn environmental networks argued that the agency retains an outdated development perspective. The networks highlighted MIGA's inconsistency in identifying (but not disseminating) environmental impact assessments for category A projects, with no assessment required or information provided for category B or C projects. The networks argued that it is

clearly unsatisfactory for a publicly-financed development institution . . .
This has led many organizations to conclude that MIGA has little interest in conforming its policies and practices with the World Bank's . . . and
has led many to conclude that MIGA should no longer function as part
of the World Bank Group.[22]

Direct socialization continued in 2003 when the network published a report
stating MIGA is non-transparent and has weak safeguards for a World Bank
Group organization – claims which MIGA rejects (Environmental Defense
et al. 2003: 4; MIGA 2004).[23] The correspondence between the network and
the agency illustrates how the organization shifted over time, first ignoring,
then rejecting the network's criticisms, finally engaging with them. MIGA
has instituted new procedures and measures such as the OEU, an institution
akin to IFC's Operations Evaluation Group.[24] While this is an important
evaluative measure it remains to be seen what impact this will have on
the organization's operations. Arguably, MIGA instituted these policies in
response to external pressure rather than because it perceived environmental
policies and procedures as ends in themselves.

Thus far we have examined networks attempts at direct socialization. Yet
the networks also engaged in indirect socialization. Indeed, the network
is active in politicizing the need for the CAO to overlook IFC *and MIGA*
operations with the support of the US Executive Director. Moreover, the
Friends of the Earth claimed success in influencing the US Congress to
limit funding for MIGA's capital increase in 2001 (providing $5 of the
$10 million requested) as a means of coercive pressure for organizational
reform. However there is no evidence of this impacting on the organization.[25]

Adopting and reviewing safeguard policies does not constitute an identity
shift. Arguably MIGA does not see itself as a sustainable political risk
insurer. Indeed, sustainability is not part of its mission statement and it has
only recently begun to release information on its environmental activities.
Notably MIGA now discloses its environmental assessments of category A,
and some category B projects (MIGA 2005b: 15). However, there are only
three permanent staff to apply and monitor MIGA's environmental and
social safeguards even though it now states that it monitors projects during
their implementation (MIGA 2005b: 15). Environmental networks maintain
that there is no evidence of an identity change within MIGA. Elsewhere
environmental networks described MIGA as an 'ostrich' in opting not
to engage with them (Park 2005a). Since Yukiko Omura became the new
Executive Vice President in May 2004 there has been a distinct shift in
MIGA–network relations. Omura instituted annual meetings with NGOs on
environmental and social issues, although environmental networks argue
that these are 'not productive' and that 'MIGA is not taking environmental
and social standards seriously.'[26] This compares with how environmental
networks view IFC: they recognize IFC has done more to operationalize
environmental and social protection and in making it 'key' to their

operations.[27] Indeed, the networks point to MIGA's lack of information on its purported environmental shift as an unwillingness to engage on how to improve MIGA's environmental sustainability. Some activists argue that socialization has failed and MIGA should not exist.[28]

Equally important is MIGA's response to the CAO. The CAO office has described MIGA as a 'closed book' on environmental and social concerns compared with IFC because of its professional identity (Park 2007a). In a 2003 report the CAO recommended that MIGA should determine whether it maintains its 'do no harm' approach or whether it should 'ensure closer convergence with IFC's broader sustainability remit' (CAO 2003b: iv). MIGA has not addressed issues outlined in the CAO's 2002 review of its environmental standards (although it has begun reviewing its policies and procedures after IFC's performance standards) and has not therefore internalized environmental norms (CAO 2002b).

Early confrontations between the network and MIGA may be the initial phase of the socialization process, where conflict challenges the organiza-tion's norms and creates room for discussion. MIGA's relations with the networks in the late 1990s are the opposite of IFC–network relations at the same time. MIGA was vociferous in opposing criticisms that it is not environmental, although there has been a recent softening of its relations with environmental networks. Environmental networks attempted to social-ize the organizations both directly and indirectly through their projects and policies. While MIGA adopted IFC's environmental and social performance standards in October 2007 and now engages with environmental networks (thus opening the way for the further socialization of environmental norms), compared to IFC it has not internalized environmental ideas.

Conclusion

This chapter posited that environmental groups directly and indirectly through powerful member states socialize international organizations to internalize environmental ideas. It analysed how environmental norms were diffused within IFC by assessing its projects and policies. IFC transformed and spread environmental ideas through its operations.[29] In comparison, environmental norms have not been internalized within MIGA, which has only recently attempted to engage with environmental networks. Environ-mental norms have not been internalized within MIGA as a result of the socialization process with environmental networks. Environmental norms remain at odds with the agency's political risk identity. Yet this chapter demonstrated how interactive processes between environmental networks, states and international organizations can lead to international organiza-tions, in corporate dominated industries, becoming part of the broader global environmental governance structure. By spreading environmental norms to organizations such as IFC, and attempting to do so with MIGA, environmental networks are helping to create new structures. Specifically, environmental networks are contributing to establishing new regimes on environmental issues led by international organizations with different mandates but increasingly with environmental identities. Understanding how socialization shapes international organizations' identities is therefore crucial to constructing global environmental governance.

Notes

1 For an earlier version of this argument see Park 2007a.
2 To ignore how ideas shape material pressure would be to overlook the normative capacity of environmental networks in influencing other actor's ideas and identities.
3 Letter from Grupo de Action por el BioBio (GABB) representing 13 Chilean environmental and social groups to President Preston 4/2/92; Letter from Natural Resources Defense Council (NRDC) representing 25 NGOs to President Preston, 20/4/92.
4 Letter from International Rivers Network (IRN) to the US Executive Director, 17/4/91.
5 GABB's limited chronology of events 'does not list numerous other letters, FAX or phone contacts, or meetings with Pangue, US Treasury, US Directors Office, NGO groups, the press and the public' (GABB, 1995: attachment 1).
6 Statement by the US Alternative Executive Director to the IFC Board of Directors, December 17/12/ 92.
7 Letter from the US Alternative Executive Director to Erupresa Electrecan Pangue S.A, 3/4/92.
8 Letter from President Wolfensohn to Minister of Finance, Chile, 6/2/97.
9 The *Financial Times*, 'World Bank Arm Warns Endesa', 21/2/97: 3.
10 MIGA used IFC safeguard policies at this stage.
11 Letter from a Member of US Congress to IFC President, dated June 28/6/91; Keck and Sikkink 1998: 149.
12 Interview with NGO Liaison Officer, IFC, 19/9/01.
13 Interview with a Bank Information Center (BIC) activist, 21/9/01.
14 Interview with an CAO Officer, IFC, 14/9/01.
15 Interview with NGO Liaison Officer, IFC, 19/9/01.
16 This is now known as the Independent Evaluation Group or IEG.
17 Interview with BIC activist, 21/9/01.
18 Interview with Conservation International activist, 18/10/01; Interview with Friends of the Earth (FoE) activist, 26/9/01.
19 Interview with Environmental Defense (EDF) activist 14/02/06; Interview with BIC activist 15/02/06.
20 Letter by MIGA to FoE, 26/7/01.
21 Letter by MIGA to FoE, 28/9/01.
22 Letter from FoE, Urgewald and Reform the World Bank Campaign to MIGA's Corporate Relations Group, 3/4/02.
23 MIGA, Response to NGO stakeholder comments, note 64, public discussion ending 5 February 1999, online: <http://www.miga.org> (accessed 2 December 2003, last updated 2003).
24 The OEU is now also part of the IEG.
25 Friends of the Earth, 'Multilateral Investment Guarantee Agency Fact sheet,' online <http://www.foe.org> (accessed 2 December 2003, last updated 2003).
26 Interview with staff member of BIC, 15/02/06.
27 Interview with EDF staff member, 14/02/06.

28 Interview with a staff member of BIC, 21/9/01; Interview with staff member of BIC, 15/02/06.
29 Confidential interview with FoE activist, dated 26 September 2001.

References

Barnett, M. and Duvall, R. (2005) *Power in Global Governance*, Cambridge: Cambridge University Press.

Barnett, M. and Finnemore, M. (2004) *Rules for the World: International Organizations in World Politics*, Ithaca, NY: Cornell University Press.

Bosshard, P. (1996a) 'The Private Sector Lending of the World Bank Group: Issues and Challenges', January 1996, The Berne Declaration, Switzerland, online. Available HTTP: <http://www.2.access.ch/evb/bd/privlend.htm> (accessed 20 January 2003, last updated 1999).

Bosshard, P. (1996b) 'A Case Study about MIGA's Lihir Island Goldmine Project in Papua New Guinea', February 1996, The Berne Declaration, Switzerland, online. Available HTTP: <http://www.2.access.ch/evb/bd/privlend.htm> (accessed 20 January 2003, last updated 1999).

Commission on Global Governance (1995) *Our Global Neighbourhood*, Oxford and New York: Oxford University Press.

Compliance Advisor Ombudsman (CAO) (2002a) 'Review of IFC's Safeguard Policies: Draft for Comment', *CAO Office Report*, Washington DC: IFC and MIGA, online. Available HTTP: <http://www.cao-ombudsman.org/env> (accessed: September 2002, last updated September 2002).

CAO (2002b) 'Insuring Responsible Investments: A Review of the Application of MIGA's Environmental and Social Review Procedures', *CAO Office Report*, Washington DC: IFC and MIGA, online. Available HTTP: <http://www.cao-ombudsman.org/env> (accessed December 2002, last updated December 2002).

CAO (2003a) 'Assessment by the Officer of the Compliance Advisor/Ombudsman in relation to a Complaint Filed against IFC's Investment in Endesa Pangue S.A', *CAO Assessment Report May 2003*, Washington DC: IFC and MIGA.

CAO (2003b) 'Extracting Sustainable Advantage? A Review of How Sustainability Issues have been Dealt with in Recent IFC and MIGA Extractive Industry Projects', online. Available HTTP: <http://www.cao-ombudsman.org/html> (accessed July 2006, last updated 2004).

Down to Earth (2001) 'The Multilateral Investment Guarantee Agency (MIGA): Whose Interests are Served and at What Cost?' *Down to Earth Fact Sheet Series 16*, online. Available HTTP: <http://www.dte.gn.apc.org/> (accessed 21 January 2003, last updated 2002).

Downing, T. (1996) 'A Participatory Interim Evaluation of the Pehuen Foundation', *IFC 2067*, AGRA Earth and Environment: Downing and Associates.

Environmental Defense, Friends of the Earth, and the International Rivers Fund (2003) 'Gambling with People's Lives: What the World Bank's New "High Risk/ High Reward Strategy" Means for the Poor and the Environment', online. Available HTTP: <http://www.environmentaldefense.org> (accessed 2 December 2003, last updated September 2003).

Finnemore, M. (1996) *National Interests in International Society*, Ithaca, NY and London: Cornell University Press.

Finnemore, M. and Sikkink, K. (2001) 'Taking Stock: The Constructivist Research

Program in International Relations and Comparative Politics', *Annual Review of Political Science*, 4: 391–416.

Ford, L. (2003) 'Challenging Global Environmental Governance: Social Movement Agency and Global Civil Society', *Global Environmental Politics*, 3(2): 120–34.

Friends of the Earth, Urgewald, and Campagna per la Riforma della Banca Mondiale (2001) 'Risky Business: How the World Bank's Insurance Arm Fails the Poor and Harms the Environment', Washington DC: Friends of the Earth.

Goldman, M. (2005) *Imperial Nature: The World Bank and Struggles for Social Justice in the Age of Globalization*, New Haven, CT and London: Yale University Press.

Grupo de Action por el BioBio (GABB) (1995) 'The BioBio Dams in Chile: Violations of World Bank Policies and Lack of Accountability at the International Finance Corporation', Claim before the Inspection Panel and Petition before IFC Board of Executive Directors, Chile: GABB.

Hair, J. (1997) 'Pangue Hydroelectric Project (Chile): An Independent Review of the International Finance Corporation's Compliance with Applicable World Bank Group Environment and Social Requirements', *IFC Internal Review*, Washington DC: IFC.

International Finance Corporation (IFC) (1992) 'IFC Board Approves Pangue Dam,' *IFC Press Release No 92/32*.

IFC (2002a) 'Strategic Directions,' Confidential Report to the Board of Directors, International Finance Corporation 8 March 2002.

IFC (2002b) *Basic Facts About IFC*, online. Available HTTP: <http://www.ifc.org/about/> (accessed 3 December 2002, last updated 2002).

IFC (2005) *Annual Report volume one*, online. Available HTTP: <http://www.ifc.org/about/> (accessed 17 March 2006, last updated 2005).

Johnston, A.I. (2001) 'Treating International Institutions as Social Environments', *International Studies Quarterly*, 45(4): 487–515.

Keck, M. and Sikkink, K. (1998) *Activists Beyond Borders: Advocacy Networks in International Politics*, Ithaca, NY and London: Cornell University Press.

Koslowski, R., and Kratochwil, F. (1994) 'Understanding Change in International Politics: The Soviet Empire's Demise and the International System', *International Organization*, 48(2): 215–47.

Krasner, S., (1983) *International Regimes*, Ithaca, NY and London: Cornell University Press.

Leith, D. (2003) *The Politics of Power: Freeport in Suharto's Indonesia*, Honolulu: University of Hawaii Press.

Liebenthal, A., Michelitsch, R. and Tarazona, E. (2003) 'Extractive Industries and Sustainable Development: An Evaluation of the World Bank Group Experience – Annex E MIGA's Experience', Operations Evaluation Department, Operations Evaluation Group, Operations Evaluation Unit, online. Available HTTP: <http://www.miga.org/> (accessed 2 December 2003, last updated 2003).

Multilateral Investment Guarantee Agency (MIGA) (2001) *MIGA: The First Ten Years*, online. Available HTTP: <http://www.miga.org/> (accessed 12 June 2001, last updated 2001).

MIGA (2003) *Annual Report 2003*, Washington DC: MIGA.

MIGA (2005a) 'About MIGA: Our Development Impact and Priorities', online. Available HTTP: <http://www.miga.org/> (accessed 17 March 2006, last updated 2006).

MIGA (2005b) *Annual Report 2005*, Washington DC: MIGA.

Nielson, D. and Tierney, M. (2003) 'Delegation to International Organizations: Agency Theory and World Bank Environmental Reforms', *International Organization*, 57(2): 241–76.

Operations Evaluation Unit (2003) *A Report on Operations Evaluation in MIGA*, online. Available HTTP: <http://www.miga.org/> (accessed 2 December 2003, last updated 2003).

Overseas Private Investment Corporation (1999) 'OPIC Environmental Handbook – April 1999'. <http://www.opic.gov/> (accessed 28 January 2003, last updated 1999).

Park, S. (2005a) 'Norm Diffusion within International Organizations: A Case Study of the World Bank', *Journal of International Relations and Development*, 8(2): 114–41.

Park, S. (2005b) 'How Transnational Environmental Advocacy Networks Socialise IFIs: A Case Study of the International Finance Corporation' *Global Environmental Politics*, 5(4): 95–119.

Park, S. (2007a) 'Becoming Green: Diffusing Sustainable Development Norms throughout the World Bank Group', in Stone, D. and Wright, C. (eds) *The World Bank and Governance: A Decade of Reform and Reaction*, London: Routledge.

Park, S. (2007b) 'The World Bank Group: Championing Sustainable Development Norms?' *Global Governance*, 13(4): 535–56.

Paterson, M., Humphreys, D. and Pettiford, L. (2003) 'Conceptualising Global Environmental Governance: From Inter-State Regimes to Counter-Hegemonic Struggles', *Global Environmental Politics*, 3(2): 1–10.

Price, R. (1998) 'Reversing the Gun Cites: Transnational Civil Society Targets Land Mines', *International Organization*, 52(3): 613–32.

Robinson, S. (1998) *Comment From Dr. Scott Robinson, IFC Consultant in the Planning Stage of the Pangue Project*, American Anthropological Association, online. Available HTTP: <http://ameranthassn.org/pehuenc2.htm> (accessed September 1998, last updated 1998).

Rosenau, J. and Czempiel, E. (1992) *Governance without Government: Order and Change in World Politics*, Cambridge and New York: Cambridge University Press.

Van Veldhuizen, H. (2000) 'Multilateral Investment Guarantee Agency', *Environment Matters – IFC Annual Newsletter*, Washington DC: World Bank.

West, G. (1999) 'Political Risk Investment Insurance: A Renaissance', *Journal of Project Finance*, 5(2): 27–36.

West, G. and Tarazona, E. (2001) *Investment Insurance and Developmental Impact: Evaluating MIGA's Experience*, Washington DC: The World Bank Group.

Wiener, A. (2003) 'Constructivism: The Limits of Bridging Gaps', *Journal of International Relations and Development*, 6(3): 252–75.

Wirth, D. (1998) 'Partnership Advocacy in World Bank Environmental Reform', in Fox, J. and Brown, D. (eds) *The Struggle for Accountability: The World Bank, NGOs and Grassroots Movements*, Cambridge, MA: MIT Press.

World Bank (2001) 'MIGA Corporate Overview', *World Bank Development News: Issue Briefs*, online. Available HTTP: <http://www.worldbank.org/html/extdr/pb/miga.htm> (accessed 5 June 2001, last updated 2001).

6 The European Union and the 'external' dimension of sustainable development

Ambitious promises but disappointing outcomes?

Camilla Adelle and Andrew Jordan

Introduction

Sustainable development is now a fundamental goal of the European Union (EU). In its 2001 Sustainable Development Strategy the EU formally recognized that sustainable development includes the simultaneous pursuit of social, environmental *and* economic objectives within the Union. In addition, it stated that all EU policies 'must actively support efforts by other countries – particularly those in the developing world – to achieve development that is more sustainable' (CEC 2001a: 9). The EU has a positive (but not entirely unblemished) track record of attempting to address internal environmental issues such as pollution and biodiversity loss, as well as problems such as climate change and ozone depletion that have truly global consequences (Coffey and Baldock 2003; Jordan 2005). However, this is not enough: the EU must also take into account the effect of its internal policies (e.g. the Common Agricultural Policy) on the ability of other countries to develop more sustainably, especially those in the developing world. After all, if sustainable development within the EU involves 'exporting' problems to other areas then, by definition, it is not genuinely sustainable in an intra- or inter-generational sense. This was accepted by the then EU Environment Commissioner, Margot Wallstrom in 2003, when she warned that 'our credibility will suffer if unsustainable trends [in the EU] persist, or if our policies have detrimental impacts outside the EU, in particular on the development opportunities of the poorest countries' (Wallstrom 2003). The EU's determination to respond to this challenge was reaffirmed in the Johannesburg Plan of Implementation and in its own 'external Sustainable Development Strategy' (CEC 2002a) and related documents such as the report on *The World Summit on Sustainable Development one year on: implementing our commitments* (CEC 2003a).

This attempt to marry the so-called 'external' and 'internal' dimensions of sustainability is politically highly ambitious, which sets the EU apart from other broadly comparable political entities, notably the United States. However, its emergence and implementation has, until recently, received much less political and scholarly attention (but see Borrell and Hubbard 2000; Sporrong *et al.* 2002; Coffey and Baldock 2003). There is, of course, an emerging literature on what the EU has done internally to address the sustainability challenge (Baker *et al.* 1997; Jordan and O'Riordan 2004; Lafferty 2004), or through linked initiatives such as those concerning environmental policy integration (Lenschow 2002a; Jordan and Schout 2006; Jordan *et al.* 2006). Other scholars have also begun to document the EU's input to sustainability policy-making at the international level (Oberthür 1999; Sbragia 2002; Lightfoot and Burchill 2004).

This chapter therefore attempts to examine how the EU (which we perceive to be a highly sophisticated international organization that exhibits many important features of statehood such as a parliament and a legally supreme court) has interpreted its commitment to sustainable development. Our main focus is on the conceptualization and implementation of the 'external dimension' of sustainable development. Section 2 traces the historical evolution of the EU's thinking in this area from one which originally championed environmental policy, through to one on sustainable development, to one that could be loosely termed 'global sustainable development' (i.e. linking internal and external dimensions of sustainability in EU's borders). Section 3 sets out some of the EU's commitments to support sustainable development in developing countries through *inter alia* its international agreements and own internal development policies. The main implementing mechanisms for sustainable development in the EU include the Cardiff process of inter-sectoral environmental policy integration, the Sustainable Development Strategy and the EU's new (post 2002) impact assessment procedure governing all new policy proposals. In section 4 we examine each of them to gauge how well they are currently picking up and addressing the external dimension. Section 5 summarizes our main arguments in the light of the four themes raised by the editors in their opening chapter.

The EU's interpretation of sustainable development

The EU has adopted the Brundtland definition of sustainable development either in full e.g. in its Sustainable Development Strategy (but outside of the main text) (e.g. CEC 2001a) or, more usually, implicitly (e.g. CEC 2002a). Within this, the EU's conception focuses on inter-generational equity (i.e. the environment), mainly operationalized through the integration of the environment into other policies spheres, a process which has come to be known as EPI or environmental policy integration (Jordan and Lenschow 2000; Lenschow 2002a and b). From a pragmatic point of view, the European Commission felt comfortable about adopting this interpretation having spent the previous two decades building up an extensive corpus of environmental legislation.

Environmental policy integration was, of course, one of the operational principles of sustainable development advocated by the Brundtland Report:

'Those responsible for managing natural resources and protecting the environment are institutionally separate from those responsible for managing the
economy. The real world of interlocked economic and ecological systems
will not change; the policies and institutions concerned must' (WCED 1987:
310). Although environmental policy integration does not itself constitute
sustainable development it is undoubtedly an 'indispensable part of the
concept of sustainable development' (Lafferty and Hovden 2003: 2). Thus,
when the concept of sustainable development gained international acceptance in the late 1980s and 1990s, Directorate General (DG) Environment
turned to the concept of environmental policy integration, which it used to
push other parts of the Commission and the EU to implement sustainable
development. We can see this reflected in the EU's creation of the Cardiff
process. This Council-led process first started in 1998 and eventually involved
nine sectors preparing strategies to integrate the environment into their
policy planning. It can also be seen in the Commission's decision to tackle
sustainability through the adoption of the Fifth Environmental Action
Programme. The emphasis on the environmental pillar of sustainable development could be 'justified on the basis that environmental concerns have
persistently been underplayed in other policies, despite the fact that long-term
social and economic development depends on a functioning environment'
(EEA 2004: 16).

However, by the late 1990s and early 2000s recognition that the implementation of sustainable development requires a much broader range of factors
to be considered had begun to take root. This change in emphasis can be seen
in the appearance (some 15 years *after* the publication of the Brundtland
Report) of the 2001 Sustainable Development Strategy (CEC 2001a) and a
new impact assessment regime governing the appraisal of new Commission
proposals. In a document attached to the Sustainable Development Strategy,
the Commission argued that: 'sustainable development must strike a balance
between the economic, social and environmental objectives of society, in
order to maximize well-being in the present, without compromising the
ability of future generations to meet their needs' (CEC 2002a: 3).

Although the integration of these three pillars was implicit in the
Brundtland definition of sustainable development, this interpretation became
more popular after it had been endorsed by the 1992 Rio conference (COWI
2004). By changing its emphasis, the EU tried to emphasize that 'sustainable
development is more than a purely environmental concept', which poses a
fundamental challenge to the organization of the economy and society (CEC
2001b). However, this new interpretation immediately created a headache for
an ongoing integration-type exercise such as Cardiff. Put simply, were the
sectors involved supposed to integrate the environment into sectoral policies
as a contribution to sustainable development, *or* to integrate all three pillars
into sectoral policies (Fergusson *et al.* 2001)? Unfortunately, this important
conceptual matter has never been satisfactorily resolved.

The adoption of both the Brundtland definition and the emphasis on the three pillars of sustainable development is hugely significant with regards to how the EU acts. Baker *et al.* (1997: 28–9) suggested that the adoption of the Brundtland definition allowed:

> The EU as a whole to commit itself to the reconciliation of economic and environmental interests, while at the same time allowing Member States as well as individual DGs within the Commission a great deal of latitude with respect to their choice of policy options to put this commitment into practice.

At the same time, the three-pillar interpretation of sustainable development also leaves significant scope for flexibility in interpretations of what counts as sustainable development. While the Sustainable Development Strategy speaks of 'difficult trade-offs' between the three pillars and notes that the three pillars should be 'balanced' (CEC 2001a: 4), guidance on precisely how this should be achieved, is rarely given. More often than not, this balancing process is shaped by the political conflicts between different actors, each of which has its own (often 'sectoral') interpretation of what sustainability means. When 'balancing' the three pillars, DG Environment tends to focus mostly on environmental issues having extensive experience of and a legal mandate for environemntal matters (see above), whereas the other DGs focus more on issues relating to the other two pillars (but especially the economic ones). Rightly or wrongly, the sectors often perceive environmental concerns to be a constraint on economic growth and social cohesion, and therefore something to be minimized (COWI 2004). Within the Commission, there is 'a widespread belief that the promotion of sustainable development is the business of those who deal with the environment', i.e. DG Environment, the Environment Council of national ministers and the European Environment Agency (European Commission 1994, in Baker 2000: 314). According to Dalal-Clayton (2004: 6), some Commission officials even regard sustainable development as a 'Trojan horse' used by the environmental parts of the EU to dupe them into taking on the environmental agenda.

This lack of agreement is graphically illustrated by the wording of the Conclusions drafted by Heads of State meeting at the Goteborg European Council in June 2001. This meeting is often identified as marking the point at which the EU started to take sustainability seriously. But the statement agreed by heads of state reads: 'The European Council agrees a strategy for sustainable development which completes the Union's political commitment to economic and social renewal, adds a third, environmental dimension to the Lisbon strategy and establishes a new approach to policy making' (European Council 2001). The Lisbon strategy is, of course, the EU's long-term programme for enhancing jobs and growth. The conclusions appear to suggest that the Sustainable Development Strategy will be grafted onto it as an environmental 'add-on', rather than the three pillars working together under the banner of sustainable development (COWI 2004).

While the EU's interpretation of sustainable development within its own borders maybe narrow, it does at least seek to implement it over a relatively extensive geographical area. Since the early 1990s, the EU has also sought to 'carry the sustainable development flag in the international scene' (Baldock 2003: 7). This followed a political declaration made by the European Council in 1990 that the EU should 'exploit to the full its moral, economic and political authority' in order to accelerate international efforts to solve global problems, to promote sustainable development and respect for the global commons (European Council 1990). By doing this, it hoped to 'strengthen its normative international base and shape the concept of sus-tainability in a manner reflecting its own aims and objectives' (Lightfoot and Burchill 2004: 338). The 1992 UN Conference on Environment and Development in Rio gave the EU an early opportunity to put this leadership to the test, particularly given the lack of US leadership in environmental matters at this time (Baker 2000: 308). Indeed, the EU believed it could be an honest 'broker' in the formulation of new international environmental agreements. More importantly, it also sought to generate entirely 'new alli-ances between industrialized and developing countries' around the broader issue of sustainable development (European Commission 1996, in Baker 2000: 309).

The EU's attempts to adopt a leading position continued in the run up to the 2002 World Summit on Sustainable Development, where the EU believed it had 'a responsibility to show leadership throughout the preparations . . . at the conference itself' (CEC 2001a: 2). However, the agenda in Johannesburg raised many problems for the EU because it reflected (much more so than Rio), a broader, multi-sectoral interpretation of sustainable development that well beyond the contours of its existing environmental and sustainability policies (Lightfoot and Burchill 2004). Significantly, although the EU tried to adopt a three-pillared understanding of sustainable development, it did not fully embrace Brundtland's message about privileging the needs of the present, and especially those in the developing world, i.e the external dimen-sion, although it did rush out a special communication on its external responsibilities entitled *A Global Partnership for Sustainable Development* just before the Johannesburg meeting (see below). Nonetheless, it is fair to say that until that point, international development issues had remained somewhat separate from the EU's – and notably DG Environment's – under-standing of sustainable development (Coffey and Baldock 2003).

The next section briefly sets out how the EU has started to commit itself to support what might be termed 'global sustainable development'. In contrast to the EU's traditional, quite introspective interpretation of sustainable development, this new way of thinking seeks to link poverty reduction in the developing world with the pursuit of sustainable development in the EU 25. This perforce involves addressing the impacts that the EU has on these countries, e.g. through agricultural subsidies undermining the livelihood of farmers in developing countries etc.

The EU's commitment to global sustainable development

The 2001 Goteburg Council meeting adopted the Sustainable Development Strategy and, importantly for our purposes, it also called upon the Commission to develop a Communication on its external dimensions to lay before the World Summit on Sustainable Development. This was produced by an inter-service group involving officials from DG Development, Environment and Trade as well as the Secretariat General of the European Commission. As there was so little time (essentially September 2001 to early 2002), many important issues were not properly resolved.

The first draft, which was produced by DG Development, apparently tried to make poverty reduction the main focus. However, this proved to be wholly unacceptable to both DG Trade and DG Environment. In fact, it was obvious that while they were all broadly committed to the principle of sustainable development, the three DGs had very 'different objectives, agendas and territories to defend' (Dalal-Clayton 2004: 16). To help smooth over these tensions, the DG for External Relations joined the group as a mediator. The final document, *Towards a Global Partnership for Sustainable Development*, was eventually released on 13 February 2002 (CEC 2002a). It contained six sets of priority objectives and actions, namely: trade for sustainable development; fighting poverty; natural resources; policy coherence; governance; and financing sustainable development.

The EU now regards the four large global development agreements: the Millennium Development Goals, the World Summit on Sustainable Development, the Doha Development Agenda of the WTO negotiations, and the Monterrey Consensus, as 'mutually supportive processes and essential building blocks of a worldwide partnership for sustainable development' (CEC 2004: 4). The increasingly dominant theme of all these partnerships, to which the EU is a party (and which it has in many respects played an active role in shaping), is poverty reduction. In particular, the first Millennium Development Goal and the Johannesburg Plan of Implementation (the main outcome of the World Summit on Sustainable Development) is aimed at eradicating extreme poverty; the headline target is to halve (between 1990 and 2015) the proportion of people whose income is less than $1 a day (UN 2000; WSSD 2002). These international commitments to global sustainable development are mirrored in a number of internal strategic documents such as the EU Development Policy and the EU Sustainable Development Strategy. For instance, a priority objective of the 'external Sustainable Development Strategy', *A Global Partnership for Sustainable Development*, is to 'attain the International Development Targets and the Millennium Development Goals, in particular the target of halving extreme poverty in the world by 2015' (CEC 2002a: 9) while the overall objective of the EU Development Policy is the reduction and eventual eradication of poverty (CEC 2000).

However, the EU has only just started to put these external commitments on sustainable development into practice. Doing so will require it to include the internal and external dimensions across all sectors of policy-making (FOEE 2002). The Sustainable Development Strategy acknowledges this, when it states:

> Sustainable Development should become the central objective of all sectors and policies. This means that policy makers must identify likely spillovers – good and bad – onto other policy areas and take them into account. Careful assessment of the full effects of a policy proposal must include estimates of its economic, environmental and social impacts inside and outside the EU.
>
> (CEC 2001a: 6)

We have already shown that the EU's broad interpretation and implementation of sustainable development continues to emphasize the environmental pillar and the internal aspects. The next section examines how far the EU has succeeded in translating this aspiration into daily policy-making in the various sectors and levels of the EU. In particular, we look at a number of implementing instruments, to see how well they are picking up and reconciling the internal and external sustainability dimensions of sectoral policies. These instruments are as follows:

- *The Treaties of the European Union*: these help to organize the EU, by setting out the things it should do and how it should go about achieving them (Church and Phinnemore 2002). In other words, they are currently the closest thing that the EU has to a written constitution.
- *Environmental Action Programmes*: these chart the future strategic direction of the EU's environmental policy. Moreover, they 'provide the detail on the content of the EU environemntal policy agenda that is so obviously lacking in the Treaties' (McCormick 2001: 88).
- *The Cardiff process*: a so-called Partnership for Integration launched in 1998 through which the different sectoral formations of the Council of Ministers develop and update strategies to give effect to 'environmental integration and sustainable development' in their sector (European Council 1998: 13).
- *The EU Sustainable Development Strategy*: in 1997 the EU and the other signatories of the Rio Declaration committed themselves to producing sustainable development strategies in time for the Johannesburg Summit. The EU's Sustainable Development Strategy was eventually adopted in June 2001.
- *Impact assessment*: from 2003 all major policy proposals produced by the Commission should undergo a policy appraisal that aims to identify its likely positive and negative impacts (including potential economic, social and environmental consequences). This commitment reflects both a drive for better regulation within the Commission and also a request

for sustainability impact assessment made by heads of state at the 2001 Goteborg European Council (see above).

- *The Thematic Strategies*: the Sixth Environmental Action Programme, which was adopted in 2002, aims to pursue a more thematic approach, instead of dealing with specific pollutants or economic sectors as has been the case in the past. During 2005, the Commission drew up thematic strategies to tackle seven key cross-cutting environmental issues, such as air pollution and the marine environment. In so doing, it tried to identify synergies with existing sectoral policies, the Lisbon strategy and the Sustainable Development Strategy.
- *Informal organizational structures*: these aim to coordinate policy in pursuit of sustainable development. They include the *sustainable development / environment units* embedded in the various DGs of the Commission, the *Green Diplomacy Network* of environmental experts in foreign ministries and DG for external relations, which brings together national and EU officials in order to better coordinate international relations.
- *Various ongoing policy reform efforts which are relevant to global sustainable development*: these include reforms to the Common Agricultural Policy and the Common Fisheries Policy.

It is worth noting before we look at each instrument in detail that they have developed in an *ad hoc* manner over the last decade or so. Instead of one single instrument to implement sustainable development, there are now many different instruments. If anything, there is a *'piling up* of strategies . . . that are insufficiently harmonized with one another' (Hinterberger and Zacherl 2003: 32). For instance, the EU now has not one, but *two* long-term environmental strategies (the Sustainable Development Strategy and the Sixth Environmental Action Plan) and two cross-sectoral integration processes – Lisbon and Cardiff, not to mention many other strategic activities with a strong sustainability dimension, such as the ongoing reforms of the Common Agricultural Policy and the Structural Funds.

The EU's implementation of global sustainable development

Treaties

The main articles in the Amsterdam Treaty referring to sustainable development, namely Articles 2 and 6,[1] do not specifically mention the external dimension. It is also interesting that very little action has flowed from Article 178 of the Maastricht Treaty, which states that all policies that are likely to affect developing countries should 'take account of' the objectives of the development policy. This article is not generally connected to the sustainable development debate and no formal mechanisms have ever been set up to implement it (unlike Article 6, which triggered the Cardiff process). Williams (2004) points out that while the development cooperation title in the treaties appears no less prescriptive than the environment title, its provisions appear to be have been taken less seriously by the Community, perhaps because development policy is seen as purely external.

Environmental Action Programmes

Both the fifth and the sixth Environmental Action Programmes (published in 1993 and 2001 respectively) devote space to exploring the EU's role in the international context. The fifth noted the 'special responsibility of the Community and its constituent Members States to encourage and participate in international action to combat global environmental problems' (Official Journal 1993) and covers the major global environmental threats such as climate change, ozone layer depletion and biodiversity loss, etc. Its also set out the EU's positive attitude to global partnership and regional cooperation in seeking to address these issues. The sixth Environmental Action Plan demonstrates a more sophisticated understanding of the problem. Importantly, it concentrates much less on laying out the issues and more on linking (i.e. coordinating) the EU's role in shaping and responding to the global sustainability agenda. However, beyond recognizing its responsibility to adopt a leadership role in international environmental diplomacy, neither the fifth nor the sixth plans really drew out the links between the external and internal dimension of environmental protection and/or sustainability (but see the discussion of the Thematic Strategies, below).

The Cardiff process

Several reviews of the integration strategies produced by the sectoral formations of the Council noted a widespread failure to consider (let alone address) the external dimension (Fergusson *et al.* 2001; Opoku 2003). Fergusson *et al.* (2001: 10) described the strategies as 'weak in relation to the external dimension, even in areas where this is clearly a major issue'. For example the fisheries strategy dedicates considerable space to international fisheries management but does not discuss the impacts of the Common Fisheries Policy on developing countries. Similarly, another review (Opoku 2003) found that while the agriculture strategy mentions 'the legitimate concerns of the rural world' in World Trade Organisation (WTO) negotiations, it does not elaborate on the impacts on developing countries, which according to some lobbying groups (e.g. Oxfam 2002), have an extremely detrimental impact on farmers' livelihoods. Meanwhile, the strategy produced by the Economic and Finance Council sees the global dimension to sustainable development solely in terms of threats to the EU economic competitiveness. Furthermore, it assumes that because external trade (defined as that with non-EU or EEA states) amounts to such a small percentage of total EU trade, its impacts must be of minor importance (Opoku 2003).

The Sustainable Development Strategy

One of the most significant criticisms of the Sustainable Development Strategy was that it almost totally neglected the external dimension (only one paragraph mentioned developing countries). It is unclear whether the task force which produced the strategy was even aware of the need to address the external dimension but took a decision to leave it aside, or whether it did not even realize that there was one (Dalal-Clayton 2004). Either way, the main pressure to include the external dimension came from the NGO community, most notably the European Office of World Wide Fund for Nature (WWF) and the Institute for European Environmental Policy (IEEP). WWF produced a consultation paper on the Sustainable Development Strategy in 2001 and a follow-up response in April 2001. Despite these demands from civil society, in the end the Sustainable Development Strategy focused almost exclusively on the European perspective (Tanasescu 2006). An 'external sustainable development strategy' was not added until 2002 (see above).

The additional document on the external dimension produced in the run-up to the Johannesburg conference (see above) was also criticized for glossing over many of the EU's impacts on the developing world (IIED and RING 2004). Others pointed out that it was not intimately connected to the main body of the original (2001) Sustainable Development Strategy, with its predominantly internal focus (Coffey and Baldock 2003). It is also obvious that the annual review process for the Sustainable Development Strategy in the Spring reviews of the Lisbon process (a strategy for employment and economic growth) is inadequate for the EU's internal environment let alone its impact on the external environment (Coffey and Baldock 2003). Many interested parties hoped that the 2005/6 review process would be used to address this lack of integration between the external and internal dimensions (Dalal-Clayton 2004; IIED and RING 2004). This expectation was supported by the presidency conclusions of the spring council 2005 which called for a new Sustainable Development Strategy to be presented at the end of 2005 which 'fully integrate[d] the internal and external dimensions' (European Council 2005). In the end, the 'renewed' Sustainable Development Strategy (European Council 2006) adopted by the Council in June 2006, contained a two-page section of objectives and targets on 'Global Poverty and Sustainable Development Challenges'. Although this pledged to 'include sustainable development concerns into all EU external policies' (European Council 2006: 21), it mainly reiterated the EU's support for relevant international agreements (e.g. the Monterrey Consensus and the Millennium Declaration) and it did not acknowledge at all the impacts of internal EU policies on the developing world.

Impact assessment

The impact assessment regime is still relatively new and will take time to bed in. Nonetheless, early evaluations do suggest that it is paying very little attention to external impacts on sustainable development (Wilkinson *et al.* 2004; Adelle *et al.* 2006). Yet the original guidelines issued by the Commission in 2002 (subsequently updated in 2005) emphasize the importance of considering impacts falling outside the EU (CEC n.d.: 24; CEC 2005a: 28). In fact, the title page of the original guidelines prominently displays the following quote from the EU Sustainable Development Strategy: 'Careful assessment of the full effects of a policy proposal must include estimates of its economic, environmental and social impacts inside *and outside the EU*' (CEC 2001a) (emphasis added). However, the updated (2005) guidelines gave a stronger emphasis on the need to support economic competitiveness in the EU and avoid over-prescriptive legislation. Adelle *et al.* (2006) found that only the impact assessments which were carried out on policy proposals that were obviously external (e.g. such as that on promoting human rights through development cooperation (CEC 2003b)), included an adequate assessment of the external dimension. They also found that consultation with developing countries and development NGOs was weak.

The Thematic Strategies

There is some evidence that the networks developing around the seven themes have grappled with the external dimension (ENDS 2004). Four of the five Thematic Strategies published by the beginning of 2006 contained a section on the external dimension (or, as it was termed, the 'international dimension'). In general, this section mainly covers the EU's contribution to negotiating and implementing international *environmental* agreements. Even in the strategy that arguably has the most obvious external dimensions, namely that addressing the sustainable use of natural resources (WWF 2005: 3) makes only passing references to the global impacts of natural resources (CEC 2005b). Likewise, although the marine Thematic Strategy does mention the sustainability of fisheries agreements with developing countries, it does not elaborate on this. In general, it is geared towards addressing the deteriorating state of Europe's marine environment rather than the impacts of the EU's policies on developing countries (CEC 2005c)).

Informal organizational structures

Neither the *sustainable development units* nor the *Green Diplomacy Network* of environmental experts in foreign ministries have really championed the external dimensions of sustainable development. However, the external relations family (DG RELEX) and the Inter-service Quality Group have arguably made more of an impact. The external relations 'family' was set up in 1995 to help coordinate the EU's role in external relations. DG for External Relations operates as a inter-service consultation mechanism with civil servants from the different external relations members (DG Development; DG Trade; DG External Relations; DG Enlargement; Humanitarian Aid Office; EuropeAid

Co-operation Office). However, the external relations family has been critized because it focuses only on *new* external EU policies, i.e. it misses some key incoherence issues arising from internal community policies and existing policies (OECD 2002: 70).

The Inter-service Quality Support Group comprises members from DG Development, DG External Relations, DG Trade, DG Enlargement and Humanitarian Aid Office Europe Aid. It was established in 2001 to monitor all Country Strategy Papers for countries in receipt of EU development assistance, including how well they achieve wider policy coherence. However, ActionAid Alliance, a network of international development NGOs, claims that it has 'certainly raised the profile of policy coherence within the Commission, but its impacts on Country Strategy Papers has yet to be felt' (ActionAid Alliance 2003: 5). A Commission staff working paper published in November 2002 states that although the overall 'policy mix' was mentioned in the vast majority of documents, the analysis was rarely taken very far, in particular with regard to trade and fisheries (CEC 2002b: 17).

Policy developments

The reform of the Common Agricultural Policy is often justified by the EU in relation to environmental imperatives, but critics continue to argue that they have not gone fast or far enough. For example, ActionAid Alliance believes they are 'piece-meal reforms [which] offer little, if any benefit to the world's poor, particularly since they allow the provision of public aid to agriculture in ways which are designed not to reduce overall levels of EU production' (ActionAid Alliance 2003: 7). ActionAid emphasizes that reductions in intervention prices are accompanied by increased direct aid payments enabling prices to be charged for agricultural products which do not reflect the underlying costs of production (ActionAid Alliance 2003). This debate between NGOs and the Common Agricultural Policy supporters continues to slowly rumble on as do the Common Agricultural Policy reforms themselves. Be that as it may, what is particularly interesting for our purposes is that these policy reforms have often stemmed from pressure exerted by other countries through the WTO, rather because of the implementation of sustainability-related mechanisms (see above) to address the external dimension of sustainable development.

Meanwhile, as part of the reform of the Common Fisheries Policy, the Commission presented a Communication on an Integrated Framework for Fisheries Partnership Agreements in December 2002 (CEC 2002c), which will replace the old access agreements. This change in approach recognizes the need for better knowledge on the financial, economic, institutional, environmental and social impact of a fisheries agreement on the partner country prior to the opening of negotiations. In addition, from 2003 onwards a broader set of Sustainability Impact Assessments (i.e. *not* impact assessments – see above) have been carried out on new partnership agreements. While the

EU has not considered withdrawing from these access agreements altogether, claiming that the EU would be replaced by something less responsible, 'many of the ambitions set out in the Communication (CEC 2002c) should lead to a substantial improvement of the current situation' (IEEP 2003: 3). However, critics are concerned about the EU's willingness to conclude more agreements with developing countries in the future. 'The Commission's rather candid statement about wanting to maintain a European presence in distant waters should perhaps be a warning to those expecting fundamental change to follow from any agreement on the Communication' (IEEP 2003: 4).

Conclusions

Over the last twenty years, the EU has taken significant strides forward in the way in which it thinks about and seeks to implement sustainable development. Throughout the first twenty years of EU environmental policy-making (1970–1990), the primary focus was on maintaining and, where possible improving, environmental quality within the EU's borders via the large corpus of environmental Directives and Regulations. As in most other comparable jurisdictions, sustainable development was only weakly present in policy discourses. In the 1990s, the EU commited itself much more strongly to the concept of sustainable development. But DG Environment in particular conceived of this first and foremost as an *environmental* concept which, until surprisingly recently, it sought to implement through the predominantly environmental principle of environmental policy integration. In the 2000s, the EU began to take a closer interest in what we have referred to as the global sustainable development agenda. However, the EU is still struggling to adapt its internal structures and policies to give effect to this broader interpretation of sustainable development. It is worrying that newer mechanisms such as the impact assessment (which explicitly state that external impacts are of interest) are not performing significantly better than some of the older mechanisms which predate the EU's rhetorical commitment to global sustainable development. But as the sectors have gradually become more aware of the potential, long-term implications of Article 6, so they have made ever-stronger attempts to neutralize them. The environmental policy journal *ENDS Daily* (2004) recently concluded that 'the debate [is now] . . . less of integrating environment into sectoral policies, and more of reverse integrating competitiveness into EU environmental policies.' Witness, for example, the virtual death of the Cardiff process, the rising prominence of the Lisbon and Better Regulation agendas, and DG Environment's search for less intrusive approaches to implementing EPI predominantly at member state level (Jordan and Schout 2006).

And yet, thinking about and addressing the external dimension of sustainable development is as crucial, if not more so, than in the early 1990s. Authors working in the social justice field place 'social justice *at the core* of sustainable development' (Langhelle 2000: 299). Taking their cue from

Brundtland's social democratic interpretation of sustainable development, they see the issue of intra-generational equity (i.e. the needs of the world's poor, primarily those in developing countries) as the main priority in relation to sustainable development (Jacobs 1999; Langhelle 2000; Neefjes 2000; Agyeman *et al.* 2003). On this view, environmental sustainability on its own is a necessary, but insufficient, condition of sustainable development.

Regardless of how sustainability is defined and interpreted, the EU remains a key player. Indeed, 'on many key issues, the EU is part of the problem rather than the solution' (FOEE 2002). Many actors around the world are increasingly looking towards the EU to exercise leadership in the environment and development field, but the EU finds itself grappling with issues of internal policy coordination which hinder its own pursuit of sustainable development (Lightfoot and Burchill 2004). At a time when the concept of sustainable development is itself in danger of being over-shadowed by the competitiveness agenda of the Lisbon agenda, this import-ant but much neglected dimension of sustainable development is in danger of slipping off the political and scholarly agenda in Europe, before it has received a full airing.

What, then, does the EU's response to sustainable development reveal about the wider themes raised in Chapter 1? The first and most important thing to point out is that the EU is neither an international organization nor a state as conventionally understood. It has more sophisticated institutional bodies (not least a directly elected Parliament and a European Court of Justice), many more policy responsibilities and much more complex decision-making than most other supranational bodies in the world. These make the EU a highly sophisticated 'political system but not a state' (Hix 2005: 2). It has been variously described as a 'partial' or 'part-polity' (Sbragia 2004) – a 'quasi-federation' (Weale 1995).

Given these attributes, one would probably expect the EU to have a more sophisticated and effective set of policy delivery mechanisms than the other international organizations analysed in this book. We have listed some of them in this chapter. However, we have also shown how many of them have struggled to get an adequate grip on the sustainability agenda. In terms of *effects*, the EU has undoubtedly succeeded in raising and maintaining the political profile of the sustainability agenda not only internationally, but also internally amongst its member states. The underlying problem, of course, is that sustainability is an exceedingly complex policy challenge that cannot possibly be resolved purely by the EU and certainly not by DG Environment, which has understandably tried to take the lead in develop-ing EU environmental policy. The EU certainly needs the support of its member states, especially in relation to policy sectors where it does not exercise as much policy competence, such as transport and energy. The member states have pledged themselves individually to address sustain-ability, but none have been entirely successful at implementing it (Lafferty 2004). Similarly, DG Environment has found it more difficult to pursue cross-cutting issues such as sustainability and even EPI than 'old-fashioned' environment policy, where it could operate rather more independently of the other sectoral DGs.

In relation to the question of *design* and *vertical interplay*, the EU demonstrates what appears when supranational bodies are given the power to initiate new legislation and thereby shape political agendas, but when Member States remain the primary implementing bodies: in short, an extensive implementation deficit (Jordan 2002). The EU's administrative capacity to get things done should be understood as being 'an amalgam of the European and the national, marked by interpenetration and interdependence' (Kassim 2003: 161). On the positive side, this allows the EU (and especially DG Environment) to be an international pathfinder in terms of the definition and interpretation of policy challenges like climate change and (the external dimensions of) sustainability. But on the downside, it often struggles to put these into effect, lacking as it does many of the administrative and legal capacities held by states.

Finally, there is the issue of *integration*. In many respects, this chapter offers a neat case study in the law, politics and administration of cross-sectoral (dis)integration because sustainability is an interconnected problem *par excellence*. Indeed, it well be *the* most cross-cutting policy issue of our time. Policy coordination is notoriously difficult for *any* policy system to achieve – it is 'ever sought, but always just beyond reach' (Rhodes 2000: 359). But for an international organization – even a highly sophisticated example like the EU – it is especially challenging. As the EU has become larger, institutionally denser and more multi-levelled, so the perceived need to act in a joined-up manner has grown (Jordan and Schout 2006). The EU has an extremely fluid and almost constantly expanding agenda of policy problems (Peters and Wright 2001: 158), each of which bring together many actors, sectors and member states in a complex game of three-dimensional chess. As the EU's administrative capacity is relatively weak in comparison to its member states, cross-cutting policy challenges like sustainability need to be backed by especially strong and sustained political leadership if they are to have a long-lasting effect. In spite of high-level commitments to implement sustainability both internally and externally, the EU's political leadership (that is the Commission President and the heads of state) seem too preoccupied with pursuing the narrower issue of economic competitiveness to promote the economic pillar of sustainability – witness, for example, the current focus of the Lisbon agenda on 'jobs and growth' in Europe. Interpreting the failure to reconcile the internal and external dimensions of policy-making as being the product of variable political will and leadership *or* of weak administrative capacities, rather misses the point, because the two are as mutually interdependent in the EU as they are in many other policy systems.

Note

1 Article 6 of the Amsterdam Treaty states that: 'Environmental protection requirements must be integrated into the definition and implementation of the Communities policies . . . in particular with a view to promoting sustainable development.' The concept of sustainable development is also enshrined in the Preamble
and in the objectives of the Amsterdam Treaty as well as featuring in Article 2 of
the Treaty, which lays down the tasks of the Community.

References

ActionAid Alliance (2003) *Policy (In)Coherence in European Union Support to Developing Countries: A Three Country Case Study*, Brussels: ActionAid Alliance.

Adelle, C., Hertin, J. and Jordan, A. (2006) 'Sustainable Development "Outside" the European Union: What Role for Impact Assessment?', *European Environment*, 16: 57–72.

Agyeman, J., Bullard, R. and Evans, B. (2003) 'Joined-up thinking: bringing together sustainability, environmental justice and equity', in Agyeman, J. *et al.* (eds) *Just Sustainabilities Development in an Unequal World*, London: Earthscan.

Baker, S. (2000) 'The European Union: Integration, Competition, Growth – and Sustainability', in Lafferty, W. and Meadowcroft, J. (eds) *Implementing Sustainable Development Strategies and Initiatives in High Consumption Societies*, Oxford: Oxford University Press.

Baker, S., Kousis, M., Richardson, D. and Young, S. (1997) 'Introduction: The Theory and Practice of Sustainable Development in the EU', in Baker, S. *et al.* (eds) *The Politics of Sustainable Development: Theory, Policy and Practice within the EU*, London: Routledge.

Baldock, D. (2003) 'The EU Sustainable Development Strategy: From Lisbon to Goteborg and Beyond – An Evaluation of Progress', report prepared for the European Economic and Social Committee, Brussels: Institute for European Environmental Policy.

Borrell, B. and Hubbard, L. (2000) *Global Economic Effects of the EU Common Agricultural Policy*, Oxford: Institute of Economic Affairs.

Commission of the European Community (CEC) (no date) *Impact Assessment in the Commission: Guidelines*, Brussels: Commission of the European Community.

CEC (2000) 'The European Community's Development Policy', *COM (2000) 212*, Brussels: Commission of the European Union.

CEC (2001a) 'A Sustainable Europe for a Better World: A European Union Strategy for Sustainable Development', *COM (2001) 264*, Brussels: Commission of the European Community.

CEC (2001b) 'Consultation Paper for the Preparation of a European Union Strategy for Sustainable Development', *SEC (2001) 517*, Brussels: Commission of the European Union.

CEC (2001c) 'Ten Years after Rio: Preparing for the World Summit on Sustainable Development in 2002', *COM (2001) 53*, Brussels: Commission of the European Union.

CEC (2002a) 'Towards a Global Partnership for Sustainable Development', *COM (2002) 82*, Brussels: Commission of the European Union.

CEC (2002b) 'Progress Report on the Implementation of the Common Framework for Country Strategy Papers', *SEC (2002) 1279*, Brussels: Commission of the European Union.

CEC (2002c) 'An Integrated Framework for Fisheries Partnership Agreements with Third Countries', *COM (2002) 637*, Brussels: Commission of the European Union.

CEC (2003a) 'The World Summit on Sustainable Development One Year On: Implementing our Commitments', *COM (2003) 829*, Brussels: Commission of the European Community.

CEC (2003b) 'Extended Impact Assessment on European Initiative for Democracy and Human Rights Regulations 975/1999 and 976/1999', *SEC (2003) 1170*, Brussels: Commission of the European Union.

CEC (2004) *European Commission Report on Millennium Development Goals 2000–2004*, Brussels: Commission of the European Community.

CEC (2005a) 'Impact Assessment Guidelines', *SEC (2005) 791*, Brussels: Commission of the European Union.

CEC (2005b) 'Thematic Strategy on the sustainable use of natural resources', *COM (2005) 670*, Brussels: Commission of the European Union.

CEC (2005c) 'Thematic Strategy on the Protection and Conservation of the Marine Environment', *COM (2005) 504*, Brussels: Commission of the European Union.

Church, C. and Phinnemore, D. (2002) *The Penguin Guide to the European Treaties*, London: Penguin Books.

Coffey, C. and Baldock, D. (2003) *Building a Comprehensive EU Sustainable Development Strategy – Adding the External Dimension*, London: Institute for European Environmental Policy.

COWI (2004) 'Evaluation of Approaches to Integrating Sustainability into Community Policies', report for the European Commission Secretariat General, online. Available HTTP: <http://ec.europa.eu/budget/evaluation/pdf/fin_rep_eval_app_071004_en.pdf> (accessed 19 July 2006).

Dalal-Clayton, B. (2004) *The EU Strategy for Sustainable Development: Process and Prospects*, London: International Institute for Environment and Development.

Environmental Data Services (ENDS) (2004) 'Commission Floats Idea of National Resource Allocation Plans', *ENDS Report*, 359: 58.

Environmental Data Services (ENDS) (2004 daily) 'Bid to Rescue EU Green Integration Efforts', *ENDS Daily*, 1679, 3 June.

European Council (1990) *Presidency Conclusions: Dublin European Council, 25 and 26 June 1990 (The Environmental Imperative – Declaration by the European Council)*, Brussels: Council of the European Union.

European Council (1998) *Presidency Conclusions: Cardiff European Council, 15 and 16 June 1998*, Brussels: Council of the European Union.

European Council (2001) *Presidency Conclusions: Goteborg European Council, 15 and 16 June 2001*, Brussels: Council of the European Union.

European Council (2005) *Presidency Conclusions: Brussels European Council, 16 and 17 June 2005*, Brussels: Council of the European Union.

European Council (2006) *Review of the EU Sustainable Development Strategy (EU SDS): Renewed Strategy 10117/06*, Brussels: European Council.

European Environment Agency (EEA) (2004) *Environmental Policy Integration: Looking Back, Thinking Ahead*, Copenhagen: European Environment Agency.

Fergusson, M., Coffey, C., Wilkinson, D. and Baldock, D. (2001) *The Effectiveness of EU Council Integration Strategies and Options for Carrying Forward the Cardiff Process*, London: Institute for European Environmental Policy.

Friends of the Earth Europe (FOEE) (2002) 'EU Loses Earth Summit Leadership Role', Press Release, 28 August, online. Available HTTP: <http://www.foe.co.uk/resource/press_releases/20020828143307.html>.

Hinterberger, F. and Zacherl, R. (2003) *Ways Towards Sustainability in the European Union: Beyond the European Spring Summit in 2003*, Vienna: SERI Institute.

Hix, S. (2005) *The Political Sytem of the European Union*, 2nd edition, Basingstoke: Palgrave.

Institute for European Environmental Policy (IEEP) (2003) 'CFP reform 2002', *Briefing no. 11, February 2003*, London: IIEP.

International Institute for Environment and Development and The Regional and International Networking Group (IIED and RING) (2004) *Europe: A Global Partner for Sustainable Development?*, London: IIED and RING.

Jacobs, M. (1999) 'Sustainable Development as a Contested Concept', in Dobson, A. (ed.) *Fairness and Futurity: Essays on Environmental Sustainability and Social Justice*, Oxford: Oxford University Press.

Jordan, A. (2002) 'The Implementation of EU Environmental Policy', in Jordan, A. (ed.) *Environmental Policy in the European Union: Actors, Institutions and Processes*, London: Earthscan.

Jordan, A. (2005) 'Introduction: European Union Environmental Policy', in Jordan, A. (ed.) *Environmental Policy in the European Union: Actors, Institutions and Processes*, 2nd edition, London: Earthscan.

Jordan, A. and Lenschow, A. (2000) 'Greening the European Union: What Can Be Learned from the Leaders of EU Environmental Policy?', *European Environment*, 10(3): 109–20.

Jordan, A. and O'Riordan, T. (2004) 'An Ever More Sustainable Union? Integrating Economy, Society and Environment in a Rapidly Enlarging Europe', in Koutrakou, V. (ed.) *Contemporary Issues and Debates in EU Policy*, Manchester: Manchester University Press.

Jordan, A. and Schout, A. (2006) *The Coordination of the European Union: Exploring the Capacities for Networked Governance*, Oxford: Oxford University Press.

Jordan A., Schout A., Unfried, M. and Zito, A. (2006) 'Environmental Policy: Struggling to Address a Multilevel Coordination Deficit?', in Kassim, H., Menon, A. and Peters, B.G. (eds) *Coordinating the European Union*, Lanham, MD: Rowman and Littlefield.

Kassim, H. (2003) 'The European Administration: Between Europeanization and Domestication', in Hayward, J. and Menon, A. (eds) *Governing Europe*, Oxford: Oxford University Press.

Lafferty, W. (ed.) (2004) *Governance for Sustainable Development*, Cheltenham: Edward Elgar.

Lafferty, W.M. and Hovden, E. (2003) 'Environmental Policy Integration: Towards an Analytical Framework', *Environmental Politics*, 12(3): 1–22.

Langhelle, O. (2000) 'Sustainable Development and Social Justice: Expanding the Rawlsian Framework of Global Justice', *Environmental Values*, 9: 295–323.

Lenschow, A. (2002a) 'Greening the European Union: An Introduction', in Lenschow, A. (ed.) *Environmental Policy Integration: Greening Sectoral Policies in Europe*, London: Earthscan.

Lenschow, A. (2002b) 'New Regulatory Approaches in "Greening" EU Policies', *European Law Journal*, 8: 19–37.

Lightfoot, S. and Burchill, J. (2004) 'Green Hope or Greenwash? The Actions of the

European Union at the World Summit on Sustainable Development', *Global Environmental Change*, 14: 337–44.

McCormick, J. (2001) *Environmental Policy in the European Union*, Basingstoke: Palgrave.

Neefjes, K. (2000) 'People defining their environments: a future of change', in Lee, K. *et al.* (eds) *Global Sustainable Development in the 21st century*, Edinburgh: Edinburgh University Press.

Oberthür, S. (1999) 'The EU as an International Actor: The Protection of the Ozone layer', *Journal of Common Market Studies*, 37: 641–59.

OECD (2002) *Development Co-operation Review: European Community Report by the Development Assistance Committee*, Paris: OECD.

Official Journal (1993) 'Towards Sustainability: the European Community Programme of Policy and Action in relation to the Environment and Sustainable Development', *OJ/93 C138/83*, Brussels: Commission of the European Union.

Opoku, C. (2003) 'The Cardiff Process and Sustainable Development outside the European Union', unpublished report, University of East Anglia.

Oxfam (2002) 'Europe's Double Standards: How the EU Should Reform its Trade Policies with the Developing World', *Oxfam Briefing Paper 22*, Oxfam International.

Peters, B.G. and Wright, V. (2001) 'The National Coordination of European Policy-Making', in Richardson, J. (ed.) *European Union: Power and Policy-Making*, London: Routledge.

Rhodes, R.A.W. (2000) 'The Governance Narrative: Key Findings and Lessons from the ESRC's Whitehall Programme', *Public Administration*, 78(2): 345–63.

Sbragia, A. (2002) 'Institution-building from Below and Above: The European Community in Global Environmental Politics', in Jordan, A. (ed.) *Environmental Policy in the EU: Actors, Institutions and Processes*, London: Earthscan.

Sbragia, A. (2004) 'The Future of Federalism in the European Union', keynote address delivered at the European Community Studies Canada (ECSA-C) 2004 Biennial Conference.

Sporrong, N., Coffey, C. and Bevins, K. (2002) 'Fisheries Agreements with Third Countries: Is the EU Moving Towards Sustainable Development?' IEEP Report commissioned by WWF, London: IEEP.

Tanasescu, I. (2006) 'The Political Process Leading to the Development of the EU Sustainable Development Strategy', in Pallemaerts, M. and Azmanova, A. (eds) *The European Union and Sustainable Development: Internal and External Dimensions*, Brussels: VUB Press.

United Nations (UN) (2000) *Millennium Declaration*, New York: United Nations.

Wallstrom, M. (2003) Speech Made to the Sustainable Development Inter-Group of the European Parliament, Strasbourg 24 September.

Weale, A. (1995) 'Democratic Legitimacy and the Constitution of Europe', in Bellamy, R., Bufacchi, V. and Castiglione, D. (eds) *Democracy and Constitutional Culture in the Union of Europe*, London: Lothian Foundation Press.

Wilkinson, D., Fergusson, M., Bowyer, C., Brown, J., Ladefoged, A., Monkhouse, C. and Zdanowicz, A. (2004) *Sustainable Development in the European Commission's Integrated Impact Assessments for 2003*, London: Institute for European Environmental Policy.

Williams, R. (2004) 'Community Development Cooperation Law, Sustainable

Development, and the Convention on Europe – from Dislocation to Consistency?' *The Yearbook of European Environmental Law*, 4: 303–75.

World Commission on Environment and Development (WCED) (1987) *Our Common Future*, Oxford: Oxford University Press.

World Summit on Sustainable Development (WSSD) (2002) *Plan of Implementation*, New York: United Nations.

Worldwide Fund for Nature (WWF) (2005) *Europe 2005, The Ecological Footprint*, Brussels: WWF.

Part II

International environmental programmes and secretariats

7 The role of the United Nations Environment Programme in the coordination of multilateral environmental agreements

Steinar Andresen and Kristin Rosendal

Introduction

In this chapter we discuss the extent to which the United Nations Environment Programme (UNEP) has been successful in achieving one of its main functions, the coordination of multilateral environmental agreements (MEAs). This will be discussed in relation to the biodiversity cluster.

Before specifying our approach further, we will first make some general observations on how the study of international environmental organizations fits into the broader study of global environmental governance. Over the last two decades there has been a strong research focus on international environmental regimes and attention has also been geared towards the interplay between regimes.[1] There has also been an increased interest in the study of organizations in global environmental politics – the main focus of this chapter.[2]

One key discussion among academics and policy-makers has been the idea of establishing a world environment organization in order to streamline and simplify the increasingly complex web of international environmental institutions. This idea had some political momentum before the World Summit in Johannesburg in 2002 but nothing came out of it. However, the idea is not dead, as during the 2006 UNEP Governing Council meeting, the idea was once more tabled. Our reading of this debate is, however, that at present it does not seem to be a politically feasible alternative, since major states like the United States are strongly opposed to it. In the corresponding academic discussions, there have been some strong supporters for the idea, while others have opposed it.[3]

We find it worthwhile to dwell on an important underlying point in the discussion of a world environment organization in order to clarify our position on the role of international organizations in global environmental governance: *To what extent can environmental problems be mitigated through design of international organizations?* To simplify, within the realist school of thought, the answer is simply that design does not make much of a difference, as organizations are no more than epiphenomena, a mere reflection of the will of the most powerful members. However, few realists are concerned with 'soft' issues like the environment (Mitchell 2002). Therefore, students work-ing on international institutions tend to belong either to the institutionalist or the social constructivist school of thought.[4] The former is particularly pre-occupied with the significance and role of institutions, while the latter is *also* preoccupied with the significance of norms, knowledge and learning. This leads to what seems to be a trivial – but we believe often neglected – observa-tion: *Most students of international environmental institutions and organiza-tions believe that these bodies play a significant role in deciding the effectiveness of solutions to the relevant problems.* This *may* imply a systematic overplay of their importance. That is, if one believes that 'institutions matter', one will tend to seek confirmation of one's belief, and not be as open towards other conclusions as one should according to text books in methodology. There-fore, we would like realists to take more interest in these 'soft' issue areas, in order to get a sharper discussion of the fruitfulness of the different approaches.

Still, there are considerable variations between scholars as to the signifi-cance they attribute to institutional design. Some analysts emphasize the significance of power and underline the fairly modest effect of international institutions and organizations (e.g. Miles *et al.* 2002). In a similar vein, some observers maintain that too little attention is paid to the role played by the major political and economic actors in explaining effectiveness, or rather lack of such, of international environmental institutions and organizations. The gist of the argument is that you cannot change the root causes of the problem by clever design when major actors are dragging their feet (Najam 2003). Others are more optimistic as to the significance of institutional design. They do not necessarily downplay political realities, but have a stronger belief that a strong and unified organization – for example a world environment organization – may make a positive difference in terms of effectiveness.

As to our position on this debate, and in the context of this book on international environmental organizations, we have some sympathy for both perspectives. On the one hand, we find it important to emphasize the signifi-cance of power and the dominant position of strong actors in explaining the effectiveness of international organizations.[5] To give an illustration, when the United States does not want to 'play ball' in the climate regime, the chances of an effective international climate policy is strongly reduced. Correspond-ingly, when the United States (as well as major sectors of industry) stood forward as leaders in strengthening the ozone regime, this explains a signifi-cant part of the high effectiveness of this regime and the related organiza-tions. We therefore believe that *overall the design of international institutions and organizations cannot be expected to make much of a difference to their effectiveness.*

On the other hand, we find it misguided to disregard the opportunities offered by clever design (for example Wettestad 1999 and Andresen *et al.* 2000). As researchers we cannot – and should not – attempt to influence the world political system. As individuals we may regret the lack of environmental enthusiasm on the part of many key actors. Yet it is the role of policy-makers and civil society to exert pressure on these actors to do more. This is a different matter when it comes to organizational design. In dialogue with policy-makers and practitioners we can suggest changes that may make *some* positive difference for the problem-solving ability of the organization in question.

UNEP is a programme and thus no traditional UN organization. Still, here we study the organizational component of UNEP as manifested by its head-quarters in Nairobi and its offices around the world. The staff of UNEP consists of bureaucrats working both as 'servants' as well as coordinators of a number of environmental regimes. It may have a positive influence on these through its expertise, knowledge and, not least, through the exercise of *authority* and as facilitator for the parties to the relevant agreement.[6] How effective is UNEP in terms of coordinating relevant multilateral environmental agreements? Does this contribute to enhancing problem-solving capacity and thereby increasing effectiveness?

It has become commonplace to define effectiveness in relation to inter-national regimes in terms of output, outcome and impact. Output refers to rules, programmes and regulations emanating from the regime while outcome refers to behavioural change – in the 'right' direction – by key target groups and as a result of the regime. Finally, impact refers to the environmental improvements in the relevant issue area following from the regime in question. Can the indicators of effectiveness from regime analysis be transferred to the analysis of international organizations? It has been suggested that these three indicators can be used for the study of international environmental organiza-tions (Biermann and Bauer 2004). This may be a sensible strategy, but some modifications may be needed in our case. First, the outcome indicator may be more problematic to apply in the study of organizations than it is regarding regimes. Less can be expected in terms of direct and tangible results following from an organization like UNEP as compared to that of a regime.[7] In a sense UNEP is further removed from the problem at hand compared to the regime and the parties to the regime, being responsible for implementing commit-ments agreed to, while UNEP provides more of a general 'super-structure'. Providing clever advice, facilitation, knowledge production as well as medi-ation may certainly be important. Yet the chain of events from the tasks of UNEP to the actual problem at hand is usually long, indirect and complex – and also exceedingly difficult to measure. Therefore, outcome as an indicator of effectiveness is difficult to apply in terms of a body like UNEP. Con-sequently we believe that output, although this only says something about the *potential* for effectiveness, is the most relevant indicator for evaluating UNEP's coordinating efforts.

In the earlier days of regime analysis, *goal achievement* was used as a yard-stick against which performance could be measured (for example Andresen and Wettestad 1995 and Bernauer 1995). This yardstick has since then been more or less discarded, not least because goals are often so vague that they are exceedingly difficult to measure performance against. Consider for example the goal of the World Health Organization 'health for all', which was not very useful as a measuring rod. Nevertheless, in this chapter we have chosen to use goal achievement as a measuring rod, as the goal of coordination is quite specific and it is feasible to measure performance in relation to this goal. Translating this indicator to the indicators outlined above, it comes closest to the output indicator, telling us something about UNEP's ability to improve the output and thereby enhance the *problem-solving ability* of the regimes in this cluster. We take as point of departure that 'coordination is good' – as this is one of the 'raisons d'être' for UNEP. In the academic literature, however, this is a rather complex and controversial question (Victor 1999).

We have relied heavily on *interviews* within the UNEP Headquarters in Nairobi, its regional office in Geneva, as well as with the relevant secretariats of MEAs.[8] By interviewing both the 'demand side' (MEA Secretariats) and the 'supply side' (UNEP) we applied a version of the *ego and alter perceptions*, i.e. how UNEP judge their own capacity in this respect and how this is judged from the other side of the fence (Arts 1998). We believe this gives a more nuanced and realistic picture than many general analyses of UNEP that tend to be somewhat stereotypically 'pro or against' UNEP.

Finally, how do we explain the performance of UNEP in this regard? Systematic and skilful analytical devices have been used in order to shed light on this question both in relation to regimes as well as to international environmental organizations (e.g. Miles *et al.* 2002 and Biermann and Bauer 2005). In this chapter we have been less ambitious, drawing upon a combination of inductive and deductive approaches. Inductively, we have relied on the many semi-structured interviews conducted: what factors have they defined to explain the performance of UNEP along this dimension? Deductively, we have relied on some of the insights drawn from the research project Environmental Regime Effectiveness, more specifically the notion of *problem-solving capacity* (elaborated in Miles *et al.* 2002). Based on this we end up with two main explanatory variables. The first is the role and position of UNEP in the UN system, that is, the strength of UNEP compared to other relevant UN bodies. The simple assumption is that the stronger UNEP is, the higher its potential to coordinate. We also include financial resources and geographical location in this dimension. The more 'centrally located' and the stronger financially, the easier coordination will be. The second more internal dimension deals with UNEP as organization, its organizational set-up and bureaucratic culture. Here we want to discuss whether UNEP is organized in a way that makes effective coordination possible and whether its organizational culture pulls in the same direction. The latter point also depends on the 'cultural fit' between UNEP and the relevant multilateral environmental agreements. With this caveat, let us turn to the evaluation of UNEP.

Assessing the effectiveness of UNEP

First a brief note on our focus on the 'biodiversity conservation cluster'. We will not go into the discussion about the potential and pitfalls of clustering MEAs (Oberthür 2002). However, a number of clusters have been identified such as 'global atmosphere', 'hazardous substance', 'marine environment' and 'biodiversity'. We have chosen the latter mainly for two reasons: First, UNEP plays a key role in this cluster and, second, it is a fairly 'mature' cluster, thereby illustrating the performance of UNEP through the various stages of development of these MEAs. The idea of identifying clusters within the larger issue areas is in itself problematic. No matter which way the lines are drawn, it will inevitably involve fencing something in and something else out, and the drawing of borders between regimes is inherently a political activity.[9] However, there is general agreement that the main multilateral environmental agreements included are: The Convention on Biological Diversity (CBD), the Ramsar Convention on Wetlands, the Convention on the Conservation of Migratory Species of Wild Animals (CMS), the World Heritage Convention (WHC), and the Convention on Trade in Endangered Species of Wild Fauna and Flora (CITES).[10] First we address briefly the question of whether they perceive a need for coordination among themselves, illustrating the need for coordination in general. Second, we look more specifically into what the secretariats of MEAs expect from UNEP in this regard and how UNEP responds.

The majority of these MEAs were established in the 1970s and are therefore in the phase of implementation. Ramsar (1972) is dedicated to stopping the loss and deterioration of wetlands. The WHC (1972) concerns both natural and cultural habitats of particular significance to humanity. The CMS (1979) aims to conserve terrestrial, marine and avian migratory species throughout their range.[11] The purpose of CITES (1973) is to ensure that listed species of wild fauna and flora do not become subject to unsustainable exploitation because of international trade. Finally, the CBD (1992) is the most encompassing convention and its mandate comprises all species and ecosystems worldwide. UNEP has formal responsibility for or affiliations with the CBD secretariat, CITES and the CMS while UNESCO administers the WHC. Ramsar is fairly independent, with the IUCN as its secretariat. A number of formal coordination activities are taking place within the biodiversity conservation cluster. There is a joint web site between CBD, CITES, CMS, WHC and Ramsar and several memoranda of understanding have been signed between the CBD and the other conventions.[12] Also, the seventh conference of the parties to the CBD in 2004 established the Biodiversity Liaison Group, including the CBD, CITES, Ramsar, CMS and WHC.

UNEP has also increased its coordination activities. In response to calls for coordination, UNEP established a Division for Environmental Conventions (DEC) in 1999. This division coordinates the MEAs, tracks inconsistencies in decisions of the COP's and seeks to streamline national reporting on biodiversity-related agreements. UNEP has been convening coordination meetings for secretariats of environmental agreements since 1994. Since 1998, the UN Office in Nairobi (UNON) offers administrative services to the secretariats of multilateral environmental agreements, including personnel and accounting services.

Formally, it appears that there is considerable coordination, but memoranda of understanding and joint web sites do not necessarily say much about the extent to which there is *real* coordination. With its comprehensive framework, the CBD could be a natural focal point for the other institutions within this cluster. The CBD differs from most of the other institutions within the conservation cluster in its strong focus on sustainable use and equitable sharing. UNEP staff agrees that it might have been more logical to see the other MEAs as protocols under this CBD umbrella – but they realize this will never happen.[13] The CBD is itself clear about not aspiring to become an overall framework convention for the biodiversity conservation conventions.[14] In addition, the CBD faces opposition both from other secretariats and from key countries. Part of the blame for the distrust is put on the secretariat of the biodiversity convention itself: CITES complains that they would like to see the CBD as a partner, but fails to achieve this due to arrogance on the part of the CBD Secretariat.[15] Part of the distrust may also stem from CITES projects not getting into the Global Environment Facility's (GEF) portfolio along with CBD projects.[16]

Another important aspect that affects the scope for coordination is the relationship between the MEAs and their conferences of the parties (COPs). Each multilateral environmental agreement maintains its own jurisdiction, each of the conferences of the parties constitute the highest authority for the convention, and the decisions on joint efforts with other multilateral environmental agreements rest with the conferences of the parties (Carstensen 2004). 'We are servants – not in the engine room.'[17] The statement has a wide application as all secretariats of MEAs look to their conferences of the parties for guidance on what to do. The most important action is at the national level. But decisions of conferences of the parties tend to put the secretariats in the crossfire, with a *double bind* message emanating from the very same member states. On one side, there are the specific demands of the member states for ever more detailed reports and on the other hand there is the pressure for more harmonization of reporting systems.

Given the double bind message from the COPs and the interlinked diversity of tasks, the secretariats of MEAs do recognize the need for coordination. But do they want UNEP to provide these services? Part of the answer is that the secretariats of MEAs seem to look more towards their conferences of the parties for guidance, rather than to UNEP. A second rough conclusion is that to the extent that the secretariats recognize a need for coordination, or any other kind of assistance, from UNEP, expectations as to what UNEP can deliver are not very high.

First, UNEP's relation to the MEA secretariats involves both administration and substance. The administrative tasks are performed by the UNON in Nairobi. This is where the heaviest criticism from the secretariats has occurred. The most annoying aspect of their work is excessive red tape and respondents agree that a major problem rests with this body. In effect, many would like the divisions and the secretariats themselves to take on more administrative tasks, rather than leaving it to UNON – and in the case of the secretariat of the biodiversity convention this has been done. The substance has to do with UNEP coordinating the MEAs. Here the scope for UNEP's role is largely influenced by the respective COPs; the multilateral environmental agreements are in general not ready for interference by UNEP. Still, the picture is not all bleak; some secretariats realize the benefits they get from their links with the UN system. There is added recognition stemming from the UN seal, and some staff of secretariats sees themselves as UN international civil servants.[18]

Secondly, to the extent that secretariats recognize a real need for coordination from UNEP, at least some of them do not expect UNEP to be able to deliver, as UNEP organizes workshops and meetings, but little substantial comes out of it. For instance, UNEP failed to consult CITES during the development of national biodiversity strategies. Echoing these views, the CBD would also like to see a more service-oriented UNEP.[19] On a similar note, Ramsar maintains that UNEP could ideally be very effective in coordinating activities on specific issue areas, but fails to play this role. However, the smaller secretariats, such as Ramsar, are in more need of various kinds of assistance from UNEP. Ramsar stresses the need for more streamlining and rationalization, which will help the secretariats to be more outreaching and assisting to the parties: 'UNEP should and could play this role in information and early warning, but is not able to.'[20] This is partly due to lack of financial resources but may also result from insufficient technical expertise and excessive emphasis on administrative matters.[21]

In sum, these are generally grave tidings for UNEP and the sentiments are not just blowing off steam. A major signal is the meeting of the conference of the parties to the biodiversity convention in 2004 that established the aforementioned Biodiversity Liaison Group between CBD, CITES, CMS, Ramsar and WHC, but without UNEP as a member (Decision VII/26). This is clearly a sore point with UNEP, which has acted as a founding father for most of these conventions. How does this relate to our theoretical perspective: what is the 'score' – or the goal achievement – of UNEP in terms of coordination of the biodiversity cluster? In answering this question we have relied primarily on interviews and based on these, the conclusion is quite negative. On a simple scale of high, medium and low, UNEP's degree of effectiveness is tentatively somewhere between low and medium. How do we account for this?

Explanation of performance

This section first analyses the relationship between UNEP and other international organizations somehow involved in the biodiversity conservation cluster. We do not systematically survey all these bodies as only a few illustrative examples will be used.

Many shoppers in the same market

In line with the overall development of MEAs, the biodiversity cluster emerged without a grand master plan – but now there is pressure from donors to coordinate. Through Governing Council decision, UNEP has a mandate to contribute to this cooperation; but does the role and position of UNEP – compared to other agencies – provide room for this?

As noted, UNEP is centrally placed in the biodiversity conservation cluster.[22] Yet while UNEP is certainly very active in this cluster, so are other international organizations. With more than 1,000 staff, 100 of whom are in their headquarters, the IUCN draws its members from states, state agencies, NGOs and personal membership. It has for several decades been heavily involved in the biodiversity conservation cluster. Both Ramsar and WHC have formal links to IUCN in their convention texts. Ramsar is co-located with IUCN in Gland, Switzerland, and has only eight staff members. IUCN supports collaboration between Ramsar and a number of other global environmental conventions, including CBD and CITES. Moreover, the IUCN secretariat and the Ramsar Bureau collaborate on stakeholder involvement in dialogues on the conservation of biological diversity through the Global Biodiversity Forum (GBF).[23] In sum, IUCN plays a significant role in coordinating the biodiversity conservation cluster.

A probably even more important actor is UNDP (and the World Bank) through their collaboration with UNEP as implementing agencies, administering the GEF. The UNEP GEF Coordination Office assists 28 countries in preparing biodiversity action plans and national reports and in accessing the CBD clearing-house mechanism, and 118 countries in preparing national biosafety frameworks. In comparison, UNDP GEF supports some 250 full-size projects and 30 medium-size projects on maintaining sustainable use in 141 countries.[24] To date, more than 3,000 biodiversity-related projects of local NGOs and community-based organizations in 73 countries have been funded through the UNDP GEF Small Grants Programme, totalling over $58 million. UNDP lists biodiversity as one of the six focal points in their Energy and Environment Practice. In sum, through capacity development, knowledge management and policy advice UNDP GEF has directed over $1.9 billion through grants and cost-sharing arrangements to developing countries for biodiversity-related projects. This also encompasses enabling activities to help countries respond to CBD obligations. It is the UNDP's regional bureaux and country offices that undertake biodiversity projects described above. UNDP has country offices in 166 countries in five global regions.

On this basis, what is the relation between UNEP, IUCN and UNDP? As IUCN performs important coordination functions in this cluster, there is a potential for synergy as well as competition and turf battles. In fact, cooperation is most pronounced. The IUCN has entered into cooperation with UNEP on monitoring and assessment. The World Conservation Monitoring Centre was originally set up by IUCN and was later placed under the auspices of UNEP. Neither IUCN nor UNEP consider the relationship as competitive. According to IUCN, the relationship is unproblematic because they have quite similar mandates but different strengths. IUCN has flexibility and UNEP has the intergovernmental mandate.[25] This view is reiterated in UNEP. It is also pointed out how the two are complementary in that they reach out to different clients and thus have a wider combined reach.[26]

There is an interesting potential for synergetic cooperation between UNEP and IUCN as the environmental sustainability issue is increasingly competing with other issues – issues that 'belong' to other international bodies.[27] The link to development has lately introduced a strain in relationships to other relevant actors. That link became manifest in Rio (1992) and was further strengthened at the Johannesburg 2002 Summit.[28] One observer claims that UNEP was strongly opposed to this trend – and in effect that UNEP to an increasing extent has been side-tracked by other UN bodies in the period after Rio.[29] This has resulted in frequent rivalry between UNEP and more development-oriented actors like the GEF and the UNDP – as well as the Commission on Sustainable Development (CSD).[30] A key IUCN source maintains that UNDP is increasing its influence through the mixed environment and development agenda – at the cost of UNEP. More concretely, IUCN would have liked to see UNEP taking the lead in implementing the Millennium Development Goals and the Biodiversity 2010 target – but UNDP dominates this process.[31] According to sources in CITES, UNEP's role has been weakened by the strategic and political decisions to establish Commission on Sustainable Development (CSD) and the GEF.[32] Key UNEP sources take a somewhat different but also realistic view of this situation, admitting that they have to compete with UNDP and the World Bank, especially in capacity building.[33]

However, there are also signs that UNEP is improving its grip on this situation. UNEP is increasing its share of GEF money within the biodiversity issue area. UNEP's GEF Division is also rising to the task – it increased from 2 to 100 staff members from 2001 to 2004 and is now 'fighting' UNDP/GEF over resources. Recently, UNEP and UNDP have concluded a memorandum of understanding (which is outwardly highly praised but judged to be without teeth by internal experts). UNEP is also collaborating increasingly with UNDP through the regional and national offices. According to central actors, UNEP is gradually succeeding in utilizing the UNDP structure through their own use of GEF funding to get footholds 'on the ground'.[34] While the World

Bank has let go quite easily of their National Environmental Action Plans, leaving the floor to UNEP's National Biodiversity Conservation Plans, the UNDP has, however, felt more pressured in this process.[35] The future test of how this tug-of-war turns out will depend very much on how UNEP is able to reorient its focus to the regional and national level. Backing up this tentative conclusion, UNEP is already quite decentralized in that some two-thirds of UNEP staff work at the regional level. UNEP's capacity to perform operatively would hence not seem to be particularly low. In most of our interviews, UNEP staff underlined that regionalization was indispensable to success in the implementation phase.

In sum, the relation with IUCN seems mainly synergetic. They complement each other, and there is probably room for even more cooperation – not least in meeting the emerging challenges from the 'development segment'. The relationship to UNDP is more mixed and by no means all negative. However, UNDP is so much bigger, the sustainability approach strengthens its position, and the fact that it is represented in almost all countries implies that UNEP is far from *the one and only coordinator* in relation to the multilateral environmental agreements. In addition, there are other actors – not least the GEF, illustrating 'the many shoppers in the market' – of which UNEP is only one – and its position is not strengthened by its geographic location and its financial status.

Geographical location and funding situation

Overall, the geographical location of Nairobi has made it more difficult for UNEP to perform its coordination role more generally and in relation to the biodiversity more specifically (cf. also Ivanova, this volume). Some of the problems caused by this are the general efficiency as well as problems of recruiting and keeping experts. As the CSD and GEF are located in New York and Washington DC respectively, this has added to the weakening of UNEP vis-à-vis UNDP and the World Bank. Regarding UNEP in relation to the distribution of the multilateral environmental agreements, the geographical distribution of biodiversity cluster headquarters is almost complete, but none of them is very close to Nairobi.[36] On a positive note, the Nairobi location provided for a very strong support for UNEP among developing countries, especially in the early period. In itself it was extremely important to make the Group of 77 realize that environmental problems were also relevant for them (Najam 2005). That is, the location may contribute to lower effectiveness, but increase legitimacy for the large majority of states in the world – an often neglected point in effectiveness analyses (Andresen and Hey 2005).

To some extent, UNEP may compensate for lack of control and large geographical distances through the regional offices and through appointing the central staff of the secretariats belonging to UNEP. Concerning the regional trend, the UNEP Division for Regional Conventions is now the second largest within UNEP, next to its Division of the Global Environment Facility (DGEF), and it is important in enhancing implementation. The division notices a greater recognition of UNEP within the UNDP structure in that UNEP provides added value.[37] Appointment of central staff also provides potential control, but such means of control are not always welcome by the secretariats, because such appointments are sometimes perceived to be more politically rather than professionally based. Overall the location weakens the coordinating abilities of UNEP – although there are some positive as well as mitigating factors (cf. also Ivanova, this volume).

It is widely agreed that UNEP has a very weak and unstable financial basis, even according to UN standards. This is a major point among analysts when they explain the weak performance of UNEP, linked also to the discussion of whether UNEP should be given status as a *specialized agency*. We shall not go into this debate here, but a few words on UNEP's finances are warranted.[38] After a short-lived growth around Rio 1992, support was again reduced, while it has increased somewhat under the leadership of Töpfer. Yet the overall economic picture is still rather bleak. There is also a growing trend among donors to control more of the budget as they do not trust UNEP to administer funds effectively. The GEF has increased the capacity of UNEP as it is one of the three implementing agencies but compared to the two others, UNEP is the 'little brother' (Heggelund *et al.* 2005). However, the main challenge for UNEP is that the dominant actors for various reasons do *not* want to give UNEP a financially stronger role.[39]

More recently the need for partnerships between business, green NGOs and public authorities has been underlined as a way to increase environmental funding. There are various opinions on the role of these new ventures (Najam 1999; Andonova and Levy 2003), but increased business involvement is one potential way to increase funding. The World Business Council for Sustainable Development (WBCSD), a coalition of 170 international companies, is cooperating with IUCN on biodiversity (WBCSD 1997). However representatives of the WBCSD preferred collaboration with NGOs, as NGOs provided good accountability and UNEP was regarded as close to invisible and irrelevant by the WBCSD.[40] This view to some extent is substantiated by environmental NGOs as WWF agrees that working with NGOs and business is much quicker than working through the UNEP.[41]

Thus, the funding situation of UNEP is weak, primarily due to the lacking willingness of the member states to change this situation. The weak financial basis clearly reduces the coordinating capacity of UNEP. However, this is not only a question of lacking economic resources.

The organization and bureaucratic culture of UNEP

The MEAs are not very open for interference by UNEP as they regard their COPs as the legitimate source of policy advice. At the same time, UNEP's Governing Council has decided that UNEP shall coordinate the multilateral environmental agreements. As one of our interviewees in UNEP put it, 'this is not an easy process'.[42]

First, a major difficulty seems to stem from the internal organization of UNEP. Töpfer introduced reorganization from issue-specific to a functional division of labour between the UNEP divisions. This may have solved some problems, but according to our respondents, new problems appeared, as responsibility for each issue became split between all divisions. UNEP divisions fight among themselves to get credit for projects; they all have separate budgets and hence they are unable to cooperate on projects.[43] In some instances, the divisions also hamper the optimal utilization of technical expertise in an issue area, as staff have become spread out between them. Also, the strong growth of UNEP's GEF division has not only had positive implications for UNEP. It has become rather dominant and unruly and other divisions have not benefited from this development.

Second, the most widespread explanation for lacking success is that UNEP keeps failing to ask the right service-oriented question of 'What can we do for you?' Instead UNEP still keeps up the old top-down strategy of concocting plans for the MEAs that they do not need and do not want. In other words, UNEP is stuck in the initiation phase as the founding father and has so far been unable to enter the implementation phase as the multilateral environmental agreement has reached adulthood.[44]

This perceived lack of service-orientation may also stem from the bureaucratic culture in UNEP. Most of the MEA secretariats have limited staff. UNEP therefore provides specialized support, such as media support, and this is perceived as positive.[45] However, a lot of time goes to red tape and detail questions. UNEP staff are very much ready to agree that the relationship between UNEP and secretariats is often constrained by red tape and that UNEP should reduce this type of activity.[46] We are not in a position to judge whether this level of bureaucracy is unavoidable – considering it is a small UN body located in a developing country. However, based on the interviews, the bureaucratic culture of UNEP is perceived to weaken its ability to coordinate the MEAs. Differences between some of the more technically oriented MEAs like CITES and the more policy-oriented UNEP is also said to provide problems of coordination.

Our interviews in Nairobi indicate that UNEP in all divisions and at most levels of the organization is acutely aware of the need to turn from a top-down to a bottom-up approach. Many focused on the red tape in administrative functions and said that something should be done about UNON. Yet the service on substantive issues was also greatly criticized. From some of our respondents (who preferred anonymity), we have chosen a few citations: 'An impediment is the bureaucratic culture in UNEP, which dissuades creativity.' 'We do not accomplish much. We must be more service-oriented!' 'We have got the message: People are fed up with our turf wars.'[47]

In sum, major internal challenges for UNEP are its fragmented responsibility across divisions and the bureaucratic red tape. Based on our sources there is unanimity both inside and outside UNEP that it must turn from a top-down to a bottom-up approach to become more service-oriented. Such (seeming) consensus may pave the way for gradual changes in this direction. Yet considering the top-down and less than open culture in UNEP itself, this will probably take time. UNEP has been very successful in terms of agenda setting and regime formation, but this has become less important over time. New challenges of the implementation phase call for a more regional and national approach, and key respondents are aware of this. UNEP is already quite decentralized and this may be an advantage from this point of view. However, the strong position of some of the regional offices – in contrast to the rather weak position of the headquarter in Nairobi – may pose internal problems of coordination in UNEP itself. Difficult priorities both internally and externally are needed if UNEP is to be able to redirect its roles and functions more in this direction.[48]

Conclusion

UNEP is a small international organization with very limited resources, and few outside the UN bureaucracy and the relevant research community have heard about it. We know that more visible and resourceful UN organizations have not been able to perform very effectively.[49] Thus, expectations should be modest as to what can be accomplished by UNEP, a fact often forgotten in both the UN and the research community. In this chapter we have not attempted to comprehensively evaluate UNEP. Rather, we have taken one specific part of the mandate of UNEP, coordination, and looked upon this in relation to the biodiversity cluster. Effectiveness was conceived of in terms of goal achievement. Based primarily on extensive interviews we concluded that UNEP was quite some way from achieving this goal. However, the secretariats of the smaller multilateral environmental agreements were more satisfied with the role of UNEP than the bigger ones. This may point to a more structural problem facing UNEP as it has traditionally been well equipped as a 'founding father' for new institutions, but has not really been able to keep the 'children in the nest when they are ready to fly', as one respondent put it.[50] In short, to create new institutions is usually not very controversial, but mature and growing institutions simply do not want to be controlled or coordinated. Still, UNEP's score regarding coordination is quite low. We explain this by three factors. First, although UNEP is *formally* the main coordinating actor, there are other relevant actors that have more resources and also very relevant competence. There are examples of synergies, not the least between UNEP and IUCN, but turf battles are more prominent, and UNEP has not profited from the stronger link between environment and the development. Second, UNEP's location as well as its strained funds explains modest performance. Third, internal organization and bureaucratic culture have also contributed to the rather modest score in terms of coordination.

These perceptions are to a large extent shared also by our respondents in UNEP's headquarters in Nairobi.

In line with our theoretical perspective, this does not mean that all would have been well within the biodiversity cluster if UNEP had been more effective. The main reason for success or failure of these multilateral environmental agreements can be found elsewhere, but a more effective UNEP could have contributed to enhancing the problem-solving capacity of this cluster. This somewhat gloomy conclusion does not mean that the work of UNEP in this regard is useless. To use the traditional counterfactual reasoning, we think most of these MEAs are somewhat better off due to the efforts of UNEP. The most important question, however, is whether UNEP could have done any better, given all the above-mentioned constraints, through clever institutional design. The most frequently mentioned remedy is to provide for an improved and more stable financial basis. We believe this is probably not at present a feasible alternative. What about moving UNEP to Bonn or New York and applying purely merit systems of recruitment and fire and hire like in Microsoft? This may have increased effectiveness, but UNEP is part of 'real world UN' and such major changes are hardly possible. However, we do think there is potential for improvements even within the present realities. Some of them we have hinted at, like concentrating more resources in terms of bottom-up think tank assistance and scrapping the old top-down culture. Also, UNEP needs to focus more on the main challenge in global environmental governance today, namely implementation on the ground. True, UNEP is no major operative body and cannot, and should not, have offices in most countries like UNDP. Still, there is an important niche where UNEP can assist countries through its considerable experience and expertise in environmental management.

Notes

1 See Victor *et al.* 1998; Young 1999; Miles *et al.* 2002. The most comprehensive effort on interaction so far is Oberthür and Gehring 2006.
2 The most systematic effort has been the MANUS Project (Biermann and Siebenhüner 2008).
3 A comprehensive overview of the various positions has been presented by Biermann 2002, Biermann and Bauer 2005 and Mee 2005.
4 For a discussion of the position of various schools of thought in relation to international organizations, see Bauer 2006.
5 This observation is based on findings from the most comprehensive study of environmental regime effectiveness that we are aware of so far, Miles *et al.* 2002.
6 For a discussion on the role of secretariats more generally as well their role in specific regimes, see Bauer 2006 and Andresen and Skjærseth 1999.
7 We do not argue that this holds for all IEOs. It may for example be different for the IMO, being more of an operative body.
8 We sent our main questions to the respondents beforehand. The interviews were semi-structured and in most cases the interviewees were very open. As some of the questions were of quite a delicate political nature, however, some respondents chose to remain anonymous while most accepted openness.

9 See e.g. Rosendal 2001a and 2001b on different clusters involving the CBD.
10 <http://www.biodiv.org/convention/partners-websites.asp>
11 We have not looked systematically at the roles of CMS and WHC.
12 For a detailed overview, see Rosendal and Andresen 2003.
13 Interview with NN, UNEP Information Unit for Conventions (UNEP/IUC), Geneva, 25 September 2003.
14 Interview with NN, CBD Secretariat, Montreal, 16 March 2004.
15 Interview with NN2, CITES Secretariat, Geneva, 24 September 2003.
16 Interview with NN2, CITES Secretariat, Geneva, 24 September 2003.
17 Interview with NN, Ramsar, 6 September 2004.
18 Interview with NN2, CITES Secretariat, Geneva, 24 September 2003.
19 Interview with NN, CBD Secretariat, Montreal, 16 March 2004.
20 Interview with NN, Ramsar, 6 September 2004.
21 For example, CITES was able to bring about the improved management of shared sturgeon species which is something UNEP had tried to do for a number of years. Interview with NN2, CITES Secretariat, Geneva, 24 September 2003.
22 For an overview of the various formal coordinating roles of UNEP in this cluster, see Rosendal and Andresen 2003.
23 Based on data from YBICED 2003/2004 (Thommessen and Stokke (2003/4)).
24 To learn more, visit <http://www.undp.org/gef> and <http://www.undp.org/biodiversity>
25 Interview with Martha Chouchena, Head of Policy, Biodiversity and International Agreements Unit, IUCN, 23 September 2003.
26 Interview with NN, UNEP Information Unit for Conventions (UNEP/IUC), Geneva, 25 September 2003.
27 Interview with Martha Chouchena, Head of Policy, Biodiversity and International Agreements Unit, IUCN, 23 September 2003.
28 The traditional preservation ideology basically believes in protecting species and ecosystems from mankind by establishing nature reserves. The introduction of the concept of environmental sustainability may be regarded as an effort to revive focus on the long-term links between environment and development.
29 Corroborated by interviews in the Climate Change Secretariat, 23 October 2003.
30 For an analysis of the effectiveness of CSD, see Kaasa 2005.
31 Interview with Martha Chouchena, Head of Policy, Biodiversity and International Agreements Unit, IUCN, 23 September 2003.
32 Interview with NN2, CITES Secretariat, Geneva, 24 September 2003.
33 The establishment of the GEF was more important, as it took away the role that was intended for UNEP. 'UNEP got a smaller part of the bigger pie.' Interview with Michael Williams, UNEP Information Unit for Conventions (UNEP/IUC), Geneva, 25 September 2003.
34 Interviews with Petter Johan Schei, FNI (January 2005); NN1 and NN2, DGEF, UNEP, Nairobi, November 2004.
35 Interview with NN1, DGEF, UNEP, Nairobi, November 2004.
36 For an overview, see Rosendal and Andresen 2003.
37 Interview with Zhijia Wang, Deputy Director, Division of Regional Cooperation and Monika Wehrle-MacDevette, DRC, Nairobi, Kenya 25 November 2004.
38 For a detailed overview of the development of the financial status of UNEP, see Mee 2005.
39 For example, UNEP worked hard to gain control over the ozone fund, but it was placed in Montreal – with no UNEP control whatsoever.
40 Interview with James Griffiths, Director, Sustainable Forest Products Industry and Biodiversity, World Business Council for Sustainable Development, Geneva, 26 September 2003.

41 Interview with Aimee Gonzales, Senior Policy Advisor to WWF, Gland, 6 September 2004.
42 Interview with NN, DEC Interlinkages and synergies, UNEP, November 2004.
43 Interview with NN, Atmosphere and Desertification Convention Units, DEC, UNEP, Nairobi, Kenya 23 November 2004.
44 Interviews with NN, DEC, DECI, DGEF, Nairobi, Kenya 23 November 2004.
45 Interview with NN, UNEP Information Unit for Conventions (UNEP/IUC), Geneva, 25 September 2003.
46 'They do have a point though – when any request for home leave needs to be approved in Nairobi, we do need to remove some of those irritants. We also need to recognize that UNEP's strengths are not on general administration'. Interview with NN, UNEP Information Unit for Conventions (UNEP/IUC), Geneva, 25 September 2003.
47 Interviews with NN, DEC, DECI, DGEF, Nairobi, Kenya 23 November 2004.
48 Interviews with NN (DEC; Interlinkages and Synergies), NN (Regional Office of Africa to UNEP), NN1 and NN2 (DGEF), Zhijia Wang and Monika Wehrle-MacDevette (DRC), NN (DEC and DEPI), NN (DEC), and NN (headquarters).
49 WHO is a one example of a UN body with low effectiveness during most of the 1990s, not least due to weak leadership (Andresen 2002).
50 Interview with NN, UNEP Information Unit for Conventions (UNEP/IUC), Geneva, 25 September 2003.

References

Andonova, L.B. and Levy, M.A. (2003) 'Franchising Global Governance: Making Sense of the Johannesburg Type II Partnership', *Yearbook of International Cooperation on Environment and Development:* 19–32.
Andresen, S. (2002) 'Leadership Change in the World Health Organisation: Potential for Increased Effectiveness?', *FNI Report 08/2002*, Lysaker: FNI.
Andresen, S. and Hey, E. (2005) 'The Effectiveness and Legitimacy of International Environmental Institutions', *International Environmental Agreements*, 5(3) 2005: 211–26.
Andresen, S. and Skjærseth, J.B (1999) *Background Paper to the UNU Conference,* Lysaker: CICERO.
Andresen, S. and Wettestad, J. (1995) 'International Problem Solving Effectiveness: The Oslo Project Story so far', *International Environmental Affairs*, 7: 127–49.
Andresen, S., Skodvin, T., Underdal, A. and Wettestad, J. (2000) *Science and Politics in International Environmental Regimes between Integrity and Involvement*, Manchester: Manchester University Press.
Arts, B. (1998) *The Political Influence of Global NGOs. Case Studies on the Climate and Biodiversity Conventions*, Utrecht: International Books.
Bauer, S. (2006) 'Does Bureaucracy Really Matter? The Authority of Intergovernmental Treaty Secretariats in Global Environmental Politics', *Global Environmental Politics*, 6(1): 23–49.
Bernauer, T. (1995) 'The Effect of International Environmental Institutions: How We Might Learn More', *International Organizations*, 49(2): 351–77.
Biermann, F. (2002) 'Strengthening Green Global Governance in a Disparate World Society. Would a World Environment Organisation Benefit the South?', *International Environmental Agreements: Politics, Law and Economics*, 2: 297–315.
Biermann F. and Bauer, S. (2004) 'Assessing the Effectiveness of Intergovernmental

Organisations in International Environmental Politics', *Global Environmental Change*, 14: 189–93.

Biermann, F. and Bauer, S. (2005) (eds) *A World Environmental Organisation: Solution or Threat for Effective International Environmental Governance*, Aldershot, UK and Burlington, VT: Ashgate.

Biermann, F. and Siebenhüner, B. (2008) (eds) *Managers of Global Change. Explaining the Influence of International Environmental Bureaucracies*, Cambridge, MA: MIT Press (forthcoming).

Carstensen, J. (2004) 'EC Environmental Law and Multilateral Environmental Agreements for Europe', UNITAR paper on the EU environmental *acquis*.

Heggelund, G., Andresen, S. and Ying, S. (2005) 'Performance of the Global Environmental Facility (GEF) in China: Achievements and Challenges as Seen by the Chinese', *International Environmental Agreements: Politics, Law and Economics*: 323–48.

Kaasa, S. (2005) 'The Commission on Sustainable Development', *FNI Report 5/2005*, Lysaker: FNI.

Mitchell, R. (2002) 'International Environment', in Risse, T., Simmons, B.A. and Carlsnaer, W. (eds) *Handbook of International Relations*, London: Sage Publications.

Mee, L. (2005) 'The Role of UNEP and UNDP in Multilateral Environmental Agreements', *International Environmental Agreements*, 5(3): 227–63.

Miles, E.L., Underdal, A. Andresen, S., Wettestad, J., Skjærseth, J.B. and Carlin, E.M. (2002) *Environmental Regime Effectiveness: Confronting Theory with Evidence*, Cambridge, MA: MIT Press.

Najam, A. (1999) 'World Business Council for Sustainable Development: The Greening of Business or a Greenwash?', in Bergesen, H.O., Parmann, G. and Thommessen, Ø.B. (eds) *Yearbook of International Co-operation on Environment and Development 1999/2000*, London: Earthscan.

Najam, A. (2003) 'The Case against a New International Environmental Organization', *Global Governance*, 9(3): 367–84.

Najam, A. (2005) 'Developing Countries and Global Environmental Governance: From Contestation to Participation and Engagement', *International Environmental Agreements*, 5(3): 303–21.

Oberthür, S. (2002) 'Clustering of Multilateral Environmental Agreements: Potentials and Limitations', *International Environmental Agreements*, 2: 317–40.

Oberthür, S. and Gehring, T. (2006) *Institutional Interaction in International and EU International Environmental Governance*, Cambridge, MA: MIT Press.

Rosendal, G.K. (2001a) 'Impacts of Overlapping International Regimes: The Case of Biodiversity', *Global Governance*, 7: 95–117.

Rosendal G.K. (2001b) 'Overlapping International Regimes: The Forum on Forests (IFF) between Climate Change and Biodiversity', *International Environmental Agreements: Politics, Law and Economics*, 1(4): 447–68.

Rosendal, G.K. and Andresen, S. (2003) 'UNEP's role in Enhancing Problem-Solving Capacity in Multilateral Environmental Agreements: Coordination and Assistance in the Biodiversity Conservation Cluster', *FNI Report 10/2003*, Lysaker: FNI.

Thommessen, Ø.B. and Stokke, O.S. (eds) (2003/04) *Yearbook of International Cooperation on Environment and Development*, Lysaker and London: The Fridtjof Nansen Institute and Earthscan.

Victor, D. (1999) 'The Market of International Environmental Protection Services and the Perils of Coordination', background paper at the UNU Tokyo 1999 Conference.

Victor, D., Raustiala, K. and Skolnikoff, E. (eds) (1998) *The Implementation and Effectiveness of International Environmental Commitments*, Cambridge MA: MIT Press.

Wettestad, J. (1999) *Designing Effective International Regimes: The Key Conditions*, Cheltenham, UK: Edward Elgar.

World Business Council for Sustainable Development (WBCSD) (1997) *Business and Biodiversity: A Guide for the Private Sector*, report written with International Union for Conservation of Nature and Natural Resources (IUCN), Geneva: WBCSD, IUCN.

Young, O.R. (ed.) (1999) *The Effectiveness of International Environmental Regimes*, Cambridge, MA: MIT Press.

8 UNEP as anchor organization for the global environment

Maria Ivanova[1]

Introduction

In the context of increasing ecological, economic and political interdependence, international organizations have evolved from simple mechanisms for state cooperation to central actors in world politics and active agents of global change. However, while the number of institutions, policies and programmes charged with stewardship of the global commons has risen dramatically over the last thirty years, the state of the global environment continues to show negative trends and increasing risks (Speth 2004; Berruga and Maurer 2006). As a result, scholars and politicians alike have called for measures to strengthen the global environmental governance system (Esty and Ivanova 2002b; Speth 2003, 2004; Desai 2004; Kanie and Haas 2004) and, in turn, transform the United Nations Environment Programme (UNEP) into a more powerful global environmental organization.[2]

Contemporary reform initiatives for environmental governance have focused on UNEP to a great extent – some suggesting fairly modest changes such as the proposal by the French and German governments to establish a UN Environment Organization (UNEO) and others offering a more comprehensive reform agenda like the proposals for a WEO (World Environment Organization), GEO (Global Environmental Organization) and GEM (Global Environmental Mechanism).[3] Institutional reform, however, must ultimately be rooted in an understanding of where and why UNEP has succeeded and failed in order to identify leverage points for improved effectiveness, efficiency and equity.

Currently, the debate on global environmental governance reform has artificially divided the environmental governance academic community into 'friends' and 'foes' of UNEP, rather than opening analytical avenues for constructive critique and refinement of theoretical assumptions. Analysts of UNEP offer a wide range of opinions regarding the effectiveness of the organization. It is considered by some as 'one of the most impressive UN organizations in terms of its actual achievements' (Najam 2001), 'relatively effective' (Conca 1995 cited in Najam 2003) and 'given its mandate, its resources and its authority . . . a remarkable success' (von Moltke 1996). It is also characterized as 'relatively obsolete, eclipsed in resources and prestige' (Haas 2004), 'under-funded, over-loaded and remote' (ibid.), a 'peanut-sized' (Speth 2002) 'weak agency' (von Moltke 1996) with 'wasted scarce resources [and] a credibility gap' (United Nations 1997). Yet, as Bauer and Biermann have found, few of the normative statements are grounded in systematic evidence and '[b]oth proponents and opponents of a world environment organization [have] had to build their arguments in most cases on the basis of personal experiences, theoretical deliberation and normative visions, rather than on the findings of empirically-based research' (Biermann and Bauer 2005).

In this chapter, I evaluate UNEP's performance more systematically by examining the core functions UNEP performs as an anchor organization. Anchor organizations are the primary, though not the only, international organizations in a global issue area. They typically perform three main functions: (1) overseeing the monitoring, assessment and reporting on the state of the issue in their purview; (2) setting an agenda for action and managing the process of determining standards, policies and guidelines; and (3) developing institutional capacity to address existing and emerging problems (Figure 8.1). Anchor organizations define the problems, develop new policy ideas and programmes, manage crises and set priorities for shared activities that would not exist otherwise (Barnett and Finnemore 2004: 156).

The analysis thus focuses on UNEP's performance in monitoring and assessment, agenda-setting and policy processes, and capacity development,

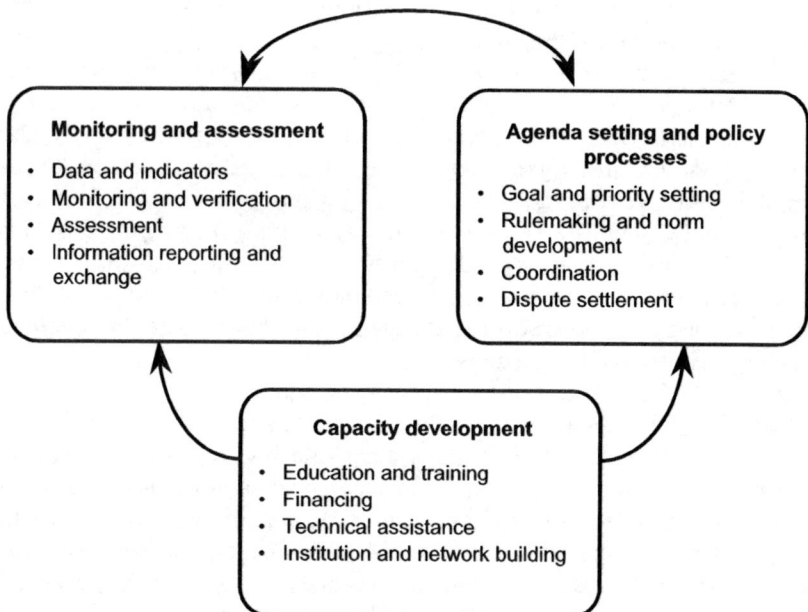

Monitoring and assessment

- Data and indicators
- Monitoring and verification
- Assessment
- Information reporting and exchange

Agenda setting and policy processes

- Goal and priority setting
- Rulemaking and norm development
- Coordination
- Dispute settlement

Capacity development

- Education and training
- Financing
- Technical assistance
- Institution and network building

Figure 8.1 Main functions for an anchor organization.

and concludes that UNEP's performance is mixed. While the organization was set up as the anchor in global environmental governance, it has not been able to meet all such expectations for a number of reasons. I identify four key factors that have limited UNEP's ability to fulfil its mandate: formal status, governance, financing structure, and location. In the context of current political processes for UN reform in the international environmental governance arena, this analysis seeks to glean lessons for the architects of the environmental governance system for the twenty-first century.

UNEP's performance as an anchor organization

UNEP was created in 1972 as the core – or anchor organization – for the global environment to gather and transmit information, catalyse action and coordinate environmental activities within the UN system. UNEP was established in response to a common understanding that 'the work in the field of environment needed a common outlook and direction' (Rydbeck 1972) and that it was necessary to create

> a central coordinating mechanism in the United Nations to provide political and conceptual leadership, to contemplate methods of avoiding or reducing global environmental risks, of working out joint norms and of avoiding or settling conflicts between states on environmental matters. This coordinating mechanism needed to be given enough authority and resources to ensure effective co-ordination of ongoing and planned activities.
>
> (Rydbeck 1972)

Over the years, however, international environmental responsibilities have spread across multiple organizations, including UNEP and close to a dozen other UN bodies (such as the Commission for Sustainable Development, the World Meteorological Organization, the Food and Agriculture Organization, the UN Educational, Scientific and Cultural Organization, and others). Adding to this fragmentation are the independent secretariats and governing bodies of the numerous environmental conventions. The practical result has been a series of jurisdictional overlaps, gaps and 'treaty congestion' (Brown Weiss 1995) leading to unproductive duplication, competition and waste of scarce resources.

By contrast, other international collective action issues such as trade, health or labour concerns have fairly well-developed and coherent organizational structure anchored in an international organization (WTO, WHO and ILO respectively). In the global environmental domain, no one organization is perceived to be 'the authority' in environmental matters and no one organization is considered to be 'in authority' to ensure coherence and effectiveness in the system. Barnett and Finnemore (2004) distinguish between being 'an authority' and 'in authority' as the two key aspects of power for international organizations. An organization is 'an authority' when it is perceived as an expert in its particular domain (for example, the WHO is an authority on global public health). An organization is 'in authority' when its rational-legal status has empowered it to perform certain functions (for example, UNHCR is in authority to protect refugees within certain legal parameters).

UNEP's mandate, defined as too broad by some and too narrow by others (von Moltke 2001b; Iwama 2004; Bauer and Biermann 2005),[4] has stayed clear and relatively focused on four core functions over the last three decades: (1) monitoring, assessment and early warning; (2) developing international norms, standards and policies; (3) coordinating the environmental activities of the UN system; and (4) building national institutional capacity. These functions clearly fall within the three categories of anchor organization responsibilities as illustrated in Figure 8.2.

In this chapter, I assess UNEP's existing role and future potential as an anchor organization for the global environment by examining the organization's performance in the three core roles of an anchor organization: (1) monitoring and assessment, (2) agenda-setting and managing policy processes, and (3) capacity development.

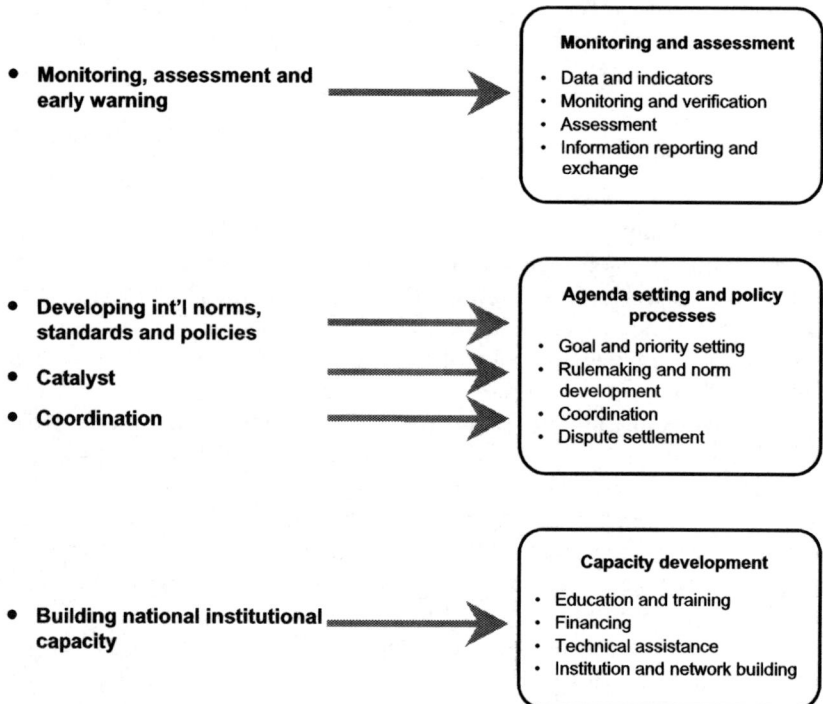

- **Monitoring, assessment and early warning**

Monitoring and assessment
- Data and indicators
- Monitoring and verification
- Assessment
- Information reporting and exchange

- **Developing int'l norms, standards and policies**
- **Catalyst**
- **Coordination**

Agenda setting and policy processes
- Goal and priority setting
- Rulemaking and norm development
- Coordination
- Dispute settlement

- **Building national institutional capacity**

Capacity development
- Education and training
- Financing
- Technical assistance
- Institution and network building

Figure 8.2 Functions of UNEP's mandate and anchor organizations.

Monitoring and assessment

UNEP was established to 'keep under review the world environmental situation' and 'promote the contribution of the relevant international scientific and other professional communities to the acquisition, assessment and exchange of environmental knowledge and information' (UN 1972a). In the area of monitoring and surveillance UNEP is expected to 'provide policy advice, early warning information on environmental threats and to catalyze and promote international cooperation and action, based on the best scientific and technical capabilities available' (UNEP 1997b). UNEP does not perform any direct monitoring and surveillance of its own. Rather, it collects, collates, analyses and integrates data from UN agencies and other organizations – including convention secretariats, universities, science institutes and non-governmental organizations – to form broader environmental assessments.

UNEP is considered relatively effective in its assessment of global environmental issues (Haas 2004). Its flagship environmental assessment publication, the *Global Environmental Outlook* (GEO), has been recognized as 'one of the two most respected environmental outlook publications currently available' (UNEP 2005c: 11). The GEO process has become an important model to develop and improve the scientific credibility, political relevance and legitimacy of UNEP's assessment function (UNEP 2005f: 12). The GEO uses an approach based on collaborating centres, involving universities, research centres, international institutes and non-governmental organizations in 30 countries representing regions around the world. It also employs a periodic review process through an online user survey soliciting external feedback and an informal, self-reflective internal review.

This 'comprehensive global state of the environment report' (UNEP/ GRID-Arendal 2005) has been widely cited as useful for identifying major emerging environmental issues and for placing national issues in a broader perspective, raising the awareness of policy-makers, scientists and the general public on the large-scale processes and trends regarding the global environment. The most important contribution of the GEO process has been in influencing policy formulation, catalysing action and developing institutional capacity. Regional governmental forums and national governments have adopted GEO methodology for the production and improvement of their state of the environment reporting. In countries where no such reporting was carried out (Barbados, Cameroon, Congo, Costa Rica, Cuba, Gabon, Ghana, Peru and Senegal, among others) the GEO process has catalysed national State of the Environment reports. Several collaborating centres reported that participation in the GEO process has improved the quality of products and services offered, increased satisfaction among centre stakeholders and enhanced their credibility and reputation. In some centres it has also helped to develop new skills and knowledge for staff members and to attract additional staff. It is important to note, however, that these are self-reported trends. A more accurate measure of enhanced credibility and reputation would be through a survey of change in perception by organizations working with the UNEP collaborating centres.

One of the GEO's key limitations is the lack of comparative data across countries. While the report provides comprehensive information by issue and geographic area, it does not show the comparative performances of countries around the world in addressing environmental challenges. The data, therefore, are not used to their full capacity for informing policy decisions. As an intergovernmental organization, UNEP has faced political pressure from countries to not include cross-country comparisons. UNDP, however, has tackled that challenge and its *Human Development Report* is a highly acclaimed publication. Recent efforts at developing environmental sustainability indicators illustrate the power of comparison across jurisdictions. For example, the Environmental Sustainability Index (ESI) and Environmental Performance Index (EPI), developed by the Yale Center for Environmental Law and Policy and the Center for International Earth Science Information Network (CIESIN) at Columbia University, benchmark the ability of nations to protect the environment.[5] With 76 data sets compiled into 21 indicators, the Environmental Sustainability Index ranks 146 countries in environmental stewardship, allowing comparison across a range of issues. The Environmental Performance Index employs a distance-to-target approach to gauge a country's current performance on the major components of environmental health and ecosystem vitality. Measuring environmental quality in absolute terms is arguably impossible. But relative measures are achievable. National governments find it useful to compare their performance with that of others that are similarly situated. Identifying leaders and laggards pressures under-performing countries to improve results. No country scores very high or very low on all indicators. Therefore, 'every society has something to learn from benchmarking its environmental performance against relevant peer countries' (Esty *et al.* 2005: 2). UNEP is the natural forum for creating a coherent international system for environmental information and assessment. It offers the advantage of building on an existing organization with a clear mandate to serve as an information clearing-house and with a relatively strong scientific track record. UNEP's work, however, has not yet become the standard for quality, relevance, timeliness and accessibility.

While the GEO process and outputs are notable, a number of strategic challenges remain and improvements are necessary to enhance UNEP's monitoring and assessment function. Fragmentation and the resulting duplication among UNEP's various monitoring and assessment activities have prevented it from becoming the anchor organization for the environment. Inadequate quality of incoming and outgoing information lead to unreliable output and relevance (UNEP 2004a: 13). Missing data limit UNEP's ability to compile complete international environmental assessments, draw conclusions and make scientifically based policy recommendations, sometimes compromising the credibility of its work (UNEP 2004a: 23). In the GEO process these problems are largely due to the lack of sufficient capacity and resource constraints. Methodological issues related to data management and analysis, indicator development and integrated policy analysis have also further hampered information quality. Addressing many of today's pressing environmental issues requires integrating socio-economic factors with more traditional environmental science data, thus creating a demand for a more comprehensive approach and extensive institutional capacity in both the contributing and receiving organizations. Therefore, while UNEP has made significant improvements in providing information about its work to the public, significant institutional investment is required to enhance this core function.

Agenda-setting and managing policy processes

A second core function of an anchor organization is agenda-setting and management of intergovernmental processes to address critical issues and to gain agreement on standards, policies and guidelines. UNEP was designed as an advocacy organization at the international level. It was expected to be proactive and set the global agenda by identifying emerging concerns and galvanizing action around them from government, international organizations, NGOs and business. Setting goals and priorities and coordinating efforts for their attainment have, however, been problematic for UNEP.

UNEP's anchor role also demands that it serves as the centre of gravity in a complex system of international environmental governance. Resolution 2997 of 1972 clearly outlined UNEP's coordination function to 'provide general policy guidance for the direction and co-ordination of environmental programmes within the United Nations system' (United Nations 1972a) and endowed the organization with specific institutional mechanisms by establishing an Environmental Coordination Board.[6] With the increasing number of treaties and organizations responsible for their administration, coordination of overlapping efforts has emerged as an issue of paramount importance. UNEP has not succeeded in becoming the central forum for debate and deliberation in the environmental field, like the WTO for trade or the WHO for health. Moreover, in contrast to other international organizations, including the International Maritime Organization, the International Labour Organization and the UN Economic Commission for Europe, UNEP has not been able to provide an organizational home for the conventions that have emerged under its aegis. This fragmentation of policy processes, however, has had a largely detrimental impact on the effectiveness of global environmental governance (Bernstein and Ivanova 2006).

Some analysts have called UNEP a victim of its own success since most multilateral environmental agreements came into existence as a result of UNEP's catalytic role. In the last thirty years, UNEP has played a highly regarded lead role in establishing an extensive system of international environmental law (Haas 2004) through the creation of conventions and soft-law guidelines for a wide range of sectors. Despite the successful creation of international agreements, 'the flourishing of new international institutions poses problems of coordination, eroding responsibilities and resulting in duplication of work as well as increased demand upon ministries and government' (United Nations 1998). Once launched, the conventions became autonomous entities – each with its own conference of the parties, secretariat and associated subsidiary bodies that have autonomous influence often exceeding that of UNEP.

UNEP has undertaken efforts at greater coherence and coordination of the numerous conventions but with limited success. For example, UNEP initiated a process of harmonization of reporting requirements for the five biodiversity-related conventions (Convention on Biological Diversity, CITES, Convention on Migratory Species, the Ramsar Convention on Wetlands and the World Heritage Convention) and the two regional seas conventions with biodiversity related protocols (Barcelona and the Cartagena Conventions). While a common website and a biodiversity clearing-house mechanism have been established, there has been little substantive progress toward the practical implementation of a common reporting framework.

Coordination of the environmental activities of international organizations has also posed a significant challenge. The constant creation, abolishment and recreation of coordination mechanisms to assist UNEP in this anchor role illustrate the magnitude of the problem. The Environmental Coordination Board was established in 1972 by General Assembly Resolution 2997. In 1977, General Assembly Resolution 32/197 on the restructuring of the economic and social sectors of the United Nations merged the Environmental Coordination Board under the Administrative Committee on Co-ordination (ACC). Subsequently, each agency assigned a Designated Official on Environment Matters (DOEM) to coordinate environmental activities with the executive director of UNEP. In 1995, UNEP abolished the DOEM and substituted the Inter-Agency Environment Management Group (IAEMG). This group only met twice and was replaced by the Environment Management Group (EMG) in 1999. The EMG has not yet lived up to its potential as a joint coordinating body within the UN system largely independent of UNEP.

Four key reasons help to explain the coordination challenge. First, the explosion in the number of international organizations has overwhelmed the series of UNEP-driven coordination bodies and mechanisms, which have yielded few results. As often pointed out by UN officials, 'everyone wants to coordinate but no one wants to be coordinated.' Second, other UN bodies have refused to accept UNEP's mandate to coordinate all environmental activities in the UN system due to 'institutional seniority'. A number of UN bodies (ILO, FAO, UNESCO, WHO, WMO, IMCO, IAEA, ICAO and UNDP) possessed environmental responsibilities before UNEP was created and thus feel less of a need to defer to UNEP. Third, the fear of losing certain parts of one's work programme, budget and staff if duplication were eliminated leads agencies to jealously guard their 'sovereignty' without a view of the broader public good. Fourth, UNEP's approach to coordination was perceived as controlling and threatening. For example, UNEP's earliest heavy-handed attempts (mid- to late 1970s) at coordination drove the WMO to send out a memo warning others of 'this upstart agency's plans to take over everyone's work'. This has led to strained relations and turf wars among the agencies, compromising UNEP's role as an anchor organization with the mandate to manage broader policy processes. Subsequently, 'UNEP could no more be expected to "coordinate" the system-wide activities of the UN than could a medieval monarch "coordinate" his feudal barons' (Imber 1993: 83 cited in Najam 2003).

The existence of a clear and coherent institutional vision has enabled international organizations other than UNEP to serve as stronger anchor organizations in their fields. The WHO, for example, has been able to reject funds that do not advance its long-term strategic vision and instead focus government contributions on a set of key priorities. UNEP's attempts to cover a vast number of priorities, often under pressure from governments, and its risk-averse attitude have prevented it from establishing a solid brand name that would give it the freedom to act as a leader by setting the global environmental agenda and taking action to attain it. Without a long-term strategy for accomplishing goals, it is difficult to raise the necessary funds. As the Office for Internal and Oversight Services observed in 1997, a vicious circle of limited funds and limited effectiveness had deterred UNEP from enlarging its visionary capacity and raising the necessary resources throughout much of its existence (United Nations 1997).

Although considerable improvements have been initiated in the last few years, a sense of prioritization is still lacking.[7] UNEP's planning process is in many ways driven by the influence of individual states asserting their own priorities. The organization's dependence on voluntary contributions creates governance challenges, particularly with respect to the establishment of priorities, allocation of resources and execution of programmes. The ultimate result of UNEP's limited ability to perform the role of anchor organization in agenda-setting and management of policy processes has been proliferation of institutional arrangements, meetings and agendas and 'substantial overlaps, unrecognized linkages and gaps' (UNEP and Environmental Management Group 2005), hampering policy coherence as well as synergy and amplifying the negative impact of already limited resources (UNEP 2001b).

Capacity development

UNEP has begun to reinvent its work programmes to appeal to donors and recipients alike by putting a new emphasis on capacity development initiatives. Although UNEP's mandate clearly prescribes its core strategies to be normative and catalytic, the organization now views implementation as its primary strategy (UNEP 2005b, para. 58). With a small staff and minimal resources, however, UNEP is no match for agencies like UNDP or the World

Bank. With field offices in every country around the world, annual budgets in the billions and strong reputations, UNDP and the World Bank set the agenda, locally as well as globally. UNEP does not have the capacity to function as a full-fledged operational agency. However, a purely normative role is also insufficient and even unnecessary, as concrete results are increasingly needed. The pressures to continue moving in a more operational direction will continue to grow and a balance between the normative and the operational will need to be struck.

There is an overall 'treaty fatigue' as governments have become overloaded with meetings, reports, policy documents, and reporting requirements for the numerous multilateral environmental conventions. Governments, in particular those of developing countries, increasingly call for concrete assistance with implementation, for financial and technical support in implementing existing agreements rather than the development of new ones. In addition, concrete accomplishments on the ground are the clearest evidence of success and completed projects have become the hard currency for governments. It is therefore much easier to mobilize funds for tangible products than for normative or catalytic activities. However, by shifting from a normative and catalytic function to an implementation and operational role, UNEP has moved from being proactive to being reactive. The focus on implementation – while critical and necessary – has put an emphasis on reacting to specific country needs and circumstances. Many capacity-building projects are requested by governments, compelling UNEP to pursue the work although it lacks the human and financial capacity to do so effectively.[8]

UNEP recognizes these challenges in finding a balance between its normative mandate and the operational demands it faces. The High-Level Open-Ended Intergovernmental Working Group was established in March 2004 to improve UNEP's capacity-building efforts, resulting in the adoption of the Bali Strategic Plan for Technology Support and Capacity Building (UNEP 2005a). The essence of the Bali Plan lies in coordination, cooperation and partnerships. The strategic premise is that efforts should build on existing organizations and be 'coordinated, linked and integrated with other sustainable development initiatives through existing coordination mechanisms' (UNEP 2005a, para. 5). Given UNEP's track record in coordination, however, the prospects for success are limited at best. The Plan underlines the need for improved inter-agency coordination and cooperation based on transparent and reliable information. It does not, however, clarify the respective roles for UNEP, UNDP and the World Bank, which have become more like competitors than partners.

In sum, UNEP has a clear mandate to perform the anchor role in global environmental governance but has done so with only partial success. It has been relatively effective in two key areas – monitoring and scientific assessment and launching policy processes for environmental agreements. It has also often served as the only international partner of frequently marginalized environment ministries in many countries and provided a critical forum where they can meet their counterparts. However, UNEP has largely fallen short in managing policy processes in a coherent and coordinated fashion for a number of resons discussed below. It has failed to establish itself as the organizational home for the numerous international environmental conventions. And without a centre of gravity, the system of international environmental governance has grown increasingly complex and fragmented.

Explaining (in)effectiveness

Several key factors have constrained UNEP's performance as anchor organization for the global environment. First, UNEP's status as a programme rather than a specialized agency within the UN system has limited its authority and standing. Second, UNEP's governance arrangements, including the Committee of Permanent Representatives and the Governing Council, have constrained its autonomy and leadership. Third, UNEP's financing structure has led to complete dependence on voluntary funds resulting in a high degree of unpredictability and volatility of resources as well as openness to excessive member state influence on the organization's agenda. Finally, UNEP's location away from the centres of international political activity have hampered its ability to effectively coordinate the UN's environmental activities, to assert itself as the central actor in global environmental governance and to attract and retain the most highly qualified policy staff.

Formal status

In the UN hierarchy, programmes have the least independence and authority as they are subsidiary organs of the General Assembly. Specialized agencies, on the other hand, are separate, autonomous intergovernmental organizations with governing bodies independent of the UN Secretariat and the General Assembly.[9] Besides their role in elaborating common vision, rules and standards, they also perform many operational activities within the particular sector they govern. The vision for UNEP in 1972, however, was for a new type of governing body.

UNEP was not intentionally constituted as a programme in order to diminish its power (Ivanova 2007). Recognizing the complex nature of environmental issues, governments sought to create a lean, flexible and agile entity that could pull together the relevant expertise housed in the various agencies and deploy it effectively. The new entity was expected to grow into its mandate as it proved its effectiveness and be 'essentially flexible and evolutionary so as to permit adaptation to changing needs and circumstances' (United Nations 1972b). The establishment of UNEP as a specialized agency was deemed counterproductive, since it would make the environment another 'sector' and marginalize it. As Maurice Strong, the Secretary General of the 1972 Stockholm Conference, put it, the core functions could 'only be performed at the international level by a body which is not tied to any individual sectoral or operational responsibilities and is able to take an objective overall view of the technical and policy implications arising from a variety of multidisciplinary factors' (United Nations 1972b). Furthermore, there was a strong sense of disillusionment with the unwieldy bureaucracy of the UN specialized agencies. This new body was designed to operate at the core of the UN system – best accomplished with the status of a programme, rather than a specialized agency, which, with their semi-autonomous governing mechanisms, operate on the periphery of the UN system.

While not intentionally diminishing UNEP's power, the decision to constitute it as a programme rather than a specialized agency has impacted its authority. UNEP has not been able to establish the autonomy necessary to become an effective anchor organization for the global environment. As new organizations sprang up across various levels of governance and many existing ones added substantial environmental mandates, UNEP could claim little authority over them. For example, the creation of the Commission on Sustainable Development and the Global Environment Facility after the Rio Earth Summit in the early 1990s marginalized UNEP politically and eclipsed it financially. In addition, the increased emphasis on environmental work at the World Bank, while commendable, also led to overlap with UNEP activities. UNEP was unable to coordinate and create synergies among the multiple bodies in the environmental arena as its political power and resources were dwarfed by newer organizations. Thus, while the choice of organizational form did not seek to incapacitate UNEP, the effect has been largely negative. As one senior UNEP official exclaimed, UNEP 'just does not have a voice in front of the larger UN agencies'.

Governance

Ultimately, UNEP's governance structure serves two very distinct roles: (1) the external functions of advancing international environmental governance by monitoring global environmental trends, setting a consensus global environmental agenda and establishing global priorities and (2) the internal responsibility of overseeing UNEP's programme, budget and operations. UNEP's governance structure conflates these two roles. The Governing Council is responsible for both setting the global environmental agenda and elaborating UNEP's work programme and budget. This leads to overly politicized institutional governance and a work programme that reflects a compilation of individual states' interests rather than a focused, strategic vision. It also prevents UNEP from exercising leadership in international environmental governance more broadly, as no long-term, bold vision for the system can be elaborated and implemented.

Three separate bodies share governance responsibilities for UNEP: the Governing Council comprised of 58 member states, the Secretariat headed by the executive director, and the Committee of Permanent Representatives (CPR) comprised of ambassadors to Kenya serving as Permanent Representatives to UNEP. Few other international agencies possess governance bodies resembling the CPR whose responsibilities include reviewing UNEP's draft programme of work and budget, monitoring the implementation of Governing Council decisions and preparing draft decisions for consideration by the Council (UNEP 1997). In most cases, international organizations are governed by an assembly responsible for establishing broad policy priorities (the equivalent of the Governing Council) and a smaller executive board charged with operational responsibilities. The committee of permanent representatives at UNEP, however, comprises representatives from all member states of the United Nations willing to participate as well as of specialized agencies and the European Union.[10] More often than not, however, these representatives possess little environmental knowledge and expertise and are responsible for a number of other areas.[11] The CPR considerably limits the autonomy and power of the secretariat in Nairobi either through direct intervention in UNEP's work (meeting four times a year to discuss the work programme and budget) or through influence on UNEP's staff, whose loyalties often lie with their national governments. Since advancement within the ranks of national administrations is often contingent on a good recommendation from the ambassador at one's duty station, there is considerable pressure for UNEP staff to pursue narrow national interests within the organization.

These complex governance arrangements further affect UNEP's work since the final say on decisions regarding the work programme and budget lies not with the CPR, which constantly oversees UNEP's operations, but with the Governing Council. Meeting once a year, the Governing Council is supposed to both craft a visionary agenda for international environmental governance at the global scale and set the parameters within which UNEP is allowed to operate, i.e. its biennial programme of work and budget. Typically, a person other than the permanent representative in Nairobi represents the country at the governing council, often the environmental minister who flies to Kenya specifically for the week-long session. Even though a permanent representative to UNEP might have worked on a particular aspect of the work programme for months, his or her recommendations and decisions could be contested by the national representative under this arrangement. In this context, the governance structure of UNEP has unnecessarily hampered effective performance creating significant duplication of effort and even conflicting priorities. Without a clarification of CPR's relationship with the Governing Council, there will be little room for substantially improving UNEP's performance.

Financing structure

UNEP's limited financial resources are another key reason analysts use to explain UNEP's ineffectiveness (von Moltke 1996; Najam 2003). UNEP's annual budget of $215 million (including all contributions: Environment

Fund, earmarked contributions and trust funds) is indeed miniscule compared to UNDP's $3.2 billion and to EPA's $7.6 billion. However, it is larger than the budget of the WTO. Figure 8.3 compares the annual budgets of several major international organizations.

While the disparity in resources is striking, the nominal sum of the budget is a symptom of the problem. The root cause of UNEP's problems is the organization's particular financial structure. Unlike many other international organizations whose budgets are based on predictable mandatory assessed contributions, UNEP is completely dependent on the voluntary contributions of individual states. This unreliable and highly discretionary financial arrangement allows for individual donors to dictate UNEP's priorities, which has resulted in a fragmentation of UNEP's activities and a lack of clear prioritization. Furthermore, UNEP's financial stability, ability to plan beyond the current budget cycle and autonomy are compromised, thus instilling a risk-averse attitude within the organization's leadership.

In the past ten years, contributions to the Environment Fund have dropped 36 per cent and have decreased in real terms since the 1970s and 1980s. Contributions to trust and earmarked funds directing UNEP into specific activities, on the other hand, have increased dramatically. The proportion of restricted financing now comprises more than two-thirds of UNEP's revenue as shown in Figure 8.4.[12]

This illustrates two important aspects that explain the political dynamics and consequences for UNEP's performance. First, the decline in contributions to the Environment Fund shows that confidence in UNEP has diminished.

2006 IO Budgets

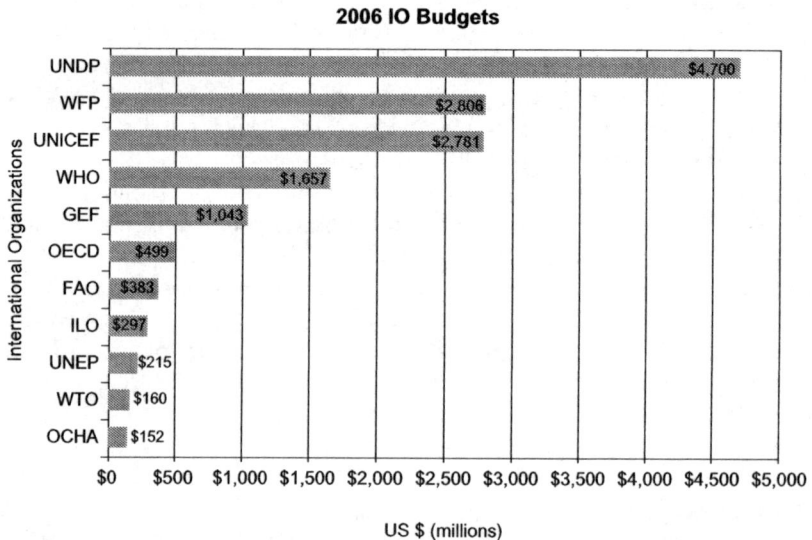

UNDP	$4,700
WFP	$2,806
UNICEF	$2,781
WHO	$1,657
GEF	$1,043
OECD	$499
FAO	$383
ILO	$297
UNEP	$215
WTO	$160
OCHA	$152

International Organizations

US $ (millions)

Figure 8.3 Comparative organizational annual budgets.

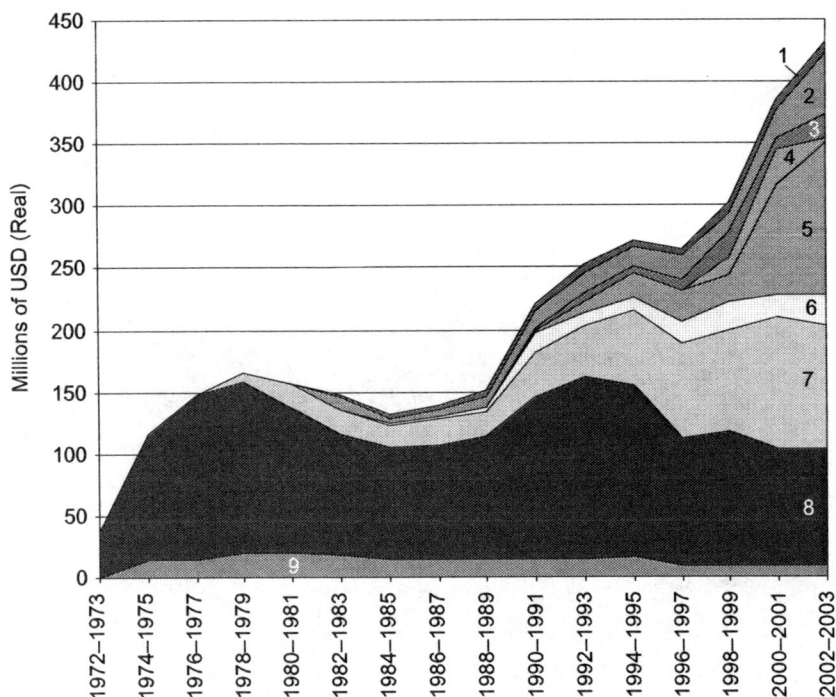

1	Other (incl. JPO)	6	Techn. Cooperation Funds
2	Earmarked contributions	7	General Trust Funds
3	UNEP support to MF	8	Environment Fund
4	UN Foundation	9	UN regular budget
5	GEF		

Figure 8.4 Total UNEP biennial income from 1973 to 2003 in real 2000 US dollars.
Source: Ivanova 2005.

The secretariat is deprived of power to initiate and carry out programmes it deems necessary and urgent. The second key trend – a three-fold increase in overall funding since the 1980s, including trust funds, earmarked contributions and other revenues – shows recognition of the need for international mechanisms and UNEP in particular in addressing environmental concerns.

The diversification trend in financial contributions is clearly illustrated in Figure 8.5, which depicts funding from the top five donors to UNEP: the United States (historically the top donor), Japan, Germany, the United Kingdom and Sweden. For all countries, contributions have shifted from the Environment Fund to other earmarked mechanisms and are now currently roughly equal.[13]

Under the leadership of former Executive Director Klaus Töpfer (1997–2005), UNEP made significant progress in attracting financial resources. The

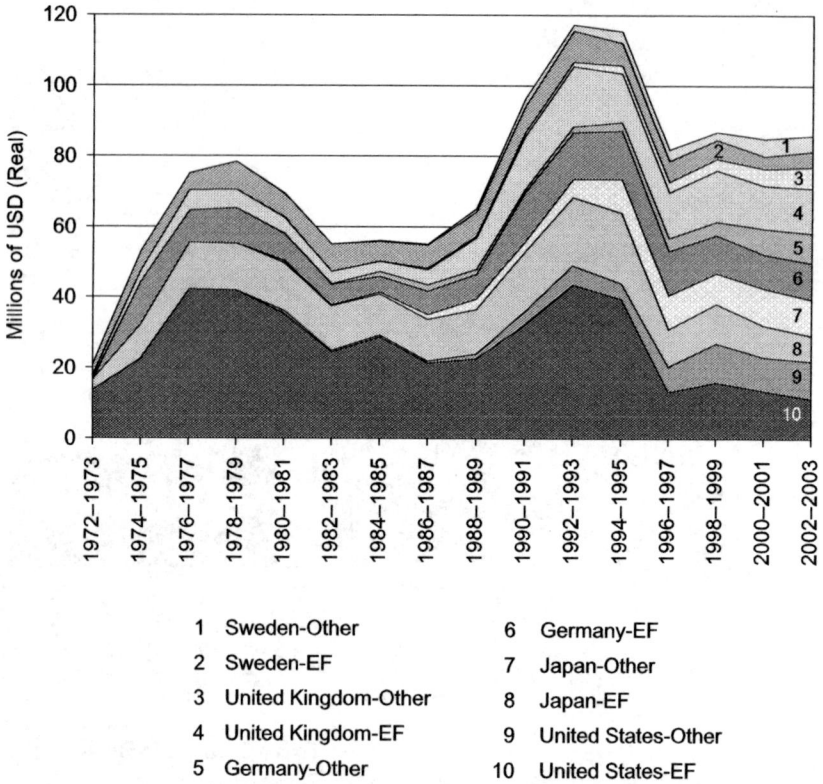

Figure 8.5 Top five donor contributions to UNEP in real 2000 US dollars.
Source: Ivanova 2005.

pilot phase of the voluntary indicative scale of contributions instituted in 2002 has broadened the donor base and encouraged many countries to increase their contributions. In 2003, over 100 countries contributed to UNEP – twice as many as in the mid-1990s – though most amounts were miniscule. A number of countries have also increased their contributions compared to the mid-1990s. Canada's contributions to the Environment Fund, for example, increased from a record low of $662,000 (USD) in 1997 to almost $2 million in 2004.

Location

UNEP is the only UN agency headquartered in the developing world with the exception of UN Habitat, which is also in Nairobi and which was headed by the executive director of UNEP until 2000. The decision to locate UNEP in Nairobi was not a 'strategic necessity without which developing countries might have never accepted an environmental organ to be created' (Najam

2003: 374). Nor was it a way to marginalize the organization and 'cannibalize its mandate' (von Moltke 1996: 54).[14] It was not ill intended, premeditated or the result of a secret bargain. Quite the opposite: it was the outcome of an open ballot vote at the General Assembly in November 1972. Solidarity among developing countries, which outnumbered developed countries by far, led to a decisive vote in favour of Nairobi. The decision was openly political, seeking to affirm the role of developing countries as equal partners in multilateral affairs (Ivanova 2007).

UNEP's location has influenced the organization significantly. Its ability to effectively coordinate and catalyze environmental action has been inhibited by its geographical isolation from other relevant UN operations, inadequate long-distance communication and transportation infrastructure and lack of sufficient face-to-face interaction with counterparts in other agencies and treaty secretariats. UNEP's headquarters are located far outside the dense political activity 'hotspots', posing a challenge to its ability to fulfil the coordination role specified in its mandate (Ivanova 2006). UNEP's offices in Paris, New York and Geneva, however, have tried to step into the liaison role. Their 'proximity to other organizations and important governments seems to make these programs among the brighter lights of UNEP achievement' (Eastby 1984).

It is important to note that the location constrains particularly UNEP's coordination function and that for other aspects of UNEP's mandate – such as capacity building – the location may present an opportunity rather than a challenge. UNEP's expertise in institution building is greatly needed in Africa. However, pressing environmental challenges demand immediate on-the-ground action – a mandate that UNEP does not possess. A demand for greater operational responsibilities for UNEP has thus emerged both from the developing world and from the organization's staff.

The most important consequence of UNEP's location is the inability to attract and retain top-notch staff with the policy expertise and experience necessary to make the organization the leading authority in the environmental field. Nairobi is not necessarily a desirable location for the staff with the expertise and management qualities that UNEP needs. The increasingly treacherous security situation exacerbates this problem. In addition, the remoteness of UNEP from the international organizations it was charged to coordinate has required frequent travel by the executive director and many senior staff, imposing a significant financial burden, but most importantly, creating a leadership vacuum due to prolonged absences from Nairobi. Effective management of the organization requires that the leadership be present and responsive to staff needs and organizational priorities (Ivanova 2007).

Conclusion

Collective action in response to global environmental challenges continues to fall short of needs and expectations (Speth 2004). The question, therefore, is not *whether* to revitalize the global environmental regime, but *how*. The integrated and interdependent nature of the current set of environmental challenges contrasts sharply with the fragmented and uncoordinated nature of the organizations we rely upon for solutions. Yet, political emphasis is increasingly being placed on working within existing organizations rather than attempting bold new designs. As former UN Secretary-General Kofi Annan urged in his 2005 report *In Larger Freedom*:

> [i]t is now high time to consider a more integrated structure for environmental standard-setting, scientific discussion and monitoring treaty compliance. This should be built on existing institutions, such as the United Nations Environment Programme, as well as the treaty bodies and specialized agencies.
>
> (United Nations 2005, para. 212)

UNEP is still the leading international organization in the environmental domain. Only UNEP's mandate adequately reflects all the functions of an anchor organization. It is the natural forum for the creation of a coherent international system for environmental monitoring, assessment, information and analysis. However, UNEP can no longer aspire to the lead role for *every* environmental issue. Expertise within the system has been diffused over the past thirty years with the proliferation of other international organizations and non-governmental organizations in the environmental arena. Instead, UNEP could effectively lay the foundation for a policy forum where various clusters of agencies and networks convene to negotiate and exchange experience. A more strategic, prioritized and long-term capacity development approach, drawing on UNEP's comparative advantage as an information clearing-house and a policy forum, rather than an operational agency, could facilitate the implementation of multilateral environmental agreements.

The initiative by the French and German governments to create a United Nations Environment Organization may provide the impetus for a restructuring of the system. Simply upgrading UNEP into a UNEO, however, will not suffice. In fact, the UNEO vision does not substantially depart from the existing UNEP mandate. The proposal for UNEO addresses most of the functions necessary for an effective anchor organization for the environment, but fails to make any significant upgrade from the status quo in terms of mandate. The question therefore becomes whether a UNEO would be better equipped to effectively perform these functions.

Today's reformers face issues regarding the formal status, governance, financing and location of a new international environmental organization just as the founding members of the global environmental governance system did in 1972. Analysis of UNEP's performance starkly illustrates that unless these key structural issues are addressed, little progress in the environmental domain is possible.

Notes

1 An earlier draft was produced for the Secretariat of the International Task Force on Global Public Goods and published as a report by the Yale School of Forestry and Environmental Studies. The author gratefully acknowledges research assistance and comments from Christine Kim, as well as comments and suggestions from Raymond Clémençon, Jane Coppock, Mohamed El-Ashry, Daniel Esty, Harris Gleckman, Kaitlin Gregg, Laura Hess, Christine Hogan, Katell Le Goulven, Jessica Marsden, Frits Schlingemann, Alex Shakow and Gus Speth on previous versions of this work.

2 In earlier work, the author uses the term 'anchor institution'. For the purpose of consistency and greater theoretical clarity, the term organization is used throughout this book. Thus, 'anchor institution' has been substituted by 'anchor organization'.

3 For proposals for a World Environmental Organization (WEO), see Biermann 2000, 2001, 2002a, 2002b; Biermann and Bauer 2004, 2005; Charnovitz 2002. For a Global Environment Organization (GEO) see Esty 1994, 2000; Runge 2001; Ruggiero 1998. For a Global Environmental Mechanism (GEM) see Esty and Ivanova 2002a.

4 For example, von Moltke (2001b) characterizes UNEP's mandate as impossible, Iwama (2004) as 'narrow mandate of a "catalyst"' and Bauer and Biermann (2004) as 'insufficient mandate'.

5 See <http://www.yale.edu/esi and www.yale.edu/epi>.

6 The Environmental Co-ordination Board (ECB) was made up of executive heads of the UN agencies under the chairmanship of the UNEP executive director and mandated to meet periodically to ensure 'co-operation and co-ordination among all bodies concerned in the implementation of environmental programmes'. In addition, the ECB was responsible for reporting annually to UNEP's Governing Council and fell under the auspices of the Administrative Committee on Coordination.

7 The 2006–7 UNEP Draft Programme of Work, for example, contains a detailed description of outputs for subprogrammes and comprises a vast array of projects, publications, meetings, processes, services, symposia, studies and training events. These are largely limited, *ad hoc* and often short-term initiatives established independently of one another, rather than a set of harmonized initiatives developed to accomplish a set of focused priorities. See <http://www.unep.org/gc/gc23/index-flash.asp>.

8 Availability of funding from the Global Environment Facility (GEF) to three implementing agencies, namely the World Bank, UNDP and UNEP, has also pushed UNEP toward increased operational activities. Since the late 1990s, the GEF has accounted for the largest increase in UNEP's income and the GEF division in UNEP has developed as an almost autonomous body.

9 Some of the specialized agencies include the Food and Agriculture Organization (FAO), World Health Organization (WHO), World Meteorological Organization (WMO), International Bank for Reconstruction and Development (World Bank), International Maritime Organization (IMO), UN Educational, Scientific and Cultural Organization (UNESCO) and UN Industrial Development Organization (UNIDO).

10 As of 2005, there were 87 countries with permanent missions to UNEP and thus representatives on the Committee of Permanent Representatives.

11 The United States and Sweden have specially appointed Permanent Representatives, often with solid environmental backgrounds, whose only responsibility is to work with UNEP.

12 Financial analysis performed by Lisa DeBock and Jamie Fergusson of the Yale

research team based on documentation provided by UNEP (DeBock and Fergusson 2004)

13 Financial analysis performed by Lisa DeBock and Jamie Fergusson of the Yale research team based on documentation provided by UNEP

14 Von Moltke asserts, 'lacking enthusiastic supporters, UNEP's mandate was cannibalized. The principal means of achieving this goal was to provide limited funds divided between a minimal institutional budget and a modest "Fund", to assign it a "catalytic" function and to locate it away from the decision-making centres of the UN system.'

References

Barnett, M. and Finnemore, M. (2004) *Rules for the World: International Organizations in Global Politics*. Ithaca, NY: Cornell University Press.

Bauer, S. and Biermann, F. (2004) 'Does Effective International Environmental Governance Require a World Environment Organization? The State of the Debate Prior to the Report of the High-Level Panel on Reforming the United Nations', Global Governance Working Paper No. 13, Amsterdam, Berlin, Oldenburg, Potsdam: The Global Governance Project.

Bauer, S. and Biermann, F. (2005) 'The Debate on a World Environment Organization: An Introduction', in Biermann, F. and Bauer, S. (eds) *A World Environment Organization: Solution or Threat for Effective International Environmental Governance*, Aldershot: Ashgate.

Bernstein, S. and Ivanova, M. (2007) 'Institutional Fragmentation and Normative Compromise in Global Environmental Governance: What Prospect for Re-Embedding?, in Bernstein, S. and Pauly, L.W. *Global Governance: Towards a New Grand Compromise?*, Albany, NY: SUNY Press.

Berruga, E. and Maurer, P. (2006) *Co-Chairmen's Summary of the Informal Consultative Process on the Institutional Framework for the UN's Environmental Activities*, New York.

Biermann, F. (2000) 'The case for a world environment organization', *Environment*, 42(9): 22–31.

Biermann, F. (2001) 'The emerging debate on the need for a world environment organisation: a commentary', *Global Environmental Politics*, 1(1): 45–55.

Biermann, F. (2002a) 'Green Global Governance: The case for a World Environment Organisation', *New Economy*, 9(2): 82–86.

Biermann, F. (2002b) 'Strengthening Green Global Governance in a Disparate World Society: Would a World Environment Organisation Benefit the South?', *International Environmental Agreements: Politics, Law and Economics*, (2): 297–315.

Biermann, F. and Bauer, S. (2004) 'Does Effective International Environmental Governance Require a World Environment Organization? The State of the Debate Prior to the Report of the High-Level Panel on Reforming the United Nations', *Global Governance Working Paper Nr. 13*, Amsterdam, Berlin, Oldenburg, Potsdam: The Global Governance Project.

Biermann, F. and Bauer, S. (2005) *A World Environment Organization: Solution or Threat for Effective International Environmental Governance?*, Aldershot, UK: Ashgate.

Brown Weiss, E. (1995) 'International Environmental Law: Contemporary Issues and the Emergence of a New World Order', *Georgetown Law Journal*, 81(1) (March): 675–693.

Charnovitz, S. (2002) 'A World Environment Organization', *Columbia Journal of Environmental Law*, 27(323): 323–362.

Conca, K. (1995) 'Greening the United Nations: environmental organisations and the UN system', *Third World Quarterly*, 16(3): 441–457.

DeBock, L. and Fergusson, J. (2004) 'UNEP's Financial Performance', Yale School of Forestry and Environmental Studies.

Desai, B. (2004) 'Blueprints for Strengthening International Environmental Institutions', in Desai, B. (ed.) *Institutionalizing International Environmental Law*, Ardsley, NY: Transnational Publishers, 221–273.

Eastby, J.H. (1984) 'David Mitrany's Approach to Politics: Functionalism in Theory and Practice', PhD dissertation, University of Virginia.

Esty, D.C. (1994) 'The Case for a Global Environmental Organization', in Kenen, P.B. (ed.) *Managing the World Economy: Fifty Years After Bretton Woods*, Washington, DC: Institute for International Economics.

Esty, D.C. (2000) 'International Governance at the Global Level: The Value of Creating a Global Environmental Organization', *Environment Matters*, Annual Review 1999–2000: 12–15.

Esty, D.C. and Ivanova, M. (eds) (2002a) *Global Environmental Governance: Options and Opportunities*. New Haven, CT: Yale School of Forestry and Environmental Studies.

Esty, D.C. and Ivanova, M. (2002b) 'Revitalizing Global Environmental Governance: A Function-Driven Approach', in Esty, D. and Ivanova, M. (eds) *Global Environmental Governance: Options and Opportunities*, New Haven, CT: Yale School of Forestry and Environmental Studies.

Esty, D.C., Levy, M.A., Srebotnjak, T. and de Sherbinin, A. (2005) *2005 Environmental Sustainability Index: Benchmarking National Environmental Stewardship*. New Haven, CT: Yale Center for Environmental Law and Policy.

Global Environment Facility (2008) *What Is the GEF?: GEF Funding*. Available online at www.gefweb.org/What_is_the_GEF/what_is_the_gef.html#Funding.

Haas, P.M. (2004) 'Addressing the Global Governance Deficit', *Global Environmental Politics*, 4(4): 1–15.

Ivanova, M. (2006) 'Understanding UNEP: Myths and Realities in Global Environmental Governance', PhD dissertation, New Haven, CT: Yale University.

Ivanova, M. (2007) 'Designing the United Nations Environment Programme: A story of compromise and confrontation', *International Environmental Agreements: Politics, Law, and Economics*, 7(3): 337–361.

Iwama, T. (2004) 'Multilateral Environmental Institutions and Coordinating Mechanisms', in Kanie, N. and Haas, P.M. *Emerging Forces in Environmental Governance*, Tokyo, New York, Paris: United Nations University Press.

Kanie, N. and Haas, P.M.(eds) (2004) *Emerging Forces in Environmental Governance*, Tokyo, New York, Paris: United Nations University Press.

Najam, A. (2001) 'Vision 2020: Towards Better Global Governance', 2020 Global Architecture Visions Conference, University of Victoria, Canada: Centre for Global Studies.

Najam, A. (2003) 'The Case against a New International Environmental Organization', *Global Governance*, 9(3): 367.

Organization for Economic Cooperation and Development (2007) *OECD Annual Report 2007*. Available online at http://www.oecd.org/dataoecd/34/33/38528123.pdf.

Ruggiero, R. (1998) 'A Global System for the Next Fifty Years', Address to the Royal Institute of International Affairs, London: Royal Institute of International Affairs.

Runge, C.F. (2001) 'A Global Environmental Organization (GEO) and the World Trading System', *Journal of World Trade*, 35(4): 399–426.

Rydbeck, O. (1972) 'Statement by Ambassador Olof Rydbeck in the Preparatory Committee for the United Nations Conference on the Human Environment, Fourth Session', New York: Permanent Mission of Sweden to the United Nations.

Shakow, A. (2005) 'Review of Global Public Goods Anchor Institutions', Draft Paper prepared for the International Task Force on Global Public Goods (September)

Speth, J.G. (2002) 'The Global Environmental Agenda: Origins and Prospects', in Esty, D.C. and Ivanova, M. (eds) *Global Environmental Governance: Options and Opportunities*, New Haven, CT: Yale School of Forestry and Environmental Studies.

Speth, J.G. (ed.) (2003) *Worlds Apart: Globalization and the Environment*, Washington, DC: Island Press.

Speth, J.G. (2004) *Red Sky at Morning: America and the Crisis of the Global Environment*, New Haven, CT: Yale University Press.

UN (1972a) General Assembly Resolution 2977 (XXVII): Institutional and Financial Arrangements for International Environmental Cooperation.

UN (1972b) 'International Organizational Implications of Action Proposals: Conference on the Human Environment: Report by the Secretary-General', A/CONF.48/11/Add.1 (January 10), Stockholm: Official Record.

UN (1997) 'Review of the United Nations Environment Programme (UNEP) and the Administrative Practices of its Secretariat, including the United Nations Office in Nairobi (UNON)', *Report of the Secretary-General on the Activities of the Office of Internal Oversight Services (A/51/810)*.

UN (1998) Convention on the Prior Informed Consent (PIC) Procedure for Certain Hazardous Chemicals and Pesticides in International Trade.

UN (2005) 'In Larger Freedom: Towards Development, Security and Human Rights for All', *Report of the Secretary-General*. Available online at <http://www.un.org/largerfreedom/>.

UNEP (1997) 'Governing Council Decision 19/32: Governance of the United Nations Environment Programme'. Available online at <http://www.unep.org/Documents.Multilingual/Default.asp?DocumentID=96&ArticleID=1456&l=en>.

UNEP Governing Council (1997) Nairobi Declaration on the Role and Mandate of UNEP. Held in Nairobi from January 27–February 7. 19th Session. UNEP/GC19/1/1997.

UNEP (2001) 'Improving International Environmental Governance among Multilateral Environmental Agreements: Negotiable Terms for Further Discussion: A Policy Paper', UNEP/IGM/2/4. Bonn, Germany: UNEP.

UNEP (2004) 'Global Environmental Outlook: User Profile and Impact Study', (August), Nairobi: UNEP.

UNEP (2005a) 'Bali Strategic Plan for Technology Support and Capacity Building', online. Available online at <http://www.unep.org/GC/GC23/documents/GC23-6-add-1.pdf>.

UNEP (2005b) 'Environment Fund Budgets: Proposed Biennial Programme and Support Budget for 2006–2007'; 'Report of the Advisory Committee on Administrative and Budgetary Questions'; 'State of the Environment and Contribution of the United Nations Environment Programme in Addressing

Substantive Environmental Challenges: Report of the Executive Director'. Available online at <http://www.unep.org/GC/GC23/documents/GC23-8.pdf>.

UNEP (2005c) 'Synthesis of Responses on Strengthening the Scientific Base of the United Nations Environment Programme', UNEP/SI/IGC/2, Nairobi: UNEP.

UNEP and Environment Management Group (2005) Environment Management Group Homepage, UNEP; EMG 2005. Available online at http://www.unemg.org.

UNEP/GRID-Arendal (2006) UNEP/GRID, Arendal Homepage 2005 [cited 17 August 2006]. Available online at http://www.grida.no/.

United Nations Children's Fund (2006) *Annual Report 2006*. Available online at http://www.unicef.org/about/annualreport/files/Annual_Report_2006.pdf.

United Nations Development Programme (2006) *Global Partnership for Development: United Nations Development Programme Annual Report 2006*. Available online at http://www.undp.org/publications/annualreport2006/english-report.pdf.

United Nations Office for the Coordination of Humanitarian Affairs (2006) *OCHA in 2006: Activities and Extra-Budgetary Funding Requirements*. Available online at http://ochaonline.un.org/About%20OCHA/OCHAin2008/2006/tabid/1144/Default.aspx.

von Moltke, K. (1996) 'Why UNEP Matters', *Green Globe Yearbook 1996*, Oxford: Oxford University Press.

von Moltke, K. (2001) 'The Organization of the Impossible', *Global Environmental Politics*, 1(1) (February): 23–28.

World Food Programme (2007) *WFP's Operational Requirements, Shortfalls, and Priorities for 2007*. Available online at http://www.wfp.org/appeals/Current_Shortfalls/documents/2007/Operational_Requirements_2007_Feb.pdf.

World Health Organization (2006) *Proposed Programme Budget 2006–2007*. Available online at http://www.who.int/gb/ebwha/pdf_files/PB2006/Intro-en.pdf.

World Trade Organization (2006) *The WTO Secretariat and Budget for 2006*. Available online at http://www.wto.org/english/thewto_e/secre_e/budget06_e.htm.

9 Treaty secretariats in global environmental governance

Steffen Bauer, Per-Olof Busch and Bernd Siebenhüner

Introduction

Virtually all multilateral agreements provide for a treaty secretariat to help governments coordinate their efforts. Andresen and Skjærseth (1999: 2) define a treaty secretariat as a specific type of an international organization 'established by the relevant parties to assist them in fulfilling the goals of the treaty'. Such secretariats take shape as international bureaucracies that are being operated by international civil servants. So far, little attention has been paid to their specific role in international governance (see Bauer 2006 and Sandford 1992, 1994 for exceptions). Commonly treaty secretariats are perceived as a minor feature of the wider regime that provides the norms, rules and procedures for international cooperation. To better understand the specific functions, capabilities and roles of these bureaucracies in international governance we compare and discuss the influence of three treaty secretariats in the environmental realm: the United Nations Framework Convention on Climate Change (UNFCCC), the United Nations Convention to Combat Desertification (UNCCD), and the Convention on Biological Diversity (CBD).

Our analysis starts from the assumption that treaty secretariats as well as the secretariats of bigger intergovernmental organizations such as the World Bank or the World Health Organization are actors in their own right. They can influence international political processes and change the behaviour of national governments, other intergovernmental agencies, non-governmental organizations, and so on. Although international bureaucracies act on behalf of states, they are not passive tools in the hands of governments. They actively interfere with their environment as the bureaucratic actors that they tend to become (see Barnett and Finnemore 1999). International civil servants commonly pursue the objective of their organization rather than being a puppet of the national government of their origin (see Mouritzen 1990; Sandford 1994; Yi-Chong and Weller 2004). This is not to deny, however, that their freedom to act is considerably circumscribed by national governments.

In general, international bureaucracies can be shown to influence international political processes on three dimensions: cognitive, normative and executive (Biermann and Bauer 2005). They may act as 'knowledge-brokers' which gather, synthesize, process and disseminate scientific or other forms of knowledge and thereby change the knowledge or belief systems of other actors (the cognitive dimension). They may perform as 'negotiation-facilitators' which create, support and shape norm-building processes for issue-specific international cooperation and thereby can influence the outcomes of international cooperation (the normative dimension). And they may operate as 'capacity-builders' which assist countries in their efforts to implement international agreements and thereby help countries to comply with international rules or even shape domestic policies (the executive dimension). Unlike the bureaucracies of bigger intergovernmental organizations, however, treaty secretariats are typically neither mandated nor equipped to perform meaningful executive functions. Since this observation applies to each of the cases presented in this chapter, we restrict our comparative analysis to patterns of influence on the cognitive and normative dimensions.

To explain any observed cognitive or normative influence and variation across the three secretariats, we explore the explanatory potential of four factors which have been identified to affect the capability of international bureaucracies to change the behaviour of other actors: the structure of the underlying problem, bureaucratic authority, organizational culture, and leadership. These factors have been derived from different bodies of literature, namely International Relations, organizational theories and management studies (see Biermann and Bauer 2005 in greater detail). The structure of the underlying problem refers to the stakes and costs involved in addressing or not addressing a given problem, its saliency and urgency, and its complexity in terms of the availability and feasibility of solutions. Bureaucratic authority, in our understanding, entails the ability of an international bureaucracy to generate influence without the use of sanctions or coercive means, e.g. by persuading other actors through argumentation or analytical, political and technical expertise to voluntarily adhere to its proposals and advice as opposed to exercising power (see Bauer 2006 in greater detail). Organizational culture includes the processes of decision-making, professional cultures and the backgrounds of staff members in the international bureaucracy. Leadership is defined as the specific behaviour of staff members within the international bureaucracy and vis-à-vis external actors. This relates in particular, but not exclusively, to the bureaucracy's executive level. In the following case studies, we investigate to what extent each of these factors has affected the secretariats' potential to generate the influence observed and in how far differences in these factors explain the observed variation.

Other factors which are supposed to explain the influences of international bureaucracies and their variation, namely the formal structures as well as the legal and institutional setting within which international bureaucracies operate (see Biermann and Bauer 2005), can be reasonably excluded as irrelevant in explaining any observed variation in the influences of the three secretariats we examine. Given that all three secretariats are part of the UN system, the formal structures and core administrative functions such as the management of human resources, reporting procedures, accounting, controlling and so on follow the same general guidelines. Likewise, the legal and institutional settings of the secretariats are highly similar as reflected by the wording of their mandates.

The influence of treaty secretariats in global environmental governance

Data for the following case studies was gathered during research visits to the respective secretariats by the authors in 2003 and 2004. Some thirty personal and telephone interviews with senior and programme officers from all three secretariats provided insights into the internal functions of the bureaucracies and the perceptions of their influence. An international expert online survey provided data on external perspectives on the secretariats and their actual influence (see Tarradell 2005 for further details). Each case study begins with a description of the cognitive and normative influence which is followed by an examination of the relevance of the explanatory factors outlined above.

The climate secretariat

In 1992, the UN Conference on Environment and Development adopted the UN Framework Convention on Climate Change, also establishing its secretariat. What followed has been described as 'one of the most ambitious treaties ever adopted' (Oberthür and Ott 1999: 95) and 'the most profound and important global agreement of the late twentieth century' (Grubb *et al.* 1999: xxxiii). In another nine years of intense and highly controversial negotiations often verging on the brink of failure, governments agreed upon two other landmark agreements of the climate regime: the Kyoto Protocol (1997) and the Marrakech Accords (2001).

The overall influence of the secretariat, however, is limited. While the secretariat exerted some influence with regard to both cognitive and normative dimensions, it would be exaggerated to attribute to it a substantial independent bearing on knowledge generation, the scientific understanding of climate change, public and scientific discourses or political negotiations. In general, its influence is rather limited to technical – as opposed to political – dimensions of the climate regime.

Cognitive influence: back-up server

The secretariat's cognitive influence is limited to the utilization by stakeholders of the largely factual and descriptive information and documentation that the secretariat provides on climate change related issues, the negotiation and implementation process. In analytical, political and scientific assessments and related discourses, policy-makers, negotiators and other stakeholders – including media, science and civil society – often draw on information that is compiled and disseminated by the secretariat. In an internal review of the secretariat's activities parties expressed their general satisfaction with the information and documents provided by the secretariat. At the same time they requested additional informatory and documentary support from the secretariat (Grubb *et al.* 1999: xxxiii), thereby underscoring the value they attach to the information. Other stakeholders have judged the information to be useful and relevant as well. In a survey about the secretariat's online database on the development and transfer of climate friendly technologies 85 per cent of 303 respondents from 81 countries found the information useful and relevant to their work (UNFCCC 2005). The high frequency of visits to the secretariat's homepage, where all relevant data and documents on the climate regime are available, supports this assessment. In 2004, the secretariat estimated that at least 50,000 people around the globe closely follow the climate regime process by utilizing information posted on its website.

Normative influence: technical assistance

A review of the scholarly analyses of the climate negotiations suggests that the secretariat lacks a measurable influence, in the sense that it has not independently shaped the political outcomes of the negotiations (e.g. Grubb *et al.* 1999; Oberthür and Ott 1999; Grubb and Yamin 2001; Ott 2001b; Schröder 2001; Vrolijk 2002; Depledge 2005). Likewise, programme officers are hesitant in attributing any kind of influence on political agreements to the secretariat. Instead the secretariat's role in the negotiations has been largely restricted to facilitation and support. Three functions of the secretariat can be distinguished in that respect.

First of all, the secretariat has facilitated negotiations through the provision of technical advice and has assisted parties in their efforts to identify approaches acceptable to them. Yamin and Depledge (2005: 432, 507) view the secretariat as important and pivotal in that respect (see also Depledge 2005: 73). Confirming this judgement, parties have on a number of occasions expressed their general appreciation for the secretariat's role and advice in the negotiations (e.g. IISD 1996: 11; IISD 2000: 17; IISD 2001: 11, 12; IISD 2003: 2; UNFCCC 2004; IISD 2005a: 18). For example, the adoption of the implementation rules for the Kyoto Protocol in Marrakech, the so-called Marrakech Accords, has been partially attributed to the advice provided by the secretariat. The secretariat helped parties to make sense of the complex and largely technical issues, and to embark on the final stage of negotiations (Ott 2001a). During the negotiation of the Kyoto Protocol the secretariat, together with Chair Raul Estrada, contributed to the identification of options, which eventually enabled parties to reach consensus (Depledge 2005: 154). It made indispensable contributions in the preparation of the negotiating text which was positively received by a majority of parties (Grubb *et al.* 1999:

64; Oberthür and Ott 1999: 83, 85; see also Depledge 2005: 68, 73). Conversely, the failure of parties to agree on the implementation rules of the Kyoto Protocol at the earlier meeting in The Hague has been partially explained by the limited involvement of the secretariat in the development of proposals (Depledge 2005: 159–61).

Secondly, the secretariat has facilitated negotiations through effective procedural and time management. For example, the adoption of the so-called Geneva Ministerial Declaration in 1996 has partially been credited to the secretariat's 'skilful support' in the procedural management (Ott 2001b; see also Depledge 2005: 68, 162). Likewise, during the negotiations of the Kyoto Protocol the effective maintenance of time pressure by the secretariat and Chair Estrada is perceived as an important success factor (Oberthür and Ott 1999: 54).

Thirdly, the secretariat has facilitated negotiations by providing good logistics. In their submissions to an internal review of the secretariat's performance, parties 'generally appreciated the work of the secretariat in organizing sessions and meetings' and praised the logistics in general (Depledge 2005). In the climate regime these tasks are particularly challenging given the high number of participants. By 2005, sessions of the conference of the parties and its subsidiary bodies had been attended by over 82,000 delegates of parties, representatives of observer states, intergovernmental organizations, non-governmental organizations and journalists.

In sum, the evidence suggests that the secretariat helps parties to achieve what they want to achieve and makes political agreements among the parties actually work in terms of functioning technical systems and procedures. Ultimately, however, the negotiation processes and any kind of political decisions are driven by the parties.

Explanations: the strait-jacket of climate politics

The structure of the underlying problem constitutes the main reason for the limitations of the secretariat's influence. Climate change is commonly described as a 'malign problem' (e.g. Miles *et al.* 2002; Depledge 2005). Responses to global warming involve higher stakes than any other international environmental agreement. Although climate change is predominantly perceived as environmental challenge, effective responses are expected to have comparatively drastic consequences for the prevailing mode of economic and social development which has been pursued ever since the industrial revolution (Depledge 2005: 20). Ultimately, they may culminate in a new international economic order (Oberthür and Ott 1999; Ott 2001b: 278). Oberthür and Ott (1999) argue that, as a consequence, climate change has been elevated to the sphere of 'high politics' in international relations. At the domestic level, responses to climate change are seen to involve hard politics (e.g. Nitze 1994: 190; Lee 1999: 279; Andresen and Butenschon 2001: 351), including concerns about economic growth and competitiveness (Depledge

2005: 32). These high stakes have motivated parties to be extremely wary of any of the secretariat's activities. Parties impose severe constraints on the secretariat's role and rule out initiatives by the secretariat, thereby considerably limiting the leeway of the secretariat to exert any influence.

When the secretariat prepares any kind of information, e.g. on parties' compliance with their obligations, it has been restricted to process factual information which is exclusively provided by parties. Parties do not want the secretariat to assess political implications of this information – leaving aside any kind of criticism (Depledge 2005: 68). When the secretariat prepares input to the negotiations, e.g. draft decisions or negotiating texts, it is not tolerated by parties if it advocates own ideas (Depledge 2005: 85). They immediately react if the secretariat presents input that contradicts positions and interests of parties, puts an undue emphasis on particular approaches and aspects of a given problem, or favours one group of parties over another. In particular if the input is related to politically controversial questions these constraints become evident. Scope for ideas or proposals developed by the secretariat is limited to technical questions, if at all. Even then, the secretariat is only able to give advice indirectly through the presiding officers responsible for the conduct of negotiations (Depledge 2005: 66–7). This procedure makes the secretariat heavily dependent on the presiding officers' will to introduce its input into the negotiations (Yamin and Depledge 2005: 507).

That staff at all levels have internalized the expectations of parties and the resulting lack of leadership further explains the limitation of its influence. In fact, the secretariat has accepted the parties' definitions of boundaries and 'has very rarely attempted to exercise open substantive leadership by brokering agreements among parties' (Depledge 2005: 73). Staff strove to ensure that the secretariat is perceived as an impartial body that is not favouring one party's views over those of another, or advocating particular approaches. Staff deliberately abstain from assuming openly a proactive role. The reluctance, often unwillingness, of staff to attribute any kind of influence to the secretariat underscores this assessment. At best influence was reworded into facilitation or support. This lack of strong leadership is reflected in but also partially related to the philosophy of the first executive secretary, Michael Zammit Cutajar. He urged staff to abstain from any proactive and intrusive involvement in the negotiation and implementation of the climate regime (Depledge 2007). Paradoxically, the maintenance of this impartiality is an important, if not indispensable prerequisite for the secretariat's ability to exert any influence at all. 'Perceptions of partiality within the secretariat would be a ... persistent problem that could put the whole process in jeopardy' (Depledge 2005: 65).

The most important source of the secretariat's influence is, however, its bureaucratic authority. Its cognitive influence is simply due to the fact that the secretariat is the only authoritative source of information on the climate regime. More importantly, its expertise enables the secretariat to provide authoritative input on any substantive or procedural issue in the regime. Staff are able to carry out targeted analyses on specific negotiation and implementation issues (Yamin and Depledge 2005: 485), as well as to counsel presiding officers on the negotiation management. This ability is mainly a result of the profound knowledge in the secretariat of political sensitivities and technical issues which has been accumulated in the secretariat since its creation (Depledge 2005: 72–3). The full-time occupation in the secretariat with almost any conceivable issue related to the climate regime has resulted in 'informational asymmetry' between staff and government officials. Government officials often lack time for a comparable preparation. Or they change positions, and officials who take over the responsibility have first of all to become acquainted with the climate regime process.

The desertification secretariat

Unlike the climate convention and the biodiversity convention, both of which were opened for ratification at the 1992 Rio Summit, the UN Convention to Combat Desertification is the single one of the three 'Rio Conventions' for which negotiations were actually triggered at Rio. Only coming into force in 1996, the desertification convention is the youngest treaty in our sample. Its secretariat has been looking for an active role in the convention process ever since it was established. By so doing it has attracted criticism from those who wish to see a treaty secretariat confined to a strictly instrumental role at the service of its treaty parties. At the same time it has undeniably been influential.

Cognitive influence: globalizing desertification

The secretariat effectively maintains the concept of desertification enshrined in the convention and contributes actively to how it is being interpreted. The significance thereof for the global discourse on desertification must not be underrated. Indeed, the cognitive framing of 'desertification' as opposed to 'land degradation' bears considerable implications for the interpretation of the convention and its implementation. In particular, the use of this specific terminology affects how the non-expert stakeholder perceives the problem that is being addressed (Corell 1999: 53). Secretariat officials are even prepared to acknowledge that desertification may be a rather misleading term for the phenomenon of dryland degradation. However, the desertification secretariat is effectively conserving the desertification trademark and ensures that its usage is vividly promoted, notably so by public outreach activities.

In a similar vein, the secretariat played a lead role in shifting the global understanding of desertification from being a regional problem into a global commons problem. This transformation is a striking example for the power of discourse with tangible material implications. By framing desertification as a global problem, projects under the convention have now become eligible for funding through the multi-billion Global Environment Facility. Indeed, the establishment of a distinct programme on sustainable land management of the Global Environment Facility in the wake of the 2002 World Summit of Sustainable Development is a major concession of the donor countries vis-à-vis the developing world. African countries, in particular, had pushed for it ever since the establishment of the Global Environment Facility in 1994. While it is not feasible to precisely measure the specific impact of the secretariat in bringing this about, it can be shown, however, that it has consistently backed the issue by keeping it on the agenda of relevant intergovernmental bodies. In fact, the secretariat regards itself as a contributor to this end and argues that granting accessibility to the Global Environment Facility was an overdue step to make up for the lack of a genuine convention-financing mechanism.

Normative influence: advancing institutionalization

In line with its mandate and the general objectives of the convention, the secretariat's efforts to further and solidify the institutionalization of the convention process are characterized by a strong regional focus. Indeed, the establishment of strong links with 'affected regions' – coordinated by the secretariat's regional action facilitators for Africa, Asia and Latin-America – have helped the desertification secretariat to progressively advance the institutionalization of the convention. Pushing ahead, the secretariat seeks to expand and strengthen regional coordination units that have been developed to improve intra-regional cooperation with a view to the implementation of regional action plans. While the secretariat has, predictably, been successful in mustering support for this endeavour within affected country regions, donor country parties are wary of institutional duplication and question the added value of regional coordination units. Critical considerations of whether and how the role of existing units should be expanded and whether additional ones are desirable were thus put on the agendas of recent conferences of parties (see IISD 2003: 8; IISD 2005b: 10).

The creation of the Committee for the Review of the Implementation of the Convention (CRIC) is even better suited to illustrate the secretariat's proactive role in furthering the institutionalization of the convention. The idea of setting up a distinct subsidiary body that would assist parties to review progress in the implementation of the convention was first suggested from within the desertification secretariat, which is eager to see the desertification convention on an equal footing with both the climate change and biodiversity conventions. It thus triggered the creation of an additional institution that was initially perceived to be at odds with the interests of major donor parties but came to be accepted as a potentially useful complementation to the regime – despite continuous criticism on a number of details (see IISD 2002: 13–14). Since its 2002 inaugural session, two more meetings of the CRIC have been held with a mixed record: the second meeting was held back-to-back with the sixth conference of parties at Havana in 2003 and suffered from the highly politicized atmosphere of the overall meeting; the third meeting, held in Bonn in May 2005, saw little substantive progress but was felt to be a helpful exercise to reinvigorate momentum after the dubious outcome of the Havana meeting (see IISD 2005c: 19–20). Irrespective of the committee's future role, it can reasonably be said to have contributed to the institutionalization of the convention process by requiring governments to focus on questions pertaining to the implementation of the convention.

The most striking example of secretariat interference with the convention process is arguably the staging of a high-level segment of heads of state and government meeting during the sixth conference of parties at Havana. Irrespective of the anxiety expressed by some parties during the preparatory process, the secretariat chose to go ahead with the high-level segment which it expected to increase public attention for the convention. In the event, it actually produced a 'Havana Declaration of Heads of States and Governments'. However, it came at the cost of considerable quarrels between the secretariat and major developed countries, including the European Union. In particular, the secretariat drew heavy criticism because it failed to account for political sensitivities of developed countries in setting the stage for controversial leaders from several developing countries. So, while noteworthy influence need to be acknowledged, parties have since sought to tighten their control over the activities and resources of the secretariat.

Explanations: global discourse, regional problem

A notable implication pertaining to the post-Rio emergence of the convention is that it has been framed as a sustainable development treaty rather than as an environmental treaty in the narrow sense. This point is emphasized time and again by secretariat officers and by parties from the developing world. Indeed, poverty eradication – a policy objective central to developing countries – is prominently anchored in the convention as an essential precondition for the 'combat' against desertification to be effective (see also UNCCD 1995, 2002: Article 4, para. 2c).

As a result, although being an issue-specific convention that addresses the problem of desertification, the contents of the convention expand into an elusive complex of issues. The negotiating parties have thus created a problem structure that is rather vague. This vagueness provides those who seek to implement the convention with considerable leeway as to how to go about it. The desertification secretariat has itself benefited from that. The inherent vagueness of the convention enabled it to seek and use its room for manoeuvre and become a particularly active player within the desertification regime. The fact that many of the secretariat's professional staff have been involved in one way or another with the erstwhile negotiation of the convention, including its long-serving executive secretary Hama Arba Diallo as the head of the interim negotiations secretariat, was certainly conducive to this end. This constellation warranted considerable continuity as the negotiation process gradually evolved into the institutionalization of the actual convention. Hence, by way of utilizing its discursive capacity the secretariat itself effectively helped to mould the convention process in the way we find it today.

However, its ability to do so in the first place must be attributed to the structure of the core policy issue around which the whole convention is construed. In particular, the problem of dryland degradation is of low saliency from the perspective of the powerful parties in the industrialized world. Although it is observed all around the world, only developing countries in the world's arid and semi-arid regions are severely affected by its consequences. Hence, despite the framing of desertification as a global problem and its actual interlinkages with a variety of global issues, it essentially remains a regional problem occurring on a world-wide scale (see Bauer 2007). Land degradation does not leave everybody worse off in the sense that, for instance, global warming does. Consequently, the problem structure of desertification *per se* is unfavourable for developing countries to yield meaningful bargaining power, because the convention is of little priority to developed countries (see also Najam 2004). Thus, the former tend to appreciate a supportive role on the part of the secretariat while the latter's efforts to control the political process are comparatively weak – including allowing the secretariat a long leash, at least up until the ambivalent 2003 conference of parties at Havana.

The considerable achievements that have been made in the institutionalization of the convention and in furthering its implementation in affected regions can be partially attributed to the activities of the secretariat, notably its leadership. Rather than confining itself to 'doing its job' the secretariat has installed itself as a vocal advocate of affected country parties that actively challenges the constraints it faces by way of problem structure. The dedication to seeking opportunities to do so is largely generated at the secretariat's executive level. Indeed, executive secretary Hama Arba Diallo looms large in the history of the desertification secretariat. An experienced diplomat from Burkina Faso, he is recognized today as a charismatic international civil servant who enjoys strong support from developing countries. Notably, he is credited for a conducive role in the negotiation of the convention – particularly in the African region. Moreover, he is admired by some and loathed by others for standing up to developed country parties, as exemplified in his seeing through the High-Level Segment at Havana. While this attitude is ambivalent at least to the extent that it breaches the imperative for neutrality and thereby undermines the secretariat's overall authority, it can not be ignored in a comprehensive discussion of how the desertification secretariat affects the convention process.

In sum, the elusive scope of the problem structure in combination with its low saliency for developed countries help us to explain both the latitude and constraints within which the desertification secretariat plays its role; strong leadership is key to how the secretariat fulfils this role in a proactive, advocacy-like manner that strives for a dynamic advancement of the convention process.

The biodiversity secretariat

The secretariat of the Convention on Biological Diversity (CBD) has been established as a treaty secretariat comparable to those of the other Rio conventions on climate and desertification (Rosendal 1995; Le Prestre 2002b). Even though the mandates of these secretariats read rather similarly, the biodiversity secretariat enjoys a remarkable reputation among member countries. Thereby, it is more successful in generating normative influence compared to the climate secretariat. Several experts in the field even argue that the process of implementing the convention would not be in its current advanced state without the effective and well-respected work of the secretariat that has been described as a 'lean shark' (Siebenhüner 2007: 269). At the same time, the secretariat has hardly been able to generate significant cognitive influence.

Cognitive influence: to whom it may concern

Even though the biodiversity secretariat has neither the means nor the mandate for actual scientific research, one of its main tasks is to collect and to disseminate (scientific) knowledge. It has, however, close links with the scientific community through processes such as the Millennium Ecosystem Assessment, international scientific cooperative programmes such as DIVERSITAS, and the participation of staff members in relevant scientific symposia. The secretariat gathers scientific information on the different natural science issues of the biodiversity conservation in the various ecosystems such as mountains, wetlands, forests, etc. as well as on administrative, social, legal and economic aspects of the problems, e.g. of access and benefit sharing. This knowledge is processed and disseminated mostly to representatives of national governments and administrators. Moreover, the secretariat was actively involved in the Millennium Ecosystem Assessment.

The outcomes of these activities are limited to certain target groups that make regular use of these products. While the information provided by the secretariat is highly welcomed by most national delegates to the international negotiation bodies under the convention and by a number of representatives from non-governmental organizations, neither the scientific community at large nor business actors draw extensively on this source. What is more, the secretariat's influence on public discourse remains rather limited. Media attention to the press releases and other materials provided by the secretariat is low, although the quality of the information is, by and large, seen as scientifically credible and politically neutral. This influence can be viewed as a success of the secretariat's information policy for which trust by the parties and other stakeholders has been described as the 'most important organizational quality of a credible secretariat' (Sandford 1996: 5).

Normative influence: progress by inclusion

International cooperation and the support for negotiations and meetings is probably the field of the most obvious influence of the biodiversity secretariat. Measured by the number of participating countries, the secretariat was successful in helping to create widespread support for the Cartagena Protocol which was adopted in 2003. The secretariat's balanced and continuous efforts in facilitating dialogues and negotiations on the issue of biosafety contributed to the successful adoption of the protocol. The same holds for the successful facilitation of the preparation and negotiation process on the access and benefit provisions of the convention (Siebenhüner and Suplie 2005). In budget negotiations at each conference of parties, the secretariat's executive secretary plays a highly active role and presents cost calculations of the decisions taken to improve the quality of decision making of the budget committee and to increase governments' financial commitments.

With regard to the inclusion of non-governmental actors into the convention process, the convention designed its processes more inclusively than other UN-convention processes where non-governmental organizations are restricted to passive observer functions (Heijden 2002). For example, the secretariat promoted the inclusion of indigenous and local communities in the Working Group on Article 8j (traditional knowledge) where they now play a role similar to that of government delegates – even though they are technically still only observers. The Working Group on Article 8j process provided a platform for indigenous and local communities to articulate their concerns and interests regarding the preservation, respect and protection of traditional biodiversity-related knowledge, innovations and practices.

The secretariat was also successful in including particular issues on the agenda of other international negotiations. For instance, it is considered an achievement of the secretariat that the ecosystems approach – a prominent feature of the convention process – was adopted by other related conventions such as the Ramsar Convention on Wetlands. The secretariat was also instrumental with respect to the development of indicators for the 2010 biodiversity target and elements of the convention's programmes of work, including access to genetic resources and benefit sharing, in the WSSD Plan of Implementation. Moreover, since the fifth conference of parties in 2000 the secretariat has been entrusted with the drafting of decisions that serve as the basis for subsequent meetings of the convention bodies. Since then, many drafts, such as outputs of technical expert groups' technical assessments, have been adopted largely unchanged as prepared by the secretariat. In general, however, the influence of the secretariat decreases with the level of contestation in the respective areas of regulation. In highly contested issues such as the access and benefit-sharing provisions, secretariat drafts are regularly amended or completely redrafted by the parties.

In sum, the secretariat can be regarded as comparatively successful in fostering international cooperation in implementing the convention. It helped to organize the processes rather inclusively and is trusted by many governments as a credible and balanced facilitator of international cooperation processes. Governments as well as non-governmental organizations have changed or adapted their behaviour on the basis of their experiences with the reliable work of the secretariat which can be seen as a significant influence of the secretariat's work.

Explanations: a lean shark

Biodiversity and the combat against its loss is a highly complex environmental problem. The conservation of species as a means to preserve biodiversity also includes the protection of entire ecosystems as a functioning web of interactions among species. This also poses a challenge to international politics given the fact that most ecosystems cross national borders and biodiversity is a common interest of humankind. Moreover, economic, cultural, spiritual and aesthetical values of species are connected to species and their ecosystems. Since the preservation of ecosystems and natural habitats often requires severe changes and limitations in current land use patterns in most countries, the costs of regulation in this problem area are significant (Swanson 1999; McGraw 2002; Brand and Görg 2003).

The problem of biodiversity loss is also hardly visible and lacks public interest. Hence, public awareness is generally low as the extinction of a species is invisible and normally does not entail catastrophic repercussions. Consequently, policy-makers still have a low sensitivity to the role of biodiversity in sustainable development. The saliency of the problem for them is generally low. The secretariat's limited cognitive influence can be attributed to this characteristic of the underlying problem that does not lead to media-catching catastrophic events and large-scale damages to private and public properties.

Much of the influence observed in the normative field can be credited to the secretariat's bureaucratic authority. Like other convention secretariats, the biodiversity secretariat serves as an 'information hub' of the treaty and positions it to generate cognitive influence (Sandford 1996: 7). It has actually developed significant expertise in the field of biodiversity governance, with forty of its seventy staff members being professionals and merely thirty general service staff. Given the numerous organizational tasks in setting up conferences and meetings, this proportion indicates a rather lean administration and an emphasis on issue-specific professionals.

The secretariat's informal means of influencing governmental decisions and other stakeholders are comparatively well developed. This applies to its increasing activities in fostering communication and education on biodiversity issues. The secretariat has embarked on a policy of communication, education and public awareness. It publishes numerous documents, holds press conferences and has hired a public relations company to develop a communication strategy. All these activities combined with the external perception as a neutral and well-informed holder of expertise provide the secretariat with a significant amount of external authority that allows it to generate normative influence even beyond its mandate.

Its organizational culture complements the picture of a well-organized, respected and technocratic bureaucracy, but cannot explain the influence by itself. The composition of staff is highly heterogeneous. It is characterized by a mixture of academics and practitioners that virtually rules out any suspicion of regional, professional or other biases, although individuals with natural science backgrounds do hold a majority since the first phase of the implementation of the convention and the related work of the secretariat focused primarily on conservation issues. Decision-making procedures in the biodiversity secretariat seem to be rather centralized, with a powerful position occupied by the organization's head, the executive secretary. He holds considerable sanctioning powers over his staff members due to the short duration of most contracts and his power to extend the contracts or not.

The personal skills and abilities of the executive secretary have a significant influence on the secretariat's relationship with parties and other intergovernmental organizations and their executives. Through his dominating role in the secretariat, the executive secretary is in a position to affect the entire policy field. This requires him (or her) to develop and maintain strong informal trust-based ties to key individuals in the policy arena while at the same time ensuring neutrality and balanced action on behalf of the secretariat. The first executive secretary, Calestous Juma from Kenya, sought to establish the secretariat as an autonomous international bureaucracy, thus entering into continuous disputes with UNEP officials and its executive director. When Hamdallah Zedan, a UNEP career officer from Egypt, was appointed to succeed Juma in 1998, many observers expected an increasing level of control through the UNEP headquarters (Le Prestre 2002a). Yet, Zedan stepped up as the head of a largely autonomous international secretariat and continued on Juma's path of emancipating the secretariat from UNEP headquarters (see also Rosendal and Andresen 2004). His successor from 2006 onwards, Ahmed Djoghlaf, moves into the same direction, underlining leadership as an explanatory factor for the influence of the secretariat.

Conclusion

This chapter has looked at the secretariats of international environmental treaties not as instruments in the hands of national governments but as political actors in their own right. Our comparative survey revealed that each secretariat does indeed generate cognitive and normative influence and advances the mandate of the respective treaty. Furthermore, a clear variation in the degree of influence across the three secretariats could be observed, although they have been designed and mandated similarly and by and large fulfil similar functions. The influence of the climate secretariat was shown to be the weakest among our cases, hardly exceeding its official mandate. In comparison, the biodiversity and the desertification secretariat were capable of exerting stronger normative influence, while the cognitive influence of the desertification secretariat was found to be stronger than those of the other two secretariats.

Comparing the explanatory factors across our three cases, the structure of the underlying problem, bureaucratic authority and leadership qualify as explanatory factors given that they co-vary with the observed cognitive and normative influence. In particular leadership appears to explain the variation of influence: the desertification and biodiversity secretariat were characterized by comparatively strong leadership and were found to be more influential than the climate secretariat where a comparable leadership, if any, was missing. The structure of the underlying problem affected the capability of the secretariats to generate influence and most obviously explains variation across the climate and desertification secretariat: the high stakes involved in climate change resulted in severe constraints on the freedom of the former to act independently and limited its overall influence, whereas the vagueness of the problem of desertification and its low saliency in the developed world allowed the latter to assume a more active and influential role. Bureaucratic authority was found to be an important source of influence on the climate and biodiversity secretariats. Organizational culture instead appears to have no strong explanatory power.

Two more general findings stand out. First of all, our analyses suggest that there is no single factor which provides a satisfactory explanation for any observed influence of international bureaucracies. Rather, this influence is the result of the interplay of different explanatory variables which determine the capability of international bureaucracies to influence international political processes. Secondly, our findings revealed that the patterns and means to generate influence followed two basic schemes. The first adheres to a more technocratic mode as in the case of the climate and biodiversity secretariats. They comply in most cases with the preferences of most member states. By contrast, the desertification secretariat follows what may be labelled an advocacy approach. Its work strives to support, in particular, affected countries. At times, it may stand in strong contrast to the apparent interests of powerful developed countries. As has been shown, both approaches are capable of generating influence. Whether and why secretariats choose either one of these approaches needs to be studied further. Our findings suggest that behavioural choices for treaty secretariats are linked, in particular, to problem structure and leadership patterns.

In conclusion, this research suggests that treaty secretariats play a significant role in the institutionalization and implementation of environmental regimes. Our insight into their specific dynamics and actor quality gives rise to new questions with regard to the exact degree and spread of their influence as well as to the legitimacy and accountability of this kind of influence. They thus need to be systematically included in future studies of the complex processes of global environmental governance.

References

Andresen, S. and Butenschon, S.H. (2001) 'Norwegian Climate Policy: From Pusher to Laggard?', *International Environmental Agreements: Politics, Law and Economics*, 1(3): 337–56.

Andresen, S. and Skjaerseth, J.B. (1999) 'Can International Environmental Secretariats Promote Effective Co-operation?', United Nations University's International Conference on Synergies and Co-ordination between Multilateral Environmental Agreements, 14–16 July 1999, Tokyo, Japan.

Barnett, M.N. and Finnemore, M. (1999) 'The Politics, Power, and Pathologies of International Organizations', *International Organization*, 53(4): 699–732.

Bauer, S. (2006) 'Does Bureaucracy Really Matter? The Authority of Intergovernmental Treaty Secretariats in Global Environmental Politics', *Global Environmental Politics*, 6(1): 23–49.

Bauer, S. (2007) 'Desertification', in Robertson, R. and Scholte, J.A. (eds) *Encyclopedia of Globalization*, London: Routledge.

Biermann, F. and Bauer, S. (2005) 'Managers of Global Governance. Assessing and Explaining the Influence of International Bureaucracies', *Global Governance Working Paper Series No. 15*, Amsterdam, Berlin, Oldenburg, Potsdam: Global Governance Project.

Brand, U. and Görg, C. (2003) 'The State and the Regulation of Biodiversity. International Biopolitics and the Case of Mexico', *Geoforum*, 34: 221–33.

Corell, E. (1999) *The Negotiable Desert. Expert Knowledge in the Negotiations of the Convention to Combat Desertification*, Linköping: Linköping University.

Depledge, J. (2005) *The Organization of Global Negotiations: Constructing the Climate Change Regime*, London: Earthscan.

Depledge, J. (2007) 'A Special Relationship: Chairpersons and the Secretariat in the Climate Change Negotiations', *Global Environmental Politics* 7(1): 45–68.

Grubb, M. and Yamin, F. (2001) 'Climate Collapse at The Hague: What Happened, Why, and Where do we Go from here?', *International Affairs*, 77(2): 261–76.

Grubb, M., Vrolijk, C. and Brack, D. (1999) *The Kyoto Protocol: A Guide and Assessment*, London: Royal Institute of International Affairs, Energy and Environmental Programme.

Heijden, H.-A.v.d. (2002) 'Political Parties and NGOs in Global Environmental Politics', *International Political Science Review*, 23(2): 187–201.

International Institute for Sustainable Development (IISD) (1996) 'Report of the Meetings of the Subsidiary Bodies of the UN Framework Convention on Climate Change: 9–18 December 1996', *Earth Negotiations Bulletin*, New York: IISD.

IISD (2000) 'Summary of the Sixth Conference of the Parties to the UN Framework Convention on Climate Change: 13–25 November 2000', *Earth Negotiations Bulletin*, New York: IISD.

IISD (2001) 'Summary of the Resumed Sixth Session of the Conference of the Parties to the UN Framework Convention on Climate Change: 16–27 July 2001', *Earth Negotiations Bulletin*, New York: IISD.

IISD (2002) 'Summary of the First Session of the Committee for the Review of the Implementation of the Convention to Combat Desertification, 11–22 November 2002', *Earth Negotiations Bulletin*, New York: IISD.

IISD (2003) 'UNFCCC COP-9 Highlights: Friday, 5 December 2003', *Earth Negotiations Bulletin*, New York: IISD.

IISD (2005a) 'Summary of the Eleventh Conference of the Parties to the UN Framework Convention on Climate Change and First Conference of the Parties Serving as the Meeting of the Parties to the Kyoto Protocol: 28 November–10 December 2005', *Earth Negotiations Bulletin*, New York: IISD.

IISD (2005b) 'Summary of the Seventh Conference of the Parties to the Convention to Combat Desertification: 17–28 October 2005', *Earth Negotiations Bulletin*, New York: IISD.

IISD (2005c) 'Summary of the Third Session of the Committee for the Review of the Implementation of the Convention to Combat Desertification: 2–11 May 2005', *Earth Negotiations Bulletin*, New York: IISD.

Le Prestre, P. (2002a) 'The Operation of the CBD Convention Governance System', in Le Prestre, P. (ed.) *Governing Global Biodiversity: The Evolution and Implementation of the Convention on Biological Diversity*, Aldershot: Ashgate.

Le Prestre, P. (2002b) 'Studying the Effectiveness of the CBD', in Le Prestre, P. (ed.) *Governing Global Biodiversity: The Evolution and Implementation of the Convention on Biological Diversity*, Aldershot: Ashgate.

Lee, G. (1999) 'Environmental Policy: Too Little Too Late?', in Jones, B. (ed.) *Political Issues in Britain Today*, Manchester: Manchester University Press.

McGraw, D.M. (2002) 'The Story of the Biodiversity Convention: From Negotiation to Implementation', in Le Prestre, P. (ed.) *Governing Global Biodiversity: The Evolution and Implementation of the Convention on Biological Diversity*, Aldershot: Ashgate.

Miles, E.L., Underdal, A. *et al.* (eds) (2002) *Explaining Regime Effectiveness: Confronting Theory with Evidence*, Cambridge, MA: MIT Press.

Mouritzen, H. (1990) *The International Civil Service: A Study of Bureaucracy*, Aldershot: Dartmouth.

Najam, A. (2004) 'Dynamics of the Southern Collective: Developing Countries in Desertification Negotiations', *Global Environmental Politics*, 4(3): 128–54.

Nitze, W.A. (1994) 'A Failure of Presidential Leadership', in Mintzer, I.M. and Leonard, J.A. (eds) *Negotiating Climate Change: The Inside Story to the Rio Convention*, Cambridge: Cambridge University Press: 187–200.

Oberthür, S. and Ott, H.E. (1999) *The Kyoto Protocol: International Climate Policy for the 21st Century*, Berlin: Springer.

Ott, H.E. (2001a) 'The Bonn Agreement to the Kyoto Protocol – Paving the Way for Ratification', *International Environmental Agreements: Politics, Law and Economics*, 1(4): 469–76.

Ott, H.E. (2001b) 'Climate Change: An Important Foreign Policy Issue', *Foreign Affairs*, 77(2): 277–96.

Rosendal, G.K. (1995) 'The Convention on Biological Diversity: A Viable Instrument for Conservation and Sustainable Use?', in Thommessen, Ø.B. (ed.) *Green Globe Yearbook of International Co-Operation on Environment and Development 1995*, Oxford: Oxford University Press.

Rosendal, G.K. and Andresen, S. (2004) 'UNEP's Role in Enhancing Problem-Solving Capacity in Multilateral Environmental Agreements: Co-ordination and Assistance in the Biodiversity Conservation Cluster', *FNI Report 10/2003*, Lysaker: Fridtjof Nansen Institute.

Sandford, R. (1992) 'Secretariats and International Environmental Negotiations. Two New Models', in Susskind, L.E., Dolin, E.J. and Breslin, J.W. (eds) *International Environmental Treaty Making*, Cambridge, MA: Harvard Law School.

Sandford, R. (1994) 'International Environmental Treaty Secretariats: Stage-Hands or Actors?', in Bergesen, H.O. and Parmann, G. (eds) *Green Globe Yearbook of International Co-operation on Environment and Development 1994*, Oxford: Oxford University Press.

Sandford, R. (1996) 'International Environmental Treaty Secretariats: A Case of Neglected Potential?', *Environmental Impact Assessment Review*, 16: 3–12.

Schröder, H. (2001) *Negotiating the Kyoto Protocol: An Analysis of Negotiation Dynamics in International Negotiations*, Münster: LIT Verlag.

Siebenhüner, B. (2007) 'Administrator of Global Biodiversity: The Secretariat of the Convention on Biological Diversity', *Biodiversity and Conservation*, 16: 259–74.

Siebenhüner, B. and Suplie, J. (2005) 'Implementing the Access and Benefit Sharing Provisions of the CBD: A Case for Institutional Learning', *Ecological Economics*, 53: 507–22.

Swanson, T. (1999) 'Why Is there a Biodiversity Convention? The International Interest in Centralized Development Planning', *International Affairs*, 75(1): 307–31.

Tarradell, M. (2005) 'International Bureaucracies Influencing Global Environmental Politics: What Do Stakeholders Think?' Findings from the MANUS Senior Expert Survey [unpublished manuscript], in Amsterdam, Berlin, Oldenburg, Potsdam.

UNCCD (1995) *Down to Earth. A Simplified Guide to the Convention to Combat Desertification, Why it Is Necessary and What Is Important and Different about it*, Bonn: UNCCD.

UNCCD (2002) 'United Nations Convention to Combat Desertification in those Countries Experiencing Serious Drought and/or Desertification, particularly in Africa', Text with Annexes, and a Preface by the UNCCD Secretariat, Bonn: UNCCD.

UNFCCC (2004) 'Results of the Survey on the Effectiveness of the Use of the UNFCCC Technology Information Clearing House (TT:CLEAR)', *Note by the secretariat*, FCCC/SBSTA/2004/INF.8, 25 May 2004.

UNFCCC (2005) 'Report on the Internal Review of the Activities of the Secretariat' *Note by the Executive Secretary*, FCCC/SBI/2005/6', 11 March 2005.

Vrolijk, C. (2002) *A New Interpretation of the Kyoto Protocol. Outcomes from The Hague, Bonn and Marrakesh*, London: Royal Institute of International Affairs.

Yamin, F. and Depledge, J. (2005) *The International Climate Change Regime: A Guide to Rules, Institutions and Procedures*, Cambridge: Cambridge University Press.

Yi-Chong, X. and Weller, P. (2004) *The Governance of World Trade. International Civil Servants and the GATT/WTO*, Cheltenham, UK: Edward Elgar.

Part III

New public–private hybrid organizations

10 International organizations as entrepreneurs of environmental partnerships

Liliana B. Andonova[1]

Introduction

Public–private partnerships are an increasingly common aspect of international politics. Such agreements between states, international organizations, and non-state actors have proliferated particularly rapidly in international environmental governance (Kaul 2005; Andonova 2006). This chapter examines the growth and patterns of international environmental partnerships. In particular, it seeks to disentangle the relations between international organizations, which have been the traditional intergovernmental managers of cooperation and partnerships.

Case studies of prominent partnerships, such as the World Commission on Dams, the Global Compact, or the partnerships adopted at the 2002 World Summit on Sustainable Development (WSSD), have suggested that this is a promising new mode of governance (Reinicke and Deng 2000; Bissel 2001; Benner *et al.* 2003; Speth 2003; Ruggie 2004; Timmer and Juma 2005). Yet, we still know relatively little about the distribution of partnerships across environmental issue areas and organizations, the nature and role of different partners, and their relation to intergovernmental institutions and organizations. This chapter starts addressing some of these broad questions by focusing on one important piece of the partnership puzzle – the role of international organizations as partners. The argument posits that international organizations have been among the most active entrepreneurs of partnerships. They have steered the partnership movement in ways that respond to public pressure and strategic organizational incentives. Partnerships thus are not such a radical departure from the traditional system of intergovernmental cooperation as they may seem at first sight. They are better conceptualized as organizational innovations intended to complement and reinvent, rather than circumvent, the mandates and operations of intergovernmental organizations and regimes.

The chapter develops the argument as follows. It first discusses the structural differences and similarities between international organizations and partnerships. Then it specifies the conditions under which international organizations are more likely to engage in partnerships with non-state actors and states. The theoretical framework helps us to understand why and which international organizations have been most active as partnership entrepreneurs, and what the resulting patterns are. The empirical section examines trends in public–private environmental cooperation across several large partnership initiatives against predicted patterns. By examining a relatively large sample rather than isolated partnerships the chapter sheds empirical light on the distribution, structural variations, partner participation, political reach, and organizational embeddedness of partnerships. The chapter thus seeks to provide one of the first systematic analyses of the relationship between international environmental organizations and public–private partnerships.

International organizations and partnerships: how do they differ?

International organizations and public–private partnerships could not be more different in organizational structure. International organizations are typically relatively large bureaucracies. They are a product of intergovernmental agreements and are established to manage a set of rules, norms, and implementation procedures. International organizations are structured and managed hierarchically. Their operational mandates, objectives, and resources are determined top-down by nation states. As most organizations, international organizations also develop a set of standard procedures, organizational inertia, and organizational interests that influence their operations and relations with states (Barnett and Finnemore 2004). Modern regime theories have largely ignored international organizations as object of analysis. International organizations established to manage environmental regimes were studied largely as arenas of state interaction and a mechanism to facilitate intergovernmental cooperation but not as actors themselves (Haas *et al.* 1993). Increasingly, however, the international relations literature has been refocusing attention on these important actors in international relations, as exemplified by the emphasis placed in this volume on international environmental organizations.

Public–private partnerships do not fit comfortably within the traditional hierarchical structure of international relations and organizations. Partnerships are typically organized as networks. They involve multiple public actors (such as international organizations, states, or discrete state bureaucracies) as well as 'private' or non-state actors (including businesses, advocacy organizations, foundations, or even research institutions). Partnerships often have a minimal degree of bureaucratization. Some environmental partnerships, as we shall see in the empirical sample, have small secretariats. Others operate virtually or out of the organizational infrastructure of a leading partner or supporting organization.

Another distinctive characteristic of partnerships is their flexibility and legal voluntarism. While partnerships are not simply *ad hoc* forms of interaction or political lobbying, they involve agreements that are typically not bound by international or domestic law. Partnerships, unlike most international organizations, do not typically seek universal participation but instead focus on relatively narrow aspects of governance (Andonova 2006). For example, public–private partnerships are unlikely to be created to manage climate change in its full global complexity. However, many discrete aspects of climate management, such as carbon financing, implementation of project-based mechanisms and energy-technology transfers, have become the basis of international partnerships. The Prototype Carbon Fund, which is discussed in some detail below, targets the strengthening of financing mechanisms for carbon mitigation, rather than a broad agreement on climate change. Thus, partnerships can have multiple but usually very specific functional objectives. Some partnerships advance as a set of normative principles, such as the principles associated with the building of dams endorsed by the World Commission on Dams. Other partnerships simply seek to diffuse information, knowledge, and involvement in the best practices for environmental governance as exemplified by the Equator Initiative discussed below. Yet others have specific regulatory and implementation targets, such as the designation and protection of 12 per cent of the Brazilian Amazon, as the core of the Amazon Protected Areas Partnership between the World Bank, WWF, and the Brazilian government.

Whatever the functional objectives of public–private partnerships – norm and information diffusion, market creation, policy change, or technology diffusion – these agreements tend to seek flexible solutions for narrowly defined governance problems, with a minimalist organizational structure. The implementation of these narrowly targeted solutions is not assured by a system of laws, but by internally agreed rules and procedures. Partnerships thus establish flexible cooperation mechanisms for learning by doing, building of coalitions of the willing, and dividing a complex governance problem into its smaller components. This again is quite different from the legalistic approach of international organizations, which emphasize universal agreement or substantial participation in formally regulated and binding agreements.

Because of these differences in the structure of environmental partnerships, most studies have focused on the partnerships themselves, without exploring sufficiently their linkages to the intergovernmental system. Indeed, partnerships are often conceptualized as the alternatives to formal intergovernmental agreements and rigid bureaucratic organizations (Witte *et al.* 2003). This chapter posits that despite the structural differences, public–private partnerships cannot be neatly separated from the system of international organizations. These new mechanisms for cooperation do not simply float independently in the global governance space. More often than not, they come out of and are embedded in existing intergovernmental organizations. Thus, from the perspective of international organizations, public–private partnerships can also be conceptualized as a form of organizational innovation. In line with the emphasis on organizations in this volume, I examine public–private partnerships as organizational innovations and the conditions under which international organizations engage and support such flexible mechanisms of governance.

Why do international organizations partner?

Why would international environmental organizations, which remain the managing core of environmental regimes, share power with non-state actors through public–private partnerships? This is one of the most interesting questions related to the rise of global environmental partnerships, which so far has not been adequately addressed. This section explores the conditions for international organizations entrepreneurship and partnership for the environment. To illuminate these conditions, it builds on the insights of sociological and principal-agent models of organizational behaviour and policy change.

As scholars increasingly turn their attention to the role of international organizations as actors, they have borrowed a range of models from sociology, economics, and political science to study the behaviour of international organizations and their accountability, influence, and reforms. One set of scholars have employed principal-agent models to study the relations between states and international organizations (Pollack 1997; Nielson and Tierney 2003). Developed first in economics for the study of the firm, the principal-agent model has been applied to the study of domestic and international political institutions. When applied to international cooperation, the principal-agent model conceptualizes international organizations as agents to whom states, acting as principals, delegate authority to pursue a set of policies. It has been employed to examine primarily the mechanisms via which states control their agents, the degree and space for agency initiative in international policy-making, and the ability of principals to push through reforms consistent with their evolving interests. Other scholars have used sociological models of organizations to examine in greater depth the functioning of international organizations as bureaucracies. Such studies often emphasize the sources of organizational inertia, mission creep, or even pathologies which could hinder effective policy coordination and change (Barnett and Finnemore 2004). Focusing on the internal structure and incentives of organizations could also be helpful, however, in illuminating how international organizations respond to external demands and evolve under dual pressures from outside and within (Fox and Brown 1998; Gutner 2002).

In environmental politics, both types of organizational models have been employed to explain the greening (or the lack thereof) of international financial institutions such as the World Bank. Nielson and Tierney (2003), for example, use an extended model of delegation to track how changes in the domestic environmental preferences of the most powerful principals of the World Bank, including the US and other developed countries, have precipitated the rise of environmental projects and financing. Gutner (2002) focuses more on the interplay between external pressure and internal structure and incentives to explain the variation in the greening of the World Bank, the European Bank for Reconstruction and Development, and the European Investment Bank. Fox and Brown (1998) employ a sociologically informed framework to examine the interplay between external pressure, internal incentives, and coalition building in influencing the social and environmental accountability of the World Bank.

The theoretical models of organizations have not been widely used, however, to explore the role of other non-financial organizations in international environmental politics: neither have organizational models been employed to examine the evolution of the organizational infrastructure in environmental cooperation. The lack of attention to the role and evolution of non-financial environmental organizations can be partly explained by the fact that these organizations have hardly attracted significant public attention or contentious attacks of the type that focused on the World Bank and other financial institutions. Given the lack of visible political pressure against international environmental organizations, it becomes even more puzzling that many of these organizations are retooling and partnering with non-state actors to reinvent their missions. Indeed, organizational theories, particularly of the sociological model, imply that organizational inertia, turf battles, and standard procedures are likely to make bureaucracies averse to change and prone to inefficiencies (Barnett and Finnemore 2004). Often considerable and protracted pressure is necessary to jolt bureaucracies out of their traditional ways. Why do then international environmental organizations increasingly tread unfamiliar ground, getting involved in joint decision making and partnerships with multiple, formerly unfamiliar stakeholders?

In a broader theoretical framework that examines both the sources of political demand for and supply of public–private partnerships in global governance, I have used the principal-agent model to suggest that international organizations are likely to be, under certain conditions, among the most important entrepreneurs of partnerships (Andonova 2006). Here I build on this argument and also consider insights from the sociological perspective on organizations to elaborate why international environmental organizations, in particular, might develop an interest in public–private partnerships. In environmental regimes, international organizations typically provide specialized technical information, monitoring, capacity building, and coordination activities intended to facilitate cooperation and compliance with environmental agreements. As a principal-agent model would suggest, states determine the mandate and resources of international environmental organizations and have a variety of mechanisms to control their agents. Organizations thus vary in terms of resources and operational mandate. The United Nations Environmental Programme (UNEP), for example, has a largely technical mandate that emphasizes monitoring, diffusion of information, and in some cases the facilitation of dialogue and environmental negotiations. The United

Nations Commission on Sustainable Development (UNCSD) similarly has a largely technical mandate, albeit less focused on science and monitoring of trends compared to UNEP, but working mostly to facilitate regular inter-action and dialogue among environmental officials. Treaty secretariats, on the other hand, tend to have more issue-specific mandates related to the negoti-ation, monitoring, and implementation of environmental agreements. Their work is thus more targeted and more explicitly political. Yet other organiza-tions, such as the Multilateral Fund under the Montreal Protocol for the Protection of the Ozone Layer and the Global Environmental Facility (GEF), disburse assistance for the implementation of particular environmental con-ventions. Finally, there are organizations whose mandate is not primarily or exclusively focused on the environment, but who, rather, are involved in financial transfers or capacity building targeted at environmental policy. Examples included some of the operations of the World Bank, the European Bank for Reconstruction and Development, or the environmental support and activities provided by organizations such as the United Nations Devel-opment Programme (UNDP), the United Nations Educational, Scientific and Cultural Organization (UNESCO), and others. In sum, international environmental organizations have relatively clearly specified mandates, which can vary in their main focus from providing technical information and capacity building to facilitating and maintaining specific environmental agreements.

International environmental organizations as actors typically have a set of organizational interests. While both principal-agent and sociological models agree on this point, the two perspectives are interested in organizational incentives for different reasons. In a principal-agent framework, the interests of the agent matter only to the extent that they might differ from those of the principals, and thus might result in behaviour that is suboptimal from the principals' perspective. The principal-agent model thus provides relatively little specific guidance as to what exactly the interests of international environmental organizations might be and under what conditions they might include cooperation with non-state actors. Sociological theories of organiza-tion can complement the principal-agent model in identifying how the inter-ests of international environmental organizations might differ from those of their member states and under what conditions they might have incentives to cooperate with non-state actors.

Organizational theories suggest that, at minimum, international organiza-tions are likely to be interested in maintaining and increasing their agency budget and authority, irrespective of the preferences of states. States, at the same time, are likely to be interested in minimizing their contribution to international cooperation and organizations. Indeed, most international environmental agencies have relatively emasculated budgets. International organizations, as all bureaucracies, are also likely to maintain or expand their authority and mandate and to maintain broad public support and reputation. Environmental organizations thus might have an agency interest in averting failures of cooperation and playing an agenda-setting role to strengthen aspects of cooperation that relate to their mandates. States, on their part, might be cautious or unwilling to strengthen the role of international bureaucracies, or may have diverging preferences on issues related to the strengthening of environmental cooperation and the role of international organizations. For example, states such as Germany and France have been openly supportive of reforming and strengthening the mandate of UNEP to create a World Environmental Organization, while most of the other industrialized countries have been at best lukewarm or even in outright opposition to creating a new stronger bureaucratic centre to oversee global environmental issues. Thus, the bureaucratic interests of international organizations as agents may not fully coincide with the preferences of sovereign states, or may be more closely aligned with those of a subset of their principals.

Unpacking the organizational incentives of international environmental organizations allows us to specify conditions under which these actors might find incentives to establish new mechanisms of governance in direct collaboration with non-state actors. Several such conditions can be anticipated. To begin with, budgetary pressures or limited resources are likely to be important triggers of agency interest to attract non-state partners and thus additional resources. Increasingly, non-state actors in the commercial as well as in the non-profit sector command resources that outstrip the capacity of public budgets to support multiple policy objectives including the environment (Kaul 2005). The problem of budgetary pressure and limited resources available to international environmental organizations has been historically compounded by the inadequate intergovernmental environmental aid transfers compared to the magnitude of resources needed to implement environmental governance (Keohane and Levy 1996). We should, therefore, expect a close relationship between the variation in the willingness of states to support financially environmental cooperation and the interest of international organizations in initiating public–private partnerships as a mechanism to leverage resources.

Pressure by publics and states for greater operational effectiveness and accountability of international organizations is another potential trigger for organizational innovation through public–private partnerships. International organizations are large and visible public institutions. While some, such as the World Bank, have faced more direct advocacy pressure for reforms, other international organizations have faced more subtle but very real pressure for increased operational effectiveness while maintaining limited budgets. Indeed, while global environmental failures often result from the limited willingness of states to cooperate and follow through on their commitments, states as principals are often very eager to publicly shift the blame for cooperation failures onto the agents of cooperation. For example, at the 2002 World Summit on Sustainable Development, donor states blamed the failures of environmental governance on the ineffective implementation of existing agreements. Such framing of the issues allowed shifting the discourse toward international regimes and organizations as ineffective, rather than on states which are in fact mostly responsible for the implementation of international rules and norms.

Incentives for some form of an organizational response may be particularly strong when public scrutiny is high, while the interests of states to strengthen cooperation and support for international organizations are low (Ruggie 2003). Under such conditions, states are most likely to veil their unwillingness to make deals and commit resources behind arguments of institutional ineffectiveness, which are often seen as direct criticism of international organizations. While instances of organizational ineffectiveness do exist, it is often difficult for publics to distinguish to what extent failures in governance result from poor cooperation among states or from poor management of cooperation by international organizations. International organizations are likely, therefore, to have organizational incentives to independently craft organizational responses to public pressure within the parameters of their agency authority.

Cooperation with non-state actors through partnerships can be an attractive mode of an organizational response to financial, legitimacy, advocacy, or political pressures. Private contributions fill in the financial gaps by increasing the resources of organizations to fulfil their policy missions. Transnational environmental NGOs have had a long tradition of seeking direct cooperation with international organizations and influence in international environmental policies. Involving environmental NGOs more directly in governance through public–private partnerships may be associated with specific gains when international organizations seek to boost their public credibility and perceived effectiveness. Such gains include the leveraging of their specialized knowledge, societal reach, and external legitimacy associated with direct societal participation. The involvement of business increases the scope of the governance dialogue, as well as the access to financial and management resources. Finally, being flexible governance mechanisms, partnerships also allow to include selectively states that might be particularly interested in a specific aspect of international cooperation, thus building up gradual support through coalitions of the willing for a particular operational area. International organizations are also in the unique position to attract diverse partners as they have traditionally provided arenas that foster transnational networks. If we consider these organizational incentives, it is possible to suggest that international environmental organizations are more likely to seek partnerships with non-state actors and individual states under the following conditions:

- Budgetary or policy crises;
- Public or advocacy pressure;
- Limited willingness of states to strengthen intergovernmental cooperation and the operational capacity of international organizations.

International organizations, however, have only a limited leeway to pursue their agency interests and new mechanisms of governance in direct cooperation with non-state actors. 'Agency slack' is a concept introduced by principal-agent theory to capture the extent to which organizations have some leeway to pursue their agency interests independently of their principals. Like in other organizations, the agency slack of international organizations typically results from their specialized expertise, asymmetric information, and the presence of multiple or collective principals (Nielson and Tierney 2003). Agency slack, therefore, is likely to vary across international organizations and issue areas, according to the degree to which states are interested in and able to exert tight control over the agencies. Principal-agent analyses of organizations have examined the range of mechanisms, which principals could employ to maintain control over agent performance and outcomes, while retaining the efficiency benefits of agent specialization and slack. The principal-agent framework thus forces us to ask under what conditions international organizations might have not only interest but also enough slack to initiate partnerships with non-state actors in ways that would be sanctioned by states as their principals.

One dimension that is likely to vary along with agency slack is the extent of technical mandate and specialization of international organizations. As already discussed, in the field of environmental cooperation a number of international organizations have predominantly technical mandates that involve monitoring of environmental trends, assessment of scientific information, or capacity building. Notable examples include UNEP, the Cooperative Programme for Monitoring and Evaluation of Long-Range Transmission of Air Pollutants in Europe (EMEP), UNDP, UNCSD, and the International Panel on Climate Change (IPCC). Organizations with predominantly technical mandates are likely to have a greater agency slack for organizational innovation for several reasons. These organizations are not heavily involved in policy negotiations or enforcement-oriented monitoring. Therefore, states as principals face a lower risk of agency activism, and therefore lower incentives for tight agency control. At the same time, because of the highly technical and science-driven nature of agency activity, the benefits of specialization, delegation, and the involvement of non-state actors with relevant expertise are likely to be considerable. This is not to say that relatively technical organizations are separated from politics. But while still being political creatures, they are likely to have a higher degree of agency expertise and organizational leeway that may allow easier cooperation with non-state actors ranging from academic organizations to advocacy or business organizations.

A second dimension that is likely to vary along with agency slack is related to the extent of political contestation and relative-gains concerns across areas of cooperation. International organizations, such as the environmental treaty secretariats, which have explicitly political mandates of managing a specific set of rules and implementing procedures, are likely to have less agency slack. This would be particularly the case for secretariats operating in highly contested political issues. States are more likely to be concerned about agency activism driving policy outcomes away from their preferred points. Such organizations are likely to be more tightly controlled by principals to have less leeway for experimentation and collaboration with non-state actors (see Bauer *et al.* in this volume).

By contrast, in areas of low political contestation and broad policy agreement among states, international organizations are likely to have more space for innovation and cooperation with non-state actors. For example, the policy areas identified in the universally adopted Millennium Development Goals – poverty alleviation, health improvement, children's and women's wellbeing, and sustainable development – are likely to offer space for relevant international organizations to initiate and get involved in public–private partnerships. It is thus plausible to suggest that the relatively high concentration of partnerships in the area of environmental governance is to some degree determined by the presence of a number of technical international organizations, working on broadly agreed objectives of capacity building and sustainable development. Based on this discussion, the following conditions can be identified as allowing more agency space for public–private partnerships:

- A broader and more technical mandate of the organization;
- Less contestation and relative-gains concern among states involved in the organization;
- The implementation of broadly supported policies.

The organizational logic of public–private cooperation elaborated here has a number of observable implications. It suggests that public–private partnerships are likely to be embedded in relatively technical international environmental organizations. They are likely to support the mandates of these organizations rather than provide alternative mechanisms of governance. The partnerships' participation patterns are, furthermore, likely to reflect the strategic interests of the organizations, and their most powerful principals and strategic allies. Thus, environmental partnerships are likely to focus on relatively narrow technical areas, in which there is an interest in increasing the efficiency of cooperation through innovative mechanisms. Partnerships are less likely to address enduring yet contested governance issues in environmental politics associated with access to global decision making of traditionally disenfranchised groups or less powerful actors. The next section compares trends in environmental partnerships against the theoretical insights on the role of international organizations in shaping the leadership, partner participation, structure, and governance reach of partnership initiatives.

The sample of partnerships

To evaluate the role of international organizations in global environmental partnerships, this section examines five of the largest and most prominent partnership initiatives reflected in the academic and policy literature (Andonova and Levy 2003; Ebrahimian 2003; UNFIP 2005; Timmer and Juma 2005). These partnership initiatives include the United Nations Fund for International Partnerships (UNFIP) and the WSSD partnerships, endorsed at Johannesburg in 2002 and currently administered by the UNCSD as two of the largest initiatives with a broad portfolio of partnerships. The sample also includes the Prototype Carbon Fund (PCF) of the World Bank, the Small Grants Programmes of the Global Environment Facility (GEF), and the Equator Initiative of UNDP. These three are examples of more issue-specific partnership programmes that have attracted the attention of scholars and policy-makers. Each of the partnership initiatives considered is hosted by different international organizations: the GEF, the UN Secretariat/United Nations Foundation, UNCSD, the World Bank, and UNDP. This variation allows us to examine the relationship between partnerships and the characteristics of international organizations that host them, as well as the patterns of partnership participation and the geographical distribution. Table 10.1 summarizes the organizational base of each partnership initiative in the sample and its elements.

Each of the five partnership programmes examined here serves as a coordinating mechanism or a clearing house of a large number of partnership

Table 10.1 Sample of public–private partnership institutions for sustainable development

Host organization	Partnership programme	Year started	Environmental partnerships	% Environmental partnerships	Source
UNFIP	United Nations Fund for International Partnerships	1998	101	30	http://www.un.org/unfip/
UN CSD	WSSD Type II Partnerships	2002	321	100	http://www.un.org/esa/sustdev/partnerships/*
GEF	Small Grants Programme	1992	6,500 grants	100	http://sgp.undp.org/
World Bank	Prototype Carbon Fund	2000	128	100	http://carbonfinance.org/pcf/
UNDP	Equator Initiative	2002	75 finalists/14 prizes	100	http://www.undp.org/equatorinitiative/

Note: *Partnership information based on data published on the partnership institutions' web sites as of 24 May 2006.

projects. These partnerships are also characterized by a set of rules and organizational infrastructures that guide and influence partnership agreements. Very importantly, all partnership programmes in the sample maintain publicly accessible databases, which allow for a systematic analysis of the size, scope, and patterns of leadership, participation, and distribution of partnerships. Thus, while the partnership initiatives analysed here do not comprise the entire universe of multilateral environmental partnerships, they constitute a relatively large, representative, and randomly selected sample of such partnerships. They give us a more systematic view on the role of international organization and conditions for partnerships, which can be assessed against the theoretical model of partnerships as products of organizational entrepreneurship.

Lead international organizations of partnership initiatives

The first question which we can assess through this sample of partnership initiatives is what type of international organizations tend to lead and engage in partnerships and under what conditions. Table 10.1 reveals that four of the five major environmental partnerships examined in this chapter are embedded in UN organizations with technical or capacity-building mandates: the UN Secretariat/United Nations Foundation, UNCSD, UNEP, and GEF. Furthermore, these partnership initiatives emerged at critical junctures in the history of their host organizations. In almost all instances, the move to partnerships represented an internal effort to reinvent or fine-tune organizational mandates, as well as to strengthen the resources and public reach of the organization.

As organizational analysis might anticipate, the UN Secretariat stumbled into public–private cooperation as a mode of organizational revitalization in a period of budgetary and political crisis. In 1997, the UN experienced the biggest deficit in its history of unpaid membership dues. The US Congress had failed to approve the appropriation of the US contribution to the UN, which then accounted for roughly 30 per cent of the UN revenues. The organization faced high membership arrears, unstable budget, and criticism of ineffectiveness used by some member states, such as the US, to justify their lacklustre support. The United Nations Foundation was established the same year to administer the grant of US$ 1 billion by US entrepreneur and philanthropist Ted Turner, the largest private contribution in the history of the UN intended to support its programmes. The UN Foundation, which was established to manage the Turner grant, is probably one of the most celebrated examples of a public–private organization. In 1998, the former UN Secretary General, Kofi Annan, initiated the established UNFIP, as a partnership initiative within the UN Foundation to promote and manage public–private partnerships between UN agencies, non-state actors, and interested governments (UNFIP 2005). The UNFIP partnership programme thus resulted from an entrepreneurship on the part of the UN leadership and the private sectors. It sought to reinvent and reinvigorate both the public image and the organizational resources of the UN. UNFIP was, furthermore, established as a mechanism to elicit interest on the part of the UN organizations more broadly to take advantage of partnerships. Figure 10.1 summarizes the involvement of the UN organizations in UNFIP partnerships.

Figure 10.1 reveals that UN organizations with relatively technical and uncontested mandates have been by far the most important entrepreneurs of UNFIP partnership projects. This pattern corresponds closely to the implications of the organizational model of international organizations and partnerships. Six UN agencies have taken the lead in implementing the majority of UNFIP funded projects: the World Health Organization (WHO), the United Nations Children's Fund (UNICEF), UNDP, the United Nations Population Fund (UNFPA), UNEP, and UNESCO. Together, these six organizations have led the largest share of UNFIP supported partnerships, accounting for 81 per cent of the total UNFIP funding disbursed (Figure 10.1). The issue distribution of UNFIP partnerships reflects the mandate of its most proactive agencies. Figure 10.2 summarizes the issue distribution of UNFIP partnership projects.

Between 1998 and 2004, UNFIP supported some 101 partnerships for the environment, which represent roughly 33 per cent of all UNFIP partnerships and 25 per cent of the allocated UNFIP funding (Figure 10.2, UNFIP 2005). UNDP and UNEP have been among the most active actors in generating and

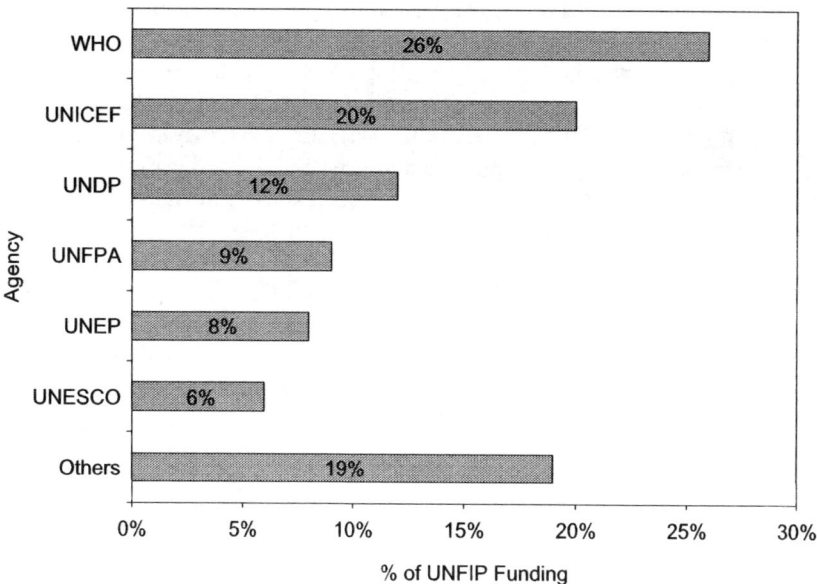

Figure 10.1 Lead UN organization in UNFIP projects (share of total funding 1998–2004).

Source: UNFIP accessed via <http://www.un.org/unfip/>, accessed May 2006.

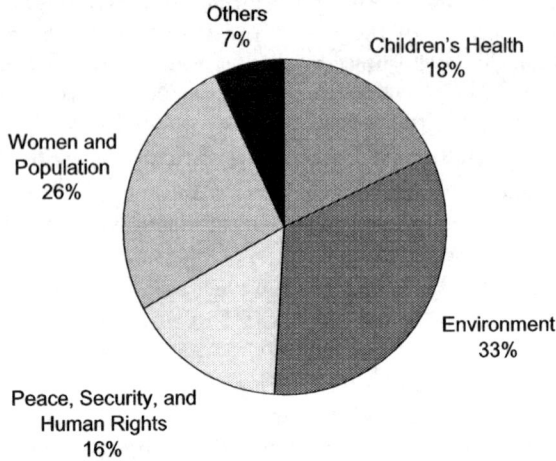

Figure 10.2 Issue distribution of UNFIP partnerships (% of total number of partnerships supported).

Source: UNFIP accessed via <http://www.un.org/unfip/>

leading UNFIP partnerships for the environment (UNFIP 2005), a pattern of organizational activism that we also see in the other environmental partnership programmes analysed here. Distinctive for both UNEP and UNDP is their highly technical and capacity-building mandate, which has given them considerably more space for technical collaboration with non-state actors. A large share of the UNFIP partnerships have also focused on issues of children's health, women, and population (Figure 10.2), in which agencies such as WHO, UNICEF, UNFPA, and UNESCO have played leading roles. Notable in this pattern is the relative absence of UN organizations that deal with more highly contested political issues such as human rights, peacekeeping, and human security, which are also among the core areas within the UN mandate. UNFIP partnerships thus tend to steer towards not just any governance gaps within the purview of the UN system, but toward relatively consensual issue areas governed by agencies with broad technical mandates. Environmental governance and capacity building have emerged as one such area of UN agency activism in generating public–private partnerships.

The WSSD partnerships are probably the most celebrated example of the increased reliance on public–private cooperation for environmental governance. This partnership initiative, similarly to UNFIP, emerged in a crisis-like situation on the eve of the Johannesburg Summit, crafted by the UN organizing bureau for the summit (Andonova and Levy 2003). States showed little willingness to increase support for international environmental cooperation and organizations in the run-up to the Johannesburg Summit. The US, as the single most powerful state in the post-Cold War world, had left the Kyoto Protocol on climate change, and was busy pointing out the implementation failures of existing environmental regimes as a reason to avoid further commitments. There was little choice for actors that sought some positive result of the WSSD other than to seek innovative and flexible solutions. The UN organizers of the conference and its Prepcom committee had particularly strong reputation incentives to avert a complete failure of the summit and weakening of public trust in the catalytic role international organizations and conferences could play in strengthening cooperation. The UN organizing bureau designed a call for public–private partnerships for sustainable development and proposed their registration as official Type II outcome, Type I outcomes being inter-governmental agreements. The UN authors of the Type II approach further specified that all partnerships proposed as part of the WSSD must go beyond existing cooperative and financial commitments. Public–private partnerships were thus packaged as additional mechanisms to strengthen the implementation of Agenda 21 at the 1992 UN conference at Rio de Janeiro, thus responding to specific criticisms of implementation failures that threatened to weaken further environmental commitments. The catalysing of organizational incentives is reflected in the fact that international organizations were not only the authors of the call for Type II outcomes at Johannesburg, but they led close to a third of the WSSD partnerships registered at the meeting, along with other pro-active actors such as transnational NGOs and the development and environmental agencies of donor countries (Andonova and Levy 2003).

The management of the WSSD partnerships following the Johannesburg Summit was delegated to UNCSD. The mandate and operational focus of UNCSD are much narrower compared to those of the other international organizations hosting the partnership initiatives in the sample. UNCSD was created immediately following the United Nations Summit on Environment and Development in Rio de Janeiro in 1992, with a mandate of 'reviewing progress in the implementation of *Agenda 21* and *the Rio Declaration on Environment and Development*'.[2] Following the World Summit on Sustainable Development, the UNCSD was also tasked with overseeing the Johannesburg Plan of Implementation and over 300 partnerships endorsed at the Johannesburg meeting. The UNCSD has thus functioned as a clearing mechanism of policy and technical information related to the recommendations of the global environmental summits, as well as a mechanism to sustain interaction and dialogue on environmental issues among policy-makers. UNCSD's focus on environmental partnerships is thus tightly connected with and came out of its mandate to implement the decisions of the Johannesburg Summit. Partnerships now represent a core activity of the organization pursued along with and often in the context of the regular intergovernmental environmental meetings.

On the eve of the Johannesburg Summit, the UNDP launched its Equator Initiative in 2002. UNDP is one of the core UN programmes focusing on development issues defined broadly to encompass different aspects of human progress and wellbeing. Its mission statement underscores the technical character and capacity-building focus of the organizations:

UNDP is the UN's global development network, an organization advocating for change and connecting countries to knowledge, experience,
and resources to help people build a better life. We are on the ground
in 166 countries, working with them on their own solutions to global and
national development challenges. As they develop local capacity, they
draw on the people of UNDP and our wide range of partners.

(UNDP URL)

UNDP follows this mission through activities in a broad range of areas –
poverty reduction, crisis recovery, women's and minority rights, environment,
and HIV/AIDS – mainly through capacity building, knowledge creation, and
networking mechanisms. UNDP activities are also quite decentralized compared to those of other UN institutions. Local UNDP offices spread
throughout the world are entrusted with a large share of operational and
implementation authority. The Equator Initiative thus grew directly out
of the organizations' technical, capacity-building mandates which seek
to link more explicitly the benefits of environmental conservation and the
benefits of poverty reduction. While the initiative cannot be credited to
specific organizational crisis or pressure, it built on the new enthusiasm for
partnerships as a mechanism to increase the reach of and support for international organizations and the type of governance they seek to promote.
In line with UNDP's knowledge-creation mission, the Equator Initiative
is organized not to create but to recognize existing public–private initiatives
that link global benefits of biodiversity conservation to local poverty reduction and sustainability. The initiative organizes a biennial call for nomination
of public–private partnerships tackling biodiversity conservation and poverty
alleviation in the biodiversity-rich equatorial countries. Biennially it awards
five prizes of US\$ 30,000 each, and also recognizes the achievements of
some 25 finalist initiatives. The programme thus seeks to strengthen collaborative governance via processes of information diffusion, public recognition, and networking among multiple actors (Timmer and Juma 2005). This
initiative fits in and strengthens the core UNDP mission of local-level
engagement and governance through capacity building and a network of
knowledge.

The other two partnership programs in the sample listed in Table 10.1
seem, at first sight, to deviate from the predicted pattern of embeddedness in
technical international organizations with relatively consensual mandates.
The PCF is an initiative of the World Bank, one of the most highly contested
intergovernmental organizations with a strong political mandate (Keck and
Sikkink 1998; Nielson and Tierney 2003). The Small Grants Programme
is an initiative of the GEF, which supports financial transfers for climate,
biodiversity, and international water projects in developing and transition
countries. The GEF is jointly operated by the World Bank, UNDP, and
UNEP, but its headquarters are within the World Bank. A second look at
organizations hosting the PCF and the Small Grants Programme would

reveal, however, that even the exceptions seem to support the general rule of entrepreneurship by relatively technical agencies or units.

The PCF emerged as an initiative of the World Bank's environmental department, a technical unit focusing on research, institutional policies, and projects dealing with sustainable development. The establishment of the PCF was proposed shortly after the Kyoto Protocol was negotiated in 1997 under the United Nations Convention for Climate Change. The Protocol introduces three flexible mechanisms: emissions trading, joint implementation (JI), and the clean development mechanism (CDM). The latter two allow the mitigation of greenhouse gas (GHG) emissions in transition and developing countries respectively, through the implementation of GHG abatement projects by industrialized countries and a negotiated transfer of emission-reduction units. The implementation of these mechanisms requires, however, a significant capacity-building effort to create institutional and financial structures both globally and within host countries to support the implementation of the Kyoto project-based mechanisms. The rationale for establishing the PCF was precisely to start building such institutional capacity in developing and transition countries, as well as to engage early on the private sector and donor countries in project-based carbon mitigation and credit transfer.[3] Expertise building and support for market-based mechanisms for environmental protection have traditionally been at the core of the World Bank's environment department mission. The executive directors of the World Bank approved the establishment of the PCF on 20 July 1999, following the initiative of the environment department. The PCF fitted nicely within the organizational priorities of the organization as an appropriate and innovative mechanism to get involved in climate-change governance. Within the organization structure of the Bank, therefore, the PCF sits within a technical unit rather than within its core lending structures.

It is also notable that the GEF Small Grants Programme was an initiative of and finds its organizational base in UNDP, rather than at the GEF headquarters in the World Bank. Established in 1995, the Small Grants Programme is one of the earliest efforts of an international environmental organization to foster partnerships with NGOs as a mechanism to gain implementation effectiveness and public legitimacy. The programme allocates a small portion of GEF funding for the purposes of supporting projects in cooperation with local NGOs and communities. The objective is to increase local capacity for the implementation of global environmental objectives as well as to increase the local 'ownership' of global environmental programmes by linking international and local benefits (Ebrahimian 2003). To achieve this, the programme seeks to support a project-based partnership with multiple local stakeholders. The Small Grants Programme was thus created within the organizational mandate of the GEF, but it sought to increase the local, grassroots purchase of this mandate through efforts directed at the immediate concerns of participating communities. Naturally, the initiative finds its organizational inspiration and home base within UNDP, which as already discussed, has an explicit capacity-building mandate and a more decentralized system of operations.

The patterns of organization leadership of the five partnership initiatives as well as of partnership projects within these initiatives reveal that environmental partnerships tend to be embedded in organizations with broad technical mandates. They are rarely created within environmental-treaty secretariats or organizations with more explicit political mandates. This clustering corresponds closely to propositions derived from the organizational model of partnerships as innovations often driven by the incentives of international organizations to reinvent and strengthen their missions. This sample reveals that organizations often respond to specific stimuli to move to public-private cooperation, such as a budgetary pressure, as in the case of UNFIP, or a threat of cooperation failure directly linked to the mandate of the organizations, as in the case of the WSSD partnership. In other instances, partnerships have been used as a tool of organizational learning-by-doing in an explicit effort to generate greater public purchase and reach of the mission of organization through the involvement of multiple stakeholders. The cluster of these partnership initiatives in the second half of the 1990s and early in the new millennium is further suggestive of a process of cross-organization learning to respond to cooperation stalemates and potential public scepticism by directly involving societal actors.

The partners of international organizations

By tracking empirical trends, the previous section has established the leading role of relatively technical international organizations in many if not all global environmental partnership programmes. Partnerships, as the terms suggests, however, involve the collaboration of multiple actors, both state and non-state. The next important empirical and policy question, therefore, is: who are the partners of international organizations in environmental governance? The partnership initiatives examined here have attracted a variety of partners, ranging from other international agencies, businesses, foundations, NGOs, and government agencies. An examination of partners in each of the five initiatives reveals that the types of partners that dominate tend to reflect the strategic objectives of the partnership programme and its host organization. Three of the partnership initiatives in the sample – the UNFIP, the WSSD Partnerships, and the PCF – appear to be strongly dominated by large transnational actors and governmental agencies of developing states, working in close cooperation with the leading international organizations.

A study of the WSSD partnerships by Andonova and Levy (2003) indicates that of some 231 public–private partnerships registered at the UNCSD website as of 2003, close to a third (29 per cent), were led by international organizations, another 26 per cent were led by developed country agencies, and about 25 per cent were led by NGOs. Thus, these three types of actors led about 80 per cent of all WSSD partnerships. A closer look at the advocacy

NGO-led initiatives also reveals that these were mostly initiatives of large transnational organizations such as the World Conservation Union, the Nature Conservancy, and the World Resources Institute, and considerably fewer were led by national or local groups. WSSD partnerships did not generate much enthusiasm among developing countries, which feared that partnerships would simply repackage existing resources, nor among business organizations which have steered to more established partnership opportunities such as those offered through the Global Compact or business organizations such as the World Business Council for Sustainable Development (Palmen 2006). By contrast, large corporate actors have a strong presence in both UNFIP and PCF partnerships. Figure 10.3 summarizes the types of UNFP and PCF partner organizations.

Figure 10.3 reveals that UNFIP has attracted powerful transnational actors as partners in governance. The list is dominated by large Western foundations, such as the BBC World Service Trust, the Bill and Melinda Gates Foundation, the Ford Foundation, the Hewlett Foundation, and the Hilton Foundation, many of which have corporate roots. Next in number are powerful multinational companies, such as Microsoft, Ericsson, CISCO Systems, Coca-Cola, and others. Partnering NGOs are also of the large transnational type, such as the World Wildlife Fund, Rotary International, Conservation International,

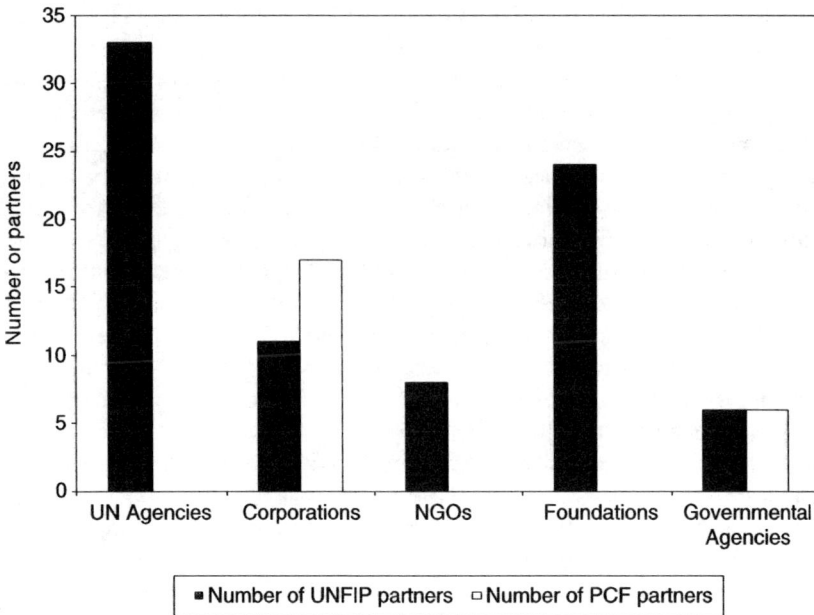

Figure 10.3 UNFIP and PCF partners by type.

Source: UNFIP accessed via <http://www.un.org/unfip/>, accessed May 2006; and Prototype Carbon Fund accessed via <http://carbonfinance.org/Router.cfm?Page=PCF>, accessed May 2006.

and others. State agencies listed as partners are virtually all large donor countries. Paradoxically, even though most UNFIP partnerships are implemented in developing countries, developing country organizations, either governmental or non-state, hardly appear on the UNFIP partnership list.

The Prototype Carbon Fund is dominated by an even narrower set of powerful actors, in this case industrialized country government agencies and energy companies. The list of partners includes the governments of Canada, Norway, Finland, the Netherlands, and the Japan Bank for International Cooperation, along with sixteen energy companies and one multinational investment bank.[4] The interests of developing and transition countries are represented broadly by the Host Country Committee established within the governance structure of the PCF. For all practical purposes, however, potential projects are proposed and negotiated by host countries governments and agencies without necessarily being directly listed as partners or represented in the governance structure of the PCF.

That large transnational actors and powerful states dominate many global environmental partnerships is an important but not very surprising trend if we take into account the driving organizational objectives behind partnerships. After all, international organizations seek partners with resources and expertise to strengthen the implementations of their mandates. One of the organizational objectives behind UNFIP, for example, has been to augment the resources available to UN organizations to implement their missions. It is precisely large NGOs, corporations, and foundations that control a sought-after mix of financial resources and expertise. These types of organizations are also more likely to have the public-relations incentives, resources, and contacts to strike deals with international organizations. Similarly, the PCF has been conceived as a mechanism to create the institutional infrastructure and a stream of carbon financing by leveraging the resources of interested actors. While developing countries are intended to be among the main beneficiaries of these partnerships initiatives, their role has remained more passive and has been overshadowed by actors with resources and transnational reach.

Despite the attraction of large and powerful partners, however, it is interesting and important to note that a number of global environmental partnerships have been designed to target the participation of small, local organizations across the globe. Both the Small Grants Programme and the Equator Initiative exemplify such an approach to partnerships. The Small Grants Programme was deliberately designed so as to attract local organizations involved in poverty alleviation and biodiversity conservation, rather than large transnational organizations. This is achieved through several mechanisms, including the disbursement of small grants of up to US$50,000, which are attractive primarily for small local organizations, rather than large transnational groups. The Programme also requires that participating organizations are involved in activities that link global environmental action to local benefits and wellbeing. This partnership initiative is, as a result, characterized by much more even participation across stakeholders and developing countries compared to the other three partnership initiatives examined in the chapter. It uses public–private partnerships as an innovative organizational mechanism to implement the mandate of the GEF in ways that increase local involvement and support of the organization. The Equator Initiative has adopted an even more decentralized approach to partnership governance. It does not seek to generate partnerships. Rather, it has created a mechanism to bring to the fore, through the competition for the Equator Prize, already existing partnerships that operate at the local level but have impact on global biodiversity management. Thus, in both initiatives, the effort to bring in local, often marginalized partners to the global arena has been informed by the objectives of the host organization, in this case UNDP, and has been achieved as a result of deliberated design. The local reach of the Small Grants Programme and of the Equator Prize notwithstanding, these two partnerships have also attracted over time willing and powerful transnational and governmental organizations as partners supporting their activities. Over the last five years, the list of the organizational partners of the Equator Initiative has grown to include the government of Canada, Conservation International, Convention on Biological Diversity (CBD), Fordham University, the German Federal Ministry for Economic Cooperation and Development (BMZ), International Development Research Centre (IDRC), the World Conservation Union (IUCN), the Nature Conservancy, Rare, Television Trust for the Environment (TVE), and the United Nations Foundation.[5] The Small Grants Programme also lists a range of institutional partners such as the United Nations Foundation, International Coral Reef Action Network, the Nile Basin Initiative, and others.

The sample of partnership initiatives considered here reveals that both the membership and the operational mechanisms of partnerships can vary considerably. The next section further explores the variation in partnership structures and the implications for assessing partnership outcomes and relations with other organizations.

Partnership structure and resources

The organizational structure of partnership programmes can frequently be traced to their original purpose and organizational base. UNFIP and the WSSD partnership programmes exemplify relatively large-scale partnership initiatives intended to stimulate and provide a broad market-like forum for partnerships among a diverse set of actors and international organizations. This structure corresponds to the original objectives of these initiatives – to induce new vigour through the involvement of the non-state sector in UN operation and in global environmental cooperation. The rules for participation are thus very broad. However, UNFIP has a much more centralized system of partnership management, partly because it serves as an arm for disbursing funding of the United Nations Foundation and leveraging it with the resources of other actors. Thus, UNFIP operates as a secretariat for UN

Foundation partnerships. Between 1998 and 2004, UNFIP supported 311 partnership projects across 122 countries with a total value of US\$ 594.3 million (UNFIP 2005). By contrast, UNCSD itself does not make or facilitate financial contribution to WSSD partnerships. Consistent with the market-like approach taken at the WSSD, the UNCSD plays the role of a clearing house for partnership information and opportunities, and encourages partnership cooperation through 'partnership fairs' at its biennial intergovernmental meetings. At best, the UNCSD has a limited role in overseeing or managing the WSSD partnerships, and does not have a designated budget to support such initiatives. Table 10.2 provides a summary of the structural characteristics of the partnerships examined in the chapter.

The other three partnership programmes considered here are organized around specific environmental issues. Their structures reflect, therefore, more narrowly defined policy objectives as well as pre-existing operational mechanisms of the host organizations. The PCF is operated by the Carbon Finance Unit of the World Bank, which serves as a secretariat of the PCF and other carbon finance activities. The PCF seeks to pool resources and political interests on the part of donor countries, the private sector, and recipient countries for financing project-based carbon mitigation. Within its six years of operation, between 2000 and 2006, it has facilitated emission-reduction purchase agreements from 31 projects, and 31 additional projects are under preparation. These emission-reduction projects and agreements have spurred cooperation among multiple public and private actors in developing and transition countries. The PCF thus operates as a parallel instrument of project-based carbon mitigation, while advancing the broad objectives of the JI and CDM mechanisms of the Kyoto Protocol. As of 2006, the PCF operated a total capital of US\$ 180 million, of which 63 per cent was contributed by private sources. Its active portfolio of US\$ 162 million covered some 25 carbon-mitigation project transactions (Table 10.2).

Table 10.2 Comparison of partnership structure and resources

Partnership programme	Partnership secretariat?	Resources disbursed	Organizing principle
UNFIP	Yes	US\$594.3mn (1998–2004)	Contracts
Small Grants Programme	Yes	US\$247.2 (1992–2007); additional US\$242.8 in partner co-financing	Contracts
PCF	Yes	\$162mn (2000–2006)	Contracts
WSSD Partnerships	No	NA	Network
Equator Initiative	No	\$420,000 (2002, 2004 prizes)	Network

Sources: <http://www.un.org/unfip/>, accessed 24 May 2006; <http://www.un.org/esa/sustdev/partnerships/>, accessed 24 May 2006; <http://sgp.undp.org/>, accessed 24 May 2006; <http://carbonfinance.org/pcf/>, accessed 24 May 2006; <http://www.undp.org/equatorinitiative/>, accessed 24 May 2006.

The GEF Small Grants Programme is operated by its central programme management team consisting of nine people based in the UNDP office in New York City. The programme, as the name suggests, disburses small grants of up to US$ 50,000, in order to elicit the interest of small organizations throughout developing and transition countries. The project proposals and the application for funding are not mediated by central governments. Instead, they are submitted directly by community, grassroots, and other non-governmental organizations to the Small Grants Programme national coordinator, typically supported by the local UNDP country office. Local partner organizations contribute with cash or in kind to the proposed project. The central programme management team functions as a quasi secretariat of the programmed task with oversight, reporting, and coordination of its activities. The largest share (60 per cent) of small grants projects addresses issues of biodiversity, while 20 per cent of the projects focus on climate change, another 6 per cent on international waters, and 14 per cent on multi-focal issues.[6] As of January 2007, the programme has provided US$ 247.2 million in support of over 7,000 small grants projects, while an estimated US$ 242.8 million were invested by other partners in cash or in-kind equivalents (Table 10.2). This financing represents a relatively thin slice of the total GEF financing since 1991, which amounts to US$ 6.8 billion in grants and over US$ 24 billion in co-financing from other sources.[7] While the UNDP Equator Initiative follows a similar objective of local involvement for global biodiversity protection, it has institutionalized an even more hands-off process in eliciting local recognition and support. The programme is the most loosely structured of all partnership initiatives considered here. It has established and relies on a global network of communication and sharing of experience among public–private partnerships targeting poverty and biodiversity. The funding supporting partnerships selected for the Equator Prize is relatively limited, amounting to some US$420,000 disbursed for the 14 Equator Prizes awarded in 2002 and 2004. The programme thus uses networks, information, and limited financing as mechanisms to increase awareness of partnership opportunities and indirectly promote the leveraging of resources toward those opportunities. As a result, this sample reveals a much greater diversity of partnership mechanisms than general discussions have considered. It has, furthermore, illustrated a very direct linkage between partnership structure, management, and budget on one hand, and the organizational basis and objectives that underpin partnership initiatives on the other hand.

Reporting partnership outcomes

Assessing the outcomes and impact of partnership is one of the most difficult tasks in studying this relatively new form of environmental governance. This is partly due to the fact that many of these initiatives are relatively recent. In addition, as partnerships emphasize a network-like, decentralized, focused, and partial approach to governance, their influence becomes an elusive target. There has hardly ever been a concerted discussion in the academic literature even on the analytical tools required to attempt an assessment of partnership impact. The present comparative survey on the role of major environmental partnership initiatives suggests at least one possible point of departure in the quest of assessing impact. Given the variety of partnership objectives and structures that we have uncovered, do partnership initiatives also diverge in the ways they report on their outcomes? Could this reporting be the starting point of comparative impact assessment? While the sample does not provide definitive answers to these questions, it again reveals some interesting variations in partnership reporting across initiatives. The three most institutionalized and centrally coordinated partnerships – the Small Grants Programme, UNFIP, and the PCF – supply by far the most extensive reporting on partnership-supported projects and their outcomes. These partnerships are quite firmly embedded in the infrastructure of existing international organizations. Indeed, they have grown directly out of that infrastructure. As a consequence, each has a quasi-secretariat, albeit with minimal staffing, and conforms to or exceeds the reporting procedures of its host international organizations. The UNFIP, the Small Grants Programme, and the PCF supply range-specific data on the supported partnerships. Each of these programmes reports its annual investment in partnerships, the aggregate outcomes, and provides project-by-project fact sheets on financing, participation, and implementation. The relatively detailed documentation on the financing and nature of each project could be taken as a starting point for further internal or external analyses of impact. These partnership initiatives seem to have used existing organizational infrastructures to achieve a level of transparency and public accountability, which could and should be further explored if we are to learn more about the impact of environmental partnerships.

Paradoxically, the WSSD Partnership Initiative, which has attracted the most attention as legitimizing public–private cooperation in global governance, has the least means to provide consistent information on the implementation or impact of partnership activities. While the UNCSD publishes the original documents registering each partnership, it has relatively few mechanisms to elicit follow-up information. Lead partners of each WSSD partnership project are the ones expected to provide updated information on financing and outcomes, which is often unavailable on the official WSSD web site. In contrast to the UNFIP, the PCF, and the Small Grants Programme, which manage partnership projects through explicit procedures and contracts, there is no contracting between UNCSD and the partnership initiatives whatsoever. The UNCSD is simply the market place and a shop window for WSSD type public–private agreements. The absence of more firm contractual embeddedness of WSSD partnerships within the intergovernmental system could potentially undermine the possibilities for external assessment and indeed the public accountability of the most visible partnership programme for the environment.

The Equator Initiative follows yet a different model of reporting partly due to its different objectives and structure. The main governance goal of the partnership is diffusion of information and support for the best local practices in conservation and poverty alleviation. The initiative has thus focused on providing information on some 25 partnerships selected biennially as finalists. A total of 75 finalist partnerships are thus featured on the UNDP's web site, covering the finalists of 2002, 2004, and 2006 rounds of competition. In addition, the initiative has commissioned a range of studies as a part of its knowledge-creation and evaluation effort, externally conducted by academic institutions.

Global environmental partnerships remain an elusive target in terms of governance impact assessment. The present review of the five partnership initiatives suggests that international organizations play an important role not only in catalysing the partnership movement, but also in assuring some degree of transparency and communication about partnership outcomes. There is a great degree of variation however, in the extent to which partnerships develop institutional mechanisms for long-term reporting and assessment of outcomes. This aspect of partnership design is important and likely to depend on the strategic objectives and organizational basis of partnerships.

Conclusion

International organizations play diverse roles in environmental governance: from being facilitators of agreements to being their monitors. Increasingly, intergovernmental organizations are also venturing into the realm of public-private cooperation. This chapter demonstrates that environmental cooperation is a particularly fertile ground for public–private partnerships for several reasons. Environmental regimes have created and rely on international organizations with highly technical mandates and enough scope to reach out to dense networks of interested non-state actors. As international organizations have faced increasing budgetary and public pressures, such relatively technical organizations have been well positioned to experiment with public-private partnerships as a mechanism to support their operational mandates, appease critics, and search for more efficient and innovative solutions to the problems which they have faced. The analysis demonstrates that partnership initiative often comes from within international organizations. As a consequence, partnerships are often guided by specific organizational objectives which find an expression in the types of partners that are reflected, as well as in the structure and mechanisms of operation and accountability that are instituted.

By examining a range of partnerships and the organizational incentives behind them, the chapter reveals a much greater diversity in environmental partnerships than previously recognized. The public–private partnership programmes reviewed here vary considerably in scope, issue orientation, and institutional structure. However, they also share important similarities.

All of these partnerships tend to be supply-driven by the resources and organizational interests of large international organizations. These partnerships have thus grown out of intergovernmental regimes, seeking to fine-tune aspects of those regimes by leveraging the resources and interests of multiple stakeholders. Despite the top-down architecture of these public–private programmes, some of the institutions have also been designed to spur domestic or local demand for public–private collaboration through a variety of mechanisms, including information, emphasis on small-scale initiatives, and linkage of global and local concerns.

International organizations are often supported in their partnership efforts by powerful governments and transnational actors similarly interested in pooling of resources in order to achieve efficiency and reputation objective. Partnerships with large powerful actors often result in predictable patterns of strategic geographic and issue concentration. International organizations also have the legitimacy and institutional basis required to elicit local participation. The ability to achieve such local reach across the globe, however, depends on careful institutional design as illustrated by the multiple mechanisms used by the Small Grants Programme to engage local actors and communities.

Understanding the variety of goals, governance structures, and partners that make environmental partnership is an important first step in analysing further their governance roles. This chapter attempts to provide such a systematic overview of partnership patterns by relating them to the system of international organizations. It demonstrates that partnerships have become an important element in the organizational landscape of environmental governance.

Notes

1 The author is grateful to Colby College and to the Jean Monnet Fellowship Programme of the European University Institute for supporting the research presented in this chapter, as well as to Daniela Andreevska for research assistance.
2 Source: UNCSD website, <http://www.un.org/esa/sustdev/csd.htm> (accessed April 2007).
3 Interviews with staff of the Environment Department, World Bank, Washington, DC, April 2002.
4 PCF online, <http://www.carbonfinance.org/pcf/> (accessed May 2006).
5 See <http://www.undp.org/equatorinitiative/partners.htm> (accessed April 2007).
6 See <http://sgp.undp.org/> (accessed February 2007).
7 See <http://www.gefweb.org/> (accessed February 2007).

References

Andonova, L. (2006) 'Globalization, Agency, and Institutional Innovation: The Rise of Public-Private Partnerships in Global Governance', Working paper of the Goldfarb Center for Public Affairs and Civic Engagement, online. Available HTTP: <http://coda.colby.edu/search/Xgoldfarb&SORT=D/Xgoldfarb&SORT=D&SUBKEY=goldfarb/1,6,6,B/frameset&FF=Xgoldfarb&SORT=D&6,6,>.

Andonova, L. and Levy, M.A. (2003) 'Franchising Global Governance: Making Sense of the Johannesburg Type II Partnerships', *Yearbook of International Co-operation on Environment and Development 2003/2004*, 19(31): 19–31.

Barnett, M. and Finnemore, M. (2004) *Rules for the World. International Organizations in Global Politics*, Ithaca, NY: Cornell University Press.

Benner, T., Reinicke, W.H. and Witte, J.M. (2003) 'Global Public Policy Networks Lessons Learned and Challenged Ahead', *Global Economics*, 21(2): 18–21.

Bissel, R.E. (2001) 'A Participatory Approach to Strategic Planning', *Environment*, 43(7): 37–40.

Ebrahimian, E. (2003) *Community Action to Address Climate Change. Case Studies Linking Sustainable Energy Use with Improved Livelihoods*, New York: GEF Small Grants Programme.

Fox, J.A. and Brown, L.D. (1998) *Struggle for Accountability: The World Bank, NGOs, and Grassroots Movements*, Cambridge, MA: MIT Press.

Gutner, T.L. (2002) *Banking on the Environment: Multilateral Development Banks and their Environmental Performance in Central and Eastern Europe*, Cambridge, MA: MIT Press.

Haas, P.M., Keohane, R.O. and Levy, M.A. (1993) *Institutions for the Earth. Sources of Effective International Environmental Protection*, Cambridge, MA: MIT Press.

Kaul, I. (2005) 'Exploring the Policy Space between Markets and States: Global Public-Private Partnerships', in Kaul, I. and Conceicao, P. (eds) *The New Public Finance: Responding to Global Challenges*, Oxford: Oxford University Press.

Keck, M. and Sikkink, K. (1998) *Activists beyond Borders. Advocacy Networks in International Politics*, Ithaca, NY: Cornell University Press.

Keohane, R.O. and Levy, M.A. (eds) (1996) *Institutions for Environmental Aid: Pitfalls and Promise*, Cambridge, MA: MIT Press.

Nielson, D.L. and Tierney, M.J. (2003) 'Delegation to International Organizations: Agency Theory and World Bank Environmental Reform', *International Organization*, 57: 241–76.

Palmen, M.F. (2006) 'The Absent Partner and the Business of Greenwash: A Study on Business Participation in Type II Sustainable Development Partnerships', Masters Thesis submitted to the Vrije Universiteit Amsterdam, The Netherlands.

Pollack, M.A. (1997) 'Delegation, Agency, and Agenda Setting in the European Community', *International Organization*, 51: 99–134.

Reinicke, W.H. and Deng, F.M. (eds) (2000) *Critical Choices. The United Nations, Networks, and the Future of Global Governance*, Ottawa: International Development Research Center.

Ruggie, J.G. (2003) 'The United Nations and Globalization. Patterns and Limits of Institutional Adaptation', *Global Governance*, 9: 301–21.

Ruggie, J.G. (2004) 'Reconstituting the Global Public Domain: Issues, Actors and Practices', *European Journal of International Relations*, 10(4): 499–531.

Speth, J.G. (2003) 'Perspective on the Johannesburg Summit', *Environment*, 45(1): 24–9.

Timmer, V. and Juma, C. (2005) 'Taking Root: Biodiversity Conservation and Poverty Reduction Come Together in the Tropics', *Environment*, 47(4): 24–41.

United Nations Development Programme (UNDP) (URL) <http://www.undp.org> (accessed March 2006).

United Nations Fund for International Partnerships (UNFIP) (2005) *Thematic Distribution of Projects Funded by the United Nations Foundation*, online. Available HTTP: <http://www.un.org/unfip/> (accessed August 2005).

Williamson, O.E. (1975) *Markets and Hierarchies, Analysis and Antitrust Implications: A Study in the Economics of Internal Organizations*, New York: Free Press.

Witte, J.M., Streck, C. and Benner, T. (eds) (2003) *Progresses or Peril? Partnerships and Networks in Global Environmental Governance. The Post-Johannesburg Agenda*, Berlin, Washington DC: Global Public Policy Institute.

11 Private governance organizations in global environmental politics

Exploring their influences

Philipp Pattberg

Introduction

The interest in organizations as a field of study within International Relations (IR) and environmental politics has resurged in recent years. However, a distinct class of organizations has been frequently overlooked in debates about the nature of global environmental governance: private organizations that do not predominantly direct their behaviour towards public actors but rather devise and implement a range of standards and regulations targeting other private actors. This empirical observation is situated within the larger context of the ongoing debate about a profound shift in global environmental governance. State-centred approaches to problem-solving are increasingly complemented by novel institutional arrangements such as public policy networks and private forms of co-regulation between NGOs and companies. These new forms of global environmental policy-making emerge at the intersection of two broader trends in world politics. First, there is the 'privatization of regulation', a transfer of regulatory tasks from public actors such as states and intergovernmental organizations to a wide range of non-state actors such as bond-rating agencies or the International Organization for Standardization (ISO). The second observable trend refers to the, real or perceived, transformation of confrontation to cooperation as the primary mode of interaction between divergent actors in world politics. In this context, partnership has been heralded as the new paradigm to overcome conflicts of interests in many different areas, from implementing international agreements (Hale and Mauzerall 2004) to securing environmental and social responsibility of corporations through rules and standards (Ruggie 2002).

As far as rules and more general norms are concerned, studies in IR and global environmental governance have primarily focused on international regimes and intergovernmental organizations that have been designed to address trans-boundary problems. Non-state actors have figured prominently on the research agenda of political scientists for more than three decades (Raustiala 1997; Keck and Sikkink 1998; Arts *et al.* 2001), but we know little about the institutionalization of governance by private, often antagonistic actors and the resulting private organizations that seem to perform similar functions to those of international organizations. The underlying assumption of this chapter is that the current process of institutionalization among a wide variety of business and non-profit actors signifies more than a greening of industry based on rationalistic interest calculations. Instead, we witness the emergence of a field of transnational organization, resulting from a variety of norm- and rule-systems on the global level, from reporting schemes to certification and environmental management standards, that exist primarily outside the international system (see Pattberg 2005). With regards to the organizational forms of the emerging transnational order, research has largely been limited to non-governmental organizations that aim at influencing state behaviour.[1] What is rather missing is a detailed assessment of a growing number of organizations active in global environmental politics, and arguably also beyond, whose primary purpose is to govern through their own rules, regulations and standards. These private governance organizations are at the centre of this chapter.

A central question with regard to newly emerging phenomena is frequently: how relevant are they? To answer this question in the case of private governance organizations, it is of central importance to assess their actual influence and the distinct ways in which they influence behaviour. Consequently, I ask: how can we assess the influence of private governance organizations in global environmental politics? What are the mechanisms through which influence is realized? The chapter proceeds in three steps. First, it analyses the shift from public to private governance and the corresponding institutionalization of cooperation between different private transnational actors that results in transnational governance organizations. Second, I discuss different possible ways to assess the influence of private organizations. I contend that three functional pathways can be distinguished through which private arrangements realize their governance task, namely regulatory, cognitive/discursive and integrative governance. Finally, I introduce an empirical case to illustrate the theoretical and conceptual claims made in the preceding part. The Coalition for Environmentally Responsible Economies (CERES) is a prime example of a private governance organization in the corporate environmental reporting and management domain.[2]

Private governance and transnational organization(s): exploring the links

Behaviour in world politics is increasingly becoming more rule-bound and institutionalized (Abbott *et al.* 2001; Goldstein *et al.* 2001). However, next to international order in the form of international regimes, conventions, treaties and international organizations, ordered rule (or in some cases ordered disorder such as transnational terrorist networks) increasingly emanates from non-state sources of authority (cf. Biersteker and Hall 2002). Within this larger context, recent studies have begun to further differentiate distinct forms of non-state, transnational organization such as public–private (Reinicke and

Deng 2000; Dingwerth 2005) and private–private rule-making partnerships (Pattberg 2004a, 2004b).

One source of the growing transnational organization is private governance. It can be defined as a form of socio-political steering in which private actors are directly involved in regulating – in the form of rules, standards or more general normative guidance – the behaviour of a distinct group of stakeholders, including business and, in a wider understanding, also public actors such as states. In addition, private governance can be understood as 'a continuing process through which conflicting or diverse interests may be accommodated and cooperative action may be taken by non-state parties' (Webb 2004: 12). In its most encompassing understanding, private governance includes formal institutions that develop rules and enforce compliance, as well as informal arrangements that individuals or organizations perceive to be in their interest. The term 'governance' is most often used to denote an indefinite process of 'governing'. However, governance also refers to the outcome of such a process, the corresponding social order that is established. In this perspective, private governance is also understood to represent a functional equivalent to public policy outcomes. Hence, private governance 'emerges at the global level where the interactions among private actors . . . give rise to institutional arrangements that structure and direct actors' behavior in an issue-specific area' (Falkner 2003: 72–3).

In addition to understanding transnational organization as a complex interaction of norms and rules in world politics that do not predominantly emanate from public sources and are not necessarily directed towards public actors such as states, the concept of transnational organization also embodies the concrete institutional forms of transnational governance, namely governance organizations. A private governance organization is neither a part of a government nor founded by public actors. Its primary purpose is to solve problems by providing an independent and private regulatory framework, often in the form of standards, guidelines and more general norms. In this respect it differs substantially from NGOs that are usually also not founded or controlled by governments but predominantly aim at changing state behaviour through lobbying or larger advocacy activities (Keck and Sikkink 1998). Private governance organizations differ from intergovernmental organizations in that they are not recognized subjects of international law and their employees are not international civil servants but private employees. However, they also share a number of similarities. Similar to intergovernmental organizations, private governance organizations are established by agreement among a number of independent organizations. To carry out their goals, an administrative body comparable to that of a treaty secretariat is set up. In addition, private governance organizations have a governing body, rely on external and internal sources of funding, possess actor qualities and are embedded within a larger institutional framework. In short, private governance organizations contribute to the establishment of rule-based behaviour at the global level through distinct rules and regulations targeting private actors, primarily business organizations. In this sense, similar questions arise with regard to their actual influence as they have been asked for intergovernmental organizations (Biermann and Siebenhüner 2009).

The influence of private governance organizations

This section proposes to analyse private governance organizations and their contribution to transnational order along the lines of three distinct functional mechanisms, namely regulatory, cognitive/discursive, and integrative governance. Before I will discuss these concepts in more detail, the following section provides a brief introduction to assessing the influence of private governance in general.

Analysing influence: how do private governance organizations matter?

In the context of this chapter, the term 'influence' is given preference over other terms used to describe behavioural changes resulting from specific activities or structures such as power or authority for several reasons (see Biermann and Siebenhüner 2009). Power carries strong connotations of force, whereas authority often invokes the association of either formal legitimation (as in the case of a public authority) or informal authorization through knowledge or belief systems (as in the case of professors or priests). 'Influence' is more neutral in this respect, defined as 'the act or power of producing an effect without apparent exertion of force or direct exercise of command' (Longman Dictionary of the English Language 1984: 754). Consequently, the sum of all effects, according to Webster's (1976: 724) something that is 'produced by an operating agent or cause; the event which follows immediately from an antecedent, called the cause; the result, consequence, or outcome', is considered the influence. In addition, the term 'influence' is also given preference over the frequently used term 'effectiveness' for two reasons. First, effectiveness is a restrictive concept when it comes to the direction of effects, because it limits the scope of analysis to those observations that contribute to goal attainment and problem-solving. Effects that display no link to addressing the principal goal of the respective institution or are counterproductive cannot be measured within the framework of effectiveness. The second reason for using 'influence' as the more encompassing and neutral term instead of 'effectiveness' is the comparative notion embedded in the latter term. Effectiveness is a relational concept; its meaning is linked to a specific point of reference, whether this point is reaching its organizational goal or reaching its organizational goal to a higher degree than a comparative case.

Scholars studying the effects of international regimes (Underdal 2002) and international organizations (Biermann and Bauer 2009) as well as scholars in the field of policy analysis (Easton 1965; Underdal 2002) agree, although in different terminology, that there are basically three different objects of measurement when it comes to analysing influence. First, *output*, referring to the actual activity of organizations and institutions such as agreeing on regulations, producing reports, conducting research or organizing meetings; second, *outcome*, understood as observable changes in the behaviour of those actors targeted by international regimes, public policies or international bureaucracies; and third, *impact*, defined as changes in economic, social or environmental parameters such as GNP, literacy rate or atmospheric carbon dioxide concentrations.

On the basis of this brief discussion, how could the influence of private governance organizations within world politics be analysed? Two complementary views can be distinguished. The first approach is to consider the influence of any private governance organization to be the aggregate of direct and indirect effects. Direct effects can be traced to the specific regulations of the organization under analysis. We can measure these direct effects by looking for behavioural changes of those actors that are within the scope of the rules. Indicators include standard-uptake (i.e. membership in private governance organizations), compliance, corrective action undertaken by the actors and the general tendency in the number of regulated actors. Taken together, these measurements can tell us in how far the rules produced by a governance organization change the behaviour of those actors that fall under the regulatory scope of this very organization. Indirect effects are induced by the rule-system as a whole and have impact on those actors not under the direct scope of private regulation. Possible indirect effects include endorsement of the governance organization and its policies by non-regulated parties, the incorporation of private rules in other existing regulatory systems, political incentives directed towards the private rule-system, and the organizational diffusion of a specific rule-system to other geographic or issue areas.

The second approach towards categorizing the influence of private organizations in world politics is to analyse the distinct characteristics of effects. First, private organizations can be expected to have normative effects resulting from the concrete rules and standards if they become socially binding to a certain extent. Second, private organizations can induce discursive effects. In this case, private rules and procedures become a point of reference in transnational debates that can only be omitted accepting high reputation costs and other strategic disadvantages. And finally, private governance organizations are expected to contribute to structural and material effects such as shifts in market shares or power relations.

Analysing the functions of private governance organizations

After having discussed the possibility of assessing the influence of private governance organizations, this section approaches the question of how private organizations realize their effects. With reference to international environmental regimes, Keohane, Haas, and Levy (1993: 21) argue that actor behaviour, in this case that of states, is affected by the three functional 'Cs': raising concern, creating a contractual environment, and increasing capacity for environmental protection. In a similar vein, I assume that the behaviour of stakeholders and other political actors is affected by three broad functions of private governance organizations. In this perspective, function is used as a heuristic term that describes the abstract influence of a social phenomenon, acknowledging that it is the product of a number of specific processes and mechanisms.

Starting with the most evident, behavioural changes result from the *regulatory function* of private governance organizations. In this view, behavioural changes can be attributed to the standards and regulations emanating from a governance organization that are directed towards business actors. Possible effects may include changes in markets and economic incentive structures, environmental improvements or deterioration, and the internalization of the respective norms. Therefore, an analysis of the regulatory function will most likely focus on the process of standard development and the different approaches taken towards putting them into practice.

Next to regulation, private governance is also achieved through a *cognitive/ discursive function*. Private governance organizations in the area of global environmental politics operate within the complex environment of scientific uncertainty. The development of adequate standards for sustainable forestry, for example, will depend on expertise in issue areas ranging from biodiversity conservation to global timber trade and consumer preferences. Brokering knowledge and organizing effective learning processes among different stakeholders is therefore key to influencing the behaviour of relevant actors. In this view, knowledge is produced and disseminated through a network of actors bound together by the overall goal of the organization. In addition, learning processes may occur that enable actors to fulfil new roles and take over new responsibilities. The cognitive function of private governance organizations may also lead to discursive changes within the specific policy community and beyond.

The third function through which private governance is thought to occur is *integration*. Several directions of influence are observable: first, international norms that are already embodied in international treaties may be partially integrated into the private governance system and thus influence actors that are not directly targeted by the international norm. Second, the direction of influence may well be focused on public actors or political systems through the endorsement of private governance, as a whole or in parts. In this perspective, behavioural changes that occur as the result of the integrative function of private governance may include public policies on the national and international level as well as instances of diffusion, endorsement or emulation of private governance by other actors of the political system such as states or international organizations.

Analysing transnational organizations: the case of CERES

Based on these discussions, I will analyse in this section as a case study the Coalition for Environmentally Responsible Economies (CERES) as the key transnational organization in the field of corporate environmental reporting and management. After briefly assessing the organizational set-up and rules established, I turn to the three functional mechanisms through which changes in the behaviour of stakeholders are achieved and political and economic incentive structures are affected.

CERES started its operations in 1989 by publishing the so-called Valdez Principles, capitalizing on the huge public outrage around the Exxon Valdez oil spill, which occurred on March 24 the same year. A group of socially responsible investors, mainly organized in the Social Investment Forum,[3] and fifteen large US environmental groups started discussing the possibility of using the power of investors (shareholder resolutions) against the power of the boardroom. The goal of CERES is to engage companies in dialogue and work towards the subsequent endorsement of environmental principles that establish a long-term corporate commitment to a continual progress in environmental performance. The ten-point code of corporate environmental conduct can be analysed as 'an environmental ethic with criteria by which investors and others can assess the environmental performance of companies' (CERES 2002a: 31).

As of 2008, more than 75 companies have endorsed the CERES Principles, including the annual reporting commitment. Among the CERES endorsers are large multinational corporations such as American Airlines, Bank of America, Coca-Cola USA, Ford Motor Company, General Motors, and Sunoco as well as small and medium-sized firms, including green companies such as The Body Shop International or Aveda Corporation. The second pillar CERES rests on is the CERES coalition, a network of around 140 organizations, including environmental advocacy groups (e.g. Conservation International; Friends of the Earth), public interest and community groups (e.g. Communities for a Better Environment; Episcopal Environmental Network), trade unions (e.g. Service Employees International Union) and foundations (e.g. the United Nations Foundation) as well as an array of investors, analysts and financial advisors representing more than $500 billion in invested capital. A board of 24 distinguished individuals governs CERES. The day-to-day operations are supervised by a president and carried out by a staff of currently 37 people located in Boston, MA. Although endorsing companies are not directly represented on the CERES board, corporate representatives participate in various committees set up by the board to develop and implement programmes and project and in this function regularly attend CERES board meetings.

Governance through regulation: managing corporate
environmental performance

The regulatory dimension of CERES as a private governance organization contains two related aspects: first, the principles, establishing a normative framework for companies to operate in; and second, a standardized format for corporate environmental reporting, defining the form and contend of public disclosure and transparency (CERES 1999a). According to CERES, 'Over the past thirteen years, CERES has emerged as the worldwide leader in standardized corporate environmental reporting and the promotion of transformed environmental management within firms' (CERES 2003a).[4]

To understand the nature of regulation in the case of corporate environmental reporting and management, I will briefly discuss the principles of corporate conduct and the standardized reporting scheme, as institutionalized in the ten-point code of environmental conduct, the CERES Principles. For example, the CERES Principles (CERES 1999b) demand the protection of the biosphere based on continual progress toward eliminating the release of substances that may damage water, air or the earth and its inhabitants (principle 1), the sustainable use of natural resources including a commitment to make sustainable use of renewable natural resources (principle 2), the reduction of waste through source reduction and recycling (principle 3), the reduction and, where possible, elimination of products that cause environmental damage or health and safety hazards (principle 6), a commitment toward environmental representation on the board of directors, as well as toward general integration of environmental practices into the everyday operations of companies (principle 9) and finally the commitment to an annual self-evaluation of progress towards these principles and the resulting public report (principle 10).

The second regulatory dimension of CERES is the commitment to public disclosure of environmental performance and improvement through an annual report. In the formative phase in the late 1980s and early 1990s, the CERES founders envisaged an independent audit procedure conducted by accountants or specialized certification organizations similar to those institutionalized in other private governance organizations.[5] However, this proposal met strong resistance from the business community and disappeared when the principles were renamed in 1992. Today, the reporting requirement takes the form of a second-party reporting scheme where rule-making and compliance reporting are separated, but not independently controlled. Compliance with the standards is mainly ensured through the threat of public withdrawal of endorsement. CERES has a review procedure in place that allows the referral of serious questions or concerns about a participating company's activities or intentions to the Engagement and Review Committee.[6] Referring to this committee and its procedures, Nash and Ehrenfeld (1997: 515) report:

CERES has developed a protocol by which it can revoke the endorser status of companies that violate the letter or spirit of its principles. CERES recently dropped the names of more than 20 companies from its list of endorsers because these firms had failed to submit CERES reports or pay membership dues. While CERES considers the remaining firms active and committed, it is prepared to take action against any endorsing company that betrays its trust.

Such actions might be caused by the company's failure to report on its constant improvements or pay the annual fee, known and deliberate falsification of the reported data and misrepresentation of the firm's relation with CERES or clear environmental mismanagement. It is important to note that the review procedures have been developed 'with the full awareness, support and participation of endorsers'.[7]

At a fairly abstract level, both aspects of CERES' regulatory dimension, the corporate code of conduct and the reporting scheme, can be considered a success. Many companies have published an environmental mission statement drawing on the original Valdez Principles.[8] To date, more than 2000 companies worldwide regularly publish environmental or sustainability reports. The CERES report form has gained so much credibility that it provides the basis for the global sustainability reporting guidelines operated by the Global Reporting Initiative. However, what are the measurable effects of this *governance through regulation*? To answer this question, I will address the development in corporate endorsement and reporting over time, performance reviews conducted by CERES and the influence of reporting on shareholder value and core business performance.

CERES' influence on companies measured by their membership in the CERES coalition is modest at first glance. After three years of intense debates and shareholder resolutions filed with major companies, only 14 companies had endorsed the CERES Principles in 1992, out of over 3000 corporations originally envisaged and approached by the founding organizations. However, CERES has been able to increase the endorsement rate over the years. In 2008, more than 75 companies are active CERES endorsers. The annual growth has been around six companies per year. In addition to business endorsing the idea behind CERES, an increasing number of civil society organizations and private foundations (e.g. the United Nations Foundation) have joined CERES and thereby increased its general acceptance.

Going beyond the plain number of endorsing companies, both the potential impact of corporations and the quality of the actual report seem to be of central importance. With regard to the first point, CERES has been rather successful at integrating large corporations that have the potential to make a difference. Next to Sunoco and GM, who are early endorsers, CERES has been able to secure the support of companies such as McDonald's and Time Warner. Endorsing companies today cover most economic sectors, from finance, to oil and gas, to automobiles, to chemical companies. With regard to the second point, available studies indicate that CERES reports perform above average compared to other standards when it comes to completeness and quality of information (Davis-Walling and Batterman 1997). In sum, CERES has a modest influence on companies through its regulatory function when measuring the standard-uptake only. However, when taking into account the companies and the sectors they represent as well as the actual quality of corporate environmental reporting, the evaluation results in a slightly more positive result.

Another way of assessing the influence of the CERES Principles on a company is looking at the detailed performance reviews CERES has conducted for their interaction with General Motors (CERES 2002b), the world's largest corporation, and Sunoco (CERES 1999c), the first Fortune 500 company to endorse the Principles. CERES developed the performance review

> as a mechanism for examining whether companies that endorsed the CERES Principles more than five years ago are achieving continuous improvement in corporate reporting, facility and product performance, and how the CERES Principles are influencing their culture, programs and policies.
>
> (CERES 2002b: 6)

At the outset of the formal collaboration between CERES and GM in 1994, both sides agreed on four areas of mutual interest for the performance review conducted in 1999/2000: public accountability (environmental reporting according to the CERES report form), plant performance (improving the environmental impacts, health and safety conditions at GM plants), product performance (improving the fuel efficiency of its fleet) and stakeholder relationships (building a lasting dialogue with CERES coalition members and other stakeholders). All of these priority areas are derived from the CERES Principles. The results of this major performance review, however, are mixed (CERES 2002b: 8–22). Addressing the issue of public accountability, GM has published eight annual environmental reports, expanding their scope from US-only to global metrics. Issues addressed cover direct company impacts as well as supply chain issues. In addition, GM is described as a leader in promoting the use of the GRI guidelines. With regard to plant performance, the report shows that GM was able to achieve improved environmental performance at the plant level over the seven years covered by the review. Significant achievement was also made in stakeholder relationships. However, and most important, GM did not show improvement in product performance with its fleet fuel performance stagnating due to higher demand for fuel-intensive automobiles. This latter observation is of particular importance when assessing the actual influence of private governance in corporate environmental reporting and management. Although the results of the GM performance review are not representative and reflect the specific situation of the company and the sector, it seems plausible to assume that performance improvements will occur in sectors that are least vulnerable to changing market conditions and poor financial performance. While environmental reporting and improving stakeholder relations are of secondary importance to the core operations of an automobile company, and plant site improvements are relatively easy to achieve in the context of constant technological improvements, GM was unable to increase its fuel efficiency because of the demand situation and global competition (CERES 2002b).

In sum, the existing performance reviews of CERES endorsers highlight that changes in business practices and corporate culture occur. However, changes seem to be distributed unevenly across issue areas. Whereas corporate environmental reporting and improvements in health, environmental and safety performance have become standard practices and corporate goals, few tangible changes have occurred in products and services. Comparative studies of corporate codes of practices come to similar conclusions. In an early review article, Nash and Ehrenfeld (1997: 519) conclude that 'codes have helped to institutionalize some significant new practices in participating firms'. With regard to CERES, interviews confirmed signs of a gradual change in the environmental consciousness of several participating firms. However, changes in products or processes that reflect this new consciousness have not been observed in the early phase of institutionalization (cf. Nash and Ehrenfeld 1997: 524).

A third possible indicator for CERES' regulatory influences are the economic effects that are generated, in particular with regard to the shareholder value and general economic performance of endorsing companies. The essential question is: can firms do well while doing good? The creation of the Dow Jones Sustainability Index and FTSE4Good can be read as a positive answer to that question. However, this corporate 'myth of CSR' it is also heavily contested (Doane 2005). Why should companies voluntarily go beyond compliance? A frequent answer is that by implementing environmental management systems and reporting on the progress achieved, companies can reduce costs that occur from waste treatment, pollution prevention, bad press and lawsuits, among other factors. More important, firms may use environmental performance as an asset in differentiation-based strategies that aim at signalling to investors and consumers that there is something unique about the company, setting it aside from competitors and thereby gaining a comparative advantage (Eisner 2004: 150). In addition, if companies are embedded in larger networks, pressure from competitors or a large market-leader can force firms to adopt existing best practices in order to compete.[9] After having argued that there is an instrumental value to corporate environmental reporting and management, the problem of causality remains. In simple terms, it is difficult to determine whether increased levels of corporate environmental responsibility cause higher returns on investment and profits in general, or whether more profitable companies are simply able to invest more of their resources in eco-friendly behaviour.

Acknowledging this difficulty, research over the past 30 years has nevertheless established clear links between good financial and environmental performance.[10] According to Eisner (2004: 149), 'there is a growing body of evidence that firms with superior environmental performance (SEP) are reaping financial rewards, although there are ongoing questions about causality'. With regard to six companies endorsing the CERES Principles, White (1996) found that it pays to be 'green'. Over a period of 48 months, the six CERES companies performed above the average of companies not using any environmental reporting scheme. In addition, qualitative data suggests that companies were able to benefit from involvement in CERES. For example, 'Sunoco believes that there is a direct correlation between HES (health, environment and safety) performance and the company's profitability' (CERES 1999c: 15). According to this account, the challenge for CERES and Sunoco has been to demonstrate to Wall Street 'the specific dollars saved over the course of the relationship' (ibid.). For example, several lawsuits were avoided through the collaboration with CERES. In sum, given the generally positive correlation between corporate environmental and economic performance and the findings on CERES companies, we can conclude that one clear influence of private governance in the environmental reporting and management domain is the improved financial performance of participating firms, although data on the full sample of CERES companies is missing.

The influence of corporate environmental reporting and management through its regulatory function can be summarized in three points. First, standard-uptake by business actors has been rather modest. However, CERES was able to steadily increase the number of endorsing companies and integrate influential global players such as GM, Ford Motor Company and McDonald's. Second, company performance reviews conducted by CERES indicate that business practices have changed as a result of endorsing the CERES Principles. However, while changes in public accountability, stakeholder relations and the environmental performance of individual plants could be observed in both reviews, no significant changes occurred in core business areas such as the fuel efficiency of GM's product range. Finally, acknowledging the fundamental problem of attributing causality to the relation between environmental and economic performance, the literature converges in its assessment that firms theoretically can do well while doing good. Therefore, adopting the CERES Principles and its annual reporting requirement potentially influences a company's core business, although specific data on the total sample of CERES endorsers is lacking and a final proof of causality is methodologically difficult.

Governance through discourse and learning: what it means to be a green company

In addition to influencing actors through its regulatory function, CERES affects actors in the corporate environmental reporting and management domain through its cognitive/discursive function. In more detail, I discuss the following aspects: (1) producing and disseminating information, (2) providing the institutional setting for learning processes, and finally (3) the diffusion of the regulatory model.

CERES uses its broad network of coalition members to produce and disseminate information on issues of key importance. One example of producing information is the recent attempt made by CERES to (re)define industry's attitude towards climate change. Within this project, CERES has produced and commissioned a range of studies that raise the issue of climate change as a risk for business and investors. For example, in a 2002 report (Innovest Strategic Value Advisors 2002: 2) CERES states:

> [t]he bottom line ... is straightforward: climate change represents a potential multi-billion dollar risk to a wide variety of U.S. businesses and industries. It should, therefore, command the same level of attention and urgency as any other business risk of this magnitude.

CERES' attempt to alter the existing discourse on climate change within the business community is also reflected in recent developments in its communications strategy.

The media strategy has been reformed starting in 2001 and now reflects the situation that CERES is often perceived as an environmental advocate, while its audience is really the companies and the financial markets. As one staff member recalls, 'the shift that CERES tries to make is really about getting our issues into the financial press; not on the environmental page, but in the business section.'[11] This attempt has been quite successful with a number of articles on the issue of climate change and business risk appearing in major US and international newspapers, including the *Wall Street Journal, Financial Times*, and the *New York Times*, in 2003 (e.g. Ball 2003a, 2003b; Burr 2003; Feder 2003a, 2003b; Murray 2003). Although these articles do not necessarily mention CERES, they make a strong case for the issue of relating climate change with investor risks. The *Wall Street Journal* for example comments (Ball 2003a): 'Here's what companies' directors have to worry about these days: accounting scandals ... earnings problems ... oh, and global warming.' And the *Financial Times* recalls:

> There was a time when the most prominent voices in the debate on climate change were environmental lobby groups, activists and non-governmental organizations. These days, however, new speakers are entering the fray: banks, insurers, investors and other organizations in the financial services sector.
>
> (Murray 2003)

These examples illustrate that CERES acted as a knowledge-producer and knowledge-broker through its reformed communications strategy. In the words of a CERES staff member, 'CERES has really driven this issue and made it into the press.'[12] This view is remarkable because, according to the same interviewee, in 2001 there would not have been an article on climate change and risk in the business press. The triggering event has been the increase in shareholder resolutions on climate change and the corresponding risk for investors. In addition, CERES has also been active in influencing a new class of actors, public pension funds, drawing on its existing coalition network. The 2003 Annual CERES Report states:

> Much of Ceres' work in 2003 culminated in the historic Institutional Investors Summit on Climate Change held at the United Nations head-quarters in New York City on November 21, 2003. There, Ceres, the State of Connecticut Treasurer's Office, and the United Nations Foundation brought together institutional investors representing more than $1 trillion in invested capital together to examine the financial risk of global climate change.
>
> (CERES 2004)

One indicator for the success of CERES' attempt to challenge the existing discourse on business and climate change can be found in the 2005 record high voting support for shareholder resolutions seeking greater analysis and disclosure from companies about the financial impacts of climate change. For example, at the 2005 corporate annual meeting of Exxon Mobil, 28.3 per cent of the shareholders supported

> a resolution requesting that the company's board of directors undertake a comprehensive review on how it will meet the greenhouse gas reductions targets in countries participating in the Kyoto Protocol. The 28.3 per cent support represent 1.5 billion shares with a market value of about $83.8 billion.
>
> (CERES 2005a)

In sum, CERES' work as a knowledge and information broker has clearly affected the conversation on climate change and investor risks. In its own words (CERES 2004): 'An important Ceres communication goal is to "change the conversation" from the assumption that climate change solutions will hurt the economy to recognition that inaction is the greater business risk.'

CERES' institutional structure as a coalition of actors from diverse back-grounds clearly facilitates inter-organizational learning processes. Consider the annual CERES conference of coalition members and endorsers as an example. Until 2003, the CERES conference was nothing more than an annual gathering where people within the CERES network could meet and discuss issues of common concern. Lately, however, the conference has taken up a more high-profile role. The new conference format places more emphasis on engaging endorsing companies and coalition members in strategic projects. This organizational change is based on the recognition that CERES does not make adequate use of its wide resources. As one interviewee reports, many people in member organizations lack a clear understanding of CERES' work and the possible contribution of their own organization to this work.[13] The conference is an attempt to increase the involvement of coalition members and endorsing companies beyond participating in CERES board meetings and committee work. In addition, greater emphasis is paid to harnessing the distinct organizational knowledge of participants in workshops and discussion groups, covering topics from 'How Investors Worldwide Are Addressing Sustainability Risks and Opportunities', to 'Oil: Closing the Sustainability Gap', and 'Electric Power and Climate Change: Best Practices in Disclosure and Management' (CERES 2005b).

In addition to passively inducing environmental reporting, as in the case of the Public Environmental Reporting Initiative (PERI), CERES was also actively involved in mainstreaming, broadening and essentially globalising the model of corporate environmental reporting with the successful establishment of the Global Reporting Initiative. The GRI was set up in 1997 to harmonize and integrate existing environmental/sustainable reporting schemes. Several companies had approached CERES and raised concerns about the fragmented scope of reporting and its limited geographical reach. At the same time, the Tellus Institute, a major think tank in the field of sustainability, published its report *Green Metrics*, a study that compared existing reporting schemes and their requirements in a single matrix and identified overlaps between various schemes (White and Zinkl 1998). Based on this input, initial discussions on establishing a broader and harmonized reporting framework emerged, leading to the successful establishment of a Steering Committee in December 1997. Shortly after, UNEP became a partner institution, a development that proved decisive, both in terms of enhanced legitimacy through public participation, as well as scientific input. Until the GRI became an independent organization in 2002, CERES served as its secretariat and provided most of the financial resources. Although being a key driver of the GRI process, CERES managed to involve a range of other players in the deliberations that led to the draft GRI principles. In this context, it was of major importance that CERES had agreed on transforming the GRI into an independent organization with its own board of directors early in the process (Waddell 2002: 5–6).

To conclude, the influence of CERES through its discursive and cognitive functions can be illustrated in three points: first, CERES has considerable influence through producing and disseminating information. Its media strategy, with its focus on getting information about CERES and the risk of climate change into the business press, has been successful and can be credited with having influenced the recent increase in shareholder resolutions on climate change filed with US corporations. Second, CERES shows clear signs of being an inter-organizational learning network, mainly through its annual conference and additional deliberative exercises. Finally, CERES has forced other actors in the field to react to the general idea of corporate environmental reporting, as well as successfully initiating a global sustainable reporting scheme, the GRI.

Governance through integration: the mainstreaming of corporate sustainability reporting

The third function through which private governance is constructed in the environmental reporting and management domain can be termed integration, relating to processes of diffusion and emulation of private norms through public actors. Three distinct patterns can be observed. First, the CERES Principles have been introduced as state legislation in sub-national polities in the US, for example in the state of New Jersey. In addition, several states have passed legislation on voluntary audits, and the US Environment Protection Agency (EPA) has strengthened their guidelines on auditing and public disclosure (Weiss 2002: 104). Second, a range of public actors and agencies endorse the CERES Principles. For example, the Environmental Protection Department of Pennsylvania (2005) states:

> While industry associations like the Chemical Manufacturer's Association and the American Forest & Paper Association deserve recognition for their environmental initiatives, as do the Programs of the Global Environmental Management Initiative and the International Chamber of Commerce, these initiatives do not match the CERES Principles nor the CERES reporting process in several important respects.
> (Department of Environmental Protection Pennsylvania 2005)

The third pattern of integration relates to the upward diffusion of private rules. Three examples illustrate this point. First, the United Nations used the Valdez Principles in the design of its sustainable development guidelines for multinational corporations (Weiss 2002: 104). Second, CERES has been a key driver in launching the GRI, which today provides an encompassing reporting framework on social, economic and environmental issues for large corporations, along with small and medium-sized enterprises, NGOs and public agencies. The GRI has been endorsed by UNEP who became an early member in the formation process in 1998. The GRI is an official collaborating centre of the United Nations Environment Programme and works in cooperation with UN Secretary-General Kofi Annan's Global Compact. Hence, the idea of standardized reporting advanced by CERES and mainstreamed into the GRI can be considered to be generally endorsed and supported at the highest levels of international politics. Substantiating this claim, the idea of corporate sustainability reporting and management also received public acknowledgement at the 2002 World Summit on Sustainable Development in Johannesburg.

In sum, private rules emanating from the private governance organization CERES have been endorsed by public actors at national, international and transnational levels, including US public agencies, governments and UN programmes. The most profound impact that CERES can claim is mainstreaming the corporate environmental reporting agenda to a global sustainability reporting agenda and securing support for this development from the United Nations and the international community at large.

Conclusion: private governance organization and the emerging transnational order

This chapter argues that the recent phenomenon of private governance in global politics goes beyond common forms of private cooperation because it involves not only adjustments of behaviour towards mutual goals but also shared norms, principles and roles. As a result, private governance is believed to include private systems of rule that exist mainly outside of the international system of governance.

Within the context of academic debate about global environmental governance and international organizations, the key point is that the institutionalization of private governance leads to transnational organization as an emerging form of post-sovereign order in world politics, complementing international and predominantly state-based forms of organization. Transnational organization can be understood as the functional outcome of a multitude of governing processes, actor-constellations and transnational policies that in sum give rise to structured behaviour of different types of actors across borders and functional domains. This observation goes beyond well-known forms of coordination and cooperation between private actors. Similar to claims that the international system shows signs of becoming gradually more rule-based and legalized, I have argued that this holds true for the transnational level of world politics, too. In particular, relations between actors excluding states and international organizations have become more institutionalized. I suggest in my analysis of corporate environmental reporting and management that private governance organizations are one such source of the emerging sphere of transnational order that has been largely overlooked in most previous accounts of world politics and its shift from public to shared forms of political steering. As Djelic and Quack argue:

> The mainstream of the International Relations (IR) tradition pictures the transnational space as essentially anomic – a shapeless and structureless arena. Agents are essentially free and rational, maximizing their own interests with little burden being put on them by the space in which their action takes place.
>
> (Djelic and Quack 2003: 27)

However, the empirical analysis has shown that private governance organizations – similar to intergovernmental organizations – influence a range of actors within and beyond their formal scope through three functional mechanisms. In sum, the regulatory, cognitive and integrative functions of private governance organizations account for the observed effects, ranging from changes is norms and perceptions to changing discourses and political and economic incentive structures. Although evidence is still rather scarce, and comparative case studies using quantitative methodologies are missing, the observations presented in this chapter suggest that the transnational level of world politics is gradually becoming more institutionalized and, even more importantly, there seems to be no theoretical objection against analysing it in terms of increasing and deepening organization.

Notes

1 One notable exception is the work of Ronit and Schneider (1999) on private organizations in global governance that explicitly focuses on the provision of public goods through private business actors.
2 For a more detailed elaboration of CERES as a private rule-making organization, see Pattberg 2007.
3 The SIF is a network of actors focusing on Socially Responsible Investing (SRI), understood as the integration of personal values and societal concerns with investment decisions. See <http://www.socialinvest.org>.
4 Website document (CERES 2003a), on file with author.
5 See Pattberg 2006 on the Forest Stewardship Council as an example of a private governance organization with strict third-party auditing procedures.
6 Personal interview with CERES staff member, January 2004.
7 Website document (CERES 2003b), on file with author.
8 Personal interview with CERES board member and participant in the early formation phase, March 2004.
9 In the auto industry, for example, Daimler Chrysler, GM, Toyota and Honda quickly followed Ford in embracing the ISO 14001 standards.
10 For an excellent overview, see Raar (2001).
11 Personal interview with CERES staff member, January 2004.
12 Personal interview with CERES staff member, January 2004.
13 Personal Interview with CERES staff member, January 2004.

References

Abbott, K.W., Keohane, R.O., Moravcsik, A. Slaughter, A.-M. and Snidal, D. (2001) 'The Concept of Legalization', in Goldstein, J.L., Kahler, M., Keohane, R.O. and Slaughter, A.-M. (eds) *Legalization and World Politics*, Cambridge, MA: MIT Press.
Arts, B., Noortmann, M. and Reinalda, B. (eds) (2001) *Non-State Actors in International Relations*, Aldershot: Ashgate.
Ball, J. (2003a) 'Global Warming May Cloud Directors' Liability Coverage', *The Wall Street Journal*, Wednesday, May 7.
Ball, J. (2003b) 'State Aides Mull Pension Funds and Environment', *The Wall Street Journal*, Friday, November 21.

Biermann, F. and Siebenhuener, B. (eds) (2009) *Managers of Global Change: The Influence of International Environmental Bureaucracies*, Cambridge, MA: MIT Press.

Biersteker, T.J. and Hall, R.B. (2002) 'Private Authority as Global Governance', in Biersteker, T.J. and Hall, R.B. (eds) *The Emergence of Private Authority in Global Governance*, Cambridge: Cambridge University Press.

Burr, B.B. (2003) 'Climate Change: The New Off-balance-sheet Risk', *Pensions & Investments*, Monday, July 21.

CERES (1999a) *CERES Report Standard Form 1998*, Boston: CERES.

CERES (1999b) *Tenth Anniversary Report 1998*, Boston: CERES.

CERES (1999c) *CERES Five-Year Review of Sunoco, Inc. A Collaborative Road to Progress*, Boston: CERES.

CERES (2002a) 'Life in the Edge Environment', *Annual Report 2001*, Boston: CERES.

CERES (2002b) *CERES Performance Review of General Motors Corporation*, Boston: CERES.

CERES (2003a) *About Us: History*, online. Available HTTP: <http://www.ceres.org/about/history.htm> (accessed 11 December 2003).

CERES (2003b) *About Us: Frequently Asked Questions* 2003, online. Available HTTP: <http://www.ceres.org/about/questions.htm> (accessed 11 December 2003).

CERES (2004) *CERES 2003 Annual Report*, Boston: CERES.

CERES (2005a) *ExxonMobil Investors Give Record Voting Support to Climate Change Resolution*, online. Available HTTP: <http://www.ceres.org/news/pf.php?nid=115> (accessed 5 November 2005).

CERES (2005b) *CERES 2005 Conference: Building Equity, Reducing Risk*, online. Available HTTP: <http://www.ceres.org/events/conference/05/> (accessed 17 November 2005).

Davis-Walling, P. and Batterman, S.A. (1997) 'Environmental Reporting by the Fortune 50 Firms', *Environmental Management*, 21(6): 865–75.

Department of Environmental Protection Pennsylvania (2005) *Answer to Questions about the Ceres Principles*, online. Available HTTP: <http://www.dep.state.pa.us/deputate/pollprev/tech_assistance/toolbox/ceres/answers.htm> (accessed 3 November 2005).

Dingwerth, K. (2005) 'The Democratic Legitimacy of Public-Private Rule-Making: What Can We Learn from the World Commission on Dams?', *Global Governance*, 11(1): 65–83.

Djelic, M.-L. and Quack, S. (2003) 'Theoretical Building Blocks for a Research Agenda Linking Globalization and Institutions', in Djelic, M.-L. and Quack, S. (eds) *Globalization and Institutions. Redefining the Rules of the Economic Game*, Cheltenham: Edward Elgar.

Doane, D. (2005) *The Myth of CSR*, Stanford: Stanford Graduate School of Business.

Easton, D. (1965) *A Systems Analysis of Political Life*, New York: Wiley.

Eisner, M.A. (2004) 'Corporate Environmentalism, Regulatory Reform, and Industry Self-Regulation: Toward Genuine Regulatory Reinvention in the United States', *Governance: An International Journal of Policy, Administration, and Institutions*, 17(2): 145–67.

Falkner, R. (2003) 'Private Environmental Governance and International Relations: Exploring the Links', *Global Environmental Politics*, 3(2): 72–87.

Feder, B.J. (2003a) 'Pension Funds Plan to Press Global Warming as an Issue', *The New York Times*, Saturday, November 22.

Feder, B.J. (2003b) 'Report Faults Big Companies on Climate', *The New York Times*, Thursday, July 10.

Goldstein, J.L., Kahler, M., Keohane, R.O. and Slaughter, A.-M. (eds) (2001) *Legalization and World Politics*, Cambridge, MA: MIT Press.

Hale, T.N. and Mauzerall, D.L. (2004) 'Thinking Globally and Acting Locally: Can the Johannesburg Partnerships Coordinate Action on Sustainable Development?', *Journal of Environment & Development*, 13(3): 220–39.

Innovest Strategic Value Advisors (2002) *Value at Risk: Climate Change and the Future of Governance*, Boston: CERES.

Keck, M.E. and Sikkink, K. (1998) *Activists beyond Borders. Advocacy Networks in International Politics*, Ithaca, NY: Cornell University Press.

Keohane, R.O., Haas, P.M. and Levy, M.A. (1993) 'The Effectiveness of International Environmental Institutions', in Keohane, R.O., Haas, P.M. and Levy, M.A. (eds) *Institutions for the Earth. Sources of Effective International Environmental Protection*, Cambridge, MA: MIT Press.

Longman Dictionary of the English Language (1984) London: Longman.

Murray, S. (2003) 'New Voices Are Entering the Fray', *Financial Times*, Thursday, October 16.

Nash, J. and Ehrenfeld, J. (1997) 'Codes of Environmental Management Practice: Assessing their Potential as a Tool for Change', *Annual Review of Energy and the Environment*, 22: 487–535.

Pattberg, P. (2004a) 'Private Environmental Governance and the Sustainability Transition: Functions and Impacts of Business-NGO Partnerships', in Jacob, K., Binder, M. and Wieczorek, A. (eds) *Governance for Industrial Transformation. Proceedings of the 2003 Berlin Conference on the Human Dimension of Global Environmental Change*, Berlin: FFU.

Pattberg, P. (2004b) ' "Private-Private Partnerships" als innovative Modelle zur Regel(durch)setzung? Möglichkeiten und Grenzen eines neuen Konzeptes am Beispiel des FSC', in Brühl, T., Feldt, H., Hamm, B., Hummel, H. and Martens, J. (eds) *Unternehmen in der Weltpolitik: Politiknetzwerke, Unternehmensregeln und die Zukunft des Multilateralismus*, Bonn: Dietz.

Pattberg, P. (2005) 'The Institutionalization of Private Governance: How Business and Non-profit Organizations Agree on Transnational Rules', *Governance: An International Journal of Policy, Administration, and Institutions*, 18(4): 589–610.

Pattberg, P. (2006) 'Private Governance and the South: Lessons from Global Forest Politics', *Third World Quarterly* 27(4): 579–93.

Pattberg, P. (2007) *Private Institutions and Global Governance. The New Politics of Environmental Sustainability*, Cheltenham, UK and Northampton, MA: Edward Elgar.

Raar, J. (2001) 'Strategy and the Multiplicity of Variables Associated with Voluntary Reporting of Environmental and Economic Performance: Ullmann Revisited', paper read at Governance and Social Responsibility Conference, at School of Accounting & Finance, Deakin University, Burwood, Australia.

Raustiala, K. (1997) 'States, NGOs, and International Environmental Institutions', *International Studies Quarterly*, 41(4): 719–40.

Reinicke, W.H. and Deng, F. (eds) (2000) *Critical Choices. The United Nations, Networks, and the Future of Global Governance*, Ottawa: International Development Research Centre.

Ronit, K. and Schneider, V. (1999) 'Global Governance through Private Organizations',

Governance: An International Journal of Policy, Administration, and Institutions, 12(3): 243–66.

Ruggie, J.G. (2002) 'The Theory and Practice of Learning Networks. Corporate Social Responsibility and the Global Compact', *Journal of Corporate Citizenship*, Spring: 27–36.

Underdal, A. (2002) 'One Question, Two Answers', in Miles, E.L., Underdal, A., Andresen, S., Wettestad, J., Skjaerseth, J.B. and Carlin, E.M. (eds) *Environmental Regime Effectiveness. Confronting Theory with Evidence*, Cambridge, MA: MIT Press.

Waddell, S. (2002) *The Global Reporting Initiative: Building a Corporate Reporting Strategy Globally*, Boston: The Global Action Network Net.

Webb, K. (2004) 'Understanding the Voluntary Codes Phenomenon', in Webb, K. (ed.) *Voluntary Codes: Private Governance, the Public Interest and Innovation*, Ottawa: Carleton University.

Webster's Third New International Dictionary of the English Language (1976), Vol. I., Chicago and London: Webster.

Weiss, A.M. (2002) 'Voluntary Codes of Management: New Opportunities for Increased Corporate Accountability', in Susskind, L., Moomaw, W. and Gallagher, K. (eds) *Transboundary Environmental Negotiations. New Approaches to Global Cooperation*, San Francisco, CA: Jossey-Bass.

White, A.L. and Zinkl, D. (1998) 'Green Metrics: A Global Status Report on Standardized Corporate Environmental Reporting', Boston: Tellus Institute.

White, M.A. (1996) *Corporate Environmental Performance and Shareholder Value*, University of Virginia Online Scholarship Initiative 1996, on file with author.

12 Agility and resilience

Adaptive capacity in Friends of the Earth International and Greenpeace

Vanessa Timmer

Introduction

Non-state actors are increasingly prominent and significant players within global environmental governance regimes (Smith *et al.* 1997; Keck and Sikkink 1998; Khagram *et al.* 2002; Clark 2003b). This chapter is about two of the largest environmental organizations, Friends of the Earth International (FoEI) and Greenpeace, and about the organizational design they have adopted to remain viable over the three decades since their founding. Their continued organizational viability is a significant accomplishment given the shifting nature of their political environment and the complexity of their subject area, as well as their complex and sometimes hostile interactions with other actors in the global environmental regime. The political environment within which they operate can be considered to be complex and dynamic not least because FoEI and Greenpeace are actively and creatively working to influence and change this environment. Greenpeace and FoEI are social movement organizations (SMOs) which 'are associations of people making idealistic and moralistic claims about how human personal or group life ought to be organized' (Lofland 1996: 3). SMOs seek to alter the status quo and to 'change some element of the social structure or reward distribution, or both, of a society' (McCarthy and Zald 1977: 1218). Greenpeace and FoEI are also *transnational* social movement organizations (TSMOs). They are transnational because they organize across national boundaries to include participants from more than one country and engage in 'global level contentious politics' to influence global regimes (Smith 2005: 229). This international focus and multi-country span results in 'additional environmental and organizational complexity' (Ghoshal and Westney 2005: 5). The term 'transnational social movement organization' can be distinguished from the broader category of 'international nongovernmental organizations (INGOs)' (also referred to as transnational civil society organizations) that are private, voluntary and nonprofit but not necessarily seeking change in the status quo (Kriesberg 1997: 12; Anheier *et al.* 2001; Kaldor 2003).

As social movement organizations, FoEI and Greenpeace respond to multiple 'internal and external pressures that affect their viability, their internal structures and processes, and their ultimate success in attaining their goals' (Zald and Ash 1966: 327). Even though these two organizations are subject to a range of similar pressures, FoEI and Greenpeace have developed different *organizational designs*, which I define as a TSMO's structure – its level of formalization and degree of centralization. *Formalization* refers to 'the degree to which an SMO has an explicitly (e.g. written) scheme of organization – division of labour – that it strives to enact in its routine activities' (Lofland 1996: 142–3). *Centralization* refers to 'the degree to which an SMO's activities are devised and directed by a well-identified SMO-wide leadership as opposed to activities originating and pursued by multiple, relatively independent SMO subgroupings' (Lofland 1996: 143). As will become evident below, these structural designs can result in different strategic responses to external change. Analytically, 'formalization' and 'centralization' are variables that represent two dimensions of organizational structure; empirically, they are often combined (Staggenborg 1989; Gamson 1990; Lofland 1996). I discuss these two dimensions in parallel and compare the decentralized and informal structural design of FoEI and the relatively more centralized and formal structural design of Greenpeace. Their different structures raise the question of whether there is 'one best' organizational design for operating within a complex and dynamic environment. In a recent survey of transnational social movement forms, Smith (2005: 247) provides a possible answer to this question. Smith writes, 'over the past several decades, the form of transnational SMOs has become more decentralized and adaptive, indicating that these organizations are responding to a changing and uncertain global environment.' There is a growing consensus amongst nongovernmental organization scholars, including Smith, which equates decentralized and informal structures with maximizing adaptability within a complex and dynamic environment (e.g. Fowler 2000; Anheier and Themudo 2001; Clark 2003a). On the basis of the empirical analysis of FoEI and Greenpeace, I challenge this assumption and present two models of organizational design that are viable for maximizing adaptability.

Friends of the Earth International and Greenpeace

The comparison between Friends of the Earth International and Greenpeace is instructive because these two transnational social movement organizations share many similarities and a few key differences. As Jasanoff (2005: 29) writes, 'the comparative method works best when the entities to be compared are different enough to present interesting contrasts, yet similar enough for the variations to be disciplined.' FoEI and Greenpeace were both founded in the late 1960s in North America. Over the past three decades, they have experienced organizational growth and expansion to offices around the world while operating within a similar transnational political environment. FoEI and Greenpeace are part of the modern environmental movement that emerged in response to extensive ecosystem degradation and pollution due to industrialized human development (McCormick 1989; Carmin and Balser 2002; Doherty 2002). They share a common concern with the misuse of power by corporations and governments and the resulting environmental and social problems. Greenpeace and FoEI are active in many of the same campaigns including halting climate change, genetic engineering, deforestation, and inequitable and environmentally destructive trade practices (FoEI 2007; Greenpeace International 2007).

The tactics adopted by both organizations are a combination of confrontational activities (e.g. direct action and protests) and non-confrontational actions (e.g. lobbying and litigation); however, Greenpeace is relatively more renowned for its media-friendly direct action tactics, in which Greenpeace activists 'bear witness' to environmental crimes, 'expose environmental criminals', and engage in 'high-profile, non-violent conflict' (Greenpeace International 2008a). FoEI, in contrast, is focused on building a global grassroots movement organized in a decentralized, participatory, democratic way in order to 'liv[e] the change [they] wish to see and work ... together in solidarity' (FoEI 2005). FoEI uses relatively more institutionalized tactics (e.g. research and lobbying) to 'challenge the current model of economic and corporate globalization, and promote solutions that will help to create environmentally sustainable and socially just societies' (FoEI 2004).

In addition to differences in their tactical focus, FoEI and Greenpeace have different structural designs, with Greenpeace adopting a relatively more centralized and formal structure than FoEI (Rucht 1999; Clark 2003b: 5). FoEI members define themselves as the 'world's largest grassroots environmental network, uniting 69 diverse national member groups and some 5,000 local activist groups on every continent' (FoEI 2008a). Greenpeace is 'a global environmental organization, consisting of Greenpeace International (Stichting Greenpeace Council) in Amsterdam, and 27 national and regional offices around the world, providing a presence in 41 countries' (Greenpeace International 2008b). Similar to FoEI, Greenpeace national offices are granted a degree of autonomy with regard to national activities and governance; however, unlike FoEI, major policy, campaign, and strategic decisions as well as legal use of the Greenpeace name are centrally coordinated. The rules guiding Greenpeace offices are also relatively more formalized and explicit than those guiding FoEI groups. The decentralized and informal structural design adopted by FoEI is in large part due to its commitment to participatory democracy and inclusiveness in decision-making (Carmin and Balser 2002).

After more than three decades of front-line activity, Greenpeace and FoEI can both be considered to be viable and successful organizations. In 2007, the FoEI secretariat had an income of €2.425 million and a total expenditure of €2.416 million. This income has increased substantially since the 1990s and has recently remained relatively stable. In 2007, the Greenpeace International office had an income of €42.640 million and an expenditure of €41.771 million, with the total income and expenditure of Greenpeace Worldwide at €177.021

million and €121.399 million respectively. FoEI estimates that it has 2 million members and supporters that predominately contribute to the organization through their volunteer efforts. Greenpeace has remained relatively stable since 2000 and is currently at 2.8 million members and depends on these members for their financial support. Both FoEI and Greenpeace report frequent requests to establish offices all over the world (e.g., FoEI 2004; Greenpeace International 2008c). FoEI has a policy of one member group per country and continues to slowly expand to new countries; however, Greenpeace maintains a relatively constant number of national offices, which it strategically selects or disbands based on international priorities. In addition to these indicators of success in income and membership numbers, both FoEI and Greenpeace can be considered to be effective and relevant on the basis of their reported successes. For example, in 2004, both FoEI and Greenpeace reported their role in effectively pressuring the Russian government to ratify the Kyoto Protocol to the United Nations Framework Convention on Climate Change, and in influencing the withdrawal of Monsanto's genetically modified roundup ready wheat (FoEI 2004; Greenpeace International 2005).

Effects, integration and interplay

In recent years, valuable theoretical and empirical research has been conducted to determine the impact and influence of activities of transnational social movement organizations, including FoEI and Greenpeace, particularly on global governance processes; international norm development; and international regimes such as those that have formed around the challenges of climate change and biodiversity loss (e.g. Fox and Brown 1998; Keck and Sikkink 1998; Florini 2000; Khagram *et al.* 2002; Clark 2003b). Scholars analysing the *effects* of TSMO campaigns have devised methods for analysing causal connections between TSMO activities and measurable outcomes and impacts. For example, Corell and Betsill (2001) devised an analytical framework for assessing SMO influence in international environmental negotiations by defining 'influence' as the transmittal of information that alters the receiver's actions and creating tools for identifying evidence and causal mechanisms. Initial findings from campaign effectiveness research suggest that TSMOs are effective in the international arena in a number of ways. These include forming powerful issue coalitions and networks; providing a voice for marginalized and unheard communities; presenting information and expert knowledge to global processes; pressuring and persuading governments, corporations and intergovernmental organizations to discuss issues of concern to the TSMO; shaping international norms, terms of debate and agreements; and monitoring compliance of and holding actors accountable to international treaties (Smith *et al.* 1997; Keck and Sikkink 1998; Arts *et al.* 2001; Corell and Betsill 2001; Brown and Timmer 2006). Even in cases where issues are brought to the table by other actors, SMOs appear to play a 'crucial amplifying role in the agenda-setting stage and a predominately monitoring role once implementation of serious management actions was underway' (van Eijndhoven *et al.* 2001: 187).

The environment within which TSMOs operate can be deemed to be dynamic due to shifting understanding of how to manage global environmental problems, to changing interests of actors engaged in global environmental governance, and to increasing demands placed upon TSMOs including demands to demonstrate their accountability and legitimacy. A recent study of national and international responses to the global environmental problems of acid rain, ozone depletion and climate change (Social Learning Group 2001, Vol. 2: 184–5) identified the ways in which these issues were framed as problems and how this issue framing evolved over time as new knowledge was gathered, as new actors became involved in the management of the problem, and as the issue moved from a phase of agenda setting to implementation and monitoring of social responses. The development of the issue frames was also actively shaped by the actors involved as they tried 'to change (or sustain) the prevailing issue frame' in order to forge coalitions and further their interests (Social Learning Group 2001, Vol. 2: 185). This evolution of the agenda of managing global environmental risks is not unique to atmospheric problems but is evident in other global environmental governance processes such as on the issue of biodiversity conservation (Brechin *et al.* 2003) and in the evolving global sustainable development debate (Kates *et al.* 2005).

TSMOs participating in and hoping to influence these processes need to take these shifts into account, particularly the *integration* of different global policy agendas such as environmental conservation, development, peace and security, freedom and social equity (Kates *et al.* 2005). The actors with whom TSMOs are interacting in global environmental governance processes, including representatives of government, international organizations, private sector and the media, have shifting interests according to the characteristics of the particular environmental issue and to new opportunities and demands that emerge from interacting with other actors. For example, Hoffman (2001) traces the fundamental shift in approach to environmental issues by certain companies within the oil and chemical industries, in part in response to pressures placed upon them by NGOs, towards proactive incorporation of corporate environmental responsibility into their strategies. The shift in approach by some industries and businesses has required corresponding changes in strategy from TSMOs in their interaction with the private sector (Clark 2003a).

TSMOs operate within horizontal and vertical linkages, which institutional theorists have defined as *interplay*. 'Horizontal interplay involves interactions occurring at the same level of social organizations; vertical interplay is a result of cross-scale interactions or links involving institutions located at different levels of social organization' (Young 2002: 26). Due to gains in prominence and influence, TSMOs have been faced with an increasing number of demands by the actors that they target with their advocacy activities and that they cooperate with to further their mission (Brown *et al.* 2003). Questions are posed as to the legitimacy of TSMO participation in global governance (Edwards 2000) and their accountability to diverse stakeholders (Ebrahim 2003) including donors and supporters, partners that cooperate on programmes and campaigns, targets of TSMO campaigns, TSMO staff and Board, and members (Brown *et al.* 2003). Stakeholder expectations can vary considerably across sectors and issues, and TSMOs are often confronted with combinations of stakeholder demands that are complex, often in conflict, and shifting (Brown *et al.* 2003). For example, a trend towards a partnership approach to global governance that involves government, private sector and SMO participants, has led to critiques of SMOs that continue to play their traditional role of protesting government and private sector (Juma 2002); however adopting a cooperative role raises questions about cooptation of a radical agenda (Clark 2003a). These demands evolve over time as the global environmental governance processes change and the role of TSMOs change within these processes. TSMOs are also adjusting to transformations in available technology, including the rise of the Internet as a communication and activism tool (Pickerill 2003).

TSMO missions (e.g. advancing sustainable development, ensuring equitable economic development) require the active participation of partners outside of the TSMO who have additional resources, legitimacy, power and scope of authority to produce large-scale results (Uvin *et al.* 2000). The scale of TSMO programmes requires that they must be 'co-produced' with partners whom the TSMO does not hold authority (Brown and Moore 2001). This requires TSMOs to build and participate in coalitions and networks around their particular issue area and mission. The networks and partnerships being formed to advance sustainable development are filling an institutional gap in global governance (Young 1997; Keck and Sikkink 1998; Brown *et al.* 2000; Risse 2003). The advantages of partnerships in coproducing results can outweigh the challenges that face TSMOs in bridging the many differences across the actors with whom it engages, including a diversity of ideological perspectives and political tactics, North–South tensions, cooperation and competition for scarce resources, and language and cultural barriers (Young *et al.* 1999; Ashman 2001; Batliwala 2002; Smith 2002: 505; Clark 2003a). Challenges specific to cross-sectoral partnerships include overcoming biased assumptions about the interests and behaviour of other sectors, preventing cooptation, and building multi-party accountability for partnership results (Brown *et al.* 2000: 289; Covey and Brown 2001; Brown 2002; Doh and Teegen 2003).

In sum, transnational social movement organizations such as Friends of the Earth International (FoEI) and Greenpeace operate in and interact with *a complex and dynamic political environment*, which requires Greenpeace and FoEI to scan for changes in the environment, develop appropriate strategic responses, and creatively adapt to change. Traditionally, researchers analysing the *effectiveness* of TSMOs have focused on assessing their success in specific campaigns and activities and in attaining their *output goals* (e.g. Arts *et al.* 2001); however, analysing how TSMOs achieve *long-term* success within a turbulent context requires a broader conceptualization of effectiveness. In addition to *output goals*, TSMOs also have *support goals* of ensuring their organizational viability and of building their capacity to repeatedly produce effective outputs over time (Letts *et al.* 1999: 3; Scott 2003). For the purposes of this chapter, the *adaptive capacity* of a transnational social movement organization is defined as its ability to create strategic responses to change. It is important to note that analysis of the adaptability of a social movement organization amounts to a *surrogate measure* of the overall effectiveness of a TSMO as it focuses assessment on the *capacity* of an organization for effective performance by analysing organizational features and design, rather than on assessing the outcomes and impacts of their activities. As will become evident below, adaptive capacity is a characteristic of an organization that arises over time from specific organizational designs.

Organizational design for adaptability

As stated in the introduction, the organizational design of transnational social movement organizations can be defined in terms of its level of centralization and degree of formalization. Recently, there has been a surge of scholarly and practitioner interest in how organizations in all sectors – private, governmental, intergovernmental and civil society – can design themselves effectively in an increasingly multifaceted, varied and rapidly changing environment (e.g. Brown and Eisenhardt 1998; Christensen and Overdorf 2000; Smillie and Hailey 2001). Amongst scholars researching transnational social movement organizations, there is a growing consensus that *a decentralized, informal structural design maximizes adaptability* (Fowler 2000; Anheier and Themudo 2001; Clark 2003a: 110–11; Smith 2005). To reiterate quotations from the introduction of this chapter, Smith (2005: 235) argues that a decentralized and informal structural design within a TSMO maximizes the 'ability of subgroups to adapt quickly' and accelerates decision-making by decentralizing authority. Fowler (2000: 142) argues for the advantage of decentralizing power and scope of authority within nongovernmental organizations since 'continual referrals up and down a decision-making chain reduce speed and introduce stiffness rather than flexibility'.

Anheier and Themudo (2001: 201) claim that decentralized and informal structures – which they label as 'relational' or network forms – 'are somewhat "fluid" organizations particularly suited for highly variable task environments' due to the fact that 'without central coordination for everyday management tasks and operations, decisions are made at the local levels with a minimum of costs for consultation and negotiation.' Anheier and Themudo continue by noting some of the disadvantages of the relational form, such as lack of coordination, and advantages of more centralized structures, such as sharing development costs; however, these authors conclude that 'adaptability is *maximized* when undertaken by small independent units rather than large bureaucratic structures' and 'on balance, and on largely economic grounds, the global environmental organizational environment for CSOs [civil society organizations] would favour the network form with decentralized and autonomous units' (2001: 202, emphasis added). Smith (2005: 235) similarly adopts an economic argument by stating that organizations operating transnationally adopt 'organizational structures aimed at limiting . . . transaction costs'. Clark (2003a: 110) agrees that decentralized and informal structures ['networks'] 'have clear advantages of adaptability and problemsolving' because 'they can reach decisions faster and more swiftly discover and adopt new techniques developed elsewhere.' The 'increasing flexibility and unit-autonomy while decreasing hierarchy' may result in 'less predictability and stability' but Clark (2003a: 111) argues that a network design is better able to work globally, manage strategic partnerships, respond rapidly, and manage information from 'ground realities and the grassroots' to influence global campaigns.

These scholars note a general historical trend towards decentralized and informal structures as the environment within which TSMOs operate has become increasingly complex and turbulent (Anheier and Themudo 2001: 202; Smith 2005: 237). There is a paradox here that requires explanation. Greenpeace and Friends of the Earth International both operate under similar complex and dynamic conditions and yet Greenpeace is not designed in a decentralized and informal way. The prevailing conclusion that decentralized and informal structures facilitate adaptability does not account for the ways in which more centralized and formalized structures enable the creative and strategic resolution of organizational challenges. I aim to address this theoretical gap by grouping the pressures facing FoEI and Greenpeace into four organizational challenges, presented in Table 12.1. Briefly, *tactical innovation* refers to the challenge for TSMOs of creating new tactics and of adapting tactics in order to repeatedly disrupt the status quo. TSMOs are also faced with *managing their relations with external actors* to reap the benefits of partnership while ensuring their relative independence. Building long-term adaptive capacity requires a TSMO to also address the need for *organizational maintenance* through acquiring resources in order to survive and the challenge of *managing internal conflicts and fostering a degree of cohesion* within the TSMO.

In defining these challenges, I am interested in the relationship between structural design and adaptability. How do different designs shape a TSMO's adaptive capacity? I argue that different SMO structures are deliberately chosen or emerge to reflect different 'ways in which SMOs deal with organizational problems' (Staggenborg 1989: 75). In resolving these organizational challenges, TSMOs are faced with *strategic dilemmas* since each strategic choice encompasses advantages and disadvantages and requires the TSMO to balance important tradeoffs (Rothschild and Whitt 1986: 76).

Table 12.1 Summary of four organizational challenges

Challenge	Description
1. Tactical innovation	The challenge of creatively adjusting tactics and devising new tactics in order to repeatedly respond to changing external conditions and persistently disrupt – or threaten to disrupt – the status quo.
2. Managing external relations	The challenge of negotiating partnerships with external actors in order to achieve common goals or of operating independently despite pressures to partner.
3. Organizational maintenance	The challenge of ensuring continued organizational viability through securing various combinations of financial support (money) and human power (activism) in order to survive, grow and remain relevant.
4. Managing internal relations	The challenge of facilitating internal cohesion and of managing internal conflict within a social movement organization.

First, TSMOs are faced with the challenge of *tactical innovation*. Greenpeace and FoEI rely on a set of tactics that they have deemed to be effective in achieving their goals. Since a TSMO's political environment is changing over time, 'the problem for movement organizations is to create organizational models that are sufficiently robust to stand up to opponents, but flexible enough to change with new circumstances' (Tarrow 1995: 136). McAdam (1983: 752) describes social movement organizations as engaged in an 'ongoing process of *tactical interaction*' between the SMO and their opponents. Because SMOs are, by definition, less powerful than those they target with their tactics, McAdam argues that they 'must devise protest techniques that offset their powerlessness'. McAdam notes that these techniques only 'temporarily afford challengers increased bargaining leverage' as the opponents will likely counter these tactics 'in a chess-like fashion' and re-establish their power. McAdam (1983: 752) concludes that 'to succeed over time . . . a challenger must continue to search for new and effective tactical forms.' TSMOs operating in a complex and dynamic environment need to build capacity to innovate their tactics *repeatedly* – the capacity for innovativeness – as the effectiveness of a particular tactic is often short-lived (Letts *et al.* 1999).

Second, FoEI and Greenpeace operate in a 'relational web' of different actors including governments, business and industry, international organizations and other social movement actors (Fowler 2000: 143). The need to cooperate and collaborate in partnership with other actors is in tension with the benefits of operating independently in order to enable flexibility and to ensure quality, coherent style and to carry out costly or dangerous tactics.

Sometimes independence is forced upon the TSMO even if the TSMO is willing to cooperate and collaborate with other actors. This can be due to resource competition amongst social movement actors (Cooley and Ron 2002), or due to accusations of illegitimacy or lack of accountability by potential partners (Clark 2003a: 169). There are distinct advantages in creating partnerships, particularly within complex and dynamic environments, as inter-organizational collaboration can produce 'co-evolutionary arrangements' whereby collaborating organizations jointly adapt to environmental changes through 'division of labour, mutual learning, and the diffusion of best practices' (Anheier and Themudo 2001: 206).

Third, in order to ensure their continued organizational viability, FoEI and Greenpeace face the challenge of ensuring resource support and selecting between two fundamental options: the mobilization of 'time' ('in-kind donations' of volunteer effort) or of 'money' (financial support) (Diani and Donati 1999: 15). For Clark (2003a: 111), this represents the choice between creating a 'professional ethos and fostering grassroots voluntarism'. Traditionally, SMOs depend upon recruiting a broad base of grassroots citizens into voluntary involvement and activism (McCarthy 2005: 195). In contrast, SMOs that build a *professional group* of committed activists have been criticized for becoming 'protest businesses' (Jordan and Maloney 1997: 18), suffering from 'bureaucratisation, a declining performance in relation to organizational resources, and a loss of initiative and emphasis particularly amongst the rank and file [grassroots]' (Rucht 1999: 218). Other scholars emphasize the benefits of professional staff supported by financial donations for being able to carry out the 'considerable planning and coordination' of campaigns in an efficient, routine and effective manner (Doherty 2002: 133). It is important to note that SMOs that depend on grassroots voluntarism often operate in a skilled, high-quality and 'professional' manner; however, in this categorization, a 'professional group' is relatively more formal in its structure and operations and is relatively more dependent on paid staff for delivering its activities.

Finally, a key challenge for any organization is in managing internal relations in order to foster a common identity and purpose and to resolve conflict (Schein 1985; Gamson 1990). The strategic dilemma for SMOs is in balancing the tradeoffs between the need for a unified, coherent response and the benefits of inclusive, participatory and democratic processes (Clark 2003b: 7).

The adaptive capacity of Friends of the Earth International and Greenpeace

I argue that FoEI and Greenpeace have developed different approaches to maximizing adaptability, stemming from their structural designs, in response to complex and dynamic internal and external challenges. I use the term 'adaptive *capacity*', in addition to adaptability, in order to highlight the fact that, over time, organizations elaborate and refine those strategic responses

that are deemed to provide workable and reliable solutions to key organizational challenges. Organizations typically develop a *pattern* of using those
strategic responses that repeatedly solve these challenges and support long-
term organizational viability. This pattern becomes embedded in an organization's strategies and structures and partially constrains its future strategic
responses. Although this routine response can be called into question in
situations of discontinuous and dramatic change in the environment, these
patterned strategic responses are remarkably robust. Some of this robustness
can be attributed to the fact that members of social movement organizations
predominately focus on action in pursuit of social change rather than on
reassessing the functionality of past response routines (Letts *et al.* 1999).
Different designs and corresponding strategic responses are also repeatedly
and reliably effective because it appears there is more than one viable design
for operating in a complex and dynamic environment (Young *et al.* 1999).

Based on organizational documents and scholarly studies of FoEI and
Greenpeace (e.g. Wapner 1996; Warkentin 2001; Carmin and Balser 2002;
FoEI 2007; Greenpeace International 2007), I propose that the patterns
and tendencies that these organizations exhibit can be expressed as logical
extremes, and provide insight as to 'ideal types' of adaptive capacity. Doherty
(2002: 17) writes, 'the concept of an ideal type was intended as a way of
defining characteristics that would help empirical investigation.' Ideal, in this
context, is not 'better' but represents an idea or theoretical construction
(Doherty 2002). As Lofland and Lofland (1984: 98) note, 'it is helpful to
develop ideal types in *pairs* or *polars* (that is, logically or theoretically
opposed) extremes' since 'such a pairing makes it clear that practically all
empirical instances range along a continuum between the given extremes.'
Following this approach, I identify two ideal types of adaptive capacity that
represent hypothetical and 'pure' cases of patterned responses of an organization to internal and external pressures. I have labelled these the *agility
model* and the *resilience model* based on their dynamics of organizational
change (described below). Table 12.2 provides an overview of these two
models, and serves as a guide for the discussion in this section. FoEI aligns
predominately with the agility model, and Greenpeace has developed a
predominately resilience model approach to building adaptive capacity.

Friends of the Earth International is a 'global federation of national
environmental organizations' (FoEI 2004), which have joined together under
the umbrella of an international organization in order to increase their
influence on their diverse campaign targets including their primary target, the
nation-state (Wapner 1996). I argue that FoEI member groups adopt a wide
approach to tactical innovation – which I label an *exploration* approach – by
casting their net across issues, adopting a broad array of tactics, searching
for root causes to environmental and social problems, promoting solutions
and alternatives, and working through multiple channels from local to
global scales. Although FoEI member groups are heavily engaged in autonomous national campaigns, they collaborate on a number of international

Table 12.2 Adaptive functionality of agility and resilience

Dimension	Agility	Resilience
A. *Organizational design:* *Structure*		
Formalization	informal	formal
Centralization	decentralized	centralized
B. *Strategic responses to organizational challenges*		
1 Tactical innovation	**exploration** Umbrella strategy that supports subgroup autonomy in developing tactics	**concentration** Clearly defined and internationally established tactics that are delivered through national offices and volunteers
	Adaptive functionality: Innovativeness across a wide range of tactics and developing new tactics	*Adaptive functionality:* Innovativeness within a focused range of tactics.
2 Managing external relations	**collaboration** Many collaborative links with outside partners: horizontal clusters of networks based on shared goals; voluntary cooperation rather than leverage; can be dense webs (Clark 2003b: 6)	**independence** Predominately independent: strategic partnerships; well defined; on pragmatic basis; usually not dense; emphasis on SMO's own work (Clark 2003b: 6)
	Adaptive functionality: Innovativeness and building bridges across partners	*Adaptive functionality:* Flexibility to shift partnerships when necessary
3 Organizational maintenance	**grassroots / voluntarism** Building a grassroots movement	**professional** Building a global organization
	Adaptive functionality: Responsiveness to local conditions	*Adaptive functionality:* Readiness for action
4 Managing internal relations	**participatory democracy** Cooperative, member-controlled	**unity of command** Defined institutional structure, secretariat-controlled
	Adaptive functionality: Managing for diversity	*Adaptive functionality:* Managing for coherence
C. *Dynamics of organizational change and adaptation*		
Motto	flow	restore
Tempo of adaptation	continuous	episodic

campaigns and, in 2005 and 2006, developed a federation-wide strategic plan that defines the common mission and vision of FoEI and focuses all of FoEI's core activities in four strategic areas: mobilization, resistance, transformation, and the building of a strong Friends of the Earth International (FoEI 2007). The collaborative approach extends to their interaction with other like-minded civil society groups and partners with whom they form many extensive and long-standing cooperative partnerships. As part of their mission, FoEI seeks 'to engage in vibrant campaigns, raise awareness, mobilize people and build alliances with diverse movements, linking grassroots, national and global struggles' (FoEI 2007). Voluntary grassroots activists are their primary organizational maintenance resource, and provide the ground realities for international campaigns to ensure responsiveness to changing local conditions. FoEI is driven by its ideological commitment to participatory democracy and inclusiveness through its member-controlled decentralized decision-making structures. The member groups continue to adopt a decentralized and informal structural design as they aim to exemplify the democratic values and support for diversity which they seek in broader society.

In contrast, Greenpeace has responded to complex and dynamic internal and external challenges by building a global organization that is relatively more centralized and formalized than FoEI. Greenpeace frames global environmental problems as problems of concentrated power and wealth at the international level within national governments, multinational corporations and international organizations (Carmin and Balser 2002). Greenpeace strives to build environmental awareness through non-violent direct action to confront these powerful international actors (Wapner 1996), and concentrates its efforts on fine-tuning and elaborating this direct action approach. The current Executive Director of Greenpeace International, Gerd Leipold, argues that 'being strategic means having a limited number of campaigns that are very focused' (Leipold quoted in Williamson 2005). The costly, secretive and technically challenging nature of Greenpeace's confrontational campaigns has reinforced an independent orientation – with some flexible strategic partnering – and a more centralized and formalized design. Greenpeace employs professional teams of direct action activists, scientists, communications experts, media relations personnel, and policy specialists operating under standards determined at the organizational level of the international secretariat, supported by a broad base of financial supporters. The governance structure is designed for coherence and unity of command in order to maintain 'the high level of internationalism and rigid adherence to its principles' (Greenpeace International 2008d).

Although FoEI and Greenpeace have responded very differently to key organizational challenges, they have succeeded in remaining viable and relevant under complex and dynamic conditions. Their structural design supports their strategic responses and is, in turn, reinforced and partially constrained by these choices. Each of the strategic responses that they have made represents a strategic dilemma; for example, in internal relations, as Clark (2003a: 117) writes, 'activists are both frustrated by top-down decision-making (Greenpeace has experienced this) and by losing critical opportunities because democratic processes are slow' which, to the author's knowledge, FoEI has experienced. Judging by their stable income, membership and reported campaign success, FoEI and Greenpeace have both found ways of resolving these strategic dilemmas and remaining adaptable to changing internal and external pressures. Greenpeace provides a counter example for scholars who suggest that decentralized and informal designs maximize adaptability. Greenpeace has focused its attention on gaining technical and moral legitimacy through undertaking 'professional protest' (Diani and Donati 1999) rather than on the political legitimacy associated with participatory and democratic structures (Brown and Moore 2001). Greenpeace's relatively more centralized and formal structure reduces transaction costs in a different way than FoEI's design since it supports Greenpeace's mission of being a unified, coherent, international organization with clear internal accountability structures that is refining and elaborating direct action tactics. By centralizing strategic decisions, Greenpeace increases its 'readiness for action' in response to ecological crises (Gamson 1990). In sum, Greenpeace has built adaptive capacity, but in a way that differs totally from the method used by FoEI.

I selected the terms 'agility' and 'resilience' for the two ideal types of adaptive capacity to reflect the dynamics of organizational change that accompanies each model. Although FoEI and Greenpeace have adopted routine strategic responses to external and internal challenges, these organizations are not static entities but, over time, are dynamically and creatively adjusted by their organizational members. Drawing on organizational change literature (e.g. Mintzberg and Westley 1992; Van de Ven and Poole 1995; Weick and Quinn 1999) and on systems theory (e.g. Holling 1973, 2001), I propose that the two models express themselves as two different dynamics of organizational change or adaptation. This proposition is based on Weick and Quinn (1999) and their suggestion of different 'tempos of change' defined as 'the characteristic rate, rhythm or pattern of work or activity'. Weick and Quinn (1999) distinguish between *episodic change*, defined as change that is 'infrequent, discontinuous and intentional' and *continuous change*, defined as change that is 'ongoing, evolving and cumulative'. The agility model can be summarized as organizing for constant change. I suggest the motto 'flow' because of the tendency of organizations adopting a decentralized and informal structural design to embrace change, continuously and incrementally adjust, and constantly reinvent themselves (Staber and Sydow 2002: 410). In contrast, the resilience model could be given the motto 'restore' (Holling 1973) or 'foster efficiency' (Staber and Sydow 2002: 409). Instead of organizing for flux and change, this approach buffers from those dynamics and focuses on building coherence and a degree of stability and persistence which is punctuated by periods of episodic change (Weick and Quinn 1999). This approach derives from and is supported by the adoption of a centralized and formalized structural design. The terms 'agility' and 'resilience' and their mottos are heuristics that aim to capture the structural and strategic features of the two models.

Conclusion

In a complex and dynamic political environment, the effectiveness of transnational social movement organizations, such as Friends of the Earth International and Greenpeace, is partly determined by their ability to adapt to change. In fact, Young and his colleagues (1999) propose that it is the capacity to adapt – which they define as the ability of organizations 'to find creative and flexible ways to organize and manage themselves in order to survive and work effectively' that is a distinguishing feature of nongovernmental organizations. The purpose of this chapter is to challenge the prevailing conclusion that decentralized and informal structural designs are the only forms of internal organization that maximize adaptability. The previous section outlined the ways in which Greenpeace responds to key organizational challenges with a relatively more centralized and formalized design. With this design, Greenpeace is better able to innovate its media-friendly, direct action tactics and to shift strategic partnerships, while facilitating its readiness for action and managing the coherence of its organization. FoEI's design is better suited to innovating across tactics and building long-lasting collaborative partnerships, while remaining responsive to local conditions and managing for diversity. It is important to note that although FoEI tends towards an agility model of adaptive capacity and Greenpeace tends towards the resilience model, both organizations remain creatively opportunistic in their strategic responses to change. For example, Greenpeace has adopted a number of solutions-oriented tactics, such as developing greenfreeze refrigerator technology without ozone-depleting chemicals (Rawcliffe 1998: 89), which differ from its characteristic direct action and problem-focused tactics. FoEI notes that 'the work of the international secretariat depends heavily upon volunteers'; however, FoEI has also employed a number of full-time professional staff at its secretariat, including a media coordinator, to support and strengthen the federation (FoEI 2008b).

FoEI and Greenpeace's structural designs build their adaptive capacity, and I also argue that the variation between their designs ensures the adaptability of the environmental movement as a whole (Gerlach and Hine 1970). I agree with Freeman (1979) and Staggenborg (1989) that social movements are strengthened when the diverse nodes of social movement are composed of both decentralized and informal structures *and* centralized and formalized SMOs. As Freeman states, 'the most viable movement is one with several organizations that can play different roles and pursue different strategic possibilities.' This point is echoed in Staggenborg (1989: 30), who writes, 'successful social movements are likely to include a variety of SMOs with different organizational structures' as 'different types of SMOs make different contributions to the "success" of a social movement' (see also Carmin and Balser 2002: 384). I argue that Greenpeace plays a different role within the environmental movement than FoEI and both roles have strengths and weaknesses. The main problem facing SMOs is not an inappropriate structure, i.e. failing to adopt the 'one best' generic design for maximizing adaptability, but 'the attempt to pursue strategies for which their structures are inappropriate' (Freeman 1979). These conclusions may also have implications for the structural design of global environmental governance organizations and the co-existence of decentralized, informal structures with relatively more formal and centralized structures. I encourage further research into the relationship between structural design and adaptability both within social movement organizations and within global governance structures.

References

Anheier, H.K., Glasius, M. and Kaldor, M. (eds) (2001) *Global Civil Society 2001*, Oxford: Oxford University Press.

Anheier, H.K. and Themudo, N. (2001) 'Organizational Forms of Global Civil Society: Implications of Going Global', in Anheier, H.K., Glasius, M. and Kaldor, M. (eds) *Global Civil Society 2002*, London: London School of Economics.

Arts, B., Noortmann, M. and Reinalda, B. (eds) (2001) *Non-state Actors in International Relations*, Aldershot and Burlington, VT: Ashgate.

Ashman, D. (2001) 'Strengthening North–South Partnerships for Sustainable Development', *Nonprofit and Voluntary Sector Quarterly*, 30(1): 74–98.

Batliwala, S. (2002) 'Grassroots Movements as Transnational Actors: Implications for Global Civil Society', *Voluntas: International Journal of Voluntary and Nonprofit Organizations*, 13(4): 393–410.

Brechin, S.R., Wilshusen, R., Fortwangler, C.L. and West, P.C. (eds) (2003) *Contested Nature: Promoting International Biodiversity with Social Justice in the Twenty-First Century*, Albany: State University of New York Press.

Brown, L.D. (2002) *Multiparty Social Action and Mutual Accountability*, Cambridge, MA: Hauser Center for Nonprofit Organizations, KSG, Harvard University.

Brown, L.D. and Moore, M.H. (2001) 'Accountability, Strategy, and International Non-Governmental Organizations', *Nonprofit and Voluntary Sector Quarterly*, 30: 569–87.

Brown, L.D. and Timmer, V. (2006) 'Civil Society Actors as Catalysts for Transnational Social Learning', *Voluntas: International Journal of Voluntary and Nonprofit Organizations*, 17(1): 1–16.

Brown, L.D., Khagram, S., Moore, M. and Frumkin, P. (2000) 'Globalization, NGOs, and Multisectoral Relations', in Nye, J.S. and Donahue, J.D. (eds) *Governance in a Globalizing World*, Washington DC: Brookings Institution.

Brown, L.D., Moore, M.H. and Honan, J. (2003) 'Building Strategic Accountability Systems for International NGOs', *AccountAbility Forum*, 2: 31–43.

Brown, S.L. and Eisenhardt, K.M. (1998) *Competing on the Edge: Strategy as Structured Chaos*, Boston, MA: Harvard Business School Press.

Carmin, J. and Balser, D.B. (2002) 'Selecting Repertoires of Action in Environmental Movement Organizations', *Organization and Environment*, 15(4): 365–88.

Christensen, C.M. and Overdorf, M. (2000) 'Meeting the Challenge of Disruptive Change', *Harvard Business Review*, 78(2): 66–78.

Clark, J. (2003a) *Worlds Apart: Civil Society and the Battle for Ethical Globalization*, London and Bloomfield, CT: Earthscan Publications, Kumarian Press.

Clark, J.D. (ed.) (2003b) *Globalizing Civic Engagement: Civil Society and Transnational Action*, London and Sterling, VA: Earthscan Publications.

Cooley, A. and Ron, J. (2002) 'The NGO Scramble: Organizational Insecurity and the Political Economy of Transnational Action', *International Security*, 27(1): 5–39.

Corell, E. and Betsill, M.M. (2001) 'A Comparative Look at NGO Influence in International Environmental Negotiations: Desertification and Climate Change', *Global Environmental Politics*, 1(4): 86–107.

Covey, J. and Brown, L.D. (2001) 'Critical Cooperation: An Alternative Form of Civil Society – Business Engagement', *IDR Reports 17(1)*, Boston: Institute for Development Research (IDR).

Diani, M. and Donati, P.R. (1999) 'Organizational Change in Western European Environmental Groups: A Framework for Analysis', *Environmental Politics*, 8: 13–34.

Doh, J.P. and Teegen, H. (eds) (2003) *Globalization and NGOs: Transforming Business, Government, and Society*, Westport, CT and London: Praeger.

Doherty, B. (2002) *Ideas and Actions in the Green Movement*, London and New York: Routledge.

Ebrahim, A. (2003) *NGOs and Organizational Change: Discourse, Reporting and Learning*, Cambridge: Cambridge University Press.

Edwards, M. (2000) *NGO Rights and Responsibilities: A New Deal for Global Governance*, London: The Foreign Policy Centre.

Florini, A. (2000) *The Third Force: The Rise of Transnational Civil Society*, Tokyo, Japan: Center for International Exchange, Washington DC: Carnegie Endowment for International Peace, Brookings Institution Press (distributor).

Fowler, A. (2000) *Virtuous Spiral: A Guide to Sustainability for NGOs in International Development*, London and Sterling, VA: Earthscan Publications.

Fox, J.A. and Brown, L.D. (1998) *The Struggle for Accountability: The World Bank, NGOs, and Grassroots Movements*, Cambridge, MA: MIT Press.

Freeman, J.H. (1979) 'Resource Mobilization and Strategy: A Model for Analyzing Social Movement Organization Actions', in Zald, M.N. and McCarthy, J.D. (eds) *The Dynamics of Social Movements*, Cambridge, MA: Winthrop.

Friends of the Earth International (FoEI) (2004) *Annual Report 2004: Friends of the Earth International*, Amsterdam: Friends of the Earth International.

FoEI (2005) *Outcomes of the Penang Visioning Workshop*, Amsterdam: Friends of the Earth International.

FoEI (2007) *Annual Report and Financial Report 2007: Friends of the Earth International*, Amsterdam: Friends of the Earth International.

FoEI (2008a) *Friends of the Earth International*. http://www.foei.org/en/who-we-are (accessed 29/08/08).

FoEI (2008b) *Meet the Staff*. http://www.foei.org/en/who-we-are/about/staff.html (accessed 29/08/08).

Gamson, W.A. (1990) *The Strategy of Social Protest*, Belmont, CA: Wadsworth.

Gerlach, L.P. and Hine, V.H. (1970) *People, Power, Change: Movement of Social Transformation*, New York: Bobbs-Merrill.

Ghoshal, S. and Westney, D.E. (2005) *Organizational Theory and the Multinational Corporation*, New York: Palgrave Macmillan.

Greenpeace (2005) *Greenpeace International Annual Report 2004*, Amsterdam: Greenpeace International.

Greenpeace (2007) *Greenpeace International Annual Report 2006*, Amsterdam: Greenpeace International.

Greenpeace International (2008a) *About Greenpeace*, http://www.greenpeace.org/international/about (Accessed 29/08/08).

Greenpeace International (2008b) *How is Greenpeace structured?* http://www.greenpeace.org/international/about/how-is-greenpeace-structured (Accessed 29/08/08).

Greenpeace International (2008c) *FAQ: Questions about Greenpeace in General*. http://www.greenpeace.org/international/about/faq/questions-about-greenpeace-in (Accessed 29/08/08).

Greenpeace International (2008d) *Governance Structure*. http://www.greenpeace.org/international/about/how-is-greenpeace-structured/governance-structure (Accessed 29/08/08).

Hoffman, A.J. (2001) *From Heresy to Dogma: An Institutional History of Corporate Environmentalism*, Stanford, CA: Stanford University Press.

Holling, C.S. (1973) 'Resilience and the Stability of Ecological Systems', *Annual Review of Ecology and Systems*, 4: 2–23.

Holling, C.S. (2001) 'Understanding the Complexity of Economic, Ecological and Social Systems', *Ecosystems*, 4: 390–405.

Jasanoff, S. (2005) *Designs on Nature: Science and Democracy in Europe and the United States*, Princeton, NJ and Oxford: Princeton University Press.

Jordan, G. and Maloney, W.A. (1997) *The Protest Business? Mobilizing Campaign Groups*, Manchester: Manchester University Press.

Juma, C. (2002) 'How Not to Save the World', *New Scientist*, 28 September: 24.

Kaldor, M. (2003) 'Civil Society and Accountability', *Journal of Human Development*, 4(1): 4–27.

Kates, R.W., Parris, T.M. and Leiserowitz, A.A. (2005) 'What is Sustainable Development? Goals, Indicators, Values and Practice', *Environment*, 47(3): 8–21.

Keck, M. and Sikkink, K. (1998) *Activists without Borders: Advocacy Networks in International Politics*, Ithaca, NY: Cornell University Press.

Khagram, S., Riker, J.V. and Sikkink, K. (eds) (2002) *Restructuring World Politics: Transnational Social Movements, Networks, and Norms*, Minneapolis: University of Minnesota Press.

Kriesberg, L. (1997) 'Social Movements and Global Transformation', in Smith, J., Chatfield, C. and Pagnucco, R. (eds) *Transnational Social Movements and Global Politics: Solidarity beyond the State*, Syracuse, NY: Syracuse University Press.

Letts, C.W., Ryan, W.P. and Grossman, A. (1999) *High Performance Nonprofit Organizations: Managing Upstream for Greater Impact*, New York: John Wiley.

Lofland, J. (1996) *Social Movement Organizations: Guide to Research on Insurgent Realities*, New York: Aldine de Gruyter.

Lofland, J. and Lofland, L.H. (1984) *Analyzing Social Settings: A Guide to Qualitative Observation and Analysis*, Belmont, CA: Wadsworth.

McAdam, D. (1983) 'Tactical innovation and the pace of insurgency', *American Sociological Review*, 48: 735–54.

McCarthy, J.D. (2005) 'Persistance and Change among Nationally Federated Social

Movements', in Davis, G.F., McAdam, D., Scott, R.W. and Zald, M.N. (eds) *Social Movements and Organizational Theory*, Cambridge: Cambridge University Press.

McCarthy, J.D. and Zald, M.N. (1977) 'Resource Mobilization in Social Movements: A Partial Theory', *American Journal of Sociology*, 82: 1212–41.

McCormick, J. (1989) *The Global Environmental Movement: Reclaiming Paradis*, London: Belhaven Press.

Mintzberg, H. and Westley, F. (1992) 'Cycles of Organizational Change', *Strategic Management Journal*, 13: 39–59.

Pickerill, J. (2003) *Cyberprotest: Environmental Activism Online*, Manchester and New York: Manchester University Press.

Rawcliffe, P. (1998) *Environmental Pressure Groups in Transition*, Manchester and New York: Manchester University Press.

Risse, T. (2003) 'Transnational Actors and World Politics', in Carlsnaes, W., Risse, T. and Simmons, B.A. (eds) *Handbook of International Relations*, London, Thousand Oaks, CA and New Delhi: Sage Publications.

Rothschild, J. and Whitt, J.A. (1986) *The Cooperative Workplace: Potentials and Dilemmas of Organizational Democracy and Participation*, Cambridge: Cambridge University Press.

Rucht, D. (1999) 'The Transnationalization of Social Movements: Trends, Causes, Problems', in della Porta, D., Kriesi, H. and Rucht, D. (eds) *Social Movements in a Globalizing World*, London: Macmillan Press.

Schein, E.H. (1985) *Organizational Culture and Leadership*, San Francisco, CA and London: Jossey-Bass.

Scott, R.W. (2003) *Organizations: Rational, Natural and Open Systems*, Upper Saddle River, NJ: Prentice Hall.

Smillie, I. and Hailey, J. (2001) *Managing for Change: Leadership, Strategy and Management in Asian NGOs*, London and Sterling, VA: Earthscan Publications.

Smith, J. (2002) 'Bridging Global Divides', *International Sociology*, 17(4): 505–28.

Smith, J. (2005) 'Globalization and Transnational Social Movement Organizations', in Davis, G.F., McAdam, D., Scott, R.W. and Zald, M.N. (eds) *Social Movements and Organization Theory*, Cambridge: Cambridge University Press.

Smith, J., Chatfield, C. and Pagnucco, R. (eds) (1997) *Transnational Social Movements and Global Politics: Solidarity Beyond the State*, Syracuse, NY: Syracuse University Press.

Social Learning Group (2001) *Learning to Manage Global Environmental Risks: A Comparative History of Social Responses to Climate Change, Ozone Depletion and Acid Rain*, Cambridge, MA: MIT Press.

Staber, U. and Sydow, J. (2002) 'Organizational Adaptive Capacity: A Structuration Perspective', *Journal of Management Inquiry*, 11(4): 408–24.

Staggenborg, S. (1989) 'Stability and Innovation in the Women's Movement: A Comparison of Two Movement Organizations', *Social Problems*, 36(1): 75–92.

Tarrow, S. (1995) 'Cycles of Collective Action: Between Moments of Madness and the Repertoires of Contention', in Traugott, M. (ed.) *Repertoires and Cycles of Collective Action*, Durham, NC: Duke University Press.

Uvin, P., Jain, P. and Brown, L.D. (2000) 'Think Large and Act Small: Toward a New Paradigm for NGO Scaling Up', *World Development*, 28(8): 1409–19.

Van de Ven, A.H. and Poole, M.S. (1995) 'Explaining Development and Change in Organizations', *Academy of Management Review*, 20(3): 510–40.

Van Eijndhoven, J., Clark, W.C. and Jager, J. (2001) 'The Long-term Development of

Global Environmental Risk Management: Conclusions and Implications for the Future', in Social Learning Group (ed.) *Learning to Manage Global Environmental Risks: A Functional Analysis of Social Responses to Climate Change, Ozone Depletion, and Acid Rain*, Cambridge, MA: MIT Press.

Wapner, P. (1996) *Environmental Activism and World Civic Politics*, Albany: State University of New York.

Warkentin, C. (2001) *Reshaping World Politics: NGOs, the Internet, and Global Civil Society*, Lanham, MD and Oxford: Rowman and Littlefield.

Weick, K.E. and Quinn, R.E. (1999) 'Organizational Change and Development', *Annual Review of Psychology*, 50: 361–86.

Williamson, H. (2005) 'Campaigners in a Corporate Mould', *Financial Times*, 10.

Young, D.R., Koenig, B.L., Najam, A. and Fisher, J. (1999) 'Strategy and Structure in Managing Global Associations', *Voluntas: International Journal of Voluntary and Nonprofit Organizations*, 10(4): 323–43.

Young, O.R. (ed.) (1997) *Global Governance: Drawing Insights from the Environmental Experience*, Cambridge, MA: MIT Press.

Young, O.R. (2002) *The Institutional Dimensions of Environmental Change: Fit, Interplay and Scale*, Cambridge, MA: MIT Press.

Zald, M.N. and Ash, R. (1966) 'Social Movement Organizations: Growth, Decay and Change', *Social Forces*, 44: 327–41.

13 International organizations in global environmental governance

Epilogue

Bernd Siebenhüner and Frank Biermann

This book presents a diverse group of studies of international organizations in global environmental governance. These include international organizations that had to adapt to the emergence of environmental policy as a new area of world politics and that had subsequently to develop environmental policies (Part I). The book also features studies on international organizations that have been created with the explicit mandate to deal with environmental policies (Part II). Thirdly, this volume brings several studies on new hybrid forms of organizations that are based on the involvement of non-state actors in world politics, such as public–private organizations and networks and even entirely non-state organizations, which can be, however, analysed with similar approaches as international organizations (Part III).

What are the general findings of this volume with regard to how international organizations have responded to environmental concerns, how they changed their organizational structures and activities and what influence they had in global environmental governance? Have experiences in this policy field been different from other fields? Which roles have different types of organizations played? We discuss these questions in this concluding chapter in light of the results of the contributions to this book.

The influence of international organizations

In light of current debates in international relations theory, the contributions to the first part of this book reveal interesting findings. While many international relations scholars still see international organizations as mere instruments in the hands of governments, results from the studies presented here lead to different conclusions, on three grounds.

First, they demonstrate that international organizations can have *autonomous* influence in international politics. As Dreher and Sarasola highlight, using quantitative data, the international organizations they study had significant influence on the global environment as well as on governance processes. Their regression analyses show the quantitative influence of numerous international organizations in these fields. They also demonstrate that this influence differs in kind and degree, and thus support similar findings from the qualitative study programme of nine international bureaucracies reported in Biermann and Siebenhüner (2009). On this basis, international organizations need to be seen as separate actors that have spheres of autonomous decision-making that differ from the will of the states that created them. This finding, however, spurs new questions. Many have been addressed in this book, namely the sources of autonomy of organizations and the factors that determine their influence.

Second, this book shows that the influence of organizations differs, and that the spheres of autonomy and influence of international organizations are far from clear-cut. Most forms of influence are fluid and subject to constant negotiation between representatives of international organizations and national policy-makers, nongovernmental activists or business groups. The influence of the OECD environmental policy reports largely hinges on the way national governments are allowed to participate in the process (Lehtonen, this volume). Nongovernmental groups can affect policies of the International Finance Corporation rather strongly, yet much less in the case of the Multilateral Investment Guarantee Agency under the roof of the World Bank (Park, this volume). Even rather similar international organizations, such as convention secretariats, show variance in their external influence due to the individuals in the organizations, the problem structure at hand, and the cultures of these bodies (Bauer, Busch and Siebenhüner, this volume). In sum, it is not necessarily the formal mandate that explains the degree and type of the influence of international organizations (supported by the findings in Biermann and Siebenhüner 2009).

Third, contributions in this book reveal several specificities of global environmental governance and the roles of international organizations in this field. Unlike other areas of international politics – such as international peace and security, international trade or global health governance – global environmental governance is characterized by a relatively low domestic priority in most countries. Biodiversity, for example, is an urgent and pressing problem due to the accelerating rate of loss of species. Yet with most national governments and even within environmental bureaucracies, the topic ranks low in visibility and political awareness (Bauer, Busch and Siebenhüner, this volume). It therefore comes as no surprise that the problem structure of the secretariat for the Convention on Biological Diversity limits its influence on national governments (Siebenhüner 2009). The same holds for the role of environmental issues on the agenda of the European Union (Adelle and Jordan, this volume).

Moreover, most environmental problems bring costs rather than immediate economic benefits for individuals and governments. Most benefits from environmental protection are difficult to quantify and to measure. Effectively to counter problems such as climate change, the loss of biodiversity or desertification would cost national governments and businesses significant amounts that are difficult to reserve in their budgets. In addition, public awareness of the need to combat environmental problems on a global scale is limited, and domestic policy-makers need to consider this. In this situation, international organizations can expect only limited support from national governments.

Organizational reform

Almost all contributions to this volume suggest that international organizations can play a powerful role in global environmental governance and be proponents of ambitious environmental protection. However, the effectiveness of international organizations varies according to the type and scope of the different organizations, which raises the question of governance reform. Andresen and Rosendal (this volume) analyse the role of the UN Environment Programme and describe it as highly influential in setting agendas and initiating negotiations. However, they argue that UNEP's influence is reduced when it comes to practical implementation, monitoring and sanctioning international agreements. The responsibility for administering these agreements lies with various treaty secretariats, which leaves UNEP with little direct influence.

This finding raises the question of whether UNEP should be given more responsibility for international convention processes, for example by upgrading it to a world environment organization. This question has spurred a controversial and still unresolved debate (Biermann 2000; Biermann and Bauer 2005; Ivanova, this volume). A world environment organization could function within a net of international regimes and could integrate existing environmental treaties in an overarching regime, similar to the International Labour Organization or the World Trade Organization. Critics, however, maintain that global environmental protection is too complex to be addressed by one single international organization and that larger bureaucracies do not automatically lead to more effective outcomes. Critics also argue that a large and comparatively powerful world environment organization will require much political energy. The question thus remains open how the multiple international environmental treaties can best be coordinated and how international organizations might assist governments in initiating, negotiating and implementing these agreements.

The new role of public–private cooperation

The focus on intergovernmental organizations in many debates on global governance should not deter attention from a more recent but rapidly developing phenomenon: the emergence of public–private forms of cooperation in global environmental governance. As Pattberg (this volume), Andonova (this volume) and Timmer (this volume) show, non-state organizations from the business and from the environmentalist side have gained influence and take up governance functions that have hitherto been the sole responsibility of governmental actors and intergovernmental organizations. This development can be observed in the field of nongovernmental organizations from the business side such as CERES (Pattberg, this volume), where companies have joined forces to establish general norms and standards for more sustainable management practices. Most of these new forms of business activism proclaim to go beyond the self-interest of the participating firms and to strive for better global policies. Also, environmentalist organizations such as Greenpeace and Friends of the Earth have become powerful players in global environmental governance, turning into professional political agencies that actively participate in international negotiations (Timmer, this volume).

An emerging question concerns the interaction and cooperation between different types of nongovernmental organizations and between intergovernmental and nongovernmental organizations. An example for the interplay of public and private policies is the Forest Stewardship Council, where non-state actors developed independent systems of norm setting and implementation in the absence of an intergovernmental regime (Rosendal 2001). This governance mechanism partly mimics intergovernmental rule making and has brought about a labelling scheme with high visibility and rising popularity among forest managers. Another form of public–private partnerships is analysed by Andonova (this volume), who focuses on partnership programmes that have been initiated to advance environmental objectives mostly within existing regimes. A public–private partnership is also analysed by Wright (this volume), namely the Equator Principles initiative that include an international organization (the International Finance Corporation as part of the World Bank) and over forty private banks and financial institutions. These studies show that these hybrid forms of governance must be analysed within their institutional embedding. Some take the place of international regulation, some complement existing regimes, and others provide new avenues for innovative solutions to global environmental problems.

Outlook

What can we expect in the future in the field of international organizations in global environmental governance? Are there any dominant trends? All the contributions in this book have studied current and past processes; few ventured to look into the future. However, today's choices and processes shape the development conditions of international organizations in the decades to come.

One trend seems to be strengthened, namely international cooperation through the creation of new, or the upgrading of existing, intergovernmental bodies. Numerous international organizations have been created in last decades. Several programmes and even convention secretariats have been upgraded to full-fledged international organizations with enlarged mandate and resources. For example, major international environmental agreements have been signed in the fields of desertification, biodiversity loss, climate change and others – with all of them now having their own supporting bureaucracy (Biermann and Siebenhüner 2009; Bauer, Busch and Siebenhüner, this volume).

A second trend is the rising importance of environmental problems on the international agenda. As almost all studies suggest, problems causing pressure in most environmental issue areas will become stronger in the future. Climate change, biodiversity loss and resource depletion are examples. Economic globalization, population growth and the rapid development of emerging economies such as China and India aggravate these problems and necessitate increased international cooperation. It can thus be expected that the demand for international organizations as moderators and mediators in intensified conflicts over resources and as proponents of global concerns will become even stronger.

Is this, then, the dawn of a new era of international organizations in global environmental governance? As the debate on the creation of a world environment organization shows, there is no self-sufficient mechanism that leads to stronger agencies. However, awareness of the globally connected nature of environmental problems grows. Scientists conceptualize now as an object of study the entire earth system including the atmosphere and all terrestrial and marine eco-systems (Schellnhuber and Wenzel 1998; Schellnhuber 1999). This development has called into question the existing structure of international environmental regimes and international organizations that in most cases follow a problem-centred or media-centred approach. Problems such as climate change, long-range air pollution or ozone depletion are addressed by different conventions with their own processes and organizational settings. The increasing understanding of their interplay has promoted debates on how to link existing regime processes and to mirror the interconnected nature of the earth system in (global) governance mechanisms and structures (Biermann 2007). In short, globally coordinated policies will remain crucial, and international organizations can play a key role as representatives of a global concern and as proponents of global response programmes.

In these processes, the tasks for international organizations in global environmental governance may further change. Over the last two decades, the international community was concerned with the negotiation and adoption of new international agreements in environmental governance. While these processes will continue, implementation will become a key challenge. Several international organizations such as UNEP, but also convention secretariats, have thus explicitly turned towards implementation programmes (see case studies in Biermann and Siebenhüner 2009). This practical work on the ground will give these international organizations a different role and may spur new debates, for example about the relationship between national governments and international organizations in project implementation.

Last but not least, more research on the role of international organizations in global environmental governance is needed. First, incomplete understanding of international organizations and their influence results in misleading conclusions about actual processes of global environmental governance. The traditional emphasis on states in international relations theory produces a perception of international organizations as mere passive structures established by states. Yet the findings of this book suggest that international organizations, on the contrary, do play a significant role in environmental governance that warrants further analysis (a theme that is also supported by the case studies in Biermann and Siebenhüner 2009).

Second, more research is needed with a view to improving the functioning of the organizations themselves. So far, the effectiveness of the United Nations and its specialized agencies in the field of environment and development has been subject to intense *public* debate – yet with limited academic response, especially in mainstream international relations research. If we underestimate the role of international organizations in environmental governance in either research or practice, we lose out on a potentially strong force to fight environmental degradation on national, regional and global scales. As studies in this volume have shown, international organizations can be effective and influential. Yet the book also shows that more research is called for to better understand the preconditions and the ways and means of the effectiveness international organizations – not the least in the field of global environmental governance.

References

Biermann, F. (2000) 'The Case for a World Environment Organization', *Environment*, 20: 22–31.

Biermann, F. (2007) ' "Earth System Governance" as a Crosscutting Theme of Global Change Research', *Global Environmental Change*, 17: 326–37.

Biermann, F. and Bauer, S. (eds) (2005) *A World Environment Organization. Solution or Threat for Effective International Environmental Governance?*, Aldershot: Ashgate.

Biermann, F. and Siebenhüner, B. (eds) (2009) *Managers of Global Change: The Influence of International Environmental Bureaucracies*, Cambridge, MA: MIT Press (in press).

Rosendal, G.K. (2001) 'Overlapping International Regimes. The Case of the Intergovernmental Forum on Forests (IFF) between Climate Change and Biodiversity', *International Environmental Agreements: Politics, Law and Economics*, 1: 447–68.

Schellnhuber, H.-J. (1999) 'Earth System Analysis and the Second Copernican Revolution', *Nature*, 402 (Millennium Supp. 2 Dec 1999): C19–C23.

Schellnhuber, H.-J. and Wenzel, V. (eds.) (1998) *Earth System Analysis: Integrating Science for Sustainability*, Berlin: Springer.

Siebenhüner, B. (2009) 'The Biodiversity Secretariat: Lean Shark in Troubled Waters', in Biermann, F. and Siebenhüner, B. (eds) (2009) *Managers of Global Change: The Influence of International Environmental Bureaucracies*, Cambridge, MA: MIT Press (in press).

Index